REPRESENTATIVE MEN

EDITED BY *Theodore L. Gross*

REPRESENTATIVE MEN

MEN

Cult Heroes of Our Time

Fp

THE FREE PRESS

NEW YORK

Collier-Macmillan Canada, Ltd., Toronto, Ontario
Library of Congress Catalog Card Number: 70–93112
                                                    printing number
         1   2   3   4   5   6   7   8   9   10

FOR MY MOTHER

Preface

"There is properly no history, only biography," wrote Emerson more than a century ago. Today we still regard the past in terms of representative men and analyze the present through heroes who embody the complex issues of America.

We live in a time when the television camera focuses upon the exceptional man and reveals his every scar, when newspaper interviews and gossip columns, senate investigations and never-ending exposés seem antagonistic to a cult of heroism. We want to know everything about a man—at once, in all places—and his heroic features are often lost in the rush of events. Often, but not always. The impassioned response to the deaths of President Kennedy, Robert Kennedy, Malcolm X, and Martin Luther King, Jr.; the celebration of Timothy Leary and Allen Ginsberg; the adulation of Paul Goodman and Marshall McLuhan; the intense interest in Leonard Bernstein, Elizabeth Taylor, Frank Sinatra, Jacqueline Onassis, and Jonas Salk—this concern with extraordinary people reveals our hungry needs for heroes. We want to know everything about these cult heroes so that they may appear more human; at the same time we want them to remain heroic—to raise us from all those leveling forces in modern society that frustrate and inhibit the heroic gesture.

Who have been the men and women most representative of America in the present age? What do they tell us about ourselves? Why should these individuals have captured the imagination of thousands of Americans? What mosaic of the American sensibility do these figures form? The following essays respond to these questions and reveal the kind of society in which we live, the sort of heroes who represent us.

The authors chosen to observe our representative men are analytical as well as admiring, critical and skeptical as well as

respectful. Thus James Reston's appraisal of John F. Kennedy
distinguishes his achievement from his promise; Diana Trilling's
comments on Timothy Leary and the drug cult in America represent an outsider's attitude toward this "self-inspired chemical
Moses"; Paul O'Neil's irreverent view of Jacqueline Onassis is a
refreshing antidote to the earlier hagiography of our existential
heroine; Eldridge Cleaver's remarks on the white race and its
heroes challenge all that we thought we knew about American
history. The volume that follows is consequently not one concerned with hero-worship but with heroes; and it seeks to reflect
the varied texture of contemporary America through its extraordinary men and women.

To place the representative men of our time in perspective, I
have presented a brief history of the hero as well as the observations of three stimulating thinkers: Norman Mailer, Arthur
Schlesinger, Jr., and Sidney Hook. I have then grouped particular
cult heroes of America into several categories—politics, social
commentary, race, literature, film, the arts, science, and popular
culture—although these exceptional people have an exciting
impetus for violating all categories. Norman Mailer has always
craved political power as well as the power of the written word,
even though he has "come to the middle-age conclusion" that
he is "probably better as a writer than a man of action"; William Buckley put aside his magazine and ran for mayor of
New York; Leonard Bernstein has been a commentator and composer, professor and pianist, television lecturer and conductor. In
modern America talented people reach beyond their chosen professions; this restless tendency is true of almost every cult hero
in this book. Other attributes are common to American heroes,
and in the introductions to individual sections as well as in brief
biographies of the heroes themselves, I suggest some of these
notable and pervasive characteristics.

"There is properly no history, only biography." In this sense,
Representative Men, which owes its title and its inspiration to
Emerson, can serve as a record of our moment in time. But it can
be more, for, as Thoreau reminds us, "Biography, too, is liable
to the same objections; it should be autobiography." By concen-
trating upon other people and the issues they illuminate, the

reader can perhaps discover something exceptional within himself. Man still wants to see his common nature enlarged, even glorified, in a hero who can lead him back to his prerogatives, to his humanity. He lives in a technological age which threatens the worth of his human nature, and as a modern American, he bears a great cross for having created so much so quickly. No act of discovery at the present time would seem to be more commanding than the discovery of some form of heroism within the individual himself. One turns, therefore, to the cult heroes of our time in search of that heroism—in search, finally, of oneself.

I would like to thank Lawrence Bone of The American Library in Paris for his assistance in the production of this book. Thomas O. Gay offered helpful editorial advice for which I am grateful. My deepest debt, as always, is to Selma, for all the little nameless acts of kindness and of love.

T. L. G.

Paris

Contents

xi

VIII
Science, 397

IX
Popular Culture, 425

REPRESENTATIVE MEN

The Cult of
Heroism in America:
Perspectives

□ The concept of the hero has always attracted the widest interest. Aristotle, Carlyle, Hegel, Spencer, Marx, Emerson, and scores of other thinkers have formulated various views of the hero, believing that "Universal History," as Carlyle once said, "the History of what man has accomplished in this world, is at bottom the History of Great Men who have worked here." [Although every age has emphasized different aspects of the hero, a common definition and certain common characteristics recur no matter where or when he appears. □ The hero is an exceptional person who maintains authority over average people and seeks to realize an ideal. In the pursuit of this ideal, the hero demonstrates certain characteristics. He is a courageous, active, social man whose passions are more intense than those of the people he represents; he is a man willing to dive, to take chances; he is someone finally who sees more deeply into the experiences of life than the average man. These qualities are present whenever the hero emerges, although they differ in importance at different times in history. In the classical and medieval periods the active hero yields to a more contemplative man. In the Renaissance he is well-balanced, a man like Brutus, in whom the elements were perfectly mixed. In the early nineteenth century, he is a romantic hero, like Byron's Don Juan or Goethe's Faust, someone in pursuit of an ideal that generally can never be achieved. The hero represents the age in which he lives, embodying the desires of common people, turning their dreams and nightmares into history, reflecting their finest and their least attractive attributes.]

□ America has produced its own variety of heroes. In the Puritan period, the hero was an ethical man, characterized by *pietàs*. In the eighteenth century, he was, to use Benjamin Franklin as an example, a practical man who sought the heroic ideal through self-discipline. Toward the middle of the nineteenth century he became "the American Adam," in the view

2

[R.W. B. Lewis]
of one critic, "a figure of heroic innocence and vast potentialities, poised at the start of a new history." In folklore, he
often assumed preternatural powers, like Johnny Appleseed or
Mike Fink or Davy Crockett. In the South he took the form
of the Southern Gentleman, defending his civilization against
a variety of external pressures.

□ In the eighteenth and nineteenth centuries these self-reliant
romantic heroes were compatible with the emergence of a
new nation eager to declare its cultural as well as its political
independence. Many of the nation's leaders were self-made
businessmen or statesmen or generals who had risen from
impoverished backgrounds. Their lives were predicated upon
a belief in heroism, and they rarely questioned those abstractions—honor, patriotism, glory, morality—that had shaped
their actions. But after World War I, a profound change
occurred in the thought of many Americans; writers challenged and often refuted the concept of heroism, even though
they did not abandon the hero. Hemingway's statement in
A Farewell to Arms is one expression of this view:

I was always embarrassed by the words sacred, glorious, and sacrifice and the expression in vain. We had heard them, sometimes
standing in the rain almost out of earshot, so that only the shouted
words came through, and had read them, on proclamations that
were slapped up by billposters over other proclamations, now for
a long time, and I had seen nothing sacred, and the things that
were glorious had no glory and the sacrifices were like the stock-
yards at Chicago if nothing was done with the meat except to
bury it. There were many words that you could not stand to hear
and finally only the names of places had dignity. Certain numbers
were the same way and certain dates and these with the names
of the places were all you could say and have them mean anything.
Abstract words such as glory, honor, courage, or hallow were obscene beside the concrete names of villages, the numbers of roads,
the names of rivers, the numbers of regiments and the dates.

☐ Hemingway speaks of a lost idealism that had a great influence on many of the cult heroes in this book. Mailer, Baldwin, Kennedy, McLuhan, Lowell, Malcolm X, and others grew up in the twenties and thirties, and formed their personal conception of the hero in direct reaction to their predecessors. They lived through an economic depression and another war and achieved their greatest powers in the 1950's and the 1960's when the mass media seemed to threaten the growth of the hero in America. In the shadow of Hemingway's work—and one would naturally associate Hemingway with T. S. Eliot, Albert Camus, and a host of other European authors—the antihero dominated the literary as well as the social imagination of people. After World War II, the politicians seemed compatible with this vision: there was, as Arthur Schlesinger, Jr., suggests, a "decline of greatness."

☐ But the wheel of history turned in the sixties, and only four years after Schlesinger had spoken of the dearth of great cult heroes in America and the world, he had to modify his views and state that "the older American faith in leadership and diversity and contention and individualism and experiment and irreverence is beginning to reassert itself." The deaths of John F. Kennedy, Malcolm X, Robert F. Kennedy, and Martin Luther King, Jr.; the concentration on love and power in the work of Norman Mailer, James Baldwin, and J. D. Salinger; the influence of Timothy Leary, Herbert Marcuse, Bob Dylan, and Allen Ginsberg on young people; the rise of black power and student power—these social and literary phenomena point to the conflict between a belief in the heroic ideal, indeed an aggressive desire to have it realized, and the forces of America that tend to destroy individualism, discourage idealism, and blur the human differences that once made America a unique country, full of contradictions but confident, in Whitman's words, that it was large, it contained "multitudes."

☐ The images which contemporary writers use to characterize

the conflict between idealism and authority change, according to the writer: Mailer's Superman and the Supermarket or Cannibals and Christians; Schlesinger's politics of hope and politics of despair; Sidney Hook's limitation and possibility; Cleaver's white villains and black idealists. Ours is an age of the dialogue, the interview, the drama *à deux*, the analyst and his patient, the separated dancers, the student and the administrator, the black man and the white man. Intense, extreme, almost Manichean. But whatever form the conflicts take and whatever descriptive term we invoke to understand them, the fundamental tension in America today is one between the idealism of some of its people and the power that the country has attained, between individuals who wish to preserve their idiosyncratic differences and a power structure which tends to blur all differences.]

The Existential Hero: Superman Comes to the Supermarket

NORMAN

MAILER

SINCE the First World War Americans have been leading a double life, and our history has moved on two rivers, one visible, the other underground; there has been the history of politics which is concrete, factual, practical and unbelievably dull if not for the consequences of the actions of some of these men; and there is a subterranean river of untapped, ferocious, lonely and romantic desires, that concentration of ecstasy and violence which is the dream life of the nation.

The twentieth century may yet be seen as that era when civilized man and underprivileged man were melted together into mass man, the iron and steel of the nineteenth century giving way to electronic circuits which communicated their messages into men, the unmistakable tendency of the new century seeming to be the creation of men as interchangeable as commodities, their extremes of personality singed out of existence by the psychic fields of force the communicators would impose. This loss of personality was a catastrophe to the future of the imagination, but billions of people might first benefit from it by having enough to eat—one did not know—and there remained citadels of resistance in Europe where the culture was deep and roots were visible in the architecture of the past.

Nowhere, as in America, however, was this fall from individual man to mass man felt so acutely, for America was at once the first and most prolific creator of mass communications, and the most rootless of countries, since almost no American could lay claim to the line of a family which had not once at least severed its roots by migrating here. But, if rootless, it was then the most vulnerable of countries to its own homogenization. Yet America was also the country in which the dynamic myth of the Renaissance— that every man was potentially extraordinary—knew its most passionate persistence. Simply, America was the land where people still believed in heroes: George Washington; Billy the Kid; Lincoln, Jefferson; Mark Twain, Jack London, Hemingway; Joe Louis, Dempsey, Gentleman Jim; America believed in athletes, rumrunners, aviators; even lovers, by the time Valentino died. It was a country which had grown by the leap of one hero past another— is there a county in all of our ground which does not have its legendary figure? And when the West was filled, the expansion turned inward, became part of an agitated, overexcited, superheated dream life. The film studios threw up their searchlights as the frontier was finally sealed, and the romantic possibilities of the old conquest of land turned into a vertical myth, trapped within the skull, of a new kind of heroic life, each choosing his own archetype of a neo-renaissance man, be it Barrymore, Cagney, Flynn, Bogart, Brando or Sinatra, but it was almost as if there were no peace unless one could fight well, kill well (if always with honor), love well and love many, be cool, be daring, be dashing, be wild, be wily, be resourceful, be a brave gun. And this myth, that each of us was born to be free, to wander, to have adventure and to grow on the waves of the violent, the perfumed, and the unexpected, had a force which could not be tamed no matter how the nation's regulators—politicians, medicos, policemen, professors, priests, rabbis, ministers, *idéologues*, psychoanalysts, builders, executives and endless communicators—would brick-in the modern life with hygiene upon sanity, and middle-brow homily over platitude; the myth would not die. Indeed a quarter of the nation's business must have depended upon its existence. But it stayed alive for more than that—it was as if the message in the labyrinth of the genes would insist that violence was locked with creativity, and adventure was the secret of love.

Once, in the Second World War and in the year or two which

followed, the underground river returned to earth, and the life of the nation was intense, of the present, electric; as a lady said, "That was the time when we gave parties which changed people's lives." The Forties was a decade when the speed with which one's own events occurred seemed as rapid as the history of the battle-fields, and for the mass of people in America a forced march into a new jungle of emotion was the result. The surprises, the failures, and the dangers of that life must have terrified some nerve of awareness in the power and the mass, for, as if stricken by the orgiastic vistas the myth had carried up from underground, the retreat to a more conservative existence was disorderly, the fear of communism spread like an irrational hail of boils. To anyone who could see, the excessive hysteria of the Red wave was no prepara-tion to face an enemy, but rather a terror of the national self: free-loving, lust-looting, atheistic, implacable—absurdity beyond absurdity to label communism so, for the moral products of Stalinism had been Victorian sex and a ponderous machine of material theology.

Forced underground again, deep beneath all *Reader's Digest* hospital dressings of Mental Health in Your Community, the myth continued to flow, fed by television and the film. The fissure in the national psyche widened to the danger point. The last large appearance of the myth was the vote which tricked the polls and gave Harry Truman his victory in '48. That was the last. Came the Korean War, the shadow of the H-bomb, and we were ready for the General. Uncle Harry gave way to Father, and security, regu-larity, order, and the life of no imagination were the command of the day. If one had any doubt of this, there was Joe McCarthy with his built-in treason detector, furnished by God, and the damage was done. In the totalitarian wind of those days, anyone who worked in Government formed the habit of being not too original, and many a mind atrophied from disuse and private shame. At the summit there was benevolence without leadership, regularity without vision, security without safety, rhetoric without life. The ship drifted on, that enormous warship of the United States, led by a Secretary of State whose cells were seceding to cancer, and as the world became more fantastic—Africa turning itself upside down, while some new kind of machine man was being made in China—two events occurred which stunned the confidence of America into a new night: the Russians put up their Sputnik, and Civil Rights—that reluctant gift to the American Negro, granted for its effect on foreign affairs—spewed into real life at Little Rock. The national Ego was in shock: the Russians were now in some ways our technological superiors, and we had an internal problem of subject populations equal conceivably in its difficulty to the Soviet and its satellites. The fatherly calm of the General began to seem like the uxorious mellifluences of the undertaker.

Underneath it all was a larger problem. The life of politics and the life of myth had diverged too far, and the energies of the people one knew everywhere had slowed down. Twenty years ago a post-Depression generation had gone to war and formed a lively, grousing, by times inefficient, carousing, pleasure-seeking, not altogether inadequate army. It did part of what it was supposed to do, and many, out of combat, picked up a kind of private life on the fly, and had their good time despite the yaws of the military system. But today in America the generation which respected the code of the myth was Beat, a horde of half-begotten Christs with scraggly beards, heroes none, saints all, weak before the strong, empty conformisms of the authority. The sanction for finding one's growth was no longer one's flag, one's career, one's sex, one's adventure, not even one's booze. Among the best in this newest of the generations, the myth had found its voice in marijuana, and the joke of the underground was that when the Russians came over they could never dare to occupy us for long because America was too Hip. Gallows humor. The poorer truth might be that America was too Beat, the instinct of the nation so separated from its public mind that apathy, schizophrenia, and private beatitudes might be the pride of the welcoming committee any underground could offer.

Yes, the life of politics and the life of the myth had diverged too far. There was nothing to return them to one another, no common danger, no cause, no desire, and, most essentially, no hero. It was a hero America needed, a hero central to his time, a man whose personality might suggest contradictions and mysteries which could reach into the alienated circuits of the underground, because only a hero can capture the secret imagination of a people, and so be good for the vitality of his nation; a hero embodies the fantasy and so allows each private mind the liberty to consider its fantasy and find a way to grow. Each mind can become more conscious of its desire and waste less strength in hiding from itself. Roosevelt was such a hero, and Churchill, Lenin and De Gaulle; even Hitler, to take the most odious example of this thesis, was a hero, the hero-as-monster, embodying what had become the monstrous fantasy of a people, but the horror upon which the radical mind and liberal temperament foundered was that he gave outlet to the energies of the Germans and so presented the twentieth century with an index of how horrible had become the secret heart of its desire. Roosevelt is of course a happier example of the hero; from his paralytic leg to the royal elegance of his geniality he seemed to contain the country within himself; everyone from the meanest starving cripple to an ambitious young man could expand into the optimism of an improving future because the man offered an unspoken promise of a future which would be rich. The sexual and the sex-starved, the poor, the hard-working and the imaginative well-to-do could see themselves in the President, could believe him to be like themselves. So a large part of the country was able to discover its energies because not as much was wasted in feeling that the country was a poisonous nutrient which stifled the day.

Too simple? No doubt. One tries to construct a simple model. The thesis is after all not so mysterious; it would merely nudge the notion that a hero embodies his time and is not so very much better than his time, but he is larger than life and so is capable of giving direction to the time, able to encourage a nation to discover the deepest colors of its character. At bottom the concept of the hero is antagonistic to impersonal social progress, to the belief that social ills can be solved by social legislating, for it sees a country as all-but-trapped in its character until it has a hero who reveals the character of the country to itself. The implication is that without such a hero the nation turns sluggish. Truman for

No.

example was not such a hero, he was not sufficiently larger than
life, he inspired familiarity without excitement, he was a character
but his proportions came from soap opera: Uncle Harry, full of
salty common-sense and small-minded certainty, a storekeeping
uncle.

Whereas Eisenhower has been the anti-Hero, the regulator.
Nations do not necessarily and inevitably seek for heroes. In
periods of dull anxiety, one is more likely to look for security than
a dramatic confrontation, and Eisenhower could stand as a hero
only for that large number of Americans who were most proud
of their lack of imagination. In American life, the unspoken war
of the century has taken place between the city and the small
town: the city which is dynamic, orgiastic, unsettling, explosive
and accelerating to the psyche; the small town which is rooted,
narrow, cautious and planted in the life-logic of the family. The
need of the city is to accelerate growth; the pride of the small town
is to retard it. But since America has been passing through a period
of enormous expansion since the war, the double-four years of
Dwight Eisenhower could not retard the expansion, it could only
denude it of color, character, and the development of novelty. The
small-town mind is rooted—it is rooted in the small town—and
when it attempts to direct history the results are disastrously colorless because the instrument of world power which is used by the
small-town mind is the committee. Committees do not create, they
merely proliferate, and the incredible dullness wreaked upon the
American landscape in Eisenhower's eight years has been the
triumph of the corporation. A tasteless, sexless, odorless sanctity in
architecture, manners, modes, styles has been the result. Eisenhower embodied half the needs of the nation, the needs of the
timid, the petrified, the sanctimonious, and the sluggish. What
was even worse, he did not divide the nation as a hero might
(with a dramatic dialogue as the result); he merely excluded one
part of the nation from the other. The result was an alienation
of the best minds and bravest impulses from the faltering history
which was made. America's need in those years was to take an
existential turn, to walk into the nightmare, to face into that
terrible logic of history which demanded that the country and its

people must become more extraordinary and more adventurous, or else perish, since the only alternative was to offer a false security in the power and the panacea of organized religion, family, and the FBI, a totalitarianization of the psyche by the stultifying techniques of the mass media which would seep into everyone's most private associations and so leave the country powerless against the Russians even if the denouement were to take fifty years, for in a competition between totalitarianisms the first maxim of the prize-fight managers would doubtless apply: Hungry fighters win fights.

The Decline of Greatness

ARTHUR M.
SCHLESINGER, JR.

Ours is an age without heroes—and, when we say this, we suddenly realize how spectacularly the world has changed in a generation. Most of us grew up in a time of towering personalities. For better or for worse, great men seemed to dominate our lives and shape our destiny. In the United States we had Theodore Roosevelt, Woodrow Wilson, Franklin Roosevelt. In Great Britain, there were Lloyd George and Winston Churchill. In other lands, there were Lenin, Stalin, Hitler, Mussolini, Clemenceau, Gandhi, Kemal, Sun Yat-sen. Outside of politics there were Einstein, Freud, Keynes. Some of these great men influenced the world for good, others for evil; but, whether for good or for evil, the fact that each had not died at birth made a difference, one believed, to everyone who lived after them.

Today no one bestrides our narrow world like a colossus; we have no giants who play roles which one can imagine no one else playing in their stead. There are a few figures on the margin of uniqueness, perhaps: Adenauer, Nehru, Tito, De Gaulle, Chiang Kai-shek, Mao Tse-tung. But there seem to be none in the epic style of those mighty figures of our recent past who seized history with both hands and gave it an imprint, even a direction, which it otherwise might not have had. As De Gaulle himself remarked on hearing of Stalin's death, "The age of giants is over." Whatever one thought, whether one admired or detested Roosevelt or Churchill, Stalin or Hitler, one nevertheless felt the sheer weight of such personalities on one's own existence. We feel no com-

REPRINTED BY PERMISSION OF THE PUBLISHER, HOUGHTON MIFFLIN COMPANY, FROM The Politics of Hope BY ARTHUR M. SCHLESINGER, JR. COPYRIGHT © 1962 BY ARTHUR M. SCHLESINGER, JR.

parable pressures today. President Eisenhower, with all his pleasant qualities, has more or less explicitly renounced any desire to impress his own views on history. The Macmillans, Khrushchevs, and Gronchis have measurably less specific gravity than their predecessors. Other men could be in their places as leaders of America or Britain or Russia or Italy without any change in the course of history. Why ours should thus be an age without heroes, and whether this condition is good or bad for us and for civilization are topics worthy of investigation.

Why have giants vanished from our midst? One must never neglect the role of accident in history; and accident no doubt plays a part here. But too many accidents of the same sort cease to be wholly accidental. One must inquire further. Why should our age not only be without great men but even seem actively hostile to them? Surely one reason we have so few heroes now is precisely that we had so many a generation ago. Greatness is hard for common humanity to bear. As Emerson said, "Heroism means difficulty, postponement of praise, postponement of ease, introduction of the world into the private apartment, introduction of eternity into the hours measured by the sitting-room clock." A world of heroes keeps people from living their own private lives.

Moreover, great men live dangerously. They introduce extremes into existence—extremes of good, extremes of evil—and ordinary men after a time flinch from the ultimates and yearn for undemanding security. The Second World War was the climax of an epoch of living dangerously. It is no surprise that it precipitated a universal revulsion against greatness. The war itself destroyed Hitler and Mussolini. And the architects of victory were hardly longer-lived. After the war, the British repudiated Churchill, and the Americans (with the adoption of the 22nd Amendment), Roosevelt. In due course, the French repudiated De Gaulle (they later repented, but it took the threat of civil war to bring him back); the Chinese, Chiang Kai-shek; and the Russians, Stalin. Khrushchev, in toppling Stalin from his pedestal, pronounced the general verdict against the uncommon man: the modern world, he said, had no use for the "cult of the individual." And, indeed, carried to the excesses to which the worshipers of Hitler and Stalin carried it, even to the much milder degree to which admirers of

Roosevelt and Churchill sometimes carried it, the cult of the individual was dangerous. No man is infallible, and every man needs to be reminded of this on occasion. Still, our age has gone further than this—it objects not just to hero worship but to heroes. The century of the common man has come into its own.]

This term, "common man," suggests the deeper problem. There is more involved than simply a dismissal of those colossi whom the world identified with a season of blood and agony. [The common man has always regarded the great man with mixed feelings—resentment as well as admiration, hatred as well as love. The Athenian who refused to vote for Aristides because he was so tired of hearing him called "the Just" expressed a natural reaction. Great men make small men aware of their smallness. Rancor is one of the unavowed but potent emotions of politics; and one must never forget that the envy of the have-nots can be quite as consuming when the haves have character or intelligence as it is when they have merely material possessions.

Modern democracy inadvertently gave envy new scope. While the purpose of democracy was to give everyone a fair chance to rise, its method enabled rancorous men to invoke "equality" as an excuse for cutting all down to their own level. 'I attribute the small number of distinguished men in political life," wrote Alexis de Tocqueville after visiting the United States in the 1830's, "to the ever increasing despotism of the majority. . . . The power of the majority is so absolute and irresistible that one must give up one's rights as a citizen and almost abjure one's qualities as a human being, if one intends to stray from the track which it prescribes." James Bryce even titled a chapter in his *American Commonwealth*, "Why Great Men Are Not Chosen President."

[History has shown these prophets unduly pessimistic. Distinguished men do enter American politics; great men have been chosen President. Democracy demonstrates a capability for heroic leadership quite as much as it does a tendency toward mediocrity. Yet Tocqueville and the others were correct enough in detecting the dislike of great men as a permanent potentiality in a democracy. And the evolution of industrial society appears to have given this sentiment new force. More and more of us live and work within great organizations; an influential book has already singled out the organization man as the American of the future. The bureaucratization of American life, the decline of the working class, the growth of the white-collar class, the rise of suburbia—all this has meant the increasing homogeneity of American society. Though we continue to speak of ourselves as rugged individualists, our actual life has grown more and more collective and anonymous. As a Monsanto Chemical film put it, showing a group of technicians at work in a laboratory: "No geniuses here; just a bunch of average Americans working together." Our ideal is increasingly smooth absorption into the group rather than self-realization in the old-fashioned, strong-minded, don't-give-a-damn sense. Where does the great man fit into our homogenized society?

"The greatness of England is now all collective," John Stuart Mill wrote a century ago: "individually small, we only appear capable of anything great by our habit of combining." He might have been writing about contemporary America; but where we Americans are inclined to rejoice over the superiority of the "team," Mill added somberly, "It was men of another stamp than this that made England what it has been; and men of another stamp will be needed to prevent its decline."

But was Mill right? Do individuals really have impact on history? A powerful school of philosophers has denied any importance at all to great men. Such thinkers reject heroes as a childish hangover from the days when men ascribed everything to the action of gods. History, they assert, is not made by men, but by inexorable forces or irrevocable laws: if these forces or laws do not manifest themselves through one individual, they will do so through another. What has happened already has comprehensively and absolutely decided what will happen in the future. "If there is a single human action due to free will," wrote Tolstoi, "no historical law exists, and no conception of historical events can be formed." If all this is so, obviously the presence or absence of any particular "hero" at any particular time cannot make the slightest difference.

This view of history is a form of fatalistic determinism; and Tolstoi's *War and Peace* offers one of its most eloquent statements. Why, Tolstoi asked, did millions of men in the time of Napoleon, repudiating their common sense and their human feelings, move from west to east, slaughtering their fellows? The

answers provided by historians seemed to him hopelessly superficial. His own answer was: "The war was bound to happen simply
because it was bound to happen"; all previous history prede-
termined it. Where did this leave the great men? In Tolstoi's view,
they were the most deluded figures of all. Great men, he said, "are
but the labels that serve to give a name to an event and, like
labels, they have the least possible connection with the event itself." The greater the man, "the more conspicuous is the inevitability and predestination of every act he commits." The hero, said
Tolstoi, "is the slave of history."

There are many forms of historical fatalism. Toynbee and
Spengler, with their theory of the inexorable growth and decay of
civilizations, represent one form. The Marxists, with their theory
that changes in the modes of production control the course of
history, represent another. When Khrushchev denounced the
practice of making "a hero" out of "a particular leader" and condemned the cult of the individual as "alien to the spirit of Marx-
ism-Leninism," he was speaking the true spirit of his faith. And
Marxism is not the only form of economic determinism; there are
also, for example, economic determinists of the laissez-faire school
who believe that all civilization is dependent on rigid adherence
to a certain theory of the sacredness of private property.

Fatalists differ greatly among themselves. But, however much
they differ, they unite in the conclusion that the individual plays
no role of his own in history. If they are right, then nothing could
matter less whether or not this is an age without heroes.

But they are not right. The philosophy of historical fatalism
rests on serious fallacies. For one thing, it supposes that because a
thing happens it had to happen. But causation is one matter; predestination another. The construction of a causal explanation
after an event merely renders that event in some sense intelligible.
It does not in the least show that this particular event, and no
other, had to take place; that nothing else could possibly have
occurred in its stead. The serious test of the fatalist case must be
applied before the event. The only conclusive proof of fatalism
would lie in the accurate prediction of events that have not yet
happened. And to say, with Tolstoi, that all prior history pre-
determines everything that follows is to say nothing at all. It is to

produce an explanation which applies equally to everything—and thus becomes so vague and limitless as to explain nothing.⌐

⌐Fatalism raises other difficulties. Thus it imputes reality to mystical historical "forces"—class, race, nation, the will of the people, the spirit of the times, history itself. But there are no such forces. They are merely abstractions or metaphors with no existence except in the mind of the beholder. The only evidence for them is deduction from the behavior of individuals. It is therefore the individual who constitutes the basic unit of history. And, while no individual can be wholly free—and, indeed, recent discoveries of the manifold ways in which we are unconsciously conditioned should constitute a salutary check on human vanity—one must assume the reality of an area of free choice until that assumption is challenged not by metaphysical affirmation but by verifiable proof—that is, consistently accurate prediction of the future.

Fatalism, moreover, is incompatible with human psychology and human morality. Anyone who rigorously accepted a deterministic view of life, for example, would have to abandon all notions of human responsibility, since it is manifestly unfair to praise or punish people for acts which are by definition beyond their control. But such fatalism is belied by the assumption of free choice which underlies every move we make, every word we utter, every thought we think.⌐As Sir Isaiah Berlin observes of determinism, "If we begin to take it seriously, then, indeed, the changes in our language, our moral notions, our attitudes toward one another, our views of history, of society and of everything else will be too profound to be even adumbrated." We can no more imagine what the universe of the consistent determinist would be like than we can imagine what it would be like to live in a world without time or one with seventeen-dimensional space.

⌐The historian concerned with concrete interpretation of actual events can easily demonstrate the futility of fatalism by trying to apply it to specific historical episodes. According to the extreme determinist view, no particular individual can make the slightest difference. As slaves of history, all individuals are, so to speak, interchangeable parts. If Napoleon had not led his armies across Europe, Tolstoi implies, someone else would have. William James, combating this philosophic fatalism, once asked the de-

terminists whether they really believed "the convergence of sociological pressures to have so impinged on Stratford-on-Avon about
April 23, 1564, that a W. Shakespeare, with all his mental pe-
culiarities, had to be born there." And did they further believe,
James continued, that "if the aforesaid W. Shakespeare had died of
cholera infantum, another mother at Stratford-on-Avon would
needs have engendered a duplicate copy of him to restore the so-
ciologic equilibrium?" Who could believe such stuff? Yet, if the
determinists do not mean exactly this, how can they read the individual out of history?⟧

In December 1931 a British politician, crossing Fifth Avenue
in New York between 76th and 77th streets around ten-thirty at
night, was knocked down and gravely injured by an automobile.
Fourteen months later an American politician, sitting in an open
car in Miami, Florida, was fired on by an assassin; a man standing beside him was killed. Would the next two decades of history
have been the same had Contasini's car killed Winston Churchill
in 1931 and Zangara's bullets killed Franklin Roosevelt in 1933?
Suppose, in addition, that Adolf Hitler had been killed in the
street fighting during that Munich *Putsch* of 1923, and that
Lenin and Mussolini had died at birth. Where would our century be now?

⌐Individuals, of course, must operate within limits. They cannot do everything. They cannot, for example, propel history into
directions for which the environment and the human material are
not prepared: no genius, however heroic, could have brought television to ancient Troy. Yet, as Sidney Hook has convincingly argued in his thoughtful book *The Hero in History,* great men can
count decisively "where the historical situation permits of major
alternative paths of development."

This argument between fatalism and heroism is not one on
which there is a lot to be said on both sides. The issue is far too
sharp to be straddled. Either history is rigidly determined and fore-
ordained, in which case individual striving does not matter; or it is
not, in which case there is an essential role for the hero. Analysis
of concrete episodes suggests that history is, within limits, open
and unfinished; that men have lived who did what no substitute
could ever have done; that their intervention set history on one

path rather than another. If this is so, the old maxim "There are no indispensable men" would seem another amiable fallacy. There is, then, a case for heroes.

To say that there is a case for heroes is not to say that there is a case for hero worship. The surrender of decision, the unquestioning submission to leadership, the prostration of the average man before the Great Man—these are the diseases of heroism, and they are fatal to human dignity. But, if carried too far, hero worship generates its own antidote. "Every hero," said Emerson, "becomes a bore at last." And we need not go too far. History amply shows that it is possible to have heroes without turning them into gods.

And history shows, too, that when a society, in flight from hero worship, decides to do without great men at all, it gets into troubles of its own. Our contemporary American society, for example, has little use for the individualist. Individualism implies dissent from the group; dissent implies conflict; and conflict suddenly seems divisive, un-American, and generally unbearable. Our greatest new industry is evidently the production of techniques to eliminate conflict, from positive thoughts through public relations to psychoanalysis, applied everywhere from the couch to the pulpit. Our national aspiration has become peace of mind, peace of soul. The symptomatic drug of our age is the tranquilizer. "Togetherness" is the banner under which we march into the brave new world.

Obviously society has had to evolve collective institutions to cope with problems that have grown increasingly complex and concentrated. But the collective approach can be overdone. If Khrushchev worried because his collectivist society developed a cult of the individual, maybe Americans should start worrying as our so-called individualist society develops a cult of the group. We instinctively suppose that the tough questions will be solved by an interfaith conference or an interdisciplinary research team or an interdepartmental committee or an assembly of wise men meeting at Arden House. But are not these group tactics essentially means by which individuals hedge their bets and distribute the irresponsibilities? And do they not nearly always result in the dilution of insight and the triumph of mishmash? If we are to survive, we must have ideas, vision, courage. These things are rarely produced by committees. Everything that matters in our intellectual and moral life begins with an individual confronting his own mind and conscience in a room by himself.

A bland society will never be creative.] "The amount of eccentricity in a society," said John Stuart Mill, "has generally been proportional to the amount of genius, mental vigor and moral courage it contained. That so few now dare to be eccentric marks the chief danger of the time." If this condition frightened Mill in Victorian England, it should frighten us much more. For our national apotheosis of the group means that we systematically lop off the eccentrics, the originals, the proud, imaginative, lonely people from whom new ideas come. What began as a recoil from hero worship ends as a conspiracy against creativity. If worship of great men brings us to perdition by one path, flight from great men brings us there just as surely by another. When we do not admire great men, then our instinct for admiration is likely to end by settling on ourselves. The one thing worse for democracy than hero worship is self-worship.

A free society cannot get along without heroes, because they are the most vivid means of exhibiting the power of free men. The hero exposes to all mankind unsuspected possibilities of conception, unimagined resources of strength.] "The appearance of a great man," wrote Emerson, "draws a new circle outside of our largest orbit and surprises and commands us." Carlyle likened ordinary, lethargic times, with their unbelief and perplexity, to dry, dead fuel, waiting for the lightning out of heaven to kindle it. "The great man, with his free force direct out of God's own hand, is the lightning. . . . The rest of men waited for him like fuel, and then they too would flame."

[Great men enable us to rise to our own highest potentialities. They nerve lesser men to disregard the world and trust to their own deepest instinct.] "In picking out from history our heroes," said William James, "each one of us may best fortify and inspire what creative energy may lie in his own soul. This is the last justification of hero worship." Which one of us has not gained fortitude and faith from the incarnation of ideals in men, from the wisdom of Socrates, from the wondrous creativity of Shakespeare, from the strength of Washington, from the compassion of Lincoln, and above all, perhaps, from the life and the death of Jesus? "We feed on genius," said Emerson. "Great men exist that there may be greater men."

Yet this may be only the smaller part of their service. Great men have another and larger role—to affirm human freedom against the supposed inevitabilities of history. The first hero was Prometheus, who defined the gods and thus asserted the independence and autonomy of man against all determinism. Zeus punished Prometheus, chaining him to a rock and encouraging a vulture to pluck at his vitals.

Ever since, man, like Prometheus, has warred against history. It has always been a bitter and remorseless fight; for the heavy weight of human inertia lies with fatalism. It takes a man of exceptional vision and strength and will—it takes, in short, a hero— to try to wrench history from what lesser men consider its preconceived path. And often history tortures the hero in the process, chains him to a rock and exposes him to the vulture. Yet, in the model of Prometheus, man can still hold his own against the gods. Brave men earn the right to shape their own destiny.

An age without great men is one which acquiesces in the drift of history. Such acquiescence is easy and seductive; the great appeal of fatalism, indeed, is as a refuge from the terror of responsibility. Where a belief in great men insistently reminds us that individuals can make a difference, fatalism reassures us that they can't. It thereby blesses our weakness and extenuates our failure. Fatalism, in Berlin's phrase, is "one of the great alibis" of history.

Let us not be complacent about our supposed capacity to get along without great men. If our society has lost its wish for heroes and its ability to produce them, it may well turn out to have lost everything else as well.

The Hero and Democracy

SIDNEY

HOOK

IF THE HERO is defined as an event-making individual who rede-
termines the course of history, it follows at once that a democratic community must be eternally on guard against him.

This simple, and to some unwelcome, conclusion is involved
in the very conception of a democratic society. For in such a society leadership cannot arrogate to itself heroic power. At legally
determined intervals government must draw its sanction from the
freely given consent of the governed. And so long as that consent
is *freely* given, that is, after the opposition has been heard, the
policy or action agreed upon becomes the one for which the community is responsible even though the leadership may have initiated it.[1]

The problem of leadership in a democracy is highly complex.
Its importance warrants further clarification. Our reflections in
this chapter, as distinct from the others, will be normative. They
will involve judgments of value concerning democracy and democracy's good.

An old Chinese proverb tells us "the great man is a public misfortune." The sentiment aptly expresses the experience and wisdom of a peace-loving race. Were the victims of great men's glory
to speak, not only in China but almost anywhere, they would
echo this homely judgment with sighs and tears and curses. For

REPRINTED BY PERMISSION OF THE PUBLISHER, HUMANITIES PRESS INC.,
NEW YORK, FROM *The Hero in History* BY SIDNEY HOOK.

1. For further amplification of the meaning of "freely given consent," see
Chapter thirteen of my *Reason, Social Myths and Democracy*, New York,
1941; also "The Philosophical Presuppositions of Democracy," *Ethics*, April
1942.

on the whole, heroes in history have carved out their paths of greatness by wars, conquests, revolutions, and holy crusades.

And yet this Chinese proverb epitomizes only past history, and not all of that. A great man may sometimes be a public fortune. His absence is far from being a sign that we shall be spared great misfortunes. Indeed, in face of calamity the people pray for a deliverer. Among the calamities they pray to be delivered from may be the rule of an earlier deliverer. If we were to conclude from the evil things great men have done that their greatness is the source of their evil, we should have to condemn all talent and capacity because they are often abused.

Great men, then, may be good men. And still a democracy must be suspicious of them! For essential to democracy is the participation of the governed in determining their own welfare. This participation is coupled with the *hope* that the governed will select and elect their governors wisely, that is, in such a way as to gratify as many of their needs and wants as the situation permits. But more important than this hope, which is sometimes sadly at variance with the facts, is the belief that it is more worthy of men to decide their own fate than to let others decide it for them.

The hero in a democratic community—the potentially event-making man—may sincerely believe that he accepts its underlying philosophy. But sooner or later he finds himself straining against two features of the democratic process. The first is the principle of majority rule, especially when he is convinced that the majority is wrong on a matter of great import. The second is the slowness of its operation even when he believes the majority is right.

No one believes in majority rule as a reasonable principle of decision in a family of small children, a prison, or an institution for the feeble-minded. To the extent that we accept majority rule as an essential feature of democracy, we are committed to the well-grounded belief that, on the whole, men are not infants, cretins, or criminals. But although men are capable of rationality, reason in human affairs is so much a matter of weighing interests, and interests so often are at variance with each other, that the majority's reason may be the minority's disaster. This proves that the principle of majority rule is not sufficient for democracy, not that it is unnecessary. Nor does it prove that certain rights are inalienable and absolute, for not one such right can be mentioned which under certain circumstances may not need to be abridged in the interest of other rights.

What is necessary in addition to the principle of majority rule is the recognition by every group interest in society of the legitimacy of any group interest, provided the group in question accepts the methods of *free* inquiry and democratic decision as principles of negotiating conflicts of interest. Even so the majority may be mistaken and unjust, even as the man who follows the lead of evidence may sometimes be mistaken while the man who acts blindly may be right. But the majority that provides a minority with the possibility of becoming a majority through the education of citizens by public opposition has gone as far as it can politically to meet legitimate grievance. Under the conditions indicated, the democrat who enjoys freedom of agitation must abide by the decision of the majority even when he believes it to be wrong.

This does not *in principle* justify toleration of a minority whose actual program calls for the overthrow of democratic political institutions by force of arms. Any particular minority may be tolerated on grounds of prudence or expediency, for example, where it is opposed to another minority, more dangerous at the moment, or where its suppression is likely to establish a precedent that may be extended to other minorities who are genuinely devoted to democratic processes.

The "potential hero" in a democracy sees what others do not. His will to action is stronger. His knowledge of what must be done to realize what he sees is surer. For these reasons, he finds himself, more likely than not, in a minority. His sense of his vocation impels him to fight for his insight. His loyalty to the democratic ideal compels him to make this insight the common faith of the majority. If the latter remain stubbornly intractable, his chances of heroic action, as a democrat, are lost. The hero fades into history as a "village Hamden."

Superior talent and strong vision, however, press for expression. So far as the hero does not renounce politics as a sphere of activity, his task becomes to get himself accepted by a majority. For, as a democrat, he does not dare to admit to himself or to others that he wants to make himself independent of the majority. In pursuit of a majority, he may seek to win it, broadly speaking, by the patient methods of education, relying upon the inherent reasonableness of his vision to make its way.

Insofar as he does this, and only so far, democracy is safe from the hero. This means that he courts failure. But the hero may master the arts of the demagogue and use the very instruments of democracy to debase its quality. Yet as long as democratic controls are not abolished, the hero as demagogue must still build up, cajole, and cater to the majority. He acquires a contempt for the group he leads by virtue of the methods by which he corrupts them. In the process, if his own will and insight grow uncertain and cloudy, he becomes just another politician. He is a hero who has missed his chance. But where his will and insight remain firm, the hero as demagogue must "fool" his following into accepting them. He must develop a public platform, on the basis of which he solicits confidence, and a secret program in whose behalf he uses the confidence so won. He becomes a threat to democracy. The greater his faith in himself, the more disinterested his intentions, the more fateful the issue to which his heroic vision drives him, the more insidious is the menace to the whole rationale of democracy. Particularly so if the hero or potential event-making character believes himself to be the indispensable instrument of his vision.

Until now we have assumed that the standpoint of the hero is one that cannot recommend itself to the majority in the light of free discussion and intelligent inquiry and that if it is adopted it is only in virtue of chicanery and demagogic fraud. Let us now assume that the majority is properly persuaded that the hero is right. The latter may still regard the processes of democracy as a fetter upon his calling. For these processes grind too slowly, and many things will not wait. If he is confident that he knows the community's good, and convinced that it hangs in the balance, the hero is tempted to confront it with a *fait accompli*. Well-intentioned opposition that delays and obstructs appears to him as objective betrayal, and can easily be pilloried as such. And he knows that, if he succeeds, a great deal will be forgiven him.

But need a democracy move slowly? No, for its pace can be accelerated by delegation of power to the leader or hero. Yet in the best of situations, this only mitigates the dangers of delay; it does not eliminate them. For a democracy cannot in advance delegate all its powers and remain a democracy. And the crucial situation is always one that involves the undelegated powers. Since power cannot in a democracy be delegated in perpetuity, the crucial situation may arise just when the delegation of power is up for *renewal*. Again, the delegation of power is always requested in a moment of crisis or emergency. But who is to determine when the moment is here?

The hero always presses for greater powers. It is natural to his vocation that he should do so. He is as eager to accept new powers as he is reluctant to surrender them after they are granted. And it is true that, in a troubled world, no democratic community can survive for long unless it entrusts its leader with great powers. At the same time, what it gives with reluctance, it must take back with eagerness. The timing is all—and it is not likely that the hero and the community will agree on what time it is.

There cannot be any guarantee that a leader will not usurp delegated power to carry out a heroic event-making task. But a democracy would be. foolish to refuse delegation of power for this reason if the situation is so crucial that decisive action must be taken at once. On the other hand, there may be no evidence that delegated powers will be abused. Nonetheless, a democracy would be foolish not to withdraw them promptly when the emergency is over, for they are a standing temptation to abuse and usurpation.

A democracy is imperiled not alone by its heroes, necessary as they may sometimes be for survival. It is imperiled by any group of its citizens who are more attached to the advantages or privileges they enjoy under democracy, or hope it will bring, than they are to the democratic process of bringing them about. For these groups, which set greater store on peace or prosperity or social status than they do on the methods of democracy to preserve (or modify) them, are the ones which feel justified in calling in the hero to cherish their "goods" even at the cost of democracy. An instructive example is furnished by conservative classes in western Europe who, convinced that democratic legislation had unjustly abridged the privileges of property, opened the gates to Mussolini and Hitler. True, their profession of democratic allegiance was merely lip service to begin with. But not so for the large numbers of the middle classes and even workers who constituted the mass base of Fascism. Security, fixed prices, employment meant more to them than democracy. They were to learn that when democracy goes, the goods for which it is sacrificed, without becoming more certain, are degraded in quality.

If we were to list as heroes the event-making men of the past, we should find few of them in the histories of democratic societies. It is in conformity with the genius of democratic society that this should be so.

There is great wisdom in the notorious political ingratitude of democratic communities. They usually refuse to glorify their leaders until they are dead. And the best reason for honoring these leaders is that they did not yield to the temptations of power, or that they were prepared to step down from positions of power even when they were convinced that they were right and the majority wrong.

Great men do not ask permission to be born. Nor do they ask permission of democracies to lead them. They find their own way to the tasks they feel called to fulfill, unless crushed by a hostile environment or isolated by the tide of events. Democracies do not have to seek these heroes when it seeks leaders. For if they exist, they will make themselves heard. A democracy must always be girded to protect itself against them even as it uses them, relying not on *their* intentions, which are always honorable but not infrequently messianic, but on the mechanisms of its own democratic institutions, on the plurality of centers of power and interest, and on the spirit of its education and morale.

In a democratic community education must pitch the ideal of the hero in a different key from that of the event-making man. The heroes in a democracy should be the great figures in the Pantheon of thought, the men of ideas, of social vision, of scientific achievement and artistic power. For it is these men who mould the intellectual ideals and social attitudes of the citizens, who without knowledge, quickened perception, and educated taste cannot realize the promise of democracy. If we are earnest in our belief in democracy, we must recognize that it is those who are affected by a basic policy who must pass upon it, either directly or indirectly. And if they are to pass upon it intelligently, know when to delegate power or withdraw it, and enhance the quality of political life by their participation, they must develop a sensitiveness to what is significant and what is trivial, an indifference to rhetorical bombast but a keen interest in what it conceals, an ability to isolate relevant issues and to weigh the available evidence.

The statesman in a democracy exercises his leadership by *proposing* a policy. But whether it is adopted and why depends upon the representatives of the democratic community who are chosen by individuals themselves potentially representative. A successful democracy, therefore, may honor its statesmen; but it must honor its teachers more—whether they be prophets, scientists, poets, jurists, or philosophers. The true hero of democracy, then, should be not the soldier or the political leader, great as their service may be, but the teacher—the Jeffersons, Holmeses, Deweys, Whitmans, and all others who have given the people vision, method, and knowledge.

It is the task of a democratic society to break down the invidious distinctions reflected in current linguistic usage between the hero and the masses or the average man. This can be accomplished in part by reinterpreting the meaning of the word "hero," and by recognizing that "heroes" can be made by fitting social opportunities more skillfully to specific talents. What we call "the average man" is not a biological but a social phenomenon. Human capacities are much more diversified than our social arrangements take note of.

Where we restrict social opportunities, so that only a few types of excellence are recognized, in respect to them the great mass of individuals, despite their differences, will appear as the dull, gray average. If, however, we extend social opportunities so that each person's specific talents have a stimulus to development and expression, we increase the range of possibility of distinctively significant work. From this point of view, a hero is any individual who does his work well and makes a unique contribution to the public good. It is sheer prejudice to believe that the grandeur and nobility associated with the heroic life can be found only in careers that reck little of 'human blood and suffering. Daily toil on any level has its own occasions of struggle, victory, and quiet death. A democracy should contrive its affairs, not to give one or a few the chance to reach heroic stature, but rather to take as a regulative ideal the slogan, "every man a hero."

We call this a "regulative ideal" because it would be Utopian to imagine that it could ever be literally embodied. As a regulative ideal it gives direction to policies that enable society to make the best of whatever powers are available to men.

What are the powers available to men? They are theoretically limited but practically indefinite. In the absence of an environment that encourages their expression, no one can speak with dogmatism about their nature and specific form. Nor can we be certain of the precise limit of human power without allowing for the willed effort that enables the runner to clear a hurdle that until then had been an insuperable obstacle.

A democracy should encourage the belief that all are called and all may be chosen. All may be chosen because a wisely contrived society will take as a point of departure the rich possibilities that nature herself gives through the spontaneous variations in the powers and capacities of men. These variations are the source and promise of new shoots of personality and value. The belief that all may be chosen, acted upon in a co-operating environment, may inspire the added increment of effort that often transforms promise into achievement.

II
Politics

☐ One revealing approach to the meaning of heroism in American politics is through a consideration of the hero's own view, especially when that hero expresses himself with the care of an historian. No significant politician of the postwar period was more obsessed with the meaning of courage than John F. Kennedy; indeed, he believed that political courage was the "most admirable of human virtues." The book that he wrote when he was disabled, *Profiles in Courage* (1954), deals with political heroism historically; but the pragmatic, urgent quality of the writing creates a personal confrontation between the subjects and Kennedy himself. John F. Kennedy wrote *Profiles in Courage* when he was a senator of rising importance and a politician of great ambition. His book is an interesting analysis of courage by a political leader who was attempting to measure those qualities essential to the hero in contemporary America.

☐ At the outset of his book Kennedy takes issue with Walter Lippmann's belief that democratic politicians are insecure, frightened men who succeed politically only because they "placate, appease, bribe, seduce, bamboozle, or otherwise manage to manipulate the demanding threatening elements in their constituencies." Kennedy insists that political courage is constantly manifested in the Senate chamber—indeed the "profiles" of his book are specific examples of that courage—although he does admit that there are "terrible pressures" that inhibit the politician from acting heroically.

☐ The first great pressure that discourages the politician is the necessity of compromise in political life. "The fanatics and extremists and even those conscientiously devoted to hard and fast principles," writes Kennedy, "are always disappointed at the failure of their Government to rush to implement all of those principles and to denounce those of their opponents. But the legislator has some responsibility to conciliate those opposing forces within his state and party and to represent them in the larger clash of interests on the national level; and he alone knows that there are few if any issues where all the truth and all the right and all the angels are on one side."

☐ Second, the politician naturally wants to be re-elected and as a consequence he must not alienate voters. One should not assume, Kennedy reminds the reader, that the politician acts from selfish principles alone; he may be dedicated to a courageous set of principles which, because of his defeat, may never be realized:

In no other occupation but politics is it expected that a man will sacrifice honors, prestige, and his chosen career on a single issue.

Lawyers, businessmen, teachers, doctors, all face difficult personal decisions involving their integrity—but few, if any, face them in the glare of the spotlight as do those in public office. Few, if any, face the same dread finality of the decision that confronts a Senator facing an important call of the roll.

☐ Third, the political leader must respond to the pressure of various interest groups within his own constituency. Kennedy considers the question of whether a politician has the right not to respond to the pressure of the people who have elected him, even if he disagrees with them himself. Does he not represent them? Kennedy concludes that the people of Massachusetts did not send him to Washington to be merely "a seismograph to record shifts in popular opinion. . . . The voters elected us, in short, because they had confidence in our judgment and our ability to exercise that judgment from a position where we could determine what were their own interests, as a part of the nation's interests. This may mean that we must on occasion lead, inform, correct, and sometimes even ignore constituent opinion, if we are to exercise fully that judgment for which we were elected. . . ."

☐ Kennedy concludes *Profiles in Courage* by stating that political heroism depends upon the ability of the people to tolerate independence and dissent on the part of the politician. He is keenly aware that political life in America is now reflected by mass media which, in reporting every act of the politician, discourage heroism. The conformity of American life affects all people but none so much as the politician, for he is constantly watched by everyone. The character in a drama can be a hero because his gestures, the very props he holds in his hands, are enlarged before the audience—there is a distance between him and the people who regard him. But the politician who faces a television camera or a press conference struggles against media that analyze character and thus destroy the unified conception necessary for the hero.

☐ Two of the most important issues of the fifties and sixties in America were "McCarthyism" and the Vietnam War. Both of these issues inhibited political heroism, but in very different ways. Kennedy was accused of writing *"Profiles in Courage* as an act of contrition," a biographer states, "even as unconscious self-indictment, because of Kennedy's own failure to take a position on the McCarthy censure." Still others "held that the key argument in *Profiles* was a damning indictment of the main tendency of McCarthyism—the stifling of unorthodox thought." Whatever truth there is in these opinions, Kennedy was clearly preparing himself for his political future.

☐ The overriding issue of the 1960's has been the Vietnam War. *Representative Men* emerges when disaffection with our Vietnamese policies is so widespread that it has even become popular; but this was not always the case. An interesting chapter of heroism in American culture could be written by tracing the shifting attitudes of politicians, columnists, racial leaders, entertainers, and intellectuals—the American people themselves—toward the war in South Vietnam. Such a study might well suggest—whatever political positions have been taken—that individual convictions and heroism in America today are indeed rare attributes.

John F. Kennedy

And so, my fellow Americans, ask not what your country can do for you; ask what you can do for your country.

Of all the public figures in American life during the 1960's, John F. Kennedy is most clearly the cult hero, the representative man. Rarely has one individual captured the imagination of so many people, although it was not until his death that the man became a myth. "There is a great wisdom in the notorious political ingratitude of democratic communities," Sidney Hook writes in "The Hero and Democracy." "They usually refuse to glorify their leaders until they are dead." This was the case with John F. Kennedy. During his life he was a man who grew out of a rich Irish background in Boston and spent almost his entire adulthood in political life; with his death he became the symbol of a life style that still haunts the American imagination. It is important, if we are to understand the nature of the cult hero in America, to distinguish between the man and the myth, to remember the living political leader and to understand the deified hero.

When one speaks of Kennedy's ancestors, his origins, and his upbringing, one thinks of certain institutions that have been traditionally important to Americans: the family, the church, and the nation. Born on May 29, 1917, into a family that had migrated to America in the 1840's, John F. Kennedy was the second of nine children. His family was extremely close—competitive among themselves, yet united whenever they confronted the outside world—and formed a source of strength to the growing boy. Kennedy went to an exclusive private school, Choate, where he was not an outstanding student. He entered Princeton in 1935, although he had to withdraw after his freshman year because of illness. In 1936 he attended Harvard, but he did not become a really serious student until his junior year. His father, who had made his fortune in banking and the stock market, became Ambassador to the Court of St. James while Kennedy was at Harvard; through his father, a man of strong personal character and a conservative in politics, young Kennedy grew to know some of the leading political figures of the world. In 1940 he published *Why England Slept*, a book based upon his thesis at Harvard. He served in the navy and, in his duty in the South Seas, distinguished himself for acts of heroism that demonstrated his toughness, his loyalty, and his cool response during moments of great stress.

Shortly after Kennedy returned to the United States he became a politician. His elder brother, Joe, had been killed in the war, and John became the political representative of the family. In 1946 he became a Boston Congressman; in 1952 a Massachusetts Senator; in 1960 President of the United States. In 1953 Kennedy had married Jacqueline Bouvier and the young couple, together with their two children (Caroline, born in 1957, and John, Jr., born in 1961), brought an enthusiasm and an élan to national politics that had rarely been experienced in America. He was President for only three years and, as James Reston points out in the following essay, he promised more than he delivered; but he informed the spirit of Americans with greater intensity than any other recent national politician.

John F. Kennedy's assassination on November 21, 1963, probably evoked—in the period that followed his death—greater feeling on the part of more people than the death of any other American. His assassination was as close to formal tragedy as is conceivable in a democracy. Kennedy had all the attributes of the hero: power, prestige, presence, the heroism of the warrior, affability, social standing, youth, physical attraction, religious belief, and wealth. He embodied all of these qualities with a special grace, and his death

seemed associated with the death of youth in America—
"we'll never be young again," wrote Daniel P. Moynihan,
reflecting the attitudes of millions of people. Americans experienced a kind of trauma as they watched the details of
Kennedy's death, the death of his assassin, and the ceremonial
funeral on television. Their interest clearly transcended mere
curiosity; it was close to obsession. Watching the death of the
President, of the tragic hero, seemed a psychic necessity for
the nation, one that was tantamount to the catharsis of
Greek tragedy.

But Kennedy's death had even deeper implications. It
touched upon the death of security in America: the security of
the family, the church, and the nation. The deaths of Joseph
Kennedy, John F. Kennedy, and his brother Robert Kennedy
form the modern democratic version of the destroyed House
of Atreus. Our sense of family is no longer what it once was:
children are dispersed and the young find their sense of community in colleges or other institutions. Secondly, belief in the
church or in formal religion is not so firm as it used to be:
the deaths of the Kennedys seem to support a philosophical
absurdity that is agnostic if not actually atheistic. Lastly,
patriotism—or an allegiance to the nation—has declined since
Kennedy's death. There are many other reasons, no doubt,
but the disaffection of the young has never been more
prominent than since 1963. The death of a hero always
diminishes the spirit of those people who revere him; the
death of Kennedy was uniquely American, for it diminished
—if it did not destroy—the innocence of those who had grown
more hopeful while he was President.

What Was Killed Was Not Only the President but the Promise

JAMES

RESTON

TIME seems to be trying to make amends to John Fitzgerald
Kennedy. Robbed of his years, he is being rewarded and
honored in death as he never was in life. Deprived of the
place he sought in history, he has been given in compensation a
place in legend. What was a monstrous personal and historic crime
a year ago is now something even more elemental and enduring: It
is a symbol of the tragedy and caprice of life, and it is likely to
be remembered by the novelists and the dramatists long after the
historians have gone on to other things.

Will he seem different to the historians from the way the
dramatists will see him? What are they likely to say of his conduct
of foreign affairs, domestic affairs, the Presidency itself? Are we
already confusing myth with reality, as he was always telling us
we should not do?

Probably we are, but this is only fair and maybe even natural.
For there was always something vaguely legendary about him. He
was a story-book President, younger and more handsome than
mortal politicians, remote even from his friends, graceful, almost
elegant, with poetry on his tongue and a radiant young woman at
his side.

He was a sudden and surprising person. He never did things
when other men were doing them. He went to Congress and the

FROM *The New York Times Magazine*, NOVEMBER 15, 1964; © 1964 BY
THE NEW YORK TIMES COMPANY. REPRINTED BY PERMISSION.

White House earlier than most. He married much later than his contemporaries. His war record, his political record and his personal life were marked by flashes of crisis and even by a vague premonition of tragedy. He always seemed to be striding through doors into the center of some startling triumph or disaster. He never reached his meridian: we saw him only as a rising sun.

Accordingly, it is not easy to make an estimate of his 1,000 days in the White House. He didn't have a fair chance and he didn't even give himself a fair chance. He often made his decisions alone after a series of private talks with several individuals, none of whom shared the whole process of his thought.

Oddly in one who had such an acute sense of history, he was disorderly about keeping records of what led up to his decisions, and though he had a great gift for conversation, he seems to have spent little time talking to his closest associates about how he had decided things in the past.

All this complicates the task of placing him in the catalogue of the Presidents. We do not have the record. We do not have the full story of the two Cuban crises, or his meeting with Khrushchev in Vienna, or the reasoning behind his gambles in Vietnam, or the communications that led up to the atomic test-ban treaty with the Soviets. We have only our clippings, memories, and impressions, and these can be uncertain guides.

I—Foreign Policy

Historians—and here we are in the realm of opinion—will probably rate President Kennedy's handling of foreign policy higher than his contemporaries did. It is a spotty record. He dreamed occasionally of an interdependent Atlantic world and this has become part of the legend, but the reality is that the alliance was in poor shape during most of his Administration. He courted Latin America like a thoughtful lover, but, again, the Alliance for Progress was more dream than reality.

Even so, he had a feeling for the way the world was going. He understood the challenge of change. He was fascinated by the political revolution produced by the liberation of the colonial peoples: sometimes too fascinated with it, and too inclined to give it a higher priority than it deserved. He studied and understood the intricate problems of the atomic revolution and the scientific revolution, probably better than any of his predecessors.

Yet this keen, analytical intelligence was not always a help. It enabled him to see the problems, but it often depressed him about finding the answers. I always thought—perhaps wrongly—that his intelligence made him pessimistic. The evidence that science was transforming the world seemed so clear and overwhelming to him that he was irritated by the failure of men and institutions to adapt and keep up.

In his very first State of the Union message, 10 days after he had been sworn in, he told the Congress and the nation: "Before my term has ended, we shall have to test anew whether a nation organized and governed such as ours can endure. The outcome is by no means certain. The answers are by no means clear."

His bungling of his first foreign-policy gamble, when he tried to help the Cuban refugees overthrow the Castro Government, made him all the more conscious, not only of the complexities of political decision, but of the possible consequences of failure.

The events at the Bay of Pigs contributed to his natural caution, and added to his problems with the Communists for most of the rest of his days in the White House. It is impossible to be sure about this, but I was in Vienna when he met Khrushchev shortly after the fiasco of the Bay of Pigs, and saw him 10 minutes after his meeting with the Soviet leader. He came into a dim room in the American Embassy shaken and angry. He had tried, as always, to be calm and rational with Khrushchev, to get him to define what the Soviet Union could and would not do, and Khrushchev had bullied him and threatened him with war over Berlin.

We will have to know much more about that confrontation between Kennedy and Khrushchev, one now deprived of life and the other of power, before we can be sure, but Kennedy said just enough in that room in the embassy to convince me of the following: Khrushchev had studied the events of the Bay of Pigs; he would have understood if Kennedy had left Castro alone or destroyed him; but when Kennedy was rash enough to strike at

Cuba but not bold enough to finish the job, Khrushchev decided he was dealing with an inexperienced young leader who could be intimidated and blackmailed. The Communist decision to put offensive missiles into Cuba was the final gamble of this assumption.

The missile crisis brought out what always seemed to me to be Kennedy's finest quality and produced the events on which Kennedy's place in history probably depends. There is a single fact that repeats itself in the Kennedy story like the major theme in a symphony: He was always at his best in the highest moment of crisis.

He could be ambiguous and even indecisive on secondary questions. He obviously trifled with the first Cuban crisis. He also temporized with the Vietnamese crisis, partly supporting those who wanted to intervene "to win," partly going along with those who reminded him that the French had suffered 175,000 casualties against the same Communist army, but never really defining his aims or reconciling his power with his objectives.

Yet always in his political life he acted decisively when faced with total defeat. He was supremely confident, almost presumptuous, in going for the Presidency in the first place against the opposition of the most powerful elements in his party. He was bold and effective when first Hubert Humphrey, then Harry Truman and finally Lyndon Johnson challenged him publicly during the campaign for the nomination. He probably won the Presidency in the critical debates with Richard Nixon. And this same quality came out in the missile crisis in Cuba.

Then he was, as Robert Frost had urged him to be, "more Irish than Harvard" but with a dash of Harvard intelligence, too. If the first Cuban crisis was the worst example of the uses of American power and diplomacy in this generation, the second Cuban crisis was the best. And the significance of this fact can be understood only in relation to the longer perspective of war in this century.

Twice in this century, the leaders of the free world have been confronted by the menacing power of a totalitarian state. From 1912 until 1914, and again from 1935 until 1939, Germany made a series of moves that clearly threatened the peace and order of the world, and during those critical testing periods, Britain, France and the United States failed either to raise enough military power or to show enough will power to avoid the holocaust. The resulting tragedies of the two great wars transformed the history of the world.

The Soviet decision to place long-range missiles in Cuba, capable of firing atomic rockets into almost any part of the United States, was a similar and in some ways even more ominous test. This lunge into the Western Hemisphere was clearly an effort to change the world balance of power in Moscow's favor, and Kennedy faced it at the risk of war and turned it back.

It is ironic that he went to his grave with many of his fellow countrymen condemning him for failing to get rid of all the Communists and all the defensive missiles in Cuba as well as all the offensive missiles. Yet this view has not been shared by most of the political leaders and historians of the world.

I saw Prime Minister Macmillan of Britain just before he resigned and before President Kennedy was murdered. "If Kennedy never did another thing," Macmillan remarked, "he assured his place in history by that single act. He did what we failed to do in the critical years before the two German wars."

Within a year of Kennedy's death, Khrushchev was removed from power, partly as a result of his humiliating defeat in the Cuban missile crisis, but something important and maybe even historic remained: The Communist world was relieved of the illusion that the United States would not risk atomic war to defend its vital interests. This new awareness greatly reduced the danger of miscalculating American intentions and led almost at once to the first really serious steps to bring atomic weapons under control.

II—The Home Front

Mr. Kennedy was more at ease in the larger world of diplomacy and the struggle between nations than he was in the world of Congressional politics and the struggle between contending national forces. He had more freedom of action in foreign than in domestic policy. He did not seem to mind the small talk of ceremonial meetings with heads of state or foreign students at the White House, and he had a rare combination of informality and dignity that made him very effective in this role. But blarneying with pompous Congressmen bored him and he simply would not take time to do it, as his successor, President Johnson, has with such marked success.

This was odd, in a way. He was a superb politician in planning and running a Presidential campaign, but he didn't really know the deck on Capitol Hill and he did not really like to play the political game there. Even though he spent most of his political life in the House and the Senate, he was always sort of a nonresident member of those peculiar clubs, always a back-bencher with a high truancy record and an excessive respect for the chairmen of the committees and the other elders of the Congress.

The very qualities of appearance, style and cast of mind that won him the admiration of the intellectual and diplomatic worlds somehow marked him as an outsider in his dealings with the Congress. He had little patience for the tiresome loquacity and endless details of legislation, and he never cared much for the boisterous bantering and backslapping of the cloakrooms.

He had a kind of gay magic as a political speaker, most of it as carefully contrived as it seemed spontaneous. He was good at the arts of Hollywood and Madison Avenue, and this delighted his fellow politicians, but he was a little too polished, ambitious and out of the ordinary to escape the envy and criticism of The Hill.

Congress likes typical Americans and Kennedy was not one. In his mature life, probably crossed the Atlantic more often than he crossed the Allegheny range. He never seemed at home in the West. The America he understood best was bounded by Harvard Yard, the State Department, Park Avenue and Palm Beach. His political style and humor were not based on the exaggerated language and gymnastics of the American hustings but on the gentler models of the House of Commons.

Maybe these things had nothing to do with his troubles in getting a legislative program through the Congress; maybe it was just the old stubborn resistance of the Congress to change—"the government of the living by the dead"—but the fact remains that his domestic program was in deep trouble when he was killed, and some of us despaired that Capitol Hill would ever be his field of triumph.

Part of the Kennedy legend is connected with his introduction of the most radical legislation on behalf of Negro equality in this century. But again the reality is less romantic. He did not normally like to take on anything more than he had to tackle, no matter how worthy. Oddly for a man who wrote a book celebrating the heroes of lost causes ("Profiles in Courage"), he was always saying: "Why fight if you are not sure to win?" The Negro demonstrations in the summer of 1963, however, forced his hand, and he went along when some Republican leaders and his brother Robert urged that action was necessary.

Yet, on the home front, as in the foreign field, he did start one major innovation of transcending importance. At the urging of Walter Heller, the chairman of the Council of Economic Advisors, he broke with the traditional economic concepts of Capitol Hill and plunged for a large tax cut and a planned budget deficit. Liberal economists in Europe and in the American universities had been arguing for years that it was no longer necessary to redistribute the wealth of the rich in order to elevate the poor, but that the total production of wealth could be increased to the benefit of everybody if modern technology and fiscal measures were applied.

Kennedy was not by temper a fiscal reformer. He came to the White House as a rather timid liberal, but the longer he was in office the more he cried out against the restraining economic and fiscal traditions of the past and the more he appealed to the country to deal with the world as it is. He never saw his tax bill go through; he died before it was passed. But he was largely responsible for heading the country into the most prolonged period of peacetime prosperity since the last World War. There was a recession when he took over in 1961. Unemployment was up to almost 7 per cent of the work force. There was a balance-of-payments deficit of nearly $4 billion. The outflow of gold to other countries in 1960 totaled $1.7 billion. But by the time he died, this trend had been reversed, at least in part as a result of his initiatives.

III—The Imponderables

Yet even if he turned the tide of the cold war toward the control of nuclear arms, and started the trend toward acceptance of the new economics of increased production and general prosperity, this is not the Kennedy story that is likely to be remembered. These things were only dramatic symbols of his critical mind. He was a critic of his age. He did not think we could deal with the menace of nuclear weapons unless we searched constantly for means of accommodation with the Communists. He did not think we could employ our people in the midst of a revolution in labor-saving machinery unless we changed our attitude toward Federal budgets and Federal deficits.

He did not think we could deal with the pressures of Communism, rising population, or galloping automation, or that we could contain the rising expectations of the nonwhite races and the new nations unless we moved faster to integrate the races at home and the nations of the free world abroad. In short, he did not believe we could deal effectively with a transformed world unless we transformed ourselves—our attitudes of mind and our institutions.

This was a youthful mind asking the big questions. He was not one for big plans and grand designs, though contemporary writers often professed to see such things in some of the speeches of Ted Sorensen. Incidentally, it was always difficult to tell where the soaring rhetoric of Sorensen's bolder and more liberal mind left off and the more cautious Kennedy mind picked up, but Kennedy was not a great planner.

I once asked him in a long private talk at Hyannis Port what he wanted to have achieved by the time he rode down Pennsylvania Avenue with his successor. He looked at me as if I were a dreaming child. I tried again: Did he not feel the need of some goal to help guide his day-to-day decisions and priorities? Again a ghastly pause. It was only when I turned the question to immediate, tangible problems that he seized the point and rolled off a torrent of statistics about the difficulty of organizing nations at different levels of economic development.

Yet there is a puzzle in all this. For while he wanted to transform the thought and institutions of the nation, and regarded the machinery of the Congress as almost an anachronism, he concentrated on working—not, on the whole, very successfully —with the Congress, and he never really exploited his considerable gifts as a public educator.

"Give me the right word and the right accent," said Joseph Conrad, "and I will move the world." This was Churchill's way, and nobody admired it more than Kennedy. But while he made a few glorious trial flights, something held him back, some fear of appealing to the people over the heads of the Congress, some fear of too much talk (he hated verbosity), some modesty, maybe —always so apparent in his embarrassment before applauding crowds.

The essence of the tragedy, however, is perfectly clear. What was killed in Dallas was not only the President but the promise. The death of youth and the hope of youth, of the beauty and grace and the touch of magic.

The heart of the Kennedy legend is what might have been. His intelligence made people think that the coming generation might make the world more rational. It even made it hard for the intellectuals of Europe to be anti-American. His good looks and eloquence put a brighter shine on politics, and made his world relevant and attractive to young people all over the world.

All this is apparent in the faces of the people who come to his grave daily on the Arlington hill. In the world of their dreams, Presidents would be young and heroic, with beautiful wives, and the ugly world would be transformed by their examples.

John Finley, the master of Eliot House at Harvard, sent me a letter which sums up this sense of loss better than anything else:

"No doubt like innumerable people, I feel suddenly old without Mr. and Mrs. Kennedy in the White House. On reflection, ours seems a society of older people; it takes a while to reach the top in science, law, business and most other things. Yet, paradoxically, only the young have the freshness to enjoy and not be wearied by the profusion and vitality of present American life.

"Not only by ability, but by sheer verve and joy, the Kennedys imparted their youth to everyone and put a sheen on our life that made it more youthful than it is. Mr. Johnson now seems Gary Cooper as President—'High Noon,' the poker game, the easy walk and masculine smile. But even Gary Cooper was growing older, and the companions and adversaries around the poker table reflect a less fresh, if no doubt practical and effective, mood. All will be well, I feel sure . . . but it is August, not June. . . ."

Always we come back to the same point. The tragedy of John Fitzgerald Kennedy was greater than the accomplishment, but in the end the tragedy enhances the accomplishment and revives the hope.

Thus the law of compensation operates. "The dice of God are always loaded," wrote Emerson. "For everything you have missed you have gained something else. . . . The world looks like a multiplication table, or a mathematical equation, which, turn it how you will, balances itself. . . . Every secret is told, every crime is punished, every virtue rewarded, every wrong redressed, in silence and certainty."

Richard Nixon

This is the time when the man and the moment come together.

In 1956 Robert Coughlan observed that "Throughout his career [Richard Nixon] has always risen to his opportunities. He has always shown the capacity to grow." The career of Richard Nixon was at one of its high points in 1956; as Vice President, he had shown responsibility and maturity in his support of President Eisenhower, who was suffering from various ailments. In the early 1960's Nixon's political career declined: he was defeated for the Presidency by John F. Kennedy in 1960; he lost the race for governor of California in 1962; and he settled down as a wealthy lawyer in New York. But in 1966, Nixon emerged once again as a Republican leader, supporting various candidates for state office, and in 1968 he was elected to the Presidency. As a man who had "shown the capacity to grow," as a man who had risen from defeat and public humiliation, he elicited admiration from his followers and grudging respect from his opponents.

Richard Nixon was born in Yorba Linda, California, on January 9, 1913. He was graduated from Whittier College in 1934 and Duke University Law School in 1937. Nixon returned to Whittier, California, to pursue a law career, but soon interrupted his practice with four years of service in the U.S. navy. He entered politics in 1946, when he ran against Jerry Voorhis for U.S. Congressman from the Twelfth District of California. Nixon won the election, partially because he accused Voorhis of an association with a Communist committee. After that election, Nixon became known for a militant opposition toward Communism that was often used for opportunistic purposes. As a member of the House Committee on Un-American Activities, he was largely responsible for the confrontation between Alger Hiss and Whitaker Chambers, which led to Hiss's conviction for perjury. When he ran for the Senate in 1950, he defeated Helen Gahagan Douglas by emphasizing Communist subversion in America and by accusing Mrs. Douglas of being "soft on Communism." In 1952 Nixon was selected as Dwight D. Eisenhower's Vice Presidential candidate. During the campaign he was accused of accepting an $18,000 special fund which had been raised by Southern California businessmen, and many people vehemently demanded his resignation. On a famous—some people would term it infamous—television speech he defended himself: "Regardless of what happens," he said, "I'm going to campaign up and down America until we drive the crooks and Communists and those who defend them out of Washington." Listeners supported Nixon, and he was elected Vice President on November 4, 1952; he was re-elected on November 6, 1956.

In 1960, Nixon lost the Presidency to John F. Kennedy by a narrow margin. Kennedy dominated the early sixties, but Nixon, who suffered a further defeat in the gubernatorial election of California, returned in 1966 to resume his leadership of the Republican Party. Once called "Tricky Dicky" by his opponents, he now is often characterized as the "new Nixon," a man who has grown more cautious in his public statements, more aware of the complexities of international and domestic affairs.

Richard Nixon's Mandate

ERIC

SEVAREID

RICHARD NIXON was elected the thirty-seventh President of the United States by a minority of the population. When he takes office later this month, he faces the formidable task of divining and reflecting the will of the majority. The majority did not tell him what that is, save in most general terms. They would like an end to the Vietnam war, of course, and they would like to feel safe in their homes and streets. Beyond that, they would like to dispel the haunting fear that common trust among the people, which must hold any society together, is being eroded.

They chose the man made available by our unique and inexact political processes who was not associated in their minds with the worries and the wounds of the past few years. They picked the new leader in cool blood, with little of the old enthusiasm, expecting no miracles. Their emotional relationship to him was hardly Freudian—not at all like that between the late Senator Kennedy or Senator McCarthy and young followers who seemed to expect of the federal governing establishment that it be to them as a parent or a lover. The voters picked not so much a different *man* as a different approach, or what they hope will prove to be a different approach.

It is bound to be different. The normal political cycle of action and reaction, of synthesis and antithesis makes that inevitable. Whether the new approach will serve the purpose is another question. Prophecies on that score, at this point, are foolish. Only negatives can be advanced with a measure of certainty.

A fundamental commitment that any government undertakes

REPRINTED FROM ERIC SEVAREID, "RICHARD NIXON'S MANDATE," *Saturday Review*, JANUARY 4, 1969. COPYRIGHT 1969 SATURDAY REVIEW, INC.

will not be breached soon again, in however well intended a fashion. That commitment, more fundamental than any treaty of alliance, is that the Government shall not send the young men of this country abroad to die in war unless the security and the vital interests of the United States are unmistakably concerned. Vietnam has been a violation of this commitment, a war into which we moved step by well intended step, walking backward. The new regime, because of the lessons of recent years, will adhere much more closely to a principle expressed by Winston Churchill in his very young years—that there is a definite if not always easily identified limit to what one nation can do on behalf of other nations at the expense of its own people.

The new regime will be very sparing of promises to alien societies. It will not repeat the mistake of President Kennedy, in his first official months, when he said that we would try to renovate the economies of Latin America in ten years' time, an implied promise that set some progress in motion, but excited expectation far more.

Mr. Nixon has refrained from promises of that kind even to our own people. He knows that we are in deep trouble at home not only because these social and racial problems are inherently very difficult to solve and the programs for solving them may have been hastily conceived, but also because progress itself has been outrun and discounted because of the impatient expectations stirred by the promises.

For many years now the procedure has been, first, a grand conception and heraldic slogan, whether it be the War on Poverty or the Alliance for Progress, or in Mr. Rusk's favorite term, a world order; then messages to Congress filled with very moving rhetoric; and finally large appropriations and the hasty throwing-together of another federal agency. A crusade seemed the only way to get anything started.

It cannot be done that way any more. Nixon has, in fact, not even put a label on his own regime. No "New Deal," "New Frontier," or "Great Society." He campaigned in cool blood and he was elected in the same spirit. It may well be that we have seen the end of innocence, of popular excitement in our Presidential elections, and will behave from now on much more like the Europeans in theirs—and Nixon will govern in this spirit. He could not do otherwise if he wished; he is not an exciting person and he knows it and cherishes no grand and exciting designs so far as anyone can discover.

He will try to bring about a gradual though not full withdrawal from the mainland of East Asia. He will not dare or wish to reduce American power in Europe or in the Mideast because potential flash points lie in those regions; he will try to bring our world balance of payments into better order.

He will try to find a more rigorous federal approach to diminishing crime and mass violence. He had no dramatic new ideas to offer in this respect during his campaign; I doubt that there are any. Federal financial help and expertise can be made available in the realm of police personnel and tactics; otherwise the federal role is limited. There is no magic in Nixon's naming of John N. Mitchell as the new Attorney General. Ramsey Clark struck many Washington observers as one of the better performers in that office. There is no magic in new appointments to the Supreme Court. Their decisions on the rights of defendants are not the core of the vast problem. Far more important are the tragically crowded dockets of our courts at all levels. If hundreds of new judges and courts could be created—federal, state, and municipal—we might make some progress in diminishing conventional crime.

Whether he can make serious inroads on the massive, festering, explosive matter of the crowded city slums, into which nearly 20,000,000 mostly unskilled, poorly educated, psychologically lost and alienated people, many from rural regions, have moved in the last twenty years, remains to be seen. With the best will and the best means, this is the work of a whole generation. Mr. Nixon has deeply committed himself to the method of tax credits to private enterprise, to bring their efforts at urban renovation into the picture. One writer has described this as drowning the already rich in money in order to sprinkle the poor. This prediction may be too cynical but almost no one now in Washington thinks this approach can be of more than fragmentary help.

One thing seems fairly clear: if the new President *is* obliged to revert to large federal outlays, it will have to be done by new processes and structures. The approach that began with the New Deal has exhausted itself to a certain degree; the huge, centralized federal bureau cannot deal effectively with these complex, intimate, personal, and group problems of poverty at the neighborhood level. Both power and money must begin to flow back toward the states and the municipalities. A new relationship must emerge. President Johnson, quite aware of this, called it "creative federalism." There will have to be direct grants to state and local government but there will also have to be new, trained minds dedicated to serve at these levels. A few universities and foundations are now attempting to encourage and train new talents in these directions. Political philosophies will mean little; there won't be many conservative approaches or liberal approaches; it will be social engineering.

In this process of restructuring government, regional authorities of various kinds will have to emerge, to deal with many complex and pressing problems, including our waterways and highways, air pollution, and rapid transit. The present structure is not effective; this, too, will be the work of many years.

Mr. Nixon cannot do so very much about all this in four years' time (we might be in for a period of one-term Presidents, so short has the national patience and attention span become), and he will be able to do very little indeed unless these last eight or nine years of steady economic growth continue. Eisenhower somehow survived three distinct economic recessions and survived them with the people's trust; Mr. Nixon, who has yet to win that trust, could not easily survive one. He needs some of that famous Eisenhower luck, and he is going to need, and has a right to expect, some forbearance, some benefit of the doubt from various people, including many press critics, for some time to come. He needs this because our common fate needs it.

How long this period of forbearance may last, nobody can say. Events and the President himself will decide that. It will be cut short if the Vietnam war flares up again into heavy, sustained fighting and casualties; it may be cut short if the new President tries to go ahead with the policy he stated during his campaign of striving for a bigger nuclear superiority over the Russians, which would almost certainly check the negotiations for a leveling-off that the Johnson Administration is trying to get back on the track. To go that way would strain federal financial resources almost unendurably and make impossible any massive federal attack on domestic ills. Hopefully, Nixon will quietly forget his campaign bravado.

There is something else that can cut short the Presidential honeymoon. This is the inner nature of Mr. Nixon himself; he is a conditioned-reflex personality. He is more like Lyndon Johnson than most people imagine. He, too, likes indirection; he tends instinctively to mask his moves with various disguises. It is not natural to either man to say simple, straightforward things to press or public. This is why another so-called credibility gap may develop, beginning with relations between the White House and the working press. The press was conditioned to look for hidden motives behind almost everything Mr. Johnson said and did. This lack of trust is bad business; it poisons the Washington mental climate and spreads outward to the people. Mr. Nixon, who knows he is not widely loved, has said that the people's respect is more important than their love. This may be true, but the foundation of respect is always *trust*. Mr. Nixon seems to have taken Woodrow Wilson for his personal model. It was Wilson who observed that a President the people trust can not only lead the people: he can also form them to his own views.

Mr. Nixon is a party man, far more than was Eisenhower, even more than is Mr. Johnson. He will try to work at another big task—the building and solidifying of the Republican party as the majority party of the country, which it has not been since Hoover's time, the Eisenhower interregnum notwithstanding. There seems some chance that Nixon can do this, building upon the suburbs and rural areas everywhere, and upon the Midwest, Far West, and border states, plus what he calls the "new South" in general. He will try to confine and isolate the Democrats in the big, Northeastern industrial regions.

This implies a swing to the right in this country, though not to the far or radical right as symbolized by Wallace; to the near right of center. This seems to frighten a good many intellectual liberals. Robert Lowell has written the following: "I have a gloomy premonition . . . that we will soon look back upon this troubled moment as a golden time of freedom and license to act and speculate. One feels the steely sinews of the tiger, an ascetic, 'moral,' and authoritarian reign of piety and iron."

We have never experienced a Bismarckian reign of piety and iron, and I do not think we will. If mass violence gets worse in the great cities, the police and military reaction will get more severe, because it will have to, but this ought not affect directly more than a small minority of the people. Mass crime is still crime, even when committed by those who have been cruelly shut out from the promises of American life, and it cannot be endured.

American society is not "sick," though it contains many sick individuals. An indictment cannot be drawn against a whole people. If everyone is guilty, then no one is guilty. If there *were* mass guilt, then there would have to be mass punishment, and that is beyond the thought or means of a democracy.

This is indeed a critical period, but we don't stand at Armageddon, the great, the final day of judgment on America. Most of the continuous upheaval is of a positive, not a negative, nature in its impulse. A basically healthy society is trying, for one thing, to cleanse itself of the one serious, chronic virus in its bloodstream, which is racism.

The Negro passion of our day seems to be the closest thing to a true people's revolution that this country has experienced. But it has followed the historical pattern in which revolutions do not produce change, in the first instance. Instead, change produces revolutions which then continue change. Totally ground-down masses of people do not make revolutions. They are usually set in motion by a small minority of intellectuals, in a general atmosphere of intellectual freedom, not repression, and they gather strength when changes *have* been made—such as the historic court decision on school desegregation—when light is seen at the end of the dark tunnel; that is, when *hope* is aroused.

Never in our history has there been such freedom of expression as there is today; never such concern with the downtrodden by the so-called Establishment; never such concern for youth; never such concern for defendants by police and court authority.

Many who are young will take that as an astonishing statement. That is because youth can measure in only one direction— from things as they are forward to their ideal of what things ought to be. They cannot measure backward, to things as they used to be, because they have not lived long enough, and they cannot measure laterally, to the conditions of other societies on this earth, because they have not yet had the opportunity to know them well. Older people must add these two measurements. This is the core reason why the generation gap exists and why it will always exist.

It is not our freedom that is in jeopardy, in the first instance; it is our public order. If that breaks down, freedom will be lost, and, though the young new leftists do not seem to believe it, so will the prospects for greater justice. There is a lesson of history they do not accept: any people, put to the test, will prefer order, even tyranny if it comes to that, over anarchy, because anarchy is the worst tyranny of all, in which no one's policy or program can have effect.

Public order is in some jeopardy, and so is the capacity of our institutions to deal with the pressing problems. If they press very painfully, it is not because of venality in high places or ignorance, or because of apathy on the part of the much-abused middle class. It is because in a very short period we have had a demographic revolution—millions pouring into the cities; a new scientific-industrial revolution which rapidly alters our daily lives and surroundings; a communications revolution which has intimately brought every condition and problem into everyone's ken; and an educational revolution which has made some measure of learning all but universal and which has thus encouraged extra millions to wish to play some role in the articulation or the solution of these problems.

Mass education and intimate, mass communications are turning us in the direction, at least, of direct democracy. The ancient Greeks believed that a citizenry of about 5,000 people was the manageable maximum for direct democracy. We shall see how it goes with 40,000,000 activists taking part. Public indifference to public affairs is by no means the whole problem. The problem is also of an opposite nature—too many untrained cooks in the kitchen.

One way or another, we are going to experiment our way, muddle our way through, if the world stays at peace. We *do* face a period, perhaps a long one, of a kind of guerrilla war in the big city ghettos, spasmodic in nature, often frightening in its effect. But nobody is going to "burn this country down" or "tear this country apart" as some of the militants so shrilly proclaim. We are not fundamentally a hating or oppressive people. There is still a deep evangelical streak, a true collective conscience, and it has been aroused.

The November election gave testimony to that effect. Wallace got a vote of more than 9,000,000, but most of it was geographically centered. He discovered that he was wrong in his repeated declaration that what he calls the red necks outnumber the others. The election showed very few surfacing currents of revolutionary sentiment, in spite of all the talk of the militants. The country supposedly was torn apart in spirit, its politics dangerously polarizing, yet it went right on with its normal pattern of reaction, in the test. It was reminiscent of the French people last spring. For several violent weeks they looked into the abyss of anarchism and extremism; then, given the chance of expression in another plebiscite, they went right back to de Gaulle and order and what seemed normal.

Until we do get our own house in better order, we shall not be able to play an exceptionally strong role in trying to get the world itself in better order. The existentialist faith in foreign affairs, as exemplified by the Kennedy brothers, the feeling that we do not exist in the world unless we *act* in the world—this faith is declining, as it had to. No one, anywhere, is going to believe in American promises, such as the one that we will abolish poverty in Asia, made by Mr. Johnson on his Far Eastern tour, when they see how desperately difficult it is for us to abolish poverty in our own country. Hopefully, the new Administration, along with the Congress, will undertake a truly searching re-examination of the very premises of our foreign policy of these last twenty years.

This nation is not going to go isolationist in the old-fashioned sense: we could not even if we would. But, of iron necessity, the heaviest concentration of the new Administration is going to be on our domestic affairs. Even some of our friendliest allies abroad are urging this course upon us.

This country has not yet realized itself; we have not reached our full potential. We have built a successful nation, but not yet a successful society or culture. If we could do that, we could bring to the world the greatest possible gift and blessing, and one within our real powers.

First, we must somehow find our way back to a greater measure of common trust among ourselves. This is what Senator Muskie tried to tell his audiences this autumn. We *have* to trust others, he said, even those whom we may fear and who we suspect may wish us harm. We must, each of us, take this risk. That is what built this country when you get down to it: risk— and trust.

George C. Wallace

I say segregation now, segregation tomorrow, segregation forever!

The most controversial issue of the 1968 Presidential campaign was the candidacy of George Wallace. Celebrated as a man of the people by his supporters, Wallace represented to liberals a hard-core segregationist, a new Huey Long who preyed upon the fears of the average white voter. Wallace has been the central figure in political conservatism since the decline of Barry Goldwater in 1964; his rise to national prominence in the 1968 campaign indicated that he represents a sizable proportion of the American population.

Born on August 25, 1919, in Clio, Alabama, George Wallace attended the local public schools. He excelled in sports, especially in boxing, and while attending the University of Alabama Law School, he earned money through professional boxing. After receiving his law degree in 1942, Wallace served in the U.S. air force for three years. In 1946 he became an Assistant Attorney General for Alabama. He rose from the state legislature to the judiciary to the executive branch in Alabama; in 1962 he was elected governor of the state, largely on the basis of a strong advocacy of segregation in the public school system. "When the court order comes," he told the voters of Alabama, "I am going to place myself in the position so that it must be directed against me and not some lesser official. I shall refuse to abide by any illegal federal court order, even to the point of standing in the school house door." On July 11, 1963, he fulfilled his pledge by preventing two Negro students from registering at the University of Alabama; under an executive order, however, Wallace yielded.

Wallace was an engaging and forceful politician in his early career; but he became more rigid and parochial as he realized that he would not be politically successful unless he took a strongly conservative view in regard to segregation. "Looking at his early years in the legislature," Marshall Frady, the author of *Wallace* (1968), has remarked, "one is left with a sense of exuberant promise subtly and inexorably corrupted. Many still remember him from those days as a dizzily gifted young man with an air of inevitability about him, winning and eager and dauntless, with instincts that were refreshingly simple and generous." Ambition corrupted him, according to Frady—"insatiable, impatient ambition, and that ambition led straight to the race issue."

Had but the federal judiciary been as well read on their American
and Southern history as on the peculiar sociological theories of
the left; had but they perused, even superficially, Mr. Kipling's
comment on the specific infusion of Scot fighting clan blood
into the English strain of the South; had they but studied, from
their lofty tower of impregnable authority, the demise of one
Edward I whose authority was even loftier, until he bullied a
Scottish clan called Wallace; then perhaps they would have busied
themselves with quieter and less hazardous pursuits than
encroachments on freedom guarded over by a little country judge.
But they didn't . . . and his name is Wallace . . . and therein
lies the tale. We cannot tell the ending to it; that will be written
in the days that are with us now.

—Official Inaugural Program
STATE OF ALABAMA, JANUARY 14, 1963

George Wallace: A Gross and Simple Heart

TOM

WICKER

MORE THAN four years later, we still "cannot tell the ending" to the story of George Corley Wallace, Jr., but as in
many another dark tale of the fighting clans of Scotland,
the signs and portents cannot be ignored. As an Alabama back-
country ballad called "Little Stonewall Wallace" has it:

Dixie's lookin' fer a man, now listen to me well,
I kin hear it in the song of the whippoorwill,
I kin feel it in the sigh of the ol' pine trees—
Done got herself a man, you wait an' see.

Those not attuned to the Alabama omens need not go about listening to its whippoorwills and pine trees. The state's automobile license plates have borne for years the legend "Heart of Dixie." These days, on many a shiny new sedan or muddy farm pickup truck, another plate appears beside the official one. It bears pictures of George and Lurleen Wallace on a field of stars and bars, and the simple proclamation: "Wallace Country."

An Alabamian choosing to be more specific can adorn his bumper with a tin picture of George alone, superimposed on the battle cry of the Alabama Movement—"Stand Up for America— Wallace for President." For the restrained, there is a tastefully devout plate reading simply, "Wallace—My Governor," with no picture. Nor, in Alabama, is it necessary to speculate about the politics of those whose cars carry tags in support of "One Nation Under God," although these are daring enough to present the American rather than the Confederate flag.

Lurleen Wallace was elected to replace Little Stonewall as Governor last fall with the biggest majority in the state's history, not excluding his own in 1962. When the Gardendale, Alabama, city council dismissed one Earl W. Hall as city judge, Hall said it was because he was a Republican in a one-party system "that stamps out any competition."

One of the most eminent attorneys in the state confided recently that it was not now a good thing in his profession to become known as an anti-Wallace man "if you have to try cases before a jury." Newspapers that have opposed Little Stonewall have been known to lose state-controlled liquor advertising. Patronage, of which there is a great deal in Alabama, is pointedly administered. ("Was that fellow for us?" Wallace will inquire to someone calling to advocate an appointment. "I hate not to but if folks wasn't for you, it's hard as the devil to appoint 'em.")

State Senator Robert Gilchrist, a leading opponent of Mrs. Wallace in the Democratic primary last spring, failed even to carry his home county against her. ("My little wife, a girl who used to work in a dime store, beat this big state senator in his own home town," Wallace says.) So Gilchrist "got the word from the primary," as a Wallace man put it, and led the fight for the Governor in enacting a state law that attempted to nullify the federal school desegregation guidelines.

George Wallace has assembled in the "Heart of Dixie" a political empire to which the shrewdest Alabama political observers now see no practical limit. He has not been able to do so just because, in the eminently practical politics of this place, a Governor can call up the head of an asphalt plant who sells his product to the state and get a $25,000 campaign contribution in two minutes, under the unspoken threat of taking the state's ample asphalt business elsewhere. The reason is rather that so many Alabamians believe wholeheartedly that Little Stonewall has single-handedly "stood up for us" and "put the spotlight on Alabama" as the spearhead of a "movement" that is sweeping the nation and that promises to relieve the South of the burden of civil-rights pressures and federal "dictation."

Wallace is where he is today because he is a demagogue of unique sincerity, a profound student of human nature in its earthiest order who accords to that nature his highest respect, and thus a politician who more than any in his time has touched and played upon the deepest chords of belief among his people— chords that ring as truly in him as in them. He is an artist of defeat who, from a string of unbroken reverses, has made of himself a Southern Messiah. Whether or not this is an exercise in mass delusion or the shrewdest political buildup in recent history, his wife spoke nothing but the plain truth when she said of him, "He speaks out for [the people of Alabama]. He says what they think. When he's on 'Meet the Press' they can listen to him and think, 'That's what I would say if I were up there.'"

There are about three and a half million people in Alabama. Despite their peculiar Southern heritage, they are not totally different from people elsewhere. George Wallace, in the 1964 Democratic Presidential preferential primaries in Indiana, Wisconsin, and Maryland, won from 25 to 43 per cent of the vote. These and other evidences suggest that George Wallace may speak for some large, unknown number of Americans—five million, ten million, more?—not necessarily racist, not necessarily reactionary, not necessarily stupid or vicious or ignorant, but human, concerned, determined.

A Feeling for the Folks

His first day back in his dark, paneled office in the Alabama state Capitol last winter, after the time taken out following Lurleen Wallace's smashing victory in the November election, was clear, cold, windy. Above the sparkling white building on Goat Hill, the Confederate flag snapped in the wind; the Alabama flag crackled with equal authority on the same staff; but there was no sign of the Stars and Stripes. On the columned gallery, which affords a decent view over Montgomery, a small medallion inset in the floor marks the exact spot where Jefferson Davis stood when he was sworn in as President of the Confederate States of America. Beyond enormous doors in a chilly rotunda, where beautifully designed staircases sweep upward without visible support, effusive Southern ladies distribute state maps, pamphlets, and honeyed words. A visitor from Washington is informed with insistent laughter that he must have brought the chilly weather with him. Intimidated suddenly by his own Southern background, the unquestionable primacy of ladies, and the priority on agreement, charm, affability, he agrees that indeed he must have. Alabama could not be responsible, even for its weather; it could only be an imposition.

The Governor's quarters are cramped into a new wing of the Capitol—new since Jefferson Davis, anyway. Audrey Henderson, Wallace's secretary, confined with her electric typewriter in a windowless cell, confides that someone once told her, "Honey, this used to be the janitor's closet." But that, she says proudly, was when "the Governor used to be a pretty quiet affair in Alabama"—which he is not now.

Reuben King, who heads the state's welfare program and occasionally fills in for George Wallace's administrative assistant, Cecil Jackson, points out, "In the last four years, every member of the Cabinet has been in the hospital. I've been in twice and I'm only thirty-seven years old. I tell you, when a man works as hard as the Governor does, with all that energy, you just don't feel right unless you do the same. He's down here until seven, eight at night. It just makes you feel kind of like you got to keep up with him." He sighs. "Miz Wallace, she's gonna be just the same. She's just like him, got a real feeling for the folks."

Wallace himself fidgets behind a big desk, and dashes out to his reception room periodically to shake a few hands and bandy words. (To a man from Tallahassee: "Lot of good folks over there, ain't they? I made a speech over there and told'em you got more instinct than *The New York Times*. You knew Castro was a Communist all along and *The New York Times*, they still don't believe it.") He receives particularly important visitors in the inner sanctum (to two well-regarded ladies who wanted his autograph on their copies of an admiring biography, *The Wallace Story* by Bill Jones, he confesses, "I ain't read that book yet myself"), and often answers his own phone. He dismisses the hectic atmosphere in which he works with a wave of the hand: "That's just life nowadays. Sometimes there's seventy-five people out there wantin' to see me."

Physically unimpressive, his cufflinks a bit too large, his hair too neatly waved, George Wallace still is one of those men who dominate a room by their mere presence. He is nervous, aggressive in the way of small men, assertive to a point just short of arrogance, with too much fire in him to permit wit, ease, or even backslapping. He puts in a quick call to one of his backers, apparently for no reason except to instruct him to "tell'em all hello for us. You tell all our friends, hello, hear?" He plays with a gavel, smacking its head in his palm, gouging himself with its handle; there is a cigar constantly in his hand or mouth (a box of Hav-A-Tampa Fancys Extra is within reach) and he stabs at its stub repeatedly with a variety of desk lighters, chews it, removes it to spit in the wastebasket.

"I got people finding out which office in this building Jefferson

Davis worked in," he says. "I just might move in there when
Lurleen moves in here."

Audrey announces another visitor. "I'm goin' to see that
sonovabitch for just a minute"; he dashes out, returns, flops in
the swivel chair behind the desk with its $100 State of Alabama
note under the glass, its family photos, its Air Force plane model,
its Confederate cannon model, its white leather Holy Bible, its
six pens in their stands ("No use to fill them," Audrey confides.
"The governor doesn't believe they'll write unless you dip'em
each time"), its three phones, beige, red, and a green one with
six buttons.

Everywhere he looks, there is tribute to his world and position
—the long conference table beyond his desk, the dark leather
chairs surrounding it, the color photograph behind him of two
decrepit Confederate veterans saluting the Stars and Bars in
eternal, dreamlike sunshine, the handsome green marble mantel
around the fireplace, the ornate crystal chandelier suspended
above the conference table, the magnificent portrait of Winthrop
Sargent (Governor of the Mississippi Territory, including Alabama, 1798–1800) above the mantel, and just beneath the portrait
the glorified bust of himself with the inscription: "George C.
Wallace, Governor of Alabama. He Stood for the People of
Alabama." There is a plaque that certifies him an honorary colonel
in the Gold Run Gulch Horse Guards, a Civil War cannonball,
"Presented to George C. Wallace by the Voters of Louisiana,
6–17–64."

An ancient television set perches on an ancient filing cabinet
at one end of the room and, in sharp contrast, at the other, past
rows of cracked black-leather-bottom chairs, is both a modern
dictating machine and a 1920s glass lamp. Here, amid the Southern
courthouse smells of tobacco, politics, earth, men, defeat, and
age, George Wallace in his dark conservative suit, faintly pin-
striped, his blue shirt with its pinched collar, his red, silver, blue
striped tie, his gold watchband, gold cufflinks, and gold ring,
cocks back in his chair and talks with the amazing frankness of
conviction.

"If one of these national parties don't recognize that people
are fed up with crime in the streets," he says, "and I mean people

of all races are fed up with courts and politicians coddling these criminals; if they don't realize we're tired of handing out foreign aid while nobody helps us out in Vietnam, and we're tired of helping France when they won't help us, and we're tired of folks raising money and blood for them Vietcong under academic freedom and freedom of speech while our boys get shot at—we've got to differentiate between what's dissent and academic freedom and what's treason—if the two parties continue along this liberal path, attackin' private property rights and free enterprise, a lot of people will be out of a choice and I'll give them one."

He snatches a desk lighter, snaps it three times, rejects it, grabs a match, lights the cigar stub. "Course I ain't one of these ultras who's against everything. A fellow like that couldn't get elected to office here in Alabama. I couldn't get elected on a hate-Niggras platform. Down here, we made the government the issue, not the Niggra. And it ain't just here in Alabama and the South. People everywhere are tired of the government telling them when to get up and when to go to bed. The people need to be enlightened about this and we're going to do that."

"Intellectual Morons"

Somebody calls to tell Wallace that his name is being used to solicit advertising in a magazine. He cradles the phone between shoulder and ear, grabs a lighter, jabs it against the inch-long Hav-A-Tampa Fancys Extra: "Well, I tell you, it's just as hard as the devil; I mean there ain't no way to keep people from invoking your name and I just don't know how to do it. Tell'em all hello up there for us." He hangs up, whirls, dictates a memo to someone to investigate the advertising project.

"The real problem ain't race," he continues, as if in unbroken conversation. "The real problem is these intellectual liberals who take power and oppress people. Insist they got to vote, even illiterates, and then won't let them run their own affairs when they do. Like they insist the people of Alabama don't have the morality and integrity to run their own affairs and so they got to be run for them, these guidelines and all. Why, there's more feelings against the Niggra in Chicago and New York than in Alabama. All this talk about the Klan, for instance. The only Klansman I know is ――― and he hangs around the Capitol here and you can't help but know him. But at least a Klansman will fight for his country. He don't tear up his draft card. But the Klan, it's just innocuous in size and they're just concerned with segregation, not subversiveness."

He repeats—it is a favorite theme—that it is "the intellectual liberals, who come to power and think they know everything and what's good for everybody, who oppress the people. Intellectual morons, I call'em. Sometimes theory just don't work. You got to be practical in dealing with human problems. Take Castro. Any man plowing a mule down here—and I don't mean a man plowing a mule didn't go to school—any man with a second-grade education knew Castro was bad just looking at his picture and reading what he said. Any cab driver in Montgomery—and I don't mean to throw off on them because I used to be one myself—knows more about why we're in Vietnam than a Yale professor sitting up there in his ivory tower. We got to get all this theory out of things."

But he is angered by the charge that he is just an unprincipled demagogue—for instance, that of a state senator who was quoted by Jack Nelson of the Los Angeles *Times* as saying that Wallace would be "the damnedest integrationist you ever saw if he thought that was what people wanted. He's got no sense of right or wrong about it."

A political leader, Wallace says, "sometimes has facts people can't get in everyday life. So he has to educate them; he can't just say, 'what will be popular today?' You're supposed to lead. If they think I'm just a demagogue what do they say about me and my wife? Nobody in this state but me thought she could get elected Governor. When I first got the idea I called up my friends and ever one of'em said, 'I'm for Wallace but I ain't voting for no woman.' But we just kept right on, and that little girl that used to work in a dime store got 480,000 votes in the primary and eight other candidates only got 403,000 and then she got 550,000 in the general. And if I had just listened to what people said, she never would of run.

"Anyway, the people have the facts on this encroachment on the rights of the states. They know the score on that and they're tired of it. I don't think I've changed anybody's mind. If I wasn't in tune with the people of Alabama they wouldn't have elected me Governor. Besides, they ain't no integrationists in this country if you get right down to it, except a few long-haired gals and some bearded fellows and a few college professors and preachers and even they aren't when it gets right down to their children intermarrying. But I don't talk about that stuff."

He has never, Wallace insists, "made a racist speech in my life, not unless you count being for segregation as racist. I mean I never talked against Niggras as people. I got nothing against Niggras. Southern folks had the most practical approach ever devised for this race business. So what if we had paternalism as long as we had peace and folks were satisfied? What good are equal rights if it gets folks killed and ruins everything? Why, you're safer in the worst part of Montgomery than on the New York City subway. We got less integration but more mingling and more law and order. And what most folks of all races want is law and order." Then he adds slyly, "Of course, some folks just *like* to get out and throw rocks."

At lunchtime, Wallace trots down an interior stairway to a long basement corridor leading to the Capitol cafeteria. He speaks to everyone along the way, calling the girls "honey," the men by their names.

From the cafeteria steam table he chooses chopped steak, rutabagas, canned peaches, sliced tomatoes, a pack of Fig Newtons. As he takes his seat with the office workers, a waitress rushes up with a small dish.

"I saved the Governor some okra," she confides to his guest. "It's his favorite."

"You said it, honey," Wallace says, eating a Fig Newton.

Grover Hall, the witty former editor of the Montgomery *Advertiser*, now the editor of the Richmond *News-Leader*, a close personal friend but not always a political supporter of Wallace's, joins the luncheon party. He joshes the Governor about his table manners; Wallace obviously enjoys it. "One time I was going up to Richmond to make a speech and ol' Grover told me I had to polish myself up because it would be a real cultured audience," he says. "Well, I went up there to the John Marshall Hotel and it was the most cultured, polite, well-dressed crowd I ever saw in my life and I gave 'em a real cultured talk until I started getting warmed up and then I forgot and called the Supreme Court a 'sorry, lousy, no-count outfit,' and you ought to have heard that cultured crowd stand up and cheer. People are about the same everywhere but ol' Grover here keeps trying to polish me up."

He douses the chopped steak in ketchup. "Course I talk like we all do down South," he continues. "You know—ain't got no, he don't, and all that—I know better but it's just comfortable. So I went up and was on television with Martin Luther King and I talked like I always do and there he was with that grammar and those big words. And they quoted me in the paper the next day to make it look like I don't know anything and then they quote a fellow like that that don't even know the origins of the English language."

Wallace rises to speak to an eager voter hovering over the table and Hall offers an opinion: "That fellow can read your insides quicker than any man I ever saw. He's had a hard life, dealt with a lot of juries later on. He just *knows* people. Then, too, he's dauntless. He never gives up. He's just got more persistence than anybody else."

After three years, Wallace still is noncommittal about what he and President Kennedy said to each other when they met in Alabama during the Birmingham civil-rights crisis of 1963. He is willing, however, to talk about Kennedy, whom he met at the 1956 Democratic National Convention during the exciting race for the Vice Presidential nomination.

"Everybody from the South was against Kefauver," Wallace recalls, "and for Kennedy. Alabama was caucusing at 10:00 P.M. and he had to make a speech to some other delegation at the same time so he asked me if I would take his sister to speak for him at our delegation. So I met them on the mezzanine of the Conrad Hilton Hotel and took her to the caucus and she spoke right well. I don't remember which sister that was, but I sure hope it wasn't the one that kissed Sammy Davis, Jr."

The Cops' Candidate

On the way back to his office, Wallace is stopped by an elderly, intense party named William Wood, who has driven from Chicago to Atlanta to see Senator Richard Russell of Georgia and has stopped by Montgomery on his way home. He chats with Wallace about "your Presidential candidacy in 1968" and predicts that "anybody" can beat President Johnson because his mainstays— "the Communists and the Negroes"—have turned against him.

Wallace is not impressed. "I don't see a Communist under every bed," he says, when he is back in his office. "Some of them may be behind all these riots. But I don't believe all this talk about poor folks turning Communist. It's the damn rich who turn Communist. You ever see a poor Communist? Like them Rosenberg folks and all. They were moneyed people."

He and Hall have been talking with indignation about the Selma marchers who congregated, thousands strong, before Wallace's Capitol building in 1965. "Now up in Chicago," Wallace points out, "when they started marching, they resisted 'em. And you know what happened? The federal courts restrained the marchers to only five hundred people in a city of five million. We didn't put up a bit of resistance in Montgomery and they just let 35,000 people march all over a city of 100,000. But the point is, now we can break up the next march down here after what happened in the North. We can call out the guardsmen and the police and go lay a billy club on their heads. If you're violent, they listen; if you're for law and order, they push you around."

Law and order concern everyone, he says again, and most of all the working class. "We run best in the industrial states," he says. "We got our biggest vote in sixty-four from organized labor. They're all concerned about crime and property rights. You take a working man, if he lives in a section where law and order breaks down, he can't just up and move like rich folks can. The police, too. I went out to the Governors' Conference in Los Angeles last summer and the patrolman in charge of the police assigned to the Conference came and got me to speak to the ones that was off-duty. I told them we believed in law and order in Alabama and we prosecuted criminals on Monday morning, not policemen. I told them, 'I wish you could run this country for about two years. You could straighten it out.' When I finished, the patrolman in charge told me, 'You're our Presidential candidate.'

"And when I went up to New York and they came down from Harlem and picketed me, the police drew this line in the street and they told them the first one to cross it would get his head split. And one of the police whispered to me, 'We drew that line pretty close to'em, Governor.' The police are for me everywhere. I was at another Governors' Conference in Miami when Johnson was Vice President and spoke on civil rights and the Governor sitting next to me said, 'I'm tired of this. There's two sides to that question in my state now.' That's a state would shock you if I told you the name of it."

It is midafternoon, quiet in the dark office; the phone has ceased to ring and visitors are being channeled to Reuben King. Wallace chews his cigar reflectively, gets up from his chair, leans against his desk. He gazes out of the window, across the lawns and the wide street where the Selma marchers heard Martin Luther King tell his dream, where Southerners in another, brighter time stood to see Jeff Davis take his oath. Wallace speaks quietly, rapidly, warming up now, as he did before the cultured audience in the John Marshall Hotel in Richmond.

"Of course, if I did what I'd like to do I'd pick up something and smash one of these federal judges in the head and then burn the courthouse down. But I'm too genteel. What we need in this country is some Governors that used to work up here at Birmingham in the steel mills with about a tenth-grade education. A Governor like that wouldn't be so genteel. He'd put out his orders and he'd say, 'The first man who throws a brick is a dead man. The first man who loots something that doesn't belong to him is a dead man. My orders are to shoot to kill.' "

Wallace sits down again, his black eyes snapping. "That's the way to keep law and order. If you'd killed about three that way at Watts the other forty wouldn't be dead today. But most Governors are like me. They got too much education. They're too genteel."

The Politics of Welfare

George Wallace got his start in Alabama politics when he was thirteen by knocking on doors in his hometown of Clio on behalf of a candidate for Secretary of State. The candidate lost the race but carried Clio, and Wallace has been turning public defeat into personal triumph ever since.

Vaguely recalling those days, the ideas that drove him into politics, he says that he "used to think about junior colleges and things like that." And there is little doubt that he is one of those Populist-tinged Southerners (like Lyndon Johnson) who see politics basically in terms of "something for the folks."

It is a matter of record—if little-known outside the state—that in his four years in office, for $40 million, he has built fourteen new junior colleges and fifteen new trade schools (legally desegregated but so located that some are virtually all for Negroes), launched a $100-million public-school building program, provided free textbooks for all Alabama schoolchildren, set out on the biggest road-building plan in the state's history, and borrowed $300 million for various projects. As a young state legislator, he was the author of the Wallace Industrial Development Act, one of those devices through which Southern communities are authorized to build virtually tax-free buildings and lease them to industries who will relocate, and this once-backward state is blooming economically, at least in part as a result. Wallace is proud of the diversification with which this is being achieved and cites Opelika as a city profiting from a big industry where the people are "still rural and own their own homes."

"I don't think God meant people to be all jammed up in cities," Wallace says. "No courtesy, no time, no room—that's all you get in cities. But industry don't locate in mud and dust."

He is indeed not one of those "ultras who is against everything" and if the federal government is his favorite target he is still an eager recipient of its largess. Reuben King says that there are 388 Alabamians in every one thousand of the state's population participating in welfare programs; only Louisiana has more. Eighty-five million of Alabama's $110-million welfare budget stems from

Washington, and 80 per cent of its $350-million state budget derives from federal grants of one kind or another. Between 1963 and 1966, expenditures on all Alabama school systems were doubled. There is a liberal nursing-home plan, a plan under which communities build self-liquidating medical clinics for private operation, a water-pollution act to preserve one of a river-laced state's greatest natural resources, and such ambitious projects as one that would link the Tennessee and Tombigbee rivers by a canal and thus establish an unbroken waterway route from the Great Lakes states and the Ohio River through Alabama to the Gulf of Mexico. . . .

How Strong Is the "Movement"?

No one—at least openly—predicts a decline in the Wallace popularity and power. In any case, despite his protestation that "there's no reason why somebody from Alabama wouldn't make just as good a President as somebody from New York or maybe even Texas," it is not because of his liberal achievements as Governor or his state's prosperity that George Wallace is likely to be found in the Presidential race in 1968. Welfare politics, in which his record is creditable, is not what makes him such a formidable force in Alabama, the South, perhaps elsewhere. His willingness to spend money, build schools, construct highways, is not what endears him to the right wing in America, or to the "working class" in Gary, Indiana, and Baltimore, or to the police in Los Angeles and New York.

Nor is Wallace a national political figure because he is a blatant racist—as, for instance, Theodore Bilbo was. He seems to have the traditional Southern attitude toward Negroes—a mixture of contempt, distaste, amusement, affection, and appreciation for a valuable servant. And surely he did not win his share of the vote in those Northern primaries in 1964 because of any outstanding success in coping with the civil-rights movement in Alabama.

In fact, George Wallace's reputation as the man who "stood up for Alabama"—or for the South, or for America—although it is one of two major ingredients of his political fortune, has been built almost exclusively on defeat. It has been his genius—like that of the mysterious Big Brother of 1984 who turned War into Peace—to make Defeat mean Triumph, Retreat mean Advance.

He "stood in the schoolhouse door" but the University of Alabama was integrated four hours later. In 1963, he used state troopers to block the desegregation of public schools, but Negro pupils ultimately enrolled. He once used state militiamen to stop federal marshals from serving a court order on him; the next day, he accepted the order. He resisted the federal government's school desegregation "guidelines" and caused his legislature to nullify them in Alabama; but even he does not expect the federal courts to allow this state action to stand.

From these dubious materials—from sheer defiance—Governor Wallace has built his "stand-up" reputation. He is, as Grover Hall suggested, "dauntless"—defying the federal government at every turn, without actually having stopped it. The psychological value of this exercise in defeat has been enormous. "I guess George has showed 'em," a Montgomery man said. "He don't take nothing lying down, does he?"

Thus has the notion spread through Alabama that George Wallace has started a national "movement" that will reverse the twentieth-century course of federal government and restore to the South—and other states—the right to follow their old way of life.

The Governor and those around him share this view. They take credit for setting the example that led to Ronald Reagan's election in California, the defeat of the Police Review Board in New York, the demise of the 1966 civil-rights bill in Congress. Wallace believes that George P. Mahoney, the "white-backlash" candidate for Governor of Maryland, could have won if in the last days of his campaign he had not sought to dissociate himself from George Wallace.

Thus, the Wallace Presidential plans for 1968 are well advanced. He is planning a platform which will bear down heavily on "Constitutional government" and "law and order" but which also will have a farm plank, an attack on foreign aid, strong support for the war in Vietnam, and programs for assisting the sick, the old, and the needy.

He says he is "thinking more in terms of a third party" but also talks of entering some Democratic preferential primaries—

notably California, where he believes the "movement" is strong. He will be in the race to win, he declares, but some of those who have long acquaintance with him are not sure he is all that mesmerized by the "movement."

They point out that if he can pick up some non-Southern delegates to go with those from Alabama, Mississippi, and a scattering from other Southern states, and that if he maintains his threat of a third-party candidacy, he could go to the 1968 Democratic National Convention in a powerful position to bargain about the platform and the party ticket.

Considering his showing in the three primaries in 1964, Wallace would scarcely have to argue that his third party might win just enough votes in some of the major states to change the outcome. ("Besides," he likes to say, "a man don't have to carry a state, he only needs a plurality in a three-man race to win the electoral votes.")

Still others think George Wallace's next move will not be for the Presidency at all but for the veteran Lister Hill's seat in the United States Senate in 1968. There are even those who believe he will hold back and run for the Governorship again in 1970, when he will be Constitutionally eligible.

Survival of the Fittest

Part of the reasoning of those who think he will not really run for President is that the *prospect* of doing so is so much more valuable to him than the *fact* might be. The one thing George Wallace cannot afford, they reason, is to have the "movement" exposed as not so powerful after all, not so promising; if it were put to the test nationally and failed, then what would happen to Wallace's reputation as the man who is turning the tide because he "stood up for Alabama"?

Yet, that reputation is not Little Stonewall's only political strength. As Grover Hall also pointed out, he "can read your insides quicker than any man I *ever saw*." What he has really "stood up" for is the age-old streak of "practicality" and earthy common sense in mankind. *We got to get all this theory out of things.* Why should intellectual morons come into the God-fearing South and destroy its practical racial arrangements because they think they know more than ordinary folks? *What good are equal rights if it gets folks killed and ruins everything?* In Chicago they resisted violently and got away with it. In Montgomery, they held back and were overrun. Violence and resistance, obviously, are practical, and it is only common sense that if policemen are to keep order they have to be violent. Even genteel George Wallace would really like to *smash one of these federal judges in the head and then burn the courthouse down.*

Thus, it is not so blatant a thing as racism, or even violence, but the old basic natural instincts of self-preservation, survival of the fittest, kill or be killed, that George Corley Wallace, Jr. appeals to in practical men, and he can be the ultimate demagogue not just because he is a spellbinding orator or a shrewd politician or a dauntless fighter but because he has recognized within himself, the prison of every man, the truth that William Faulkner points to on the walls of the old city jail in *Requiem for a Nun:*

"If you would peruse in unbroken—ay, overlapping—continuity the history of a community, look not in church registers and the courthouse records but beneath the successive layers of calcimine and creosote and whitewash on the walls of the jail, since only in that forcible carceration does man find the idleness in which to compose, in the gross and simple terms of his gross and simple lusts and yearnings, the gross and simple recapitulations of his gross and simple heart . . ."

Social Commentary

☐ In 1958, Norman Podhoretz published an essay, "The Article as Art," in which he suggests that the magazine article has become an important and fertile genre because authors who have traditionally written fiction find it practical and especially pertinent to the demands of the modern world. He lamented the invidious distinctions so often made between fiction and nonfiction, between "creativity" and "criticism," and concluded that we need "a return to the old idea of literature as a category that includes the best writing on any subject in any form. We need a return to this idea and we need it, I should add, most urgently of all for the sake of fiction and poetry."

☐ More than ten years have passed since Podhoretz' essay appeared, and few would dispute the validity of his argument. The best work of American authors has often been nonfiction, although, as Podhoretz points out, that term itself is indicative of the current American attitude: "We call everything that is not fiction or poetry 'non-fiction,' as though whole ranges of human thought had only a negative existence." Norman Mailer's *Advertisements for Myself, Armies of the Night*, and *Miami and the Siege of Chicago*; James Baldwin's *The Fire Next Time*; and Truman Capote's *In Cold Blood*—these works depend heavily upon acute social observation. Other writers guided by the same spirit have produced the most impressive and influential works in contemporary American literature: Edmund Wilson's *Patriotic Gore* and other books of essays; Lionel Trilling's *The Liberal Imagination*; Dwight Macdonald's *Against the American Grain*; Paul Goodman's *Growing Up Absurd*; Marshall McLuhan's *Understanding Media*; Susan Sontag's *Against Interpretation*; Herbert Marcuse's *One Dimensional Man*; David Reisman's *The Lonely Crowd*; Podhoretz' *Doings and Undoings* and *Making It*. The list is too long to reproduce in its entirety, but it forms a roster of extraordinarily varied accomplishment. When compared with the fiction, poetry, and drama of the fifties and sixties, it appears to be a greater achievement, richer in its perception of our society and more permanently valuable as literature.

Paul Goodman

Everything I do has exactly the same subject—the organism

and the environment. Anything I write on society is pragmatic—

it aims to accomplish something. . . . I am a man of letters . . . or

an artist-humanist.

In an essay entitled "Seven Heroes of the New Left" (May 1968), Lionel Abel listed those figures most charismatic to liberal students: Albert Camus, Noam Chomsky, Paul Goodman, Che Guevara, Regis Debray, Franz Fanon, and Herbert Marcuse. Goodman was classified as a "moralist" by the students, and that is perhaps as good a description as Goodman's own term of "artist-humanist." Goodman's interests are extremely varied. In the past twenty years he has been a poet, an author, a playwright, a social critic, a city planner, a pacifist, and an anarchist. Since the publication of his most famous book, *Growing Up Absurd* (1960), he has become the most active hero of the New Left, "the Joan of Arc of the Free Student Movement," and he has assumed the role of father figure to the younger generation.

Paul Goodman was born in New York City in 1911. Soon after Goodman's birth, his father suffered serious financial losses and deserted the family. His mother moved from Washington Square to a slum near Mount Sinai Hospital. Goodman was a brilliant student at Townsend Harris High School and The City College. He finished his Ph.D. work at the University of Chicago in 1940, although he did not officially receive his doctoral degree until 1954. Goodman has taught at various schools—Manumit, a progressive school in Pawling, New York, and Black Mountain College in North Carolina —but his time has been largely devoted to writing. In the

1930's he wrote more than a hundred unpublished short stories before several were accepted and printed in *New Directions*. He became a movie critic for *Partisan Review* and continued writing on diverse subjects in many different forms; but he did not achieve a national reputation until the publication of *Growing Up Absurd*, a book which explored the difficulty of growing up in America today and suggested that there is a wide discrepancy between purpose and effect, that American society no longer exists for the sake of people but for the sake of preserving its own bureaucracies. Goodman's other work includes social studies—*The Community of Scholars* (1962), *Compulsory Mis-Education* (1964), and *People or Personnel* (1965); plays—*Jonah* (1960), *The Young Disciple* (1965), and *Faustina* (1965); novels—*The Empire City* (1959) and *Making Do* (1963); books of short stories— *The Break-up of Our Camp* (1949) and *Our Visit to Niagara* (1960); literary criticism—*Kafka's Prayer* (1949) and *The Structure of Literature* (1954); television criticism for *The New Republic*; and city planning—*Communitas* (1947, 1961).

Goodman's chief subject is the degree to which bureaucracies have stifled human innocence. His appeal to the young rests upon his personal integrity, his refusal to accommodate himself to the technological society which he criticizes. "Most of my intellectual generation sold out," Goodman has said, "first to the communists and then to the organized system, so that there are very few independents around that a young man can accept as a hero. The next generation must have fathers more ideal than their own."

Goodman has been criticized for being too utopian, too condescending toward the achievements of modern technology, too impatient with the necessity of bureaucracies, and too superficial. Nevertheless he has become a kind of surrogate father to young people, and largely because of his role as utopian-pragmatist. The following essay is the introductory statement to *Growing Up Absurd* and suggests Goodman's social attitudes, the way in which he has combined the idealistic and pragmatic facets of his personality.

Growing Up Absurd

PAUL

GOODMAN

1

IN EVERY DAY'S newspaper there are stories about the two subjects that I have brought together in this book, the disgrace of
the Organized System of semimonopolies, government, advertisers, etc., and the disaffection of the growing generation. Both
are newsworthily scandalous, and for several years now both kinds
of stories have come thicker and faster. It is strange that the obvious connections between them are not played up in the newspapers; nor, in the rush of books on the follies, venality, and
stifling conformity of the Organization, has there been a book on
Youth Problems in the Organized System.

Those of the disaffected youth who are articulate, however—
for instance, the Beat or Angry young men—are quite clear about
the connection: their main topic is the "system" with which they
refuse to co-operate. They will explain that the "good" jobs are
frauds and sells, that it is intolerable to have one's style of life dictated by Personnel, that a man is a fool to work to pay installments
on a useless refrigerator for his wife, that the movies, TV, and
Book-of-the-Month Club are beneath contempt, that the Luce
publications make you sick to the stomach; and they will describe
with accuracy the cynicism and one-upping of the "typical" junior
executive. They consider it the part of reason and honor to wash
their hands of all of it.

Naturally, grown-up citizens are concerned about the beatniks
and delinquents. The school system has been subjected to criticism. And there is a lot of official talk about the need to conserve

our human resources lest Russia get ahead of us. The question is why the grownups do not, more soberly, draw the same connections as the youth. Or, since no doubt many people *are* quite clear about the connection that the structure of society that has become increasingly dominant in our country is disastrous to the growth of excellence and manliness, why don't more people speak up and say so, and initiate a change? The question is an important one and the answer is, I think, a terrible one: that people are so bemused by the way business and politics are carried on at present, with all their intricate relationships, that they have ceased to be able to imagine alternatives. We seem to have lost our genius for inventing changes to satisfy crying needs.

But this stupor is inevitably the baleful influence of the very kind of organizational network that we have: the system pre-empts the available means and capital; it buys up as much of the intelligence as it can and muffles the voices of dissent; and then it irrefutably proclaims that itself is the only possibility of society, for nothing else is thinkable. Let me give a couple of examples of how this works. Suppose (as is the case) that a group of radio and TV broadcasters, competing in the Pickwickian fashion of semimonopolies, control all the stations and channels in an area, amassing the capital and variously bribing Communications Commissioners in order to get them; and the broadcasters tailor their programs to meet the requirements of their advertisers, of the censorship, of their own slick and clique tastes, and of a broad common denominator of the audience, none of whom may be offended: they will then claim not only that the public wants the drivel that they give them, but indeed that nothing else is being created. Of course it is not! not for *these* media; why should a serious artist bother? Or suppose again (as is not quite the case) that in a group of universities only faculties are chosen that are "safe" to the businessmen trustees or the politically appointed regents, and these faculties give out all the degrees and licenses and union cards to the new generation of students, and only such universities can get Foundation or government money for research, and research is incestuously staffed by the same sponsors and according to the same policy, and they allow no one but those they choose, to have access to either the classroom or expensive apparatus: it will then be claimed that there is no other learning or professional competence; that an inspired teacher is not "solid"; that the official projects are the direction of science; that progressive education is a failure; and finally, indeed—as in Dr. James Conant's report on the high schools—that only 15 per cent of the youth are "academically talented" enough to be taught hard subjects. This preempting of the means and the brains by the organization, and the shutting out of those who do not conform, can go so far as to cause delusions, as when recently the president of Merck and Company had the effrontery to warn the Congress that its investigation of profiteering in drugs might hinder the quest of scientific knowledge! as if the spirit of Vesalius and Pasteur depended on the financial arrangements of Merck and Company.

But it is in these circumstances that people put up with a system because "there are no alternatives." And when one cannot think of anything to do, soon one ceases to think at all.

To my mind the worst feature of our present organized system of doing things is its indirectness, its blurring of the object. The idea of directly addressing crying objective public needs, like shelter or education, and using our immense and indeed *surplus* resources to satisfy them, is anathema. For in the great interlocking system of corporations people live not by attending to the job, but by status, role playing, and tenure, and they work to maximize profits, prestige, or votes regardless of utility or even public disutility—e.g., the plethora of cars has now become a public disutility, but automobile companies continue to manufacture them and persuade people to buy them. The indispensable premise of city planning, according to a vice president of Webb and Knapp, is to make a "modest long-term profit on the promoter's investment." (His exact sentence, to a meeting of young planners, was, "What we're going to have built will be built only if some developer is going to make a profit from it."!) Obviously he is not directly interested in housing people or in city convenience and beauty; he is directly interested in being a good vice president of Webb and Knapp. That is his privilege, but it is not a useful goal, and an idealistic young fellow would not want to be such a man. Another example: Some earnest liberal Congressmen are baffled "how to give Federal aid to education and not interfere in the curriculum and teaching." But when the teaching *function* is respected and assayed by the teacher's peers-in-skill, no one *can* interfere, no one would dare (just as Harvard tossed out McCarthy). The sole function of administration is to smooth the way, but in this country we have the topsy-turvy situation that a teacher must devote himself to satisfying the administrator and financier rather than to doing his job, and a universally admired teacher is fired for disobeying an administrative order that would hinder teaching. . . . Let me give another example, because I want to make this point very clear: These same Congressmen are concerned "how to discourage low-level programming in private TV stations without censorship." Their question presupposes that in communication the prior thing is the existence of networks and channels, rather than something to communicate that needs diffusing. But the prior thing *is* the program, and the only grounds for the license to the station is its ability to transmit it. Nothing could be more stupid than for the communications commission to give to people who handle the means of broadcasting the inventing of what to broadcast, and then, disturbed at the poor quality, to worry about censorship.

We live increasingly, then, in a system in which little direct attention is paid to the object, the function, the program, the task, the need; but immense attention to the role, procedure, prestige, and profit. We don't get the shelter and education because not enough mind is paid to *those* things. Naturally the system is inefficient; the overhead is high; the task is rarely done with love, style, and excitement, for such beauties emerge only from absorption in real objects; sometimes the task is not done at all; and those who could do it best become either cynical or resigned.

2

In the light of this criticism, the recent scandalous exposures of the advertisers, the government, and the corporations are heartening rather than dismaying. (I am writing in the winter of 1959–60 and we have been hearing about TV, the FCC, Title I, and the Drug Industry; by the time this is published there will be a new series.) The conditions exposed are not new, but now the public skepticism and disgust are mounting; to my ear there is even a new ring; and the investigations are being pushed further, even further than intended by the investigators. The effect of this must be to destroy for many people the image of inviolability and indispensability of the kind of system I have been discussing, to show its phony workings and inevitable dangers. It is the collapse of "public relations."

When the existing state of things is suddenly measured by people against far higher standards than they have been used to, it is no longer the case that there are no alternatives. People are forced by their better judgment to ask very basic questions: Is it possible, *how* is it possible, to have more meaning and honor in work? to put wealth to some real use? to have a high standard of living of whose quality we are not ashamed? to get social justice for those who have been shamefully left out? to have a use of leisure that is not a dismaying waste of a hundred million adults? The large group of independent people who have been out of the swim, with their old-fashioned virtues, suddenly have something admirable about them; one is surprised that they still exist, and their existence is relevant. And from the members of the Organized System itself come acute books criticizing the shortcomings of the Organized System.

It is my belief that we are going to have a change. And once the Americans can recover from their mesmerized condition and its astounding political apathy, our country will be in a most fortunate situation. For the kinds of radical changes we need are those that are appropriate to a fairly general prosperity. They are practicable. They can be summed up as simply restoring, in J. K. Galbraith's phrase, the "social balance" that we have allowed to become lopsided and runaway in the present abuse of the country's wealth. For instance, since we have a vast surplus productivity, we can turn to finding jobs that will bring out a youth's capacity, and so really conserve human resources. We can find ways to restore to the worker a say in his production, and so really do something for manly independence. Since we have a problem of what to do with leisure, we can begin to think of necessary community enterprises that want doing, and that people can enthusiastically and spontaneously throw themselves into, and be proud of the results (e.g., beautifying our hideous small towns). And perhaps thereby create us a culture again. Since we have the technology, the capital, and the labor, why should we not have livable cities? Should it be hard to bring back into society the 30 per cent who are *still* ill-fed and ill-housed, and more outcast then ever? What is necessary is directly addressing definite objective needs and using available resources to satisfy them; doing things that are worth while just because they are worth while, since we can. Politically, what we need is government in which a man offers himself as a candidate because he has a new program that he wants to effectuate, and we choose him because we want that good, and judge that he is the best man to effectuate it. Is that outlandish?

3

The present widespread concern about education is only superficially a part of the Cold War, the need to match the Russian scientists. For in the discussions, pretty soon it becomes clear that people are uneasy about, ashamed of, the world that they have given the children to grow up in. That world is not manly enough, it is not earnest enough; a grownup may be cynical (or resigned) about his own convenient adjustments, but he is by no means willing to see his children robbed of a worth-while society. With regard to the next generation, everybody always has a higher standard than the one he is used to. The standard is ceasing to be one of money and status and is becoming a standard of the worth of life. But worth, like happiness, comes from bona-fide activity and achievement.

My stratagem in this book is a simple one. I assume that the young *really* need a more worth-while world in order to grow up at all, and I confront this real need with the world that they have been getting. This is the source of their problems. *Our* problem is to remedy the disproportion. We can. Our inheritance, our immense productivity, has been pre-empted and parceled out in a kind of domainal system; but this grandiose and seemingly impregnable feudalism is vulnerable to an earnest attack. One has the persistent thought that if ten thousand people in all walks of life will stand up on their two feet and talk out and insist, we shall get back our country.

Marshall McLuhan

The medium is the massage

We live in the most complex technocracy in human history, but we have scarcely begun to understand the importance of machines in human affairs. Whereas man has traditionally learned by reading books, he now is influenced by many other means of communication: he listens to the radio and records, or watches television and the movies, or uses the telephone, computers, and other mass media. "The human family becomes one tribe again," asserts Marshall McLuhan, as men try to understand the most fruitful and beneficial use of these new media. McLuhan's famous phrase, "The medium is the message," means that the medium itself defines our technological age far more than the contents to which the medium has been put.

Born in Edmonton, Alberta, Canada, in 1911, McLuhan began his career as a typical scholar. He studied at the University of Manitoba and Cambridge University, where he did graduate work in 1939, writing a thesis on the poet Thomas Nashe. In 1936 he taught at the University of Wisconsin. "I was confronted with young Americans I was incapable of understanding," he commented later. "I felt an urgent need to study their popular culture in order to get through." His first book, *The Mechanical Bride* (1951), was an examination of "the folklore of industrial man." His next two books, *The Gutenberg Galaxy* (1952) and *Understanding Media* (1964), attempted to show how the modern age came into being. In *The Gutenberg Galaxy*, which is a study of the invention of movable type and its impact on Western civilization, McLuhan maintained that when print became more important than oral communication, the eye rather than the ear became the dominant sensory organ. In *Understanding Media*, he studied the influence of electronics on twentieth-century man and argued that the world has become, once again, a "global village."

Few social commentators have elicited so much controversy as McLuhan. Some critics feel that he is far too ready to predict the obsolescence of the book. Others cite his own writing as turgid, repetitious, and hyperbolic, a charge which McLuhan counters by acknowledging that at times he has difficulty understanding his own work. In his latest book, *The Medium Is the Massage: An Inventory of Effects* (1967), McLuhan illustrates the argument presented in *Understanding Media*. Considering himself an analyst, McLuhan has said that his primary aim is "to draw attention to the fact that a medium is not something neutral—it does something to people. It takes hold of them. It rubs them off, it massages them, it bumps them around."

The Paradox
of Marshall McLuhan

NEIL
COMPTON

I HAVE BEEN FOLLOWING the career of Marshall McLuhan for some years, and have never found him at a loss for an explanation of any phenomenon about which he is asked. But even he must sometimes be nonplussed by the extraordinary thrust which, after years in the decent obscurity of a solid academic reputation, has carried him to heights of fame exceeded only by such semi-divinities as the Beatles or the late Marilyn Monroe. Last spring, it was almost impossible for any inhabitant of North America to escape from the man or his image: his photograph appeared on the cover of both a major American newsmagazine and Canada's largest weekend supplement; cartoonists in the *New Yorker* and *Saturday Review* joked about the McLuhan craze (McLuhanacy?); NBC-TV presented an hour-long documentary on his work, and the CBC interviewed him at length on its top-rated Sunday night public affairs show. Meanwhile, *The Medium Is the Massage* was piled high in every paperback bookshop and reviewed in all the major media. After this sort of ubiquity even the sweet felicity of a jet-age academic chair, the $100,000 Albert Schweitzer Professorship in the Humanities at Fordham, must have seemed anti-climactic.

McLuhan owes his celebrity, of course, not to his formal scholarship and literary criticism, but to the apocalyptic pronouncements that have established him as "the first pop philosopher" (*New Yorker*) and "the prophet of the New Life Out There, the

REPRINTED FROM *New American Review*, NO. 2, BY PERMISSION OF THE AUTHOR.

suburbs, housing developments, Astrodomes, domed-over shopping centres, freeways, TV families, the whole world of the new technologies that stretch out to the West beyond the old cities of the East" (Tom Wolfe). Fame and adulation of this proportion are granted only to someone who tells people something they already want to hear. McLuhan would certainly deny any such intention and rightly insist that his roles as scholar and prophet are indivisible: both arise from a lifelong concern for the quality of life and art in our time and a long and passionate dedication to one or two governing ideas. Nevertheless, he is obviously winning disciples at a rate and on a scale that cannot be explained by mere rational persuasion.

The paradox is that this darling of marketing associations and the switched-on set idealizes the twelfth century, dislikes almost everything about the twentieth century to date (except its art), and has never really wavered in his loyalty to one of the most orthodox and conservative (not to say reactionary) of intellectual traditions. In his earliest published essay (*Dalhousie Review,* XVII, 1936), he praised G. K. Chesterton for seeking "to re-establish agriculture and small property, the only basis of any free culture" and blamed the intellectual confusion of the 1930's upon "Luther's anathemas against Reason, and Descartes's expressed contempt for Aristotle and Aquinas." In his later work, he drew heavily upon the Tory triumvirate of Eliot, Pound, and Wyndham Lewis, and upon Joyce's version of Thomist aesthetics and Viconian philosophy (though not, naturally, upon Joyce's political liberalism).

Because he held such views, it is not surprising that McLuhan at one time gave the impression of being a bitter man who scornfully contemplated the world about him. Today, however, he embraces the universe with an almost alarming eagerness and zest. His system of values remains very much what it has always been (at any rate since his conversion to Catholicism) but recent history has apparently transformed his pessimism into a kind of millennial optimism. In spite of repeated claims to detachment and impartiality, he has clearly invested a great deal of emotional as well as intellectual capital in his faith that we are entering an era which bears the promise of paradise in the form of an undissociated electronic culture. How this improbable conviction came to take hold of him is the subject of this article.

II

McLuhan was a pioneer in the revival of interest in rhetoric that has characterized literary scholarship during the past generation. As a result of his studies (which began with a Cambridge thesis on Thomas Nashe, the Elizabethan pamphleteer and novelist), he came to see the history of Western culture in terms of an all-embracing dualism in which "grammarians" are ranged against "dialecticians." According to this theory, the conflict began with the confrontation between the Sophists and their great antagonist Socrates. The Sophists, believing in the primacy of action over knowledge, consistently subordinated the study of logic to that of rhetoric or persuasion. By contrast, Socrates, Plato, and Aristotle insisted that "dialectics should control rhetoric, that knowledge was superior even to prudential action" ("An Ancient Quarrel in Modern America," *Classical Journal* XLI, 1945–6). On the whole, subsequent history has been on the side of the dialecticians, but McLuhan clearly sympathizes with the Sophists. For him, the achievement of a theoretical separation of knowledge from action or eloquence was not a great moment in the history of thought, but the first step in a long progress toward the fragmentation and dissolution of the human personality. (Later, as we shall see, he was to find an explanation for this development in the rise of phonetic literacy.)

McLuhan traces the opposition between exponents of the two traditions throughout two-and-a-half millennia. On one side are the grammarians Isocrates, Cicero, St. Augustine, Erasmus, Thomas Jefferson, and Woodrow Wilson (I confine myself to names mentioned by McLuhan); on the other are the dialecticians William of Ockham, Peter Abelard, Peter Ramus, Descartes, and John Dewey. The former tend to be encyclopedic (i.e., nonspecialist), forensic, practical, and their ideal image in Cicero's *doctus orator*, whose highest value is eloquence; the latter are specialist, speculative, introspective, and analytic. Prince Hal, Ulysses (in *Troilus and Cressida*—at least in I, iii), and Leopold Bloom belong with the grammarians; Henry IV, Hamlet, Sherlock Holmes, and Stephen Dedalus (much of the time) are dialecticians. (McLuhan's fondness for dualistic categories—hot and cool media, visual and acoustic space, dialecticians and grammarians—always tempts me to offer prizes for further lists of imaginatively paired opposites.)

Around this dichotomy, McLuhan builds a theory of American culture and, hence, of modern culture generally. He sees the South as a direct inheritor of the encyclopedic Ciceronian tradition ("The Southern Quality," *Sewanee Review* LV, 1947). By virtue of its conservative, Anglican heritage, the South was able to maintain vital connections with the eloquent and humanistic European ideal represented by Castiglione, Sidney, and Spenser. Passionate, nonintrospective, devoted to public life (as distinct from private life, which was nonexistent in the South), the educated Southern gentleman never became alienated from his humbler and unlearned fellow citizens. Consequently, says McLuhan, the South has the only tradition of real political thought in America.

In contrast to this vision of balanced civility, McLuhan paints a black picture of New England culture, founded as it is upon "the most destructive aberration of the Western mind—autonomous dialectics and ontological nominalism." Northern thought is repressive, impatient, fragmentary, and suffers from "elephantiasis of the will." Henry James epitomizes its materialistic individualism; in his sick world, almost all the characters are tourists, females are dominant and luxuriant, while males are timid and meager. The denatured sub-men of Northern cities, according to the McLuhan of two decades ago, "best express their helplessness by means of Negro music." He explains that "while ostensibly setting about the freeing of the slaves, they became enslaved, and found in the wailing self-pity and crooning of the Negro, a substitute for any life-style of their own." (Clearly, McLuhan's reputation for being hip must postdate this essay.)

In a world in which Southern civility was doomed by Northern barbarism, McLuhan found little to please him. Complaining of a time "when a triumphant technology croons the sickly boasts of the advertising man, when the great vaults and vistas of the human soul are obscured by images of silken glamor, and when it is plain that man lives not by bread alone but by toothpaste also," he called for a return to the values of St. Thomas (*St. Louis University Studies in Honor of St. Thomas Aquinas* I, 1943). His idea of political sanity was so remote from current practice that he seemed condemned to impotence and despair. In the course of a perverse but brilliant essay on detective fiction (for McLuhan, the epitome of debased modern literature), he suggested two improbable exemplars of political prudence: Shakespeare's Ulysses, whose speech on Order is "a scientific formula for what was happening and what continues to happen"; and Charles I, who, for the English world, will always be "a symbol of opposition to the tradesman ethos" ("Footsteps in the Sands of Crime," *Sewanee Review* LIV, 1946). Judging the world by these standards, he had to conclude that "today we not only live barbarously (human community is little more than a memory) but emotional illiteracy is almost universal." That characteristically shapeless sentence draws attention to a pathetic anomaly in McLuhan's intellectual equipment. This man who regards eloquence as one of the highest values is himself a notoriously inarticulate and inelegant stylist.

At this point, the reader might well conclude that McLuhan is no more than an extreme reactionary of a familiar type. His hatred for specialization, abstraction, and the hard urban ego, and his nostalgia for an imagined womblike pre-industrial Eden might seem to presage a career of splenetic irrelevance. However, he never allowed the apparent hopelessness of the situation to drive him to despair. His passionate love of literature (which he tends to read as prophecy or revelation) and his Catholic faith (an implicit element in his value system) presumably helped to preserve him from so deadly an intellectual sin. On the contrary, he has always insisted upon the absolute importance, first, of recognizing the existence of a crisis that involves us all willy-nilly; and, second, of trying to understand what is really going on. McLuhan's contempt for Marxism is unbounded, but he would certainly assent to the Marxist axiom that freedom lies in the recognition of necessity.

III

His favorite exemplar of this attitude, one who makes an appearance in virtually all McLuhan's books, is the sailor hero of Poe's "Descent into the Maelstrom." Caught up in an irresistible process, the sailor does not panic, but saves himself by studying the action of the whirlpool and learning to cooperate with it. McLuhan conceived *The Mechanical Bride* (1951) in this spirit. This study of "the folklore of industrial man" (in other words, advertisements, comic books, radio, and other popular media) attempts "to set the reader at the centre of the revolving picture . . . where he may observe the action. . . ." Like Poe's sailor, who finds amusement in speculating on the relative velocities of objects floating by him (and thus discovers how to escape from his predicament), the reader is invited to contemplate the images and the sardonic commentary in McLuhan's picture book as a first step toward developing a strategy for survival as an "integral" human being in the modern world.

In *The Mechanical Bride*, McLuhan repudiated the moral indignation and the nostalgia that had heretofore characterized his work. Like his exemplary hero, he tried to use the destructive energy of his environment in the service of his own creative purpose: the wisecracking, jazzy headlines and the flip, knowing tone are simply heightened versions of the language of the media tribe —as though a severe moralist were writing for a kind of uncorrupt *Variety*. The result is McLuhan's most successful act of communication, even though he now repudiates the hostile, disdainful spirit of this book. (Al Capp and Chic Young are among the few popular artists to emerge unscathed.) There has never been a more devastating analysis of the latent content of dozens of contemporary myths and images, ranging from Blondie to Superman, Best Sellers to Great Books, Humphrey Bogart to Emily Post, and from sexy automobiles to the assembly-line femininity of drum majorettes, pinup girls, and nylon-stocking models.

The energy and aplomb with which the author went about his exegetical task almost disguises from the casual reader the fact that *The Mechanical Bride* is a rather bleak and gloomy book.

The maelstrom of commercial culture is wittily charted, but there are no very convincing hints about how to escape from it. On the contrary, the idealization of twelfth-century philosophy, the sneers at coeducation, feminism, and working mothers, the dubious assertion that the rich were once more socially responsible than they are now, and the rather Victorian attitude toward corsets, brief skirts, and high heels would depress the *Bride* to the level of silly Tory propaganda if they were anything more than digressions from the main concern of the book.

Between *The Mechanical Bride* and McLuhan's next book, *The Gutenberg Galaxy* (1962), there is a gap of ten years during which his interpretation of contemporary culture (but not his basic value system) underwent a radical revision. I have no privileged knowledge of what influences wrought this transformation, but three factors were obviously important.

The first was the development of network television. Though it was published near the dawn of the TV age, most of the exhibits in the *Bride*'s chamber of horrors are drawn from the pre-video press and radio of the forties. In a sense, the book was out-of-date on the day it appeared. McLuhan would certainly say this, though most readers would probably agree that the book stands up remarkably well after sixteen years. After all, there are no sharp breaks in the history of culture, and the *Bride* herself will almost certainly still be around to celebrate her golden wedding in 2001.

Another potent influence was the work of the Canadian economist Harold A. Innis, who died in 1952, at the age of fifty-eight, just as he was adumbrating a brilliant theory of political and cultural change, based upon shifts in communications media. *Empire and Communications* (1950) and *The Bias of Communications* (1951) were published too late to influence the *Bride* but McLuhan's acknowledged debt to Innis is apparent in everything he has published since 1952. (For an excellent account of Innis's ideas and a comparison with those of McLuhan, see James W. Carey, "Harold Adams Innis and Marshall McLuhan," *Antioch Review* XXVII, 1967.)

Finally, there is McLuhan's collaboration with the American anthropologist Edmund Carpenter (then at the University of Toronto), which extended throughout most of the 1950's and recently has been renewed at Fordham. Together they published *Explorations* (1953-1959), a brilliant, eccentric, and imaginative periodical devoted to the study of communications in the widest possible definition of the word. (A selection from the journal, *Explorations in Communications,* was published in book form in 1960.)

Even if one is aware of these influences on McLuhan during this period, it is quite a shock to pass quickly from *The Mechanical Bride* to its successors, *The Gutenberg Galaxy* (1962) and *Understanding Media* (1964). The most startling difference is the change in the author's attitude toward the contemporary world. Not only has his contempt for many of the media and those who control them almost evaporated, but he tries (without complete success) to avoid assuming any intellectual posture that could be mistaken for a "point of view." His animus in both books is reserved for the civilization of the recent past and for contemporaries who are so "stunned" by their commitment to its values that they cannot see reality as in itself it really is. Above all, these books radiate confidence that history has taken a sudden shift toward the kind of society McLuhan could admire.

IV

The Gutenberg Galaxy: the Making of Typographic Man expounds a revised standard version of the gospel of history according to McLuhan. The works of Innis and a variety of lesser influences (including H. J. Chaytor, Tobias Dantzig, Siegfried Giedion, E. H. Gombrich, William Ivins, and Walter Ong) have been assimilated without altering the author's basic credo. In essence, the *Galaxy* identifies McLuhan's old heroes, the "grammarians," with a tradition of discourse based upon the spoken word; and his old enemies, the "dialecticians," with the cult of knowledge based upon alphabetic literacy. The whole theory is worked out in detail, with a wealth of quotations from primary and secondary authorities. Even those who are immune or antipathetic to McLuhanism may find a great deal of fascinating and out-of-the-way information in the pages of *The Gutenberg Galaxy.*

There are already too many explanations of McLuhan's ex-

planation of what Western culture is all about, and I have no
intention of adding to them. Nevertheless, a résumé of the argument of the *Galaxy* is necessary if we are to follow McLuhan's
development from glum reaction to eager apocalypse. In a prefa-
tory note, he eschews the linear form of a consecutive argument
for his book, and claims that it "develops a mosaic or field approach to its problems. Such a mosaic image of numerous data and
quotations in evidence offers the only practical means of revealing
causal operations in history." To dramatize this intention, he has
arranged the main body of the book in the form of 261 more or
less self-contained sections each headed with what a composition
teacher would call a topic sentence—a punning, epigrammatic, or
summarizing statement in large, bold, italic type—not unlike the
chapter headings in early-nineteenth-century novels. Theoretically,
the sections might be read in any order, like those experimental
novels that come with pages that can be shuffled like a pack of
cards. However, I don't recommend that anyone try this with *The
Gutenberg Galaxy.* The truth is that the alleged mosaic or galactic
form is little more than window dressing. McLuhan has a good
old-fashioned story to tell, and those who want to understand it
had better begin at the beginning in the square old way.

The introductory note also repudiates the idea of offering "a
series of views of fixed relationships in pictorial space"—what
McLuhan elsewhere calls a "fixed point of view." But here again,
his claim to have made free and impersonal arrangements of evidence, without bias or commitment, cannot be accepted for a
moment. Anyone who reads McLuhan's books with a degree of
care will have no difficulty in deciding where the author's sympathies lie.

In form, the *Galaxy* follows the classic pattern of tragedy.
McLuhan begins with a preposterous interpretation of *King Lear*
as "a working model of the process of denudation by which men
translated themselves from a world of roles to a world of jobs."
Wisely, he relies upon literary intimations of a pre-alphabetic
cultural Eden, rather than attempting to prove that such a condition ever actually existed; but that does not inhibit him from
describing the emergence of modern culture in terms of "the
anguish of the third dimension," "the madness and misery of the

new Renaissance life of action," and "schizophrenia [which] may be a necessary consequence of literacy." Like all proper tragedies, the book closes with intimations of restored order in an improbable electronic Arcadia of tomorrow.

In McLuhan's mythology, the Fall that alienated man from his naïve acoustic paradise (a fortunate Fall, he sometimes almost admits) was the change in the ratio of his senses brought about by the development of phonetic literacy. As more and more knowledge and experience came to be transmitted from generation to generation not by the spoken word but by its visual equivalent in inscription or manuscript, men moved farther from the muddled, communal, and involving culture of the ear toward the sharply defined, isolate individualism of the eye. Gradually, the linear, sequential, and segmented ordering of syllables and words on the page came to serve as a model for all thought, and Western culture began to take on its characteristic individualistic, analytic, and visual form—literally, its point of view.

Until the fifteenth century, aural and visual modes of thought continued to coexist in relatively fruitful tension. However, with the invention of printing (a characteristically "visual" attempt to achieve quantity, uniformity, and repeatability) the visual bias of European culture began to assume murderous proportions. All values that could not be reconciled with mathematical order, utility, or empirical rationalism were undermined and subverted. From the triumph of Gutenberg technology stems everything that McLuhan most detests about the modern world—capitalism, secularism, industrialism, nationalism, specialization, and socialism. Worse than that, those who ought to lead their fellows back to a saner mode of life—the intellectual and academic elite—are so "stunned" and brainwashed by their dependence upon print that they are incapable of understanding what is happening to them. These "bookmen of detached and private culture" mistake for reality what is really the pre-packaged, homogenized, and denatured product of assembly-line Gutenberg thought processes.

Whether or not this interpretation of Western culture is a valid one is a question that cannot be answered in a sentence or two. McLuhan's fallen visual world is similar to Blake's "single

vision and Newton's sleep," Pound's "usura," and Eliot's "dissocia-
tion of sensibility." No doubt all four myths stem from the same
sort of dissatisfaction about the way things are. However, did the
catastrophe occur in the fifth century B.C. or the fifteenth century A.D. (McLuhan), the sixteenth century (Pound), the seven-
teenth (Eliot), the early eighteenth (Blake)—or are we right to
doubt that any of these mysterious disasters ever occurred in real
life?

Those who are obstinately skeptical are unlikely to find themselves convinced by *The Gutenberg Galaxy*. McLuhan unwittingly
epitomizes the shortcomings of his own style of argument when
he quotes Ashley Montagu on primitive man: "The trouble with
the nonliterate is not that he isn't logical, but that he applies logic
too often, many times on the basis of insufficient premises." When
generalizations are erected upon isolated examples, when syllo-
gisms often have missing or undistributed middles, when connec-
tives such as "thus," "therefore," and "in this way" are used to
link tenuously related propositions, then precisians are likely to
dismiss the perpetrator of such solecisms as beneath serious consideration.

Yet most people who have read the *Galaxy* are unable to dismiss it. After every objection has been made, the book still contains a wealth of fascinating and novel material about the culture
of the past twenty-five hundred years. McLuhan may be wrong
to blame the alphabet and Gutenberg for all the ills of Western
bourgeois culture (for a man who attacks the idea of linear cause
and effect as an illusion of literacy he is sometimes surprisingly
simple-minded about it himself), but the "galaxy" he describes
certainly does exist. Most of the out-of-the-way information comes
from secondary sources, often quoted verbatim and at length; yet
for a literary scholar to discover this heterogeneous material and
perceive its relevance to the contemporary condition is a creative
achievement in itself. The theoretical (though not the ideological)
framework of the *Galaxy* is derived from Innis, but the detailed
applications—some of them brilliant, as in the discussions of
Gargantua, *Don Quixote*, and the *Dunciad*—are all McLuhan's.
Finally, if *The Gutenberg Galaxy* is a maddening and undisci-

plined contribution to the study of the role of printing in Western culture, it is also virtually the only work of its kind. Until one of us writes a better book we should be grateful to have this one.

V

In a kind of postscript, "The Galaxy Reconfigured," McLuhan suggests that we are at last beginning to understand the Gutenberg era only because "we have moved into another phase from which we can contemplate the contours of the preceding situation with ease and clarity. . . . As we experience the new electronic and organic age with ever stronger indications of its main outlines, the preceding mechanical age becomes quite intelligible." McLuhan also finds that our period of transition is not only "richer and more terrible" than that described by Patrick Cruttwell in *The Shakespearian Moment* (1955), but it is moving in the opposite direction—from fragmentation and dissolution to community and involvement. The last sentence of the *Galaxy* promises to carry on the story with another volume devoted to "*Understanding Media* in the world of our time."

In spite of the fact that it is the book that led to McLuhan's contemporary fame, *Understanding Media: The Extensions of Man* came as a disappointment to those whose interest had been whetted by the *Galaxy*. Its main ideas had been briefly outlined in the earlier volume, and their detailed application to twenty-six different "media" (including number, clothing, clocks, motorcars, typewriters, and weapons) often illuminates the subject less than it reveals deficiencies in the theory or eccentricities in the author. (I must apologize for all these visual metaphors, which perhaps betray my unfitness to cope with the phenomena under discussion.) Once again, McLuhan planned the book as a configuration of chapters readable in any order; but this made necessary a great deal of repetition, the tediousness of which is not relieved by the slapdash prose style.

Having already written at length about *Understanding Media* (*Commentary*, January, 1965), I shall not rehearse here the arguments for and against McLuhan's famous division of media into "hot" and "cool," his contention that television is "haptic" or tactile rather than "visual," or his "explanations" of Kennedy's electoral victory over Nixon, the assassination of Lee Harvey Oswald, and the sensuous superiority of mesh over sheer nylons. The aspects of the book that are relevant to our interest in the "paradox" of its author are its extreme optimism and the equally extreme determinism epitomized in the slogan The Medium is the Message.

Though something of a determinist, Harold Innis was certainly not an optimist. Some of the melancholy of his mentor's somber, clotted prose attaches to McLuhan's account of the rape of oral culture by typography in *The Gutenberg Galaxy*—though McLuhan's compulsive paronomasiac cheerfulness keeps breaking through.

Understanding Media is different. It deals with a series of phenomena that had hardly become apparent at the time of Innis's death and about which (by McLuhan's own testimony) there is far less possibility of writing authoritatively—until we move far enough into the post-electronic age (if there is to be one) to see the present era more clearly. Furthermore, no one, least of all Marshall McLuhan, can contemplate the present and the future with the same Olympian detachment we can bring to the past. In this book, he explicitly confesses a faith concerning "the ultimate harmony of being," and commits himself to that "wholeness, empathy and depth of awareness [which] is a natural adjunct of electric technology." It is easier to share his admiration for these values than his confidence that they are somehow implicit in a post-literate culture based upon the computer and the microwave relay.

McLuhan's optimism arises out of his theory that media are extensions of human organs—wheel extends foot, gun extends eye and teeth, radio extends mouth or ear, writing extends eye, and so on. In the past, every new technological development has disturbed the balance or "closure" between the various faculties. Because the extended sense exaggerates or intensifies only one element in a complex process, it leads to a systematic distortion of all experience. Eventually, men cease to be conscious that this has happened to them: like Narcissus, they mistake their own distorted reflections for reality itself. During the Gutenberg era, hypertrophy of the eye was the chief source of error. However, because electric technology differs from all other "media" by extending the whole nervous system rather than just one faculty, we are on the verge of a new era in human history, in which a proper, harmonious ratio between the senses will be restored. What is more, while the older mechanical technology was "explosive," fragmenting the personality and increasing the psychological distance between men, the new order is "implosive," healing the breach in the psyche and joining all humanity in a huge "seamless web" of instant electronic communication. McLuhan halfheartedly warns of the danger that we may sink back into a preliterate "Africa in the mind," but he is obviously much more hopeful that we shall all become secure and contented members of a utopian "global village."

What must we do to be saved? The answer is Nothing. Like a kind of megalomaniacal New Critic who takes the whole world for his poem, McLuhan insists upon the inseparability of content from form. The true content or "message" of any medium is "the change of scale or pace or pattern that it introduces into human affairs." What we usually think of as "content"—paraphrasable arguments, plots, or ideas—is "like the juicy piece of meat carried by the burglar to distract the watchdog of the mind." Those of us who worry about horror comics, TV violence, the lack of controversy in news media, and the Vietnam war are wasting our time on irrelevancies. All these "problems" (some of them illusory, in McLuhan's view) will be solved without our intervention by electronic technology. Our sole duty is to understand what is happening (even if this involves reading *Understanding Media* in which the Gutenberg medium seems hopelessly at odds with the McLuhan message).

VI

The two invariables that have helped to shape McLuhan's strange odyssey from straitlaced and pessimistic conservatism to his present euphoric and approving interest in everything from *Naked Lunch* to topless waitresses are his dislike of Protestant and capitalistic individualism, and his Catholic faith. The first is quite explicit in his early works and clearly implied in the later; the second is never allowed to intrude formally into any of his books, though it presumably accounts for McLuhan's lack of interest in ontology and his confidence in the essential harmoniousness of the creation. Only someone who believes that he has already *got* the message could be so indifferent to the problem of what it is that media mediate. He discusses the universe in the same spirit as a theologian might discuss the development of dogma of the evolution of the liturgy.

But even (or, perhaps, especially) from the standpoint of orthodox Catholic theology, there are serious lacunae in McLuhan's account of the way things are at the dawn of the electronic era—his inadequate psychology, his lack of interest in social structure, and his apparent inability to perceive the full tragic dimensions of some of the phenomena about which he writes with such flip assurance.

McLuhan appears to regard the Freudian unconscious as a simple product of Gutenberg technology. There is perhaps something to be said for this idea, but the man who would convince us of it ought to offer at least the outlines of an acceptable alternative theory of human behavior. This he does not do. On the contrary, he seems to see man as a ratio of five senses whose balance is wholly determined by outside circumstances. Granted that "elephantiasis of the will" is (or was) an endemic modern disease, it is surely going too far to try to save the patient by amputating his selfhood. McLuhan's account of how media extend or "outer" human faculties likewise makes some sense, but it is certainly no less simplemindedly mechanistic than any of the Gutenberg absurdities at which he jeers. His analogy between electric technology and the central nervous system seems a useful one until we realize that he means it literally, and he really does envisage a kind of universal electrical organism into which all men will be plugged—a prediction that involves not only bad psychology, but even worse theology.

Associated with McLuhan's strange idea of the psyche as a kind of Lockeian *tabula rasa* upon which media record their messages is his indifference to problems of political and economic power. This was not always so, as we have seen: he once ex-

pounded a kind of Chestertonian or Southern agrarian conservatism. Now, however, he seems to embrace an equally extreme and
impractical utopianism in which his old enemies Big Government
and Big Business have become the allies of avant-garde artists in
the cause of electronic togetherness. Presumably, this new confidence in the humane potentiality of the economic *status quo* owes
something to McLuhan's avowed preference for the iconic over the
analytic mode. ("Icons are not specialist fragments or aspects
but unified and compressed images of complex kind. They focus a
large region of experience in tiny compass.") Advertising, television, and Cold War ploys such as the space race all appeal to
him more than old-fashioned forms of communication or persuasion because of their iconic character. The fact that these
media may be controlled and exploited by men with petty or
sinister motives, such as speculative financiers, cosmetic manufacturers, or the military establishment does not appear to interest
him. He sees contemporary history as a kind of cosmic *Finnegans
Wake* in which some mysterious force is at work to harmonize
and reconcile the apparent conflicts. Often he tries to clinch a dubious argument by quoting an enigmatic sentence or two from
the *Wake*—but even Joyce's most ardent admirers will feel that
one does him a disservice by using his superb evocation of Europe's
collective unconscious as a kind of politico-cultural primer of the
atomic age. In fact, treating writers and artists as though they
were prophets in the vulgar Tiresias or Jules Verne sense of the
word, rather than as Isaiahs or Jeremiahs, is one of McLuhan's
least defensible habits.

While McLuhan places his faith in this kind of cosmic
aestheticism (a modern equivalent of eighteenth-century "cosmic
Toryism"?), the society in which he lives shows signs of lapsing
into technologically sophisticated chaos. Although he occasionally
evinces an awareness of this, most of the time he appears to be
so stunned by his vision of electrical Nirvana that he misses the
living reality as spectacularly as any Gutenberg somnambulist. Certainly, it would be hard to match the cocksure impercipience with
which McLuhan sets us right about many of the more agonizing
issues of our age.

Civil rights? "Many people have observed how the real integrator or leveler of white and Negro in the South was the private car and the truck, not the expression of moral points of view." Southern Negroes will be astonished to learn that General Motors really deserves the credit usually given to lunchroom sit-ins and voter registration drives, and flabbergasted to note the tense in which McLuhan couches his remark.

Rigged TV quiz shows? "Any play or poem or novel is also rigged to produce an effect . . . But . . . So great was the audience participation in the quiz shows that the directors of the show were prosecuted as con men. . . . Charles Van Doren merely got clobbered as an innocent bystander . . . Regrettably, [the investigation] simply provided a field day for the earnest moralizers. A moral point of view too often serves as a substitute for understanding in technological matters." This line of reasoning opens up tremendous opportunities for imaginative television producers: what about rigging the World Series to provide a suitable number of ninth-inning tie-breaking homers? With electronically controlled balls, and Nicklaus and Palmer cast as good and bad guys, the PGA tournament might be made even more exciting than it is. Instead of having to share riots with other networks, a progressive news producer could foment his own private disturbance in some unexpected city where only his cameras were ready for action. One would like to hear St. Thomas's views on this bit of moral analysis by his disciple.

War? This is really "a process of achieving equilibrium among unequal technologies." Nowadays, "the cold war is the real war front—a surround—involving everybody—all the time—everywhere. Whenever hot wars are *necessary* [my italics] . . . we conduct them in the backyards of the world with the old technologies." The Vietnam war is unpopular with the American people [unlike the Korean War?] because this hot conflict is being waged before the cool eyes of television cameras. I do not think that it is merely my hot liberal heart that is repelled by the cool glibness of these formulations—particularly that casual "necessary," the Western arrogance of "backyards," and the idea that helicopters, defoliants, guided missiles, and "Lazy Dog" shells are merely fragments of the "old technologies."

These defects in McLuhan's emotional and intellectual equipment were almost as discernible in his early work as they are in *Understanding Media* and *The Medium Is the Massage*. However, when he wrote in the character of a lonely defender of eloquence and reason in the midst of a debased and commercialized culture, his occasional crudities of thought or feeling did not detract from the general brilliance of his insights. Lacking any particular hope for the future, he was concerned less to proselytize than to maintain a detached and ironic awareness of what was happening.

Now that McLuhan foresees the triumph of electronic technology, dramatically reversing the cultural processes which prompted his pessimism, his intellectual energy is naturally diverted not merely from contemplation of the past to prediction of the future, but also from detachment to commitment. It is quite clear that his deep emotional investment in the expected new order stems from motives of which he himself is only partly aware and about which it would be inappropriate to speculate. He would be the first to heap scorn upon an opponent who allowed wish fulfillment to have such a distorting effect upon his view of reality. It would be better for McLuhan if his oversimplifications did not happen to coincide with the pretensions of young status-hungry advertising and television executives and producers, who eagerly provide him with a ready-made claque, exposure on the media, and a substantial income from addresses to sales conventions. The Marshall McLuhan who wrote those classic articles in the *Sewanee* and *Kenyon* reviews, *The Mechanical Bride*, and *The Gutenberg Galaxy* deserves a better fate than to become Madison Avenue's favorite philosopher.

William Buckley

*Sometimes I get so fatigued just explaining over and over what
I mean when if people would only read or listen . . .*

[Most of the cult heroes who represent some aspect of American intellectual life are liberal in their political sentiments. America has produced few conservative thinkers of great influence, and the universities as well as the mass media of today are dominated by liberals. A colorful and controversial exception is William Buckley, who graduated from Yale University, wrote a book that criticized his alma mater, became editor of *National Review* so as to launch a studious attack on liberalism in America, and in 1965 ran against John V. Lindsay for mayor of New York. Buckley is the intellectual or "radical" conservative of contemporary America, "a swinging Old Fogy," in the words of *Harper's,* "who has become a legend in his time."]

William Buckley was born on November 24, 1925, the sixth of ten children. His father, who began as a lawyer and ended as an oil tycoon, left an estimated $110,000,000 to his children at the time of his death. Buckley was brought up in France, England, and the United States. At the age of six he already had assumed the role of social polemicist: he wrote a letter to the king of England to persuade him that England should pay its war debts. Buckley was graduated from the Millbrook School in Millbrook, New York, in 1943, served in the army for two years, and entered Yale University in 1946. He soon became noted for his skill as a debater and a polemical journalist, and his fellow students sensed that he would be an important figure in American politics. He remained at the university until 1951 as a teacher of Spanish. After his graduation Buckley published *God and Man at Yale; The Superstitions of Academic Freedom* (1951) in which, as a Roman Catholic and a conservative, he criticized what he considered to be Yale's distorted curriculum.

In 1952 Buckley joined *The American Mercury* as associate editor, but he soon left to practice free-lance writing. In 1954 he published *McCarthy and His Enemies*, which was a collaboration with his brother-in-law and which has been considered an apologia for the anti-Communist tactics of Senator Joseph McCarthy. Buckley wrote other books that espoused his political conservatism—*Up from Liberalism* (1959), *Rumbles Left and Right* (1963), *The Unmaking of a Mayor* (1965), and *The Jeweler's Eye* (1968). But his ideas have received their widest circulation in the magazine, *National Review*, which he founded on November 14, 1955, and which he still edits. In recent years, Buckley has written a syndicated column that reaches more than 7,000,000 readers, and has appeared on radio and television as a skillful, challenging, and at times infuriating debater. "He comes prepared for total war," one commentator has observed, "with a startling array of oratorical weapons in his arsenal—charm, wit, verbal agility, and a faultless sense of pace and timing, plus a mesmerizing voice (cultivated upper-class WASP with Oxonian overlay) that he uses as a musical instrument, with the sibilants and lower registers reserved for the inevitable rhetorical kill. No one who has seen a Buckley performance is likely to forget it."

As an exponent of conservatism, Buckley has often sponsored an isolationist policy in foreign affairs; a deep belief in individualism and the survival of the fittest in regard to economic matters; a firm faith in Catholicism; a pride in his family; and a sharp suspicion of a centralized government. These convictions have been conveyed with a wit and sophistication rare in the political discourse of our day. However one may feel about Buckley's politics, one is never bored by their presentation.

He is an international traveler who is strong for states' rights;
a Honda "50" hot-rock who plays the clavichord; in one moment a
mixer-and-mingler with a Rotary Club grip and in the next a Grand
Duke icily looking down his nose to accept the peasants' birthday bows.
He is an author who sometimes sides with censors, and a celebrated
intellectual who has spoken of "the hoax of academic freedom"—
a swinging Old Fogy who has become a legend in his time.

God, Man, and
William J. Buckley

LARRY L.

KING

I N CASE you just got off the Greyhound, the William F. Buckley, Jr., described here is the same one who publishes *National
Review*, ran a noisy third for Mayor of New York City in 1965
on the Conservative party ticket, attacked his alma mater in *God
and Man at Yale* hardly before the ink had dried on his parchment, and who as a six-year-old boy wrote the King of England
that England had damn well better pony up her war debts. A
devout Catholic, he assayed the encyclical of Pope John XXIII
as "a venture in triviality"; a failed politician, he thinks he was
"hit by grace when political intelligence was distributed." He is a
New York East Side high-camp swell, by way of rural Connecticut,
who excites support for his aristocratic polemics even in the
lumpen wastelands of Queens. He can publicly describe a debate
opponent, Gore Vidal, as "a philosophical degenerate" only moments before privately offering to stand him to drinks. His
enemies, laid end-to-end, would reach from here to Southern
Purgatory, to which they variously damn him for inciting racial

REPRINTED FROM THE MARCH 1967 ISSUE OF *Harper's Magazine*. COPY-
RIGHT 1967, 1968 BY LARRY KING. REPRINTED BY PERMISSION OF THE STER-
LING LORD AGENCY.   •

hatred, dividing the Republican party, defaming Democracy, and betraying the John Birch Society.

Certain of New York's literati in their posh watering places speak of Buckley's "charm," "verve," and "style." He uses these in justifying U.S. bombing of Red China "on the grounds the good guys of this earth have got to keep the bad guys from getting nuclear bombs." When will the Africans be ready for self-government? "When they stop eating each other." "Segregation is not intrinsically immoral" and the Freedom March on Washington was "a mob deployment." He would abolish the graduated income tax, farm subsidies (but not the oil-depletion allowance), unemployment compensation, collective bargaining, most welfare programs, Sin in the aggregate, and, for all I know, Christmas seals. *National Review* ("My number one love") is committed "to standing athwart history yelling 'Stop!'"

[Why is Bill Buckley (consort of the late Senator Joe McCarthy, Goldwater, and Young Americans for Freedom, to throw in a little reverse guilt-by-association) the social darling of so many Establishment liberals? Irving Howe, the critic and *Dissent* editor, who sees Buckley as something fashionable to have around—the way every salon or cocktail party in the 1920s and 1930s had its adopted Parlor Pink for amusement and diversion—speculates why he "took in certain people":

"Perhaps one reason is that we have no tradition in this country of right-wing intellectuals. Think of the archetypal American reactionary and you summon an image of a stumbling primitive who wants the United States to quit the U.N., drop the bomb, bust the unions, clean up the Reds, abolish the income tax. But that someone wanting a good many of these same things could also write a paragraph of lucid prose and make a clever wisecrack was not really within the bounds of our experience. . . ."

Norman Mailer seems to find in Buckley the greatest spectacle on earth. "No other actor," Mailer has written, "can project simultaneous hints that he is in the act of playing Commodore of the Yacht Club, Joseph Goebbels, Robert Mitchum, Maverick, Savonarola, the nice prep-school kid next door, and the snows of yesteryear." John Kenneth Galbraith calls him "the only reactionary I ever met with a sense of humor." Publisher Tom Guinzburg at Viking Press, Buckley's old roommate at Yale, thinks "many liberals find Bill—well, bearable, because they sense he feels pain."

Murray Kempton finds in Buckley an admirable mixture of naïveté, sentiment, and geniality to go with his other qualities. "There are occasions," Kempton once wrote, "when Buckley tempts you to remember Macaulay's grudging compliment to Burke, which was that he generally chose his side like a fanatic and defended it like a philosopher." Even the writer Michael Harrington, who once described Buckley as "an urbane front man for the most primitive and vicious emotions in the land," speaks approvingly of his inner sense of irony, and of how remarkably relaxed he is in private.]

Beware of Amiability

Some months ago I resolved to inspect William F. Buckley, Jr., in a clinical sense. My aim was to take a personal look at Buckley's fatal charm and, having looked, to judge arbitrarily whether he has "mellowed" and "doesn't honestly believe all that jazz"—as some friendly liberals contend—or whether he really skins and eats crippled babies alive. I knew that our more obvious dissimilarities (Yale vs. Texas Tech, Skull & Bones vs. West Texas Boosters, oilman-financier father vs. dirt-farming daddy) might preclude any immediate appreciation of Mr. Buckley's subtler charms, but I was willing for him to take that risk.

I now report that Mr. Buckley can, indeed, charm the socks off a rooster; that his wit is no mere illusion; that he is an instinctive aristocrat, who, while accepting the tributes of a Park Avenue doorman, can look down his nose as if sniffing something malodorous; that he drives in Manhattan traffic as if Lin Piao and the Red Guards are in pursuit; and that he is a refined, polished gentleman who, sitting among artifacts of culture in his own home, can call a guest a son-of-a-bitch in an Oxford accent and with the cold eyes of a lynch-mob leader.

Buckley's *National Review* offices lack the luxury of his Connecticut estate or his elegant pad in New York's East 70s. The offices sprawl over three floors of a decrepit building on East 35th

Street between Third and Lexington, a neighborhood of mixed circumstances.

The elevator sneaked up to the third-floor hall littered with cardboard boxes. A middle-aged lady with dark hair cut in a severe Dutch bob greeted me in Buckley's office: he had been unavoidably detained, but do please have a seat. I sat at a long table. The lady came bearing the latest issue of *National Review*, along with a bound volume of Buckley's syndicated newspaper columns. "To get the current topics first," she instructed, "read from back to front." I said perhaps that was as good a way to read Buckley as any, smiling to show that I was really one of this earth's good guys. The secretary disappeared wordlessly, to adjoining quarters and I turned to inspect the battleground from which Bill Buckley fights against the world, liberal flesh, and the devil.

Buckley's desk was a profusion of books, papers, memos, and manuscripts. From it he directs a staff of twenty-odd, including several reformed Old Leftists whose dreams have turned to clabber, in getting the weekly word out to 97,000 readers. Photographs and paintings of sailing sloops brightened an otherwise cheerless room that has walls the exact color of Gulden's spicy brown mustard. Buckley's maps pull down from the wall; if they were all pulled down in tandem one would have a perfect view of a flat world.

The bulletin board displays Buckley's humor. (He once posted a picture of Karl Marx wearing a Goldwater button.) A telegram curled, aging, and with a dateline from somewhere out there on the wrong side of the Hudson warned: S–747 AND H.R. 1932 TO DESTROY WALTER-McCARRAN IMMIGRATION LAWS, THEREBY FLOODING AMERICA WITH 750,000 TRAINED REVOLUTIONARIES NOW WAITING TO LEAD NATIONWIDE REVOLT. GET BUSY. URGENT. A clipping from *National Review:* "Conservatives are organizing a Paean for Earl Warren. They're going to gather at the Supreme Court and Pae on him." Dear John letters from Birch Society sympathizers told of their cooled ardor following Buckley's excommunication of Robert Welch from the high priesthood of conservatism: "*You utter rat!!!* . . . Traitor! . . . Finks like you who turn their peashooters on the John Birch Society."

Buckley has more brass than seventy-six trombones come marching by, and no suspicion that he could possibly be wrong about anything. It is on the record that as a small boy Buckley (1) two days after arriving at a private school proceeded to explain the deficiencies of the institution to its startled president; (2) dictated exactly how short his sisters should be permitted to wear their skirts; (3) crashed a faculty meeting at Millbrook School to accuse a teacher of robbing him of the right to express his political views in class, then "proceeded to expound to the stunned faculty on the virtues of isolationism, the dignity of the Catholic Church, and the political ignorance of the school staff."

In 1946, at a San Antonio army base for less than forty-eight hours, Lt. William F. Buckley, Jr., wrote the Commanding General "telling him that he found a great waste of manpower, that his staff was inadequate, and expressed surprise that such things could be." Buckley was snatched from the brink of military class warfare by an intermediary who counseled him against mailing the letter.

Buckley's father (a native Texan who came up from scratch to leave a $110-million oil fortune) was no shrinking violet either. He was kicked out of Mexico after taking the wrong side of one too many revolutions, sent inter-family memos to his children advising them on everything from politics to the healthful benefits of walking, and in general exhorted them—in the words of a daughter—to become "absolutely perfect." "What this country needs," he advised his son in 1953, "is a politician who has an education and I don't know of one. There hasn't been an educated man in the Senate or House of Representatives since Sumners of Texas quit in disgust three or four years ago." Yet even a man of such strong sentiments felt constrained to write his son that he must "learn to be more moderate in the expression of your views and try to express them in a way that would give as little offense as possible."

That must have been the most wasted advice since the Prime Minister counseled Edward VIII against hanging out with divorcees. Buckley once told a crowd to Norman Mailer's face that as a political analyst Mailer "comes close to being the most ignorant man I have ever met." When Democratic nominee Abraham Beame during the Mayor's race boasted that "I was educated by the City of New York," Buckley observed—"which fact should be obvious." Buckley called Republican John Lindsay "Destiny's tot," and of Arthur Schlesinger, Jr., he has said, "No one believes anything he says, anyway." And the barb that caused his trouble with the primitive Right: "For all I know, Robert Welch thinks *I'm* a Communist plot." His passion for verbal hip-shots, combined with the imperial demeanor, inspired Buckley's sibling early on to tag him "the young Mahster," and, years later, prompted James Wechsler of the New York *Post* to say, "You allow yourself to become mellow and amiable, then suddenly you discover he is practically calling you a traitor. . . . I just won't allow myself to get amiable."

Private Message to Mailer

I was almost to the point of reading Buckley's column when he burst into his office in a great clomping of heels. He grabbed my hand to give it a healthy wring, making a two-syllable word of "Hi!", beaming as if I had at long last come with the rent money or to spring him on bail. He apologized for tardiness occasioned by a luncheon engagement in some distant cavern of the city, then called for coffee and offered cigars. Immediately he began to interview me: What was my background, what had I written, what sort of article did I propose to write about him, where did I live, was I married, what was Lyndon Johnson *really* like?

We sized each other up like two fighters in midring, Buckley hooking me with a couple of jokes and scoring with an anecdotal right-cross: "When I sent Norman Mailer a copy of my latest book I turned over to the index in the back and wrote 'Hi!' by his name. Knowing Mailer, he'll *immediately* go to the index to evaluate his own role and that 'Hi!' will just kill him!" We sipped our coffee and laughed at Norman Mailer. Buckley chuckled at a couple of my stories, didn't counterpunch when I jabbed him lightly with a couple of my Leftist wisdoms, and was such an eager host that he plopped two ersatz sweet pills into my coffee over protests that I never use sugar. He used all his equipment: the deep, rolling voice; flourishing, theatrical gestures with the cigar; the leaping eyebrows, popping eyes, and the smile that bursts suddenly to display a great sea of teeth. He was winning on points easily. Then James Wechsler's ghost warned me not to get amiable.

"Your more enthusiastic opponents," I said, "have warned me of your charm. Will you please turn it off anytime I give the hand signal?" Buckley obliged by saying that he would remain alert for my signs of distress. I wanted to ask more specific definitions, I said, of certain cloudy proposals in his book, *The Unmaking of a Mayor* (published in 1966, a year after his unsuccessful campaign against John V. Lindsay), and to quiz him on a number of points raised in earlier articles about him that I had secured from the Library of Congress. "How many articles did they send you?" he asked. Oh, maybe sixty-five or seventy. "My God!" Buckley said, "there must have been *thousands!*" Obviously the federal bureaucracy had bungled again.

In *The Unmaking of a Mayor* Buckley frets over being misquoted in the press and of being habitually misunderstood by his critics. He makes the valid point that reporters sometimes do not permit the facts to botch up an otherwise excellent story (as he several times proved by producing taped recordings of his campaign press conferences and then comparing his utterances with stories purporting to report them), and he grieves that so few took his third-party candidacy for Mayor seriously. There was that nasty accusation that he had said Harlem residents throw garbage out their windows and then wallow in it, that he encouraged cheers for Alabama peace officers who had beaten civil-rights marchers at the Selma bridge, and that he advocated "concentration camps" for nonproductive New Yorkers said to be sapping the city purse through welfare programs—lies or distortions or misquotations all.

Buckley had gone on at length in his book about *The New York Times'* attacking him for using the term "epicene resentment" in alluding to demonstrators against the war in Vietnam. The *Times* and all politicians smart enough to know what "epicene" means upbraided him for charging the demonstrators with a certain tutti-fruttiness, Buckley answering that "epicene" means sexless and, besides, he didn't mean the demonstrators: he

meant their *resentment*. Couldn't everybody see that was an in-
sinuation of a different color? Buckley replowed this old ground
with me. I then quoted him on the same subject: "I wonder how
these self-conscious *boulevardiers* of protest would have fared if
a platoon of American soldiers who have seen the gore in South
Vietnam had parachuted down into their mincing ranks?" Had
he said that? Yes, he had. Well, was not "mincing" a far more
suggestive word—and didn't it clearly designate the demonstrators themselves rather than some "resentment" they might
harbor?

"I see what you mean," Buckley said, frowning. "Your point is
that 'mincing' is a much stronger word than 'epicene.' I tend to
agree."

No, I said, my point was that he had called the demonstrators fags.

Buckley's smile was cool; he said they certainly could use me
over at *The New York Times*. No, he did not concede that he had
impugned anyone's manhood: "If one takes metaphor away from
the language—God, what have we left? Isn't political rhetoric
dull enough already?"

The telephone rang. It was a family conversation, having to
do with weekend plans, and I got this insane image of the wife
saying to the husband, "Honey, will you stop by the store and
pick up a bucket of caviar?" Suddenly Buckley clapped his hand
over the receiver and called to me, "You could, perhaps, crucify
me for the use of 'mincing' by seeking its most narrow, personal-
ized definition or application. But then *you* would be squarer
than *I* for having suggested a censure of sexual terms. So who's
to judge which of us is right? Who's to establish the standard?
It's really a matter of . . . sophistication." Buckley dipped back
to the telephone as if to signify he claimed the point.

The People on Welfare

Michael Harrington's *The Other America* is often credited
with inspiring the government's war on poverty. After debating
Buckley, Harrington concluded that his opponent "knows absolutely nothing of poverty." Harrington said he had been loaded

with facts, figures, and examples to prove his debating points, but that Buckley rebutted with "rhetoric or jokes; he simply slid by the questions." Buckley has been shielded from poverty, and the sight of its horrors. He therefore could not, Harrington implied, be a competent judge of welfare programs or pass verdict on how much help society owes the chronically poor. Did Buckley agree? I asked. No, he did not. Well, *had* he seen poverty at first hand: visited a ghetto, known the indescribable odors of a flophouse, seen the desolate camps of migratory workers, or shanty towns abandoned when the coal vein played out?

Buckley stared at me for long moments. "No," he said, "I have not. That's one of my shortcomings." He paused. "I really mean that. It *is* a shortcoming. I'm not the type to have been of any use to Associated Press, say, if I'd been in Dealy Plaza on November 22, 1963. I learn by reading. After all, you must remember that the people who write the best books on the Civil War were not at Gettysburg." Another pause, then: "So while it's true I haven't actually been *around* poverty, I think Mr. Harrington has little or no reason for judging me ignorant of the subject." He seemed nettled and, I thought, for the first time a bit unsure of his ground.

Buckley had written, "The purpose of education is to educate, not to promise a synthetic integration by numerically balancing ethnic groups in the classroom." Isn't there education I asked, in children's learning to live with, observe, or get to know as individuals children of other races? Buckley nodded, "Sure," Well, then? In tones you might use to a backward child, Buckley said, "But that's merely a *by*-product! If it happens, well and good. Education, you see, is an *intellectual* rather than a *sociological* process." He sighed. "Sometimes I get *so* fatigued just explaining over and over what I *mean* when if people would only read or listen . . ."

All right. I had read and listened to his announcement for Mayor, and many of his pronouncements during the campaign. Very funny stuff. But how could he complain of not being taken seriously enough when—asked how many votes he expected to get "conservatively speaking"—he had answered, "Conservatively speaking, one." Or, when queried on what he would do if elected, had variously answered "demand a recount," "I hadn't thought about it," and "put a net under the window of the editor of *The New York Times*"?

Buckley said that well, dammit, political dialogue was so gawddahm *dull*, so bereft of humor, so spiritless; one hoped to bring a touch of life to the game. And one knew, too, that one's serious proposals would hardly get the slightest mention in the press, so one bid for attention by making remarks which one knew would at least get one in the newspapers. After all, he had had far less campaign funds than the Democrat or Republican candidates; it was necessary to compensate by breaking into the news columns.

He added, "I made many serious proposals during the campaign, all dealing with *specific* problems of this city. The newspapers chopped them down to a few sentences, or lost them on the back pages. For instance, my transportation paper contained some *dahm* good ideas—we've a terrible, messy, almost hopeless traffic problem in New York. Among my recommendations was the now infamous, if I may call it that, crosstown bikeway. The newspapers singled the bikeway proposal out, to the exclusion of all others, making it sound extremely frivolous. It isn't frivolous at all." He brooded a moment. "From the standpoint of strategy my timing was bad. I released the transportation paper in the last tremors of the campaign. There was never any opportunity to counter the impression that the bikeway proposal was a joke."

There had been much breast-beating, if not many cerebral strokes, over Buckley's campaign proposal to encourage "nonproductive" citizens to quit New York. Resolved: that welfare recipients not infirm or tied down by small children be required to perform labors for the city* and, should they balk, that they be encouraged to seek areas where opportunity might knock louder. If they refused to go—well, their welfare grants would be discontinued. Might this not, I asked, constitute a rather unfeeling eviction of people from their chosen ground through a form of glorified blackmail?

My God, Buckley said, didn't people *want* opportunity? Besides, there probably wouldn't be all that many people involved.

---

* Buckley said this proposal has long existed on the books, though it has never been enforced.

I objected: thousands would oppose the idea on principle, or for other reasons of their right, and would not go. Buckley countered that liberals were such pessimists: maybe he had more faith in people than I did. Would he propose to enforce his decree by moving welfare-staters out at bayonet point? Ah, he said, the old "concentration camp" concept again! No, he would not want anyone to have that power, including himself. However, the law gave the city a wide latitude in establishing welfare qualification standards, he said, and the right set of standards might motivate more people to go. But some *wouldn't* be motivated, and if he should arbitrarily cut off welfare benefits wouldn't there be chaos: hungry families, evictions, more school dropouts, more crime, more festering of the wound?

Perhaps so, Buckley said. Certainly there would be many problems. How would you administer such a law? Where would you draw the line? Candidly, he answered his own questions: "I don't know. Perhaps my idealism convinced me that God and the Conservative party would find a way." He had hoped, however, that the mere introduction of the subject would inspire new thinking on the welfare problem.

Had Buckley "mellowed," as friendly liberals claim? "I suppose," he said, "there's a situation in which the Hungarian Freedom Fighter could be said to have 'mellowed,' isn't there?" The dazzling grin: "No, I don't think I've mellowed. My God, I should *hope* not. No, I think the liberals are finding it increasingly difficult to rebut the charges we make in *National Review*. There simply can't be anything wrong with the *liberal* truths, you see, so there must be something wrong with *mine*. Therefore, I can't mean half of what I say—it's merely an affectation, a pose—or I have somehow mellowed like a ripe old pear. So convenient for them, isn't it?" He leaned back in his chair, waving the cigar like a baton, vastly pleased.

Buckley founded *National Review* in 1955. Though circulation has grown from the initial 8,000 to almost 100,000, the magazine continues to lose money. (So do most political magazines with one-eyed views of the issues, whether left or right.) The editor's lecture fees, royalties from writing, and similar undertakings are largely plowed back into the magazine. Buckley led me to the bulletin board and pointed to a scroll attesting that the American Institute of Management deemed William F. Buckley, Jr., worthy of recognition for "his individual executive managerial abilities." Beaming, the honoree pointed to a connecting line he has drawn from the scroll to the document posted next to it: a financial statement showing *National Review* $2,181,222.23 in the red.

Does he feel pain or disappointment in seeing his pet causes repeatedly rejected by the electorate? "Individuals sometimes hurt me," he said, "but not events. I have almost lost the capacity to feel pain in the sense that I expect any sudden reversal of the trends. I do wish the opportunity to get *across* to more people without having to fight past their taboos, or preconceptions. I get awfully tired"—and here he slumped in his chair as if suddenly blackjacked—"simply saying, 'I didn't say that,' or, 'What I said was this.' I suppose it's all part of the hot pursuit after publishable copy."

Our talk was low-key until I remarked on charges that have been made against Buckley as a racist—one which he emphatically denies, and cites as the blackest of all smears against him during the race for Mayor. ("If I lived in South Carolina," he once said to explain his position, "I would vote for segregated schools in my community; in Stamford, where I live, I'd vote for integrated schools. I hope that if I lived in South Carolina I would take a position aimed at doing what I could to increase the opportunity of Negroes to the point where I no longer felt segregation was necessary. Maybe it would take a hundred years or ten years.") Sitting in his office, Buckley said he held no brief for militant segregationists like Lester Maddox, who chased Negroes from his Atlanta restaurant with guns and axe handles rather than serve them in compliance with civil-rights laws. "If Maddox had promised to use the axe handle, should they come into the restaurant, on LBJ, who sponsored the bill, or on Earl Warren, who ratified it," Buckley said, "it would have been easier to understand."

Into the room burst a cadre of revelers: a half-dozen members of the *National Review* staff, returning from the four-hour celebration of lunch, Buckley explaining something about a special occasion. He introduced his sister, Priscilla, who is managing editor, the art director Jim O'Bryan, a jolly man whose name was lost in the joyful noise (and who hugged against his breastbone the bronze bust of some hero unknown to me), and several young ladies whose high spirits might have been equally charged to the natural exuberance of clean-living Conservative youth and generous applications of strong waters. "Had I gone to lunch with them," Buckley said, cheerfully, "the interview would not be over —merely starting."

In my Texas twang I said, "I thank I'll mosey over to the *New Republic* and tell 'em you got some real swingers over here."

One of the young ladies reached out as if to tweak my beard. "With that accent," she said, "you wouldn't dare!"

Up Park Avenue Way

Preparing to leave his office Buckley struggled with an attaché case so stuffed with paperwork it would close only after he pressed the top down with one knee. Even then, it played jack-in-the-box with him. "A nice . . . lazy . . . weekend . . . in the country," Buckley said, fighting the locks.

He asked which way I might be going; I said I was to meet a friend at Toots Shor's. "Would you like to ride part way with me?" he asked. I accepted.

While Buckley and I talked inside his office, the Devil had invented a machine, christened it "Honda 50," and parked it in front of the elevator outside the door. "Where the hell," I asked, "did *that* thing come from?" Buckley grinned: "My staff . . . Here, will you hold this? And catch the elevator door for me?" Taking his attaché case, I said that I had now carried Lyndon B. Johnson's and William F. Buckley's bags in the same lifetime, and believed I would call it a career. Half-lifting, half-shoving the Honda 50 into the elevator, Buckley remarked that obviously I had little left to live for.

On the street, he reclaimed the attaché case to lash it to the back of the motor scooter.

"Ah . . . is *this* what you offered me a ride on?"

Buckley broke out in another grin. "Chicken?"

"Well . . ." I shifted from foot to foot, more than faintly agonized.

Curiosity overcame cowardice after a brief but spirited battle; my person was sandwiched between Mr. Buckley and his attaché case. "What happens," I mumbled, "if we fall?"

"We'll discuss that contingency when we come to it. Now, don't try to balance. That's my department."

"Is there anything I can hold on to?"

"Grip the seat," Buckley instructed. I gripped the seat, fingers curved under in the manner of someone in the last throes of arthritis. We weaved and bobbed up 35th Street, charting the uncertain course of two dawn revelers. "No, no!" Buckley admonished "Don't try to balance yourself. It's not as if one's liberalism could balance another's conservatism. The *driver* keeps it in balance."

So I sat there as we headed up Park Avenue, cotton-mouthed and feeling vulnerable and exposed. What would happen to the Conservative party, I wondered, should one of the True Believers suddenly catch a glimpse of William F. Buckley, Jr., tooling up Park Avenue on a souped-up Kiddie-Kar in the company of a popeyed, pale radical whose beard was flowing wildly in the wind; who, furthermore, believed in majority rule, and who in periodically strengthening his grip on the Honda seat inadvertently squeezed the living constitutional flesh? No doubt the Stock Market would fall and new cracks might appear on the Liberty Bell.

We hit an intersection where rush-hour cars and cabs had snarled. Buckley said, "Here's where this thing really pays off." Then we scooted between the lines of cars and cabs at an indecently reckless rate.

"Do you have Medicare?" Buckley shouted. We caromed around a sharp corner on the ramp separating the Commodore Hotel from the Heliport in the Pan Am Building, going faster than the 15-miles-per-hour recommended by Mayor Lindsay's traffic signs. We brightened a dark tunnel, gaining two car lengths when Buckley artfully cut a cab off from its intended path, and emerged just in time to make a screeching halt at a traffic light.

In front of a Park Avenue apartment house another traffic

tangle blocked our path. Wretched souls waiting under a canopy for taxis smiled on us. The uniformed doorman stepped into the street. "Do you think you could of straightened this out"—he gestured toward the snarl—"if they'd let you build your bike-way?" He moved closer, leaned in, and confided, "I done all *I* could." Buckley beamed at him down a great expanse of Roman nose.

At the next intersection a pedestrian yelled, "Hey, Mister B., what would John Lindsay say?"

A few minutes later Buckley pulled over to the curb. I climbed off the Honda while passers-by who stopped to stare made a mockery of the old saw that New Yorkers would not pause to see a free earthquake. Making Buckley a present of my clammy hand, I promised that I would not forget him as long as I lived. He disappeared down a narrow lane between two endless rows of honking automobiles.

Reagan the Politician Buckley the Actor

After his television show a few days later, at Buckley's home in the East 70s, I warily skirted the Honda mocking me from the entrance foyer and trailed the entourage, which included Robert Novak, the Washington columnist who had been Buckley's TV guest, through a large anteroom where red carpeting marched up the staircase. As we entered a well-appointed study, Buckley gestured toward a painting of his own creation and cracked, "Did you see my latest Warhol?" He spoke Spanish on the telephone before pointing the way to drinks. Somebody said we needed ice. "No," Buckley said, "I just ordered some on the telephone." Presto, a maid appeared with ice.

After a round of drinks and chit-chat (would it be Romney or Reagan in '68?; how much would the Great Society back-track in the 90th Congress?; Buckley told the back-of-Norman-Mailer's-book story again) we moved into a living room no bigger than the Carlsbad Caverns, with antiqued pieces, smartly set off by off-white and red, that did not come from Discount Gene's. It was there, over bite-sized sandwiches and wine, that I encountered a small gale. Novak remarked that "the most dissimilar campaigns"

he'd known were those of two men presumed to be at least ideological first cousins: Ronald Reagan and Buckley.

"They're both fine actors," I said, "but then again—perhaps
where Mr. Reagan talked issues, Mr. Buckley cracked jokes."

I assumed this to be a witticism, but the humor was over-
looked by Mr. Buckley.

"You son-of-a-bitch," he snapped. "You haven't read my
book!"

Where I was raised the code instructed that if somebody called
you an SOB without prefacing it with a mitigating smile, you hit
him in Memory of Mother. Mr. Buckley was as far from smiling
at the moment as I was from being named in a Codicil to his
Will. I felt the heat of blood while wondering whether to hoot
and dance in the tradition of the Old West, meanwhile probably
making a pluperfect ass of myself, or whether to pass the whole
thing off with the kind of sophisticated drawing-room worldliness
they do not teach at Texas Tech. Perhaps because it crossed my
mind that anyone who would upbraid the King of England at age
six might, at age forty, be inclined to hit back, I decided on a
policy of nonviolence.

Cleverly, I said, "No, I've read your book." Mr. Buckley's eyes
might have frosted his wine goblet. Ten minutes later he took
Novak to a crosstown party, leaving me alone with the wine, the
maid, and my memories.

"Born of Absolutes"

My personal observations of William F. Buckley, Jr., are
limited to those unusual instances cited here and to one earlier encounter at a Washington party touting his latest book—hardly
enough to pose as expert. They are, however, enough to permit
the formulation of certain impressions by one who has read all
his books, many of his articles, speeches, debates, and columns,
interviewed a number of his friends and foes, and for more than
a decade observed him at work.

Happy Hour liberals to the contrary, I am convinced that
Buckley "really believes all that jazz." He believes it because, for
one thing, he was taught from childhood to believe it as surely as

he was taught to believe the dogmas of the Catholic Church. He believes it because he is congenitally incapable of presuming himself without Solutions. He believes outside the popular political pale because of ancestral precedents: a family history boasts that four generations of Buckleys were "all prone to unpopular beliefs," and the Buckleys' reverence for ancestors is rivaled only by the Japanese.

Most of all, however, he believes it because of his limited experience with The World; he knows nothing of life in the streets. ("He has," his ex-roommate Tom Guinzburg said, "a rather child-like naïveté about many things. There are whole areas outside his experience.") When he speaks of his "distrust of public education," one must remember that he was not educated in tax-supported schools. Is it not true that a man naturally fears the unknown? Mr. Buckley has had but fleeting contact with life as most of us know it: full of social terrors, old debts, and bread crumbs. When he inspires his followers to rail against public assistance to unwed mothers and their illegitimate offspring, you must remember that he has never known (1) a girl "in trouble" who would not have the money to buy an abortion even if the law permitted, (2) a home without all-providing, all-counseling parents, or (3) a hungry child. He can call for an end to unemployment compensation because he has never drunk 20-cent beer with an out-of-work stiff drowning the pain of not having the rent or money for the milk bill. He does not, therefore, realize that to end unemployment compensation would (1) strip the last thin ribbon of hope from that man and (2) relegate him to the ultimate humility—the welfare rolls, which, in time, Mr. Buckley also would purge.

When Buckley says that if he were a South Carolinian he would vote for segregated schools, one must remember that he *is*, in truth, at least a part-time South Carolinian: a family retreat at Camden, S.C., was always full of grinning servants to welcome "the young Mastah" home from Yale or the San Antonio military-base wars. No doubt, like countless Negro cooks and butlers in the South whom I have often been told of over drinks at the Country Club, they didn't want integration "forced" on them. Perhaps this is why Buckley can advocate that South Carolina's problems be settled by South Carolinians, or Mississippi's by Mississippians, without recognizing the obvious fact that he is leaving the solutions to J. Strom Thurmond and James O. Eastland. Buckley can write, "In today's all-white neighborhoods, it is reasonable that the schools should be overwhelmingly white. In today's Negro neighborhoods, it is reasonable that they should be overwhelmingly black." "Not a word"—noted Laurence Stern in the Washington *Post*—"about improving the tired physical plants or tragically undermanned staffs in the slum schools, which Buckley would preserve in the full purity of their deprivation."

Admittedly, Buckley is a man of great energies and impressive personal accomplishments: author, lecturer, debater, editor, television personality, columnist, public figure, international ski-bug, expert sailor, and world traveler. When I remarked on this to a close friend of Buckley's, I was reminded, "Well, if you had the advantages, money, and help he has, you could be pretty productive, too. Taking nothing away from Bill, he's got research people to look up his facts, staffers to make appointments *he* wants, or to be buffers between himself and bores or pests." When Buckley drives up to his house he can abandon the scooter at the curb, and somebody will spring out to park it. He doesn't have to grocery-shop, drive the children to school in a car pool, or stand in line at the tax office while an IRS employee counts on his fingers what you owe Uncle Sam thirty minutes before the filing deadline. Buckley will never fret over whether social security will see him through to the grave, whether his children will be equipped to face the world or be accepted in it, or whether he can rescue his wife's gift from Lay Away by Christmas Eve.

He is fortunate in one sense, almost tragically unfortunate in another. Knowing how difficult it is for me to conceive of what it must be like to be rich, I think of how impossible it is for Buckley to conceive of being poor.

For some—a John F. Kennedy who could have his eyes opened by a glimpse of the wretches in Appalachia, a Nelson Rockefeller raised to ways of philanthropy, a Franklin D. Roosevelt who was pushed by personal ambitions and the accident of illness to growth beyond the bounds of *noblesse oblige*, an Averell Harriman atoning for the industrial sins of his forefathers—there is always the prospect of being smitten by humane grace, of achieving some degree of understanding, and the empathy that leads to the gnawing doubts that sire compassion and, in time, point the path to social reform. For a William F. Buckley, Jr., born to absolutes, nurtured on dogma, possessed of an ego that would shame de Gaulle, and a self-certainty that precludes even the idle thought of doubt, there is little hope of stumbling upon new truths, or even of seeing life through the other fellow's eyes, however myopic or temporary the view.

Norman Podhoretz

I was determined to take Commentary out of the hands of the largely academic types on whom it had come to rely so heavily and to bring it back into the family.

Ambition, Norman Podhoretz states in *Making It* (1968), has replaced sex as "the dirty little secret" of American society. Intellectuals and artists pretend that public success, money, power, and achievement are not their primary goals, but in fact they want recognition as desperately as all other people in the society. *Making It* is a confession of Podhoretz's own lust for social status, money, and power. As editor of *Commentary* since 1960, Podhoretz has become familiar with the important literary figures of New York, and *Making It* records the world of New York intellectuals as well as Podhoretz's own career as an editor.

Norman Podhoretz was born on January 16, 1930, in Brooklyn, New York. The son of a milkman, he grew up in the lower-middle-class neighborhood of Brownsville. He entered Columbia University and the Jewish Theological Seminary in 1946 at the age of sixteen and graduated from both institutions in 1950. With a Kellett Fellowship and a Fulbright Scholarship, Podhoretz went to Cambridge University in 1952 and fell under the influence of the great English critic, F. R. Leavis. Leavis and Lionel Trilling, Podhoretz' mentor at Columbia University, helped to shape the young man's intellectual direction and his desire to become a literary critic.

In 1952 Podhoretz returned from Cambridge and wrote

book reviews for *Commentary* magazine. The first review that received wide notice was his unfavorable reaction to Saul Bellow's *Adventures of Augie March* in 1953. After his service in the army (1953–1955), Podhoretz returned to work as assistant editor of *Commentary;* in 1956 he was made associate editor. By this time he was writing reviews for *The New Yorker* and, as he observes in *Making It,* he became "a minor literary celebrity" overnight when he wrote a negative review of Nelson Algren's *A Walk on the Wild Side* (June 2, 1956). He left *Commentary* in 1958, but only to return two years later as its editor. Podhoretz' books are *Doings and Undoings* (1964), a collection of his reviews, as well as *Making It,* an autobiographical account of his rise in the literary world of New York. These books are of interest; but it is primarily in his role as an editor that Podhoretz represents one distinct aspect of our culture.

"I determined to take *Commentary* out of the hands of the largely academic types on whom it had come to rely so heavily," Podhoretz has remarked, "and to bring it back into the family." The "family" includes those liberal thinkers who have been associated with some of the most acute social criticism written in America during the past thirty years. Since Podhoretz has been editor of *Commentary,* Paul Goodman, Dwight Macdonald, Lionel Trilling, Alfred Kazin, Hannah Arendt, Irving Howe, and other "members of the family" have appeared in the pages of the journal. *Commentary* is now one of the most important magazines in America, reflecting Podhoretz' varied interests and his keen sense of the significant trends in American intellectual and social life.

Making It:
The Brutal Bargain

NORMAN

PODHORETZ

NE OF THE longest journeys in the world is the journey
from Brooklyn to Manhattan—or at least from certain neighborhoods in Brooklyn to certain parts of Manhattan. I have
made that journey, but it is not from the experience of having
made it that I know how very great the distance is, for I started
on the road many years before I realized what I was doing, and
by the time I did realize it I was for all practical purposes already
there. At so imperceptible a pace did I travel, and with so little
awareness, that I never felt footsore or out of breath or weary
at the thought of how far I still had to go. Yet whenever anyone
who has remained back there where I started—remained not
physically but socially and culturally, for the neighborhood is now
a Negro ghetto and the Jews who have "remained" in it mostly
reside in the less affluent areas of Long Island—whenever anyone
like that happens into the world in which I now live with such
perfect ease, I can see that in his eyes I have become a fully
acculturated citizen of a country as foreign to him as China and
infinitely more frightening.

That country is sometimes called the upper middle class; and
indeed I am a member of that class, less by virtue of my income
than by virtue of the way my speech is accented, the way I dress,
the way I furnish my home, the way I entertain and am entertained, the way I educate my children—the way, quite simply,
I look and I live. It appalls me to think what an immense trans-

formation I had to work on myself in order to become what I have become: if I had known what I was doing I would surely not have been able to do it, I would surely not have wanted to. No wonder the choice had to be blind: there was a kind of treason in it—treason toward my family, treason toward my friends. In choosing the road I chose, I was pronouncing a judgment upon them, and the fact that they themselves concurred in the judgment makes the whole thing sadder but no less cruel.

When I say that the choice was blind, I mean that I was never aware—obviously not as a small child, certainly not as an adolescent, and not even as a young man already writing for publication and working on the staff of an important intellectual magazine in New York—how inextricably my "noblest" ambitions were tied to the vulgar desire to rise above the class into which I was born; nor did I understand to what an astonishing extent these ambitions were shaped and defined by the standards and values and tastes of the class into which I did not know I wanted to move. It is not that I was or am a social climber as that term is commonly used. High society interests me, if at all, only as a curiosity; I do not wish to be a member of it; and in any case, it is not, as I have learned from a small experience of contact with the very rich and fashionable, my "scene." Yet precisely because social climbing is not one of my vices (unless what might be called celebrity climbing, which very definitely *is* one of my vices, can be considered the contemporary variant of social climbing), I think there may be more than a merely personal significance in the fact that class has played so large a part both in my life and in my career.

But whether or not the significance is there, I feel certain that my long-time blindness to the part class was playing in my life was not altogether idiosyncratic. "Privilege," Robert L. Heilbroner has shrewdly observed in *The Limits of American Capitalism*, "is not an attribute we are accustomed to stress when we consider the construction of *our* social order." For a variety of reasons, says Heilbroner, "privilege under capitalism is much less 'visible,' especially to the favored groups, than privilege under other systems" like feudalism. This "invisibility" extends in America to class as well.

No one, of course, is so naïve as to believe that America is a classless society or that the force of egalitarianism—powerful as it has been in some respects—has ever been powerful enough to wipe out class distinctions altogether. There was a moment during the 1950s, to be sure, when social thought hovered on the brink of saying that the country had to all intents and purposes become a wholly middle-class society. But the emergence of the civil-rights movement in the 1960s and the concomitant discovery of the poor—to whom, in helping to discover them, Michael Harrington interestingly enough applied, in *The Other America*, the very word ("invisible") that Heilbroner later used with reference to the rich—has put at least a temporary end to that kind of talk. And yet if class has become visible again, it is only in its grossest outlines—mainly, that is, in terms of income levels—and to the degree that manners and style of life are perceived as relevant at all, it is generally in the crudest of terms. There is something in us, it would seem, which resists the idea of class. Even our novelists, working in a genre for which class has traditionally been a supreme reality, are largely indifferent to it—which is to say, blind to its importance as a factor in the life of the individual.

In my own case, the blindness to class always expressed itself in an outright and very often belligerent refusal to believe that it had anything to do with me at all. I no longer remember when or in what form I first discovered that there was such a thing as class, but whenever it was and whatever form the discovery took, it could only have coincided with the recognition that criteria existed by which I and everyone I knew were stamped as inferior: we were in the *lower* class. This was not a proposition I was willing to accept, and my way of not accepting it was to dismiss the whole idea of class as a prissy triviality.

Given the fact that I had literary ambitions even as a small boy, it was inevitable that the issue of class would sooner or later arise for me with a sharpness it would never acquire for most of my friends. But given the fact also that I was on the whole very happy to be growing up where I was, that I was fiercely patriotic about Brownsville (the spawning ground of so many famous athletes and gangsters), and that I felt genuinely patronizing toward other neighborhoods (especially the "better" ones like Crown Heights and East Flatbush which seemed by comparison

colorless and unexciting)—given the fact, in other words, that I
was not, for all that I wrote poetry and read books, an "alienated"
boy dreaming of escape, my confrontation with the issue of class
would probably have come later rather than sooner if not for an
English teacher in high school who decided that I was a gem
in the rough and took it upon herself to polish me to as high a
sheen as she could manage and I would permit.

I resisted—far less effectively, I can see now, than I then
thought, though even then I knew that she was wearing me down
far more than I would ever give her the satisfaction of admitting.
Famous throughout the school for her altogether outspoken snob-
bery, which stopped short by only a hair (and sometimes did not
stop short at all) of an old-fashioned kind of patrician anti-
Semitism, Mrs. K. was also famous for being an extremely good
teacher; indeed, I am sure that she saw no distinction between
the hopeless task of teaching the proper use of English to the
young Jewish barbarians whom fate had so unkindly deposited
into her charge and the equally hopeless task of teaching them
the proper "manners." (There were as many young Negro barbarians in her charge as Jewish ones, but I doubt that she could
ever bring herself to pay very much attention to them. As she
never hesitated to make clear, it was punishment enough for a
woman of her background—her family was old-Brooklyn and, she
would have us understand, extremely distinguished—to have
fallen among the sons of East European immigrant Jews.)

For three years, from the age of thirteen to the age of sixteen, I was her special pet, though that word is scarcely adequate
to suggest the intensity of the relationship which developed between us. It was a relationship right out of *The Corn Is Green*,
which may, for all I know, have served as her model; at any rate,
her objective was much the same as the Welsh teacher's in that
play: she was determined that I should win a scholarship to
Harvard. But whereas (an irony much to the point here) the
problem the teacher had in *The Corn Is Green* with her coal-
miner pupil in the traditional class society of Edwardian England
was strictly academic, Mrs. K.'s problem with me in the putatively
egalitarian society of New Deal America was strictly social. My
grades were very high and would obviously remain so, but what

would they avail me if I continued to go about looking and sounding like a "filthy little slum child" (the epithet she would invariably hurl at me whenever we had an argument about "manners")?

Childless herself, she worked on me like a dementedly ambitious mother with a somewhat recalcitrant son; married to a solemn and elderly man (she was then in her early forties or thereabouts), she treated me like a cruelly ungrateful adolescent lover on whom she had humiliatingly bestowed her favors. She flirted with me and flattered me, she scolded me and insulted me. Slum child, filthy little slum child, so beautiful a mind and so vulgar a personality, so exquisite in sensibility and so coarse in manner. What would she do with me, what would become of me if I persisted out of stubbornness and perversity in the disgusting ways they had taught me at home and on the streets?

To her the most offensive of these ways was the style in which I dressed: a T-shirt, tightly pegged pants and a red satin jacket with the legend "Cherokees, S.A.C." (social-athletic club) stitched in large white letters across the back. This was bad enough, but when on certain days I would appear in school wearing, as a particular ceremonial occasion required, a suit and tie, the sight of those immense padded shoulders and my white-on-white shirt would drive her to even greater heights of contempt and even lower depths of loving despair than usual. *Slum child, filthy little slum child.* I was beyond saving; I deserved no better than to wind up with all the other horrible little Jewboys in the gutter (by which she meant Brooklyn College). If only I would listen to her, the whole world could be mine: I could win a scholarship to Harvard, I could get to know the best people, I could grow up into a life of elegance and refinement and taste. Why was I so stupid as not to understand?

II

In those days it was very unusual, and possibly even against the rules, for teachers in public high schools to associate with their students after hours. Nevertheless, Mrs. K. sometimes invited me

to her home, a beautiful old brownstone located in what was
perhaps the only section in the whole of Brooklyn fashionable
enough to be intimidating. I would read her my poems and she
would tell me about her family, about the schools she had gone to,
about Vassar, about writers she had met, while her husband, of
whom I was frightened to death and who to my utter astonish-
ment turned out to be Jewish (but not, as Mrs. K. quite un-
necessarily hastened to inform me, *my* kind of Jewish), sat stiffly
and silently in an armchair across the room squinting at his newspaper through the first pince-nez I had ever seen outside the
movies. He spoke to me but once, and that was after I had read
Mrs. K. my tearful editorial for the school newspaper on the death
of Roosevelt—an effusion which provoked him into a full five-
minute harangue whose blasphemous contents would certainly
have shocked me into insensibility if I had not been even more
shocked to discover that he actually had a voice.

But Mrs. K. not only had me to her house; she also—what
was even more unusual—took me out a few times, to the Frick
Gallery and the Metropolitan Museum, and once to the theater,
where we saw a dramatization of *The Late George Apley,* a play
I imagine she deliberately chose with the not wholly mistaken
idea that it would impress upon me the glories of aristocratic
Boston.

One of our excursions into Manhattan I remember with particular vividness because she used it to bring the struggle between
us to rather a dramatic head. The familiar argument began this
time on the subway. Why, knowing that we would be spending
the afternoon together "in public," had I come to school that
morning improperly dressed? (I was, as usual, wearing my red
satin club jacket over a white T-shirt.) She realized, of course,
that I owned only one suit (this said not in compassion but in
derision) and that my poor parents had, God only knew where,
picked up the idea that it was too precious to be worn except
at one of those bar mitzvahs I was always going to. Though why,
if my parents were so worried about clothes, they had permitted
me to buy a suit which made me look like a young hoodlum, she
found it very difficult to imagine. Still, much as she would have
been embarrassed to be seen in public with a boy whose parents

allowed him to wear a zoot suit, she would have been somewhat less embarrassed than she was now by the ridiculous costume I had on. Had I no consideration for her? Had I no consideration for myself? Did I want everyone who laid eyes on me to think that I was nothing but an ill-bred little slum child?

My standard ploy in these arguments was to take the position that such things were of no concern to me: I was a poet and I had more important matters to think about than clothes. Besides, I would feel silly coming to school on an ordinary day dressed in a suit. Did Mrs. K. want me to look like one of those "creeps" from Crown Heights who were all going to become doctors? This was usually an effective counter, since Mrs. K. despised her middle-class Jewish students even more than she did the "slum children," but probably because she was growing desperate at the thought of how I would strike a Harvard interviewer (it was my senior year), she did not respond according to form on that particular occasion.

"At least," she snapped, "they reflect well on their parents."

I was accustomed to her bantering gibes at my parents, and sensing, probably, that they arose out of jealousy, I was rarely troubled by them. But this one bothered me; it went beyond banter and I did not know how to deal with it. I remember flushing, but I cannot remember what if anything I said in protest. It was the beginning of a very bad afternoon for both of us.

We had been heading for the Museum of Modern Art, but as we got off the subway, Mrs. K. announced that she had changed her mind about the museum. She was going to show me something else instead, just down the street on Fifth Avenue. This mysterious "something else" to which we proceeded in silence turned out to be the college department of an expensive clothing store, De Pinna. I do not exaggerate when I say that an actual physical dread seized me as I followed her into the store. I had never been inside such a store; it was not a store, it was enemy territory, every inch of it mined with humiliations. "I am," Mrs. K. declared in the coldest human voice I hope I shall ever hear, "going to buy you a suit that you will be able to wear at your Harvard interview." I had guessed, of course, that this was what she had in mind, and even at fifteen I understood what a fantastic act of aggression she was planning to commit against my parents and asking me to participate in. Oh no, I said in a panic (suddenly realizing that I *wanted* her to buy me that suit), I can't, my mother wouldn't like it. "You can tell her it's a birthday present. Or else I will tell her. If I tell her, I'm sure she won't object." The idea of Mrs. K. meeting my mother was more than I could bear: my mother, who spoke with a Yiddish accent and whom, until that sickening moment, I had never known I was so ready to betray.

To my immense relief and my equally immense disappointment, we left the store, finally, without buying a suit, but it was not to be the end of clothing or "manners" for me that day—not yet. There was still the ordeal of a restaurant to go through. Where I came from, people rarely ate in restaurants, not so much because most of them were too poor to afford such a luxury—although most of them certainly were—as because eating in restaurants was not regarded as a luxury at all; it was, rather, a necessity to which bachelors were pitiably condemned. A home-cooked meal was assumed to be better than anything one could possibly get in a restaurant, and considering the class of restaurants in question (they were really diners or luncheonettes), the assumption was probably correct. In the case of my own family, myself included until my late teens, the business of going to restaurants was complicated by the fact that we observed the Jewish dietary laws, and except in certain neighborhoods, few places could be found which served kosher food; in midtown Manhattan in the 1940s, I believe there were only two and both were relatively expensive. All this is by way of explaining why I had had so little experience of restaurants up to the age of fifteen and why I grew apprehensive once more when Mrs. K. decided after we left De Pinna that we should have something to eat.

The restaurant she chose was not at all an elegant one—I have, like a criminal, revisited it since—but it seemed very elegant indeed to me: enemy territory again, and this time a mine exploded in my face the minute I set foot through the door. The hostess was very sorry, but she could not seat the young gentleman without a coat and tie. If the lady wished, however, something could be arranged. The lady (visibly pleased by this unexpected—or was it expected?—object lesson) did wish, and the so recently defiant but by now utterly docile young gentleman was forthwith divested of his so recently beloved but by now thoroughly loathsome red satin jacket and provided with a much oversized white waiter's coat and a tie—which, there being no collar to a T-shirt, had to be worn around his bare neck. Thus attired, and with his face supplying the touch of red which had moments earlier been supplied by his jacket, he was led into the dining room, there to be taught the importance of proper table manners through the same pedagogic instrumentality that had worked so well in impressing him with the importance of proper dress.

Like any other pedagogic technique, however, humiliation has its limits, and Mrs. K. was to make no further progress with it that day. For I had had enough, and I was not about to risk stepping on another mine. Knowing she would subject me to still more ridicule if I made a point of my revulsion at the prospect of eating non-kosher food, I resolved to let her order for me and then to feign lack of appetite or possibly even illness when the meal was served. She did order—duck for both of us, undoubtedly because it would be a hard dish for me to manage without using my fingers.

The two portions came in deep oval-shaped dishes, swimming in a brown sauce and each with a sprig of parsley sitting on top. I had not the faintest idea of what to do—should the food be eaten directly from the oval dish or not?—nor which of the many implements on the table to do it with. But remembering that Mrs. K. herself had once advised me to watch my hostess in such a situation and then to do exactly as she did, I sat perfectly still and waited for her to make the first move. Unfortunately, Mrs. K. also remembered having taught me that trick, and determined as she was that I should be given a lesson that would force me to mend my ways, she waited too. And so we both waited, chatting amiably, pretending not to notice the food while it sat there getting colder and colder by the minute. Thanks partly to the fact that I would probably have gagged on the duck if I had tried to eat it—dietary taboos are very powerful if one has been conditioned to them—I was prepared to wait forever. And, indeed, it was Mrs. K. who broke first.

"Why aren't you eating?" she suddenly said after something like fifteen minutes had passed. "Aren't you hungry?" Not very, I answered. "Well," she said, "I think we'd better eat. The food is getting cold." Whereupon, as I watched with great fascination, she deftly captured the spring of parsley between the prongs of her serving fork, set it aside, took up her serving spoon and delicately used those two esoteric implements to transfer a piece of duck from the oval dish to her plate. I imitated the whole operation as best as I could, but not well enough to avoid splattering some partly congealed sauce onto my borrowed coat in the process. Still, things could have been worse, and having more or less successfully negotiated my way around that particular mine, I now had to cope with the problem of how to get out of eating the duck. But I need not have worried. Mrs. K. took one bite, pronounced it inedible (it must have been frozen by then), and called in quiet fury for the check.

Several months later, wearing an altered but respectably conservative suit which had been handed down to me in good condition by a bachelor uncle, I presented myself on two different occasions before interviewers from Harvard and from the Pulitzer Scholarship Committee. Some months after that, Mrs. K. had her triumph: I won the Harvard scholarship on which her heart had been so passionately set. It was not, however, large enough to cover all expenses, and since my parents could not afford to make up the difference, I was unable to accept it. My parents felt wretched but not, I think, quite as wretched as Mrs. K. For a while it looked as though I would wind up in the "gutter" of Brooklyn College after all, but then the news arrived that I had also won a Pulitzer Scholarship which paid full tuition if used at Columbia, and a small stipend besides. Everyone was consoled, even Mrs. K. Columbia was at least in the Ivy League.

The last time I saw her was shortly before my graduation from Columbia and just after a story had appeared in the *Times* announcing that I had been awarded a fellowship which was to send me to Cambridge University. Mrs. K. had passionately wanted to see me in Cambridge, Massachusetts, but Cambridge, England, was even better. We met somewhere near Columbia for a drink, and her happiness over my fellowship, it seemed to me, was if anything exceeded by her delight at discovering that I now knew enough to know that the right thing to order in a cocktail lounge was a very dry martini with lemon peel, please.

III

Looking back now at the story of my relationship with Mrs. K. strictly in the context of the issue of class, what strikes me most sharply is the astonishing rudeness of this woman to whom "manners" were of such overriding concern. (This, as I have since had some occasion to notice, is a fairly common characteristic among members of the class to which she belonged.) Though she would not have admitted it, good manners to Mrs. K. meant only one thing: conformity to a highly stylized set of surface habits and fashions which she took, quite as a matter of course, to be superior to all other styles of social behavior. But in what did their superiority consist? Were her "good" manners derived from or conducive to a greater moral sensitivity than the "bad" manners I had learned at home and on the streets of Brownsville? I rather doubt it. The "crude" behavior of my own parents, for example, was then and is still marked by a tactfulness and a delicacy that Mrs. K. simply could not have approached. It is not that she was incapable of tact and delicacy; in certain moods she was (and manners apart, she was an extraordinarily loving and generous woman). But such qualities were neither built into nor expressed by the system of manners under which she lived. She was fond of quoting Cardinal Newman's definition of a gentleman as a person who could be at ease in any company, yet if anything was clear about the manners she was trying to teach me, it was that they operated—not inadvertently but by deliberate design—to set one at ease *only* with others similarly trained and to cut one off altogether from those who were not.

While I would have been unable to formulate it in those terms at the time, I think I must have understood perfectly well what

Mrs. K. was attempting to communicate with all her talk about manners; if I had not understood it so well, I would not have resisted so fiercely. She was saying that because I was a talented boy, a better class of people stood ready to admit me into their ranks. But only on one condition: I had to signify by my general deportment that I acknowledged them as *superior* to the class of people among whom I happened to have been born. That was the bargain—take it or leave it. In resisting Mrs. K. where "manners" were concerned—just as I was later to resist many others—I was expressing my refusal to have any part of so brutal a bargain.

But the joke was on me, for what I did not understand—not in the least then and not for a long time afterward—was that in matters having to do with "art" and "culture" (the "life of the mind," as I learned to call it at Columbia), I was being offered the very same brutal bargain and accepting it with the wildest enthusiasm.

I have said that I did not, for all my bookishness, feel alienated as a boy, and this is certainly true. Far from dreaming of escape from Brownsville, I dreaded the thought of living anywhere else, and whenever my older sister, who hated the neighborhood, began begging my parents to move, it was invariably my howls of protest that kept them from giving in. For by the age of thirteen I had made it into the neighborhood big time, otherwise known as the Cherokees, S.A.C. It had by no means been easy for me, as a mediocre athlete and a notoriously good student, to win acceptance from a gang which prided itself mainly on its masculinity and its contempt for authority, but once this had been accomplished, down the drain went any reason I might earlier have had for thinking that life could be better in any other place. Not for nothing, then, did I wear that red satin jacket to school every day. It was my proudest possession, a badge of manly status, proving that I was not to be classified with the Crown Heights "creeps," even though my grades, like theirs, were high.

And yet, despite the Cherokees, it cannot be that I felt quite so securely at home in Brownsville as I remember thinking. The reason is that something extremely significant in this connection had happened to me by the time I first met Mrs. K.: without any conscious effort on my part, my speech had largely lost the characteristic neighborhood accent and was well on its way to becoming as neutrally American as I gather it now is.

Now whatever else may be involved in a nondeliberate change of accent, one thing is clear: it bespeaks a very high degree of detachment from the ethos of one's immediate surroundings. It is not a good ear alone, and perhaps not even a good ear at all, which enables a child to hear the difference between the way he and everyone else around him sound when they talk, and the way teachers and radio announcers—as it must have been in my case—sound. Most people, and especially most children, are entirely insensitive to such differences, which is why anyone who pays attention to these matters can, on the basis of a man's accent alone, often draw a reasonably accurate picture of his regional, social, and ethnic background. People who feel that they belong in their familiar surroundings—whether it be a place, a class, or a group—will invariably speak in the accent of those surroundings; in all likelihood, indeed, they will never have imagined any other possibility for themselves. Conversely, it is safe to assume that a person whose accent has undergone a radical change from childhood is a person who once had fantasies of escaping to some other world, whether or not they were ever realized.

But accent in America has more than a psychological or spiritual significance. "Her kerbstone English," said Henry Higgins of Eliza Doolittle, "will keep her in the gutter to the end of her days." Most Americans probably respond with a sense of amused democratic superiority to the idea of a society in which so trivial a thing as accent can keep a man down, and it is a good measure of our blindness to the pervasive operations of class that there has been so little consciousness of the fact that America itself is such a society. While the broadly regional accents—New England, Midwestern, Southern—enjoy more or less equal status and will not affect the economic or social chances of those who speak in them, the opposite is still surely true of any accent identifiably influenced by Yiddish, Italian, Polish, Spanish—that is, the languages of the major post-Civil War immigrant groups (among which may be included American-Irish). A man with such an accent will no longer be confined, as once he would almost automatically have been, to the working class, but unless his life, both occupational and social, is lived strictly within the milieu in whose tone of voice he speaks, his accent will at the least operate as an obstacle to be overcome (if, for example, he is a school-teacher aspiring to be a principal), and at the most as an effective barrier to advancement (if, say, he is an engineer), let alone to entry into the governing elite of the country. (For better or worse, incidentally, these accents are not a temporary phenomenon destined to disappear with the passage of the generations, no more than ethnic consciousness itself is. I have heard third-generation American Jews of East European stock speaking with thicker accents than their parents.)

Clearly, then, while fancying myself altogether at home in the world into which I was born, I was not only more detached from it than I realized; I was also taking action—and of very fundamental kind—which would eventually make it possible for me to move into some other world. Yet I still did not recognize what I was doing—not in any such terms. My ambition was to be a great and famous poet, not to live in a different community, a different class, a different "world." If I had a concrete image of what greatness would mean socially, it was probably based on the famous professional boxer from our block who had moved to a more prosperous neighborhood but still spent his leisure time hanging around the corner candy store and the local poolroom with his old friends (among whom he could, of course, experience his fame far more sharply than he could have done among his newly acquired peers).

But to each career its own sociology. Boxers, unlike poets, do not undergo a cultural change in the process of becoming boxers, and if I was not brave enough or clever enough as a boy to see the distinction, others who knew me then were. "Ten years from now, you won't even want to talk to me, you won't even recognize me if you pass me on the street," was the kind of comment I frequently heard in my teens from women in the neighborhood, friends of my mother who were fond of me and nearly as proud as she was of the high grades I was getting in school and the prizes

I was always winning. "That's crazy, you must be kidding," I would answer. They were not crazy and they were not kidding. They were simply better sociologists than I.

As, indeed, my mother herself was, for often in later years—after I had become a writer and an editor and was living only a subway ride away but in a style that was foreign to her and among people by whom she was intimidated— she would gaze wistfully at this strange creature, her son, and murmur, "I should have made him for a dentist," registering thereby her perception that whereas Jewish sons who grow up to be successes in certain occupations usually remain fixed in an accessible cultural ethos, sons who grow up into literary success are transformed almost beyond recognition and distanced almost beyond a mother's reach. My mother wanted nothing so much as for me to be a success, to be respected and admired. But she did not imagine, I think, that she would only purchase the realization of her ambition at the price of my progressive estrangement from her and her ways. Perhaps it was my guilt at the first glimmerings of this knowledge which accounted for my repression of it and for the obstinacy of the struggle I waged over "manners" with Mrs. K.

For what seemed most of all to puzzle Mrs. K., who saw no distinction between taste in poetry and taste in clothes, was that I could see no connection between the two. Mrs. K. knew that a boy from Brownsville with a taste for Keats was not long for Brownsville, and moreover would in all probability end up in the social class to which she herself belonged. How could I have explained to her that I would only be able to leave Brownsville if I could maintain the illusion that my destination was a place in some mystical country of the spirit and not a place in the upper reaches of the American class structure?

Saint Paul, who was a Jew, conceived of salvation as a world in which there would be neither Jew nor Greek, and though he may well have been the first, he was very far from the last Jew to dream such a dream of transcendence—transcendence of the actual alternative categories with which reality so stingily presents us. Not to be Jewish, but not to be Christian either; not to be a worker, but not to be a boss either; not—if I may be forgiven for injecting this banality out of my own soul into so formidable a series of fantasies—to be a slum child but not to be a snob either. How could I have explained to Mrs. K. that wearing a suit from De Pinna would for me have been something like the social equivalent of a conversion to Christianity? And how could she have explained to me that there was no socially neutral ground to be found in the United States of America, and that a distaste for the surroundings in which I was bred, and ultimately (God forgive me) even for many of the people I loved—and so a new taste for other kinds of people—how could she have explained that all this was inexorably entailed in the logic of a taste for the poetry of Keats and the painting of Cézanne and the music of Mozart?

IV
Race

☐ In the early twentieth century Negro leadership was divided between Booker T. Washington, who urged black people to develop their technological skills, and W. E. B. DuBois, who advised a more militant approach to racial oppression. Washington felt that the Negro should accommodate himself to the dominant white society, and he wrote an autobiography, *Up from Slavery* (1901), which illustrates his own triumph over poverty and injustice. Other men followed in his tradition, writing autobiographies like *Out of the House of Bondage* (1914), *In Spite of Handicap* (1916), and *Finding a Way Out* (1920), which fundamentally accepted the myth that an American simply had to embody traditional Christian virtues to become a hero.

☐ Another group of writers, however, expressed a more militant, more realistic view of the hero in American history. Frederick Douglass (in *Life and Times of Frederick Douglass*, 1881), W. E. B. DuBois (in *The Souls of Black Folk*, 1903), Richard Wright (in *Native Son*, 1941), James Baldwin (in *The Fire Next Time*, 1963), Malcolm X (in *The Autobiography of Malcolm X*, 1966), and Eldridge Cleaver (in *Soul on Ice*, 1968) underscore the contradictions between the myth of the American hero and the facts of American life, between the idealization of American heroes and the reality of black existence in American life, between the attempt of a Negro—as one native son—to realize the American dream and his discovery that it is a dream which belongs only to the white American.

☐ In the 1950's two separate phenomena occurred which hastened Negro militancy and have since led to widespread activity in racial affairs. The rise of independent—and, for the most part, colored—nations throughout the world changed the attitude of white Anglo-Saxon countries toward those people they had dominated for so long a time. Encouraged by this worldwide revolution, the United States Supreme Court insisted upon school desegregation in 1954. The events in Little

Rock, Arkansas; Montgomery, Alabama; and elsewhere in the South were the first of many similar black protests, marches, and sit-ins of the 1950's and '60's. Whereas the N.A.A.C.P., which had been organized by DuBois in 1909, had always used legal methods in pursuit of racial equality, new organizations with new leaders arose in the late 1950's. In addition to Roy Wilkins of the N.A.A.C.P., the late Martin Luther King, Jr., of the Southern Christian Leadership Conference, James Farmer of CORE, Elijah Muhammad of the Muslim movement, Malcolm X, Whitney Young of the Urban League, Stokely Carmichael of SNCC, and Eldridge Cleaver of the Black Panther movement assumed importance. No one of these men can claim to be the singular leader of all Negroes, and each of them has a distinct approach to racial justice. Five of the more articulate Negroes who represent the range and complexity of racial affairs in America are Malcolm X, Martin Luther King, Jr., James Baldwin, Stokely Carmichael, and Eldridge Cleaver. In their life and work, one begins to sense what Richard Wright meant when he claimed that "the Negro is America's metaphor."

Malcolm X

I am the angriest black man in America.

Since the middle of the nineteenth century, many Black people in America have been attracted to militant leaders and writers who have possessed the courage to challenge an oppressive White society. But these leaders—Frederick Douglass, W. E. B. DuBois, Marcus Garvey, Richard Wright, James Baldwin, and Eldridge Cleaver—have been few in number because the power of the society has been largely impregnable. Receiving so little sympathy from within American society, the Negro has asserted himself only at great personal sacrifice. Now that black militancy has become more forceful than ever before, it is perfectly natural that figures like Douglass, DuBois, and Wright should become cult heroes to young Negroes. In the 1960's many leaders arose to express the sentiments of black people, but the man who most dramatically represented the average Negro was one of the most charismatic heroes of the century—Malcolm X.

Malcolm X was born Malcolm Little on May 19, 1925, in Omaha, Nebraska. His father was very dark; his mother was the daughter of a white father and had a light complexion. Later in his life, as he writes in *The Autobiography of Malcolm X*, Malcolm X "learned to hate every drop of that white rapist's blood that is in me." His father was a follower of Marcus Garvey, the persuasive black orator of the thirties and forties who believed that Negroes should return to Africa; he was also a deeply frustrated man who argued with his wife constantly and who ultimately committed suicide, leaving the woman and her seven children in poverty.

Malcom X's mother could not contend with the humiliation of her poverty and in time she suffered a nervous breakdown. Malcolm X, who was an attentive and intelligent student in his early years, lost interest in formal education because he felt that he could never pursue the career of law successfully in white America. He was expelled from school and never returned. For a short while he lived with his stepsister in Roxbury, Massachusetts, and emulated, to use his own phrase, "slick" Negroes who seemed particularly glamorous. His life, during this period, had no real sense of direction: he was a shoe-shine boy, a busboy, a train conductor, a waiter in New York. Soon he drifted into the underworld of Harlem, running numbers, selling drugs, committing burglary. He was finally sent to prison, where in the midst of his intellectual and religious foundering he discovered the Muslim faith.

Malcolm X became a disciple of Elijah Muhammad while he was in prison. As part of his conversion, he began reading omnivorously and debating with great fervor. Released from prison in 1952, Malcolm X went to Detroit and soon became a minister in the Muslim movement. He rose rapidly and Elijah appointed him as minister of Temple Seven in New York, where he continued to preach to black people that "our *enemy* is the *white man!* . . . 'Negro' is a false label forced on you by your slavemaster! . . . The *ignorance* we of the black race here in America have, and the *self-hatred* we have, they are fine examples of what the white slavemaster has seen fit to teach us . . . So let us, black people, *separate* ourselves from this white man slavemaster, who despises us so much . . ." Malcolm X was an extraordinarily effective speaker who possessed, as he said of himself, "a psychic radar. As a doctor, with his finger against a pulse, is able to feel the heart rate, when I am up there speaking, I can *feel* the reaction to what I am saying."

Malcolm X eventually quarreled with Elijah Muhammad. The Muslim leader had been accused of adultery, and Malcolm X's faith in him was shattered. When he disobeyed a directive of Muhammad's and commented publicly on John F. Kennedy's assassination, he was silenced by the Muslim leader. In defiance, Malcolm X became a leader in his own right. He took a trip to Islam and met with the leaders of the Moslem world. When he returned he modified his racial position, convinced finally "that a blanket indictment of all white people is as wrong as when whites make blanket indictments against blacks." In 1965 he wrote his *Autobiography* because he felt that "it might prove to be a testimony of some social value." Malcolm X was absolutely without illusions: he said that he did "not expect to live long enough to read [the] book in its finished form." Within a few months his prediction was borne out; he was assassinated while delivering a public address.

Malcolm X was a cult hero to Negroes in America because he represented them in the most literal sense. A product of poverty, separated parents, and inadequate education, he spoke to black people with the authority of someone who had lived their lives. Above all he spoke as a fearless man. He was so pragmatic that his followers could believe in his idealism. As M. S. Handler writes in the introduction to *The Autobiography of Malcolm X:* "It was always a strange and moving experience to walk with Malcolm in Harlem. He was known to all. People glanced at him shyly. Sometimes Negro youngsters would ask for his autograph. It always seems to me that their affection for Malcolm was inspired by the fact that although he had become a national figure, he was still a man of the people who, they felt, would never betray them."

Malcolm X: Mission and Meaning

ROBERT

PENN

WARREN

JAMES FARMER, lately the National Director of the Committee of Racial Equality, has called Malcolm X a "very simple man." Elijah Poole, better known to the Black Muslims as Muhammad and, indeed, as Allah, called him a "star gone astray." An editorial writer of the *Saturday Evening Post* put it: "If Malcolm X were not a Negro, his autobiography would be little more than a journal of abnormal psychology, the story of a burglar, dope pusher, addict and jailbird—with a family history of insanity—who acquires messianic delusions and sets forth to preach an upside-down religion of 'brotherly' hatred." Carl Rowan, a Negro, lately the director of the United States Information Service, substantially agreed with that editorial writer when he said, in an interview after Malcolm's assassination, that he was "an ex-convict, ex-dope peddler who became a racial fanatic." Another editorial writer, that of the *Daily Times* of Lagos, Nigeria called him a martyr.

Malcolm X may have been, in varying perspectives, all these things. But he was also something else. He was a latter-day example of an old-fashioned type of American celebrated in grammar school readers, commencement addresses, and speeches at Rotary Club lunches—the man who "makes it," the man who, from humble origins and with meager education, converts, by will, intelligence, and sterling character, his liabilities into assets.

Malcolm X was of that breed of Americans, autodidacts and home-made successes, that has included Benjamin Franklin, Abraham Lincoln, P. T. Barnum, Thomas A. Edison, Booker T. Washington, Mark Twain, Henry Ford, and the Wright brothers. Malcolm X would look back on his beginnings and, in innocent joy, marvel at the distance he had come.

But in Malcolm X the old Horatio Alger story is crossed, as has often been the case, with another typical American story. America has been prodigally fruitful of hot-gospellers and prophets —from Dr. Graham and his bread, Amelia Bloomer and her bloomers, Emerson and the Oversoul, and Brigham Young, on to F.D.R. and the current Graham, Billy. Furthermore, to round out his American story and insure his fame, Malcolm X, like John Brown, Abraham Lincoln, Joseph Smith (the founder of Mormonism), and John Fitzgerald Kennedy, along with a host of lesser prophets, crowned his mission with martyrdom. Malcolm X fulfills, it would seem, all the requirements—success against odds, the role of prophet, and martyrdom—for inclusion in the American pantheon.

Malcolm Little, who was to become Malcolm X and El-Hajj Malik El-Shabazz, was born in Omaha, Nebraska, on May 19, 1925. All omens were right, and all his background. He was the seventh child of his father. One night during the pregnancy of his mother, hooded Ku Klux Klansmen, mounted and brandishing rifles and shotguns, surrounded the house, calling for the father to come out; the mother faced them down and persuaded them of the fact that her husband was not at home. The mother, a West Indian who looked white, was ashamed, not proud, of the white blood. The father, a Baptist preacher, was a militant follower of Marcus Garvey, and this was to lead to another attack on the Little home, in 1929, in Lansing, Michigan, this time by the Black Legion, which except for black robes was indistinguishable from the Klan; the house burned to the ground, while white police and firemen looked on. The memory of that night stayed with Malcolm from childhood—that and the pictures his father showed him of Marcus Garvey "riding in a fine car, a big black man dressed in a dazzling uniform with gold braid on it, and he was wearing a thrilling hat with tall plumes," and the Garveyite meetings at which his father presided and which always ended with the exhortation, "Up, you mighty race, you can accomplish what you will!" The people would chant these words after Malcolm's father.

To complete the picture of the preparation of the hero for his mission, his father, who had seen two brothers killed by white men and a third lynched, was found, one night, on a streetcar track, with skull crushed and body cut almost across. Negroes in Lansing—and the son all his life—believed that he had been attacked by white men, and then laid on the track. Malcolm always believed that he, too, would meet a violent death. When he first became aware of the long stalk, which was to end in gunfire in the Audubon Ballroom, Malcolm might accept it, then, as a fulfillment of old omens and intuitions.

In spite of the powerful image of the father, the pictures of Garvey in uniform, and the tales of black kings, Malcolm's early notion of Africa was still one "of naked savages, cannibals, monkeys and tigers and steaming jungles." He says that he never understood why. But that statement must be an example, in a form more bland than usual, of his irony, for a large part of his autobiography (*The Autobiography of Malcolm X*, with the assistance of Alex Haley, New York City: The Grove Press, 1966) is devoted to explaining *why*—that is, by the white man's "brain-washing"; and then explaining *how*, step by step, he came to the vision of another Africa, and of another self, different from the hustler, pimp, dope-addict, dope-pusher, burglar, and, by his own account, generally degraded and vice-ridden creature known as "Satan," who, in 1948, in Concord Prison, in Massachusetts, heard, in a letter from his brother Philbert, of the "natural religion for the black man." The religion was called the "Nation of Islam."

This autobiography is "told" to Alex Haley, a Negro, a retired twenty-year man of the Coast Guard turned journalist. From 1963 up to the assassination, Haley saw Malcolm for almost daily sessions when Malcolm was in New York, and sometimes accompanied him on his trips. Haley's account of this period, of how he slowly gained Malcolm's confidence and how Malcolm himself discovered the need to tell his story, is extremely inter-

esting and, though presented as an Epilogue, is an integral part
of the book; but the main narrative has the advantage of Malcolm's tone, his characteristic movement of mind, and his wit,
for Haley has succeeded admirably in capturing these qualities,
as can be checked by the recollection of Malcolm's TV appearances and conversation and by his taped speeches (*Malcolm X
Speaks: Selected Speeches and Statements*, edited by George
Breitman, New York: Merit Publishers, 1966).

The *Autobiography* and the speeches are an extraordinary
record of an extraordinary man. They are, among other things,
a record that may show a white man (or some Negroes, for Malcolm would say that many Negroes do not know the nature of
their own experience) what it means to be a Negro in America,
in this century, or at least what it so dramatically meant to one
man of unusual intelligence and powerful personality. Being a
Negro meant being "black"—even if black was no more than a
metaphor for Malcolm, who was himself "marigny," a dull yel-
lowish skin, pale enough to freckle, pale eyes, hair reddish-
coppery. He had been "Detroit Red" in his hustling days.

To be black, metaphorically or literally, meant, according to
Malcolm, to wear a badge of shame which was so mystically and
deeply accepted that all the practical injustices the white world
might visit upon the black would seem only a kind of inverted
justice, necessary in the very nature of things, the working out of
a curse. The black man had no history, no country, no identity;
he was alienated in time and place; he lived in "self-hate," and
being unable to accept "self," he therefore was willing to accept,
supine or with random violence, his fate. This was the diagnosis
of his own plight, as Malcolm learned it from the "Nation of
Islam."

As for the cure, what he found was the doctrine of the Black
Muslims. This involved a history of creation and a metaphysic
which made the black man central and dominant, and a secular
history of kingly achievement in Africa. The divine and secular
histories provided a justification for the acceptance of the black
"self." In addition, the doctrine provided an understanding of the
iniquity of the white man which would account for the black
man's present lot and would, at the same time, mobilize an un-

quenchable hate against him. Total withdrawal from the white man and all his works was the path to virtue, until the day of Armageddon when he would be destroyed. Meanwhile, until the Chosen People had been relieved of the white man's presence, the black man was presented with a practical program of life: thrift, education, cleanliness, diet (no pork, for example, pork being a "nigger" food), abstemiousness (no alcohol or tobacco), manners and courtesy, puritanical morality and reverence for the home and Muslim womanhood—a general program of "wake up, clean up, and stand up." In fact, on the practical side, in spite of the hatred of the white man and contempt for his culture, the Black Muslim doctrine smuggled into the life of the Negro slum the very virtues which had made white middle-class America what it was—i.e., successful.

After Malcolm's death Dr. Kenneth B. Clark, the Negro psychologist and the author of an important book called *Dark Ghettos*, said that he had been "cut down at the point when he seemed on the verge of achieving the position of respectability he sought." In the midst of the gospel of violence and the repudiation of the white world, even in the Black Muslim phase, there appears now and then the note of yearning. In the *Autobiography* we find, for instance, this passage: "I was the invited speaker at the Harvard Law School Forum. I happened to glance through a window. Abruptly, I realized that I was looking in the direction of the apartment house that was my old burglary group's hideout. . . . And there I stood, the invited speaker, at Harvard."

Malcolm, still in prison, gave up pork and tobacco, and undertook a program of reading in the good library there available. He read in Plato, Aristotle, Schopenhauer, Kant, Nietzsche, and the "Oriental philosophers." He read and reread the Bible, and could match quotations with a Harvard Seminary student who conducted a class for prisoners. He studied *The Loom of Language*, by Frederick Bodmer, and memorized Grimm's Law. He read Durant's *Story of Civilization*, H. G. Wells' *Outline of History*, Herodotus, Fannie Kimball, *Uncle Tom's Cabin*, Gandhi, Gregor Mendel, pamphlets of the "Abolitionist Anti-Slavery Society of New England," and J. A. Rogers' *Sex and Race*. He was trying to find the black man's place—and his own—in history, trying, in other words, to document the doctrine of the Black Muslims. He wrote regularly to Muhammad to tell what he had found. While he was still in prison Malcolm also had a vision. He had written an appeal to Muhammad to reinstate his brother Reginald, suspended as a Muslim for "improper relations" with the secretary of the New York Temple. That night he spent in desperate prayer. The next night he woke up and saw a man sitting, there in the cell, in a chair by him. "He had on a dark suit, I remember. I could see him as plainly as I see anyone I look at. He wasn't black, and he wasn't white. He was light-brown-skinned, an Asiatic cast of countenance, and he had oily black hair. . . . I had no idea whatsoever who he was. He just sat there. Then suddenly as he had come, he was gone." The color of the man in the vision is an interesting fact. So is his immobility and silence.

When Malcolm Little came out of prison, he was Malcolm X, the "X," according to the practice of the Black Muslims, standing for the true name lost long ago in Africa to take the place of the false white name that had been forced on him. He had been reborn, and he now entered upon his mission. Soon he was an accredited minister of Muhammad, the official defender of the faith and the intellectual spokesman of the movement. His success, and especially the fact that he was invited to colleges, where Muhammad would never be invited, led to jealousy and, as Malcolm reports, contributed to his "silencing" as soon as a good justification appeared.

Malcolm X was not the only man drawn from the lower depths to be reborn in the Nation of Islam. It is generally admitted that the record of rehabilitation by the Black Muslims of dope-addicts, alcoholics, prostitutes, and criminals makes any other method seem a waste of time. They have, it would seem, found the nerve center that, once touched, can radically change both the values and the way of life for a number of Negroes in America; and it is important here to use the phrase "Negroes in America" with special emphasis, and no other locution, for those redeemed by the Black Muslims are those who have been only *in,* but not *of,* America, those without country, history, or identity. The Black Muslims have found, then, a principle that, if not of universal validity (or, in one perspective, isn't it? for white as well as for black?), at least involves a truth of considerable psychological importance. That truth is, indeed, shrouded in metaphysical mumbo-jumbo, political and economic absurdity, and some murderous delusions, but even these elements have a noteworthy symbolic relation to the central truth. It is reported that Martin Luther King, after seeing Malcolm X on TV, remarked: "When he starts talking about all that's been done to us, I get a twinge of hate, of identification with him. But hate is not the only effect." A man as intelligent, as cultivated, and as experienced as James Farmer has testified in his recent book *Freedom When?* that the Black Muslims and Malcolm X have had a very important impact on his own thinking and in helping to change his basic views of the Negro Revolution, especially on the question of "blackness" and on the nature of integration and the Negro's role in an open society.

If this is the case, then the story of Malcolm X assumes an added dimension. It shows the reader the world in which that truth can operate; that is, it shows the kind of alienation to which this truth is applicable. It shows, also, the human quality of the operation, a man in the process of trying to understand his plight, and to find salvation, by that truth. But there is another aspect to the *Autobiography.* Malcolm X was a man in motion, he was a seeker, and that motion led, in the end, away from orthodox Black Muslim doctrine. The doctrine had been, he said, a straitjacket. He was now in the process of stripping away, perhaps unconsciously, the mumbo-jumbo, the absurdities, and the murderous delusions. He was trying, as it were, to locate the truth that had saved him, and divest it of the irrelevancies. In the end, he might have come to regard the religion that, after his break with the Black Muslims, he had found in Mecca as an irrelevancy, too. Certainly, just before his death he could say that his "philosophy" was still changing. Perhaps what Mecca gave him, for the time being at least, was the respectability, the authority, of the established thing. But he might have finally found that authority in himself, for he could speak as a man whose very existence was witness to what he said. Something of that purely personal authority comes through in these books.

Malcolm X had, in his last phase, lost the mystique of blackness so important to the Black Muslims; he had seen the blue-eyed and fair-haired pilgrims in Mecca. He was no longer a separatist in the absolute sense of the Black Muslims. He had become enough of an integrationist to say: "I believe in recognizing every human being as a human being . . . and when you are dealing with humanity as a family, there's no question of integration or intermarriage. It's just one human being marrying another human being or one human being living around with another human being." And just before his death he had made a down-payment on a house, in Long Island, in a largely Jewish neighborhood. He no longer saw the white man as the "white devil"—metaphysically evil; and he was ready, grudgingly, not optimistically, and with a note of threat, to grant that there was in America a chance, a last chance, for a "bloodless revolution." He was ready to work with other Negro organizations, even those which he had most derided, to try to find common ground and solutions at a practical level.

Certain ideas were, however, carried over from the Black Muslim days. The question of "identity" remained, and the question of race pride and personal self-respect divested of chauvinism, and with this the notion of "wake up, clean up, and stand up," the notion of self-reliance, self-improvement, self-discipline. If he could say such things, which smacked of the discredited philosophy of Booker T. Washington, and which few other Civil Rights leaders would dare to utter, it was because he did so in the context of his intransigence vis-à-vis the white world and his radical indictment of white society. Even in the last phase, even if he believed in "recognizing every human being as a human being," and no longer took the white man to be metaphysically evil, his indictment of white society was still radical; unless that society could really be regenerated, the chance for the "bloodless revolution" was gone.

This radical indictment leads to what may be the greatest significance of Malcolm X, his symbolic role. He was the black man who looked the white man in the eye and forgave nothing. If the white man had turned away, in shame or indifference, from the awful "forgiveness" of a Martin Luther King, he still had to face the unforgivingness, with its shattering effect on his accustomed view of himself and with the terrifying discovery, as Malcolm's rage brought his own rage forth, of the ultimate of which he himself would, under pressure, be capable. To put it another way, Malcolm X let the white man see what, from a certain perspective, he, his history, and his culture looked like. It was possible to say that that perspective was not the only one, that it did not give the whole truth about the white man, his history, and his culture, but it was not possible to say that the perspective did not carry *a* truth, a truth that was not less, but more, true for being seen from the angle of "Small's Paradise" in Harlem or of the bedroom to which "Detroit Red," the "steerer," brought the "Ivy League fathers" to be ministered to by the big black girl, whose body had been greased to make it look "shinier and blacker" and whose Amazonian hand held a small plaited whip.

On the afternoon of Sunday, February 21, 1965, at a meeting of his struggling new Organization of Afro-American Unity, in the Audubon Ballroom, on West 166th Street, in Harlem, Malcolm X rose to speak and uttered the ritual greeting, *"Asalaikum,* brothers and sisters!" He was immediately cut down by shotgun and revolver fire from assassins waiting in the front of the audience. At 3:30 at the Columbia-Presbyterian Hospital, he was pronounced dead. Three men—Talmadge Hayer, Norman 3X (Brown), and Thomas 15X (Johnson)—were arrested in the case and tried for first-degree murder. Thayer denied Black Muslim connections, but Thomas 15X was identified as a member and Norman 3X as a lieutenant in the "Fruit of Islam"—the bodyguards of Elijah Muhammad. After deliberating for twenty hours a jury found them guilty, and all three were given life sentences.

What would have been Malcolm's role had he lived? Perhaps, as some Negro leaders said shortly before his death, he had no real organization, and did not have the talent to create one. Perhaps his being in motion was only, as some held, a result of confusion of mind, a groping that could not be trusted to bring results. Perhaps, as James Farmer had put it, Malcolm, for all his talk, was not an activist; he had managed all along to be out of harm's way whenever harm was brewing, and he was afraid of the time when he "would have to chirp or get off the perch."

But perhaps the new phase of the Negro Revolution, with the violence of the great city slums, might have given him his great chance. He might have, at last, found himself in action. He might have found himself committed to blind violence, but on the other hand he might have had the power to control and canalize action and do something to reduce the danger of the Revolution's degenerating into random revolt. For, in spite of all the gospel of intransigence, Malcolm had always had a governing idea of a constructive role for the Negro, some notion of a society. After all, he had personal force, as no one who ever spent as little as ten minutes with him would have doubted: charisma, to use the fashionable word, and that to a degree possessed by no other leader except Martin Luther King. And he had one great asset which Martin Luther King does not have: he was from the lower depths and possessed the authority of one who had both suffered and conquered the depths.

Whatever the future might have held for him had he lived, his actual role was an important one, and in one sense the importance lay in his *being* rather than his *doing*. He was a man of passion, depth, and scale—and his personal story is a moving one. There is the long struggle. There is the sense of desperation and tightening entrapment as, in the last days, Malcolm recognized the dilemma developing in his situation. The "so-called moderate" Civil Rights leaders, he said, dodged him as "too militant," and the "so-called militants" dodged him as "too moderate." Haley reports that he once exclaimed "They won't let me turn the corner! I'm caught in a trap!" For there is a trap in the story, a real and lethal one. There is the gang of Black Muslims covering his every move in the Statler Hilton at Los Angeles, the mysterious Negro men who tried to get his room number at the Hilton in New York City, and the sinister telephone call to his room in the hotel the morning of his death. There is the bombing of his house, and his despairing anger when the event was widely taken as a publicity stunt. There is his remark to Haley, as he asked to read the manuscript of his book for a last, unnecessary time: "I just want to read it one more time, because I don't expect to read it in finished form"—wanting, as it were, to get a last sense of the shape of his own life as he felt the trap closing. There is, as with a final accent of pathos, the letter by his six-year-old daughter Attilah (named for the Scourge of God), written just after his death: "Dear Daddy, I love you so. O dear, O dear, I wish you wasn't dead." But entrapment and pathos was not all. He had been bred to danger. When he stepped on the platform that Sunday afternoon, in the face of odds which he had more shrewdly estimated than anybody else, he had nerve, confidence, style. He made his last gesture.

As one reads the *Autobiography*, one feels that, whatever the historical importance of Malcolm Little, his story has permanence, that it has something of tragic intensity and meaning. One feels that it is an American story bound to be remembered, to lurk in the background of popular consciousness, to reappear some day in a novel, on the stage, or on the screen. No—the right medium might be the ballad. Malcolm was a figure out of the anonymous depth of the folk, and even now, in a slum bedroom or in the shadowy corner of some bar, fingers may be tentatively picking the box, and lips fumbling to frame the words that will mean, long after our present problems are resolved and forgotten, the final fame, and the final significance.

Martin Luther King

I say to you today, my friends, that in spite of the difficulties and
frustrations of the moment I still have a dream. It is a dream
deeply rooted in the American dream.
. . . I have a dream that my four little children will one day live in
a nation where they will not be judged by the color of their skin
but by the content of their character.

In his position as a Negro leader, Martin Luther King represented the assertive man who rejected violence and acted with simple dignity and courage. He combined a deep religious faith with a realistic attitude toward the Negro's role in American society. An eloquent orator and a tireless crusader, he refused to adopt the position of the Negro militants. Since his death in 1968, no one man has appealed to so many black people as he, and racial leadership has become dangerously fragmented.

Martin Luther King was born on January 15, 1929, in Atlanta, Georgia, the second of three children. His father was an important pastor and racial leader of the community. King matured very quickly. He was graduated from high school by the age of fifteen and attended Morehouse College (1944–1948), Crozer Theological Seminary (1948–1951), and Boston University, where he was awarded a Ph.D. in systematic theology in 1955. King became a national leader in 1955, when he led the bus boycott in Montgomery, Alabama; his autobiography, *Stride Toward Freedom*, records the details of that seminal event. At this time he became committed to the teachings of Mahatma Gandhi and practiced the principle of passive resistance until his death. His trip to Ghana and India convinced him that his belief in a nonviolent approach to Civil Rights was sound. In 1957 King was elected president of the Southern Christian Leadership Conference, and in that role he continued to lead demonstrations, picket lines, boycotts, and sit-ins throughout the South. His active leadership reached its greatest point in 1963, when he delivered his eloquent speech at the peace demonstration in Washington, D.C. In 1964 he won the Nobel Peace Prize and achieved international recognition.

Martin Luther King was a practical idealist who saw human affairs in moral and religious terms. Thus he found it natural in his later years to link the struggle for racial justice with the Vietnamese War. He was sharply criticized by other Negro leaders because they felt he might be harming the cause of Negro equality within America itself; but his position has proved to be increasingly justified. When he was assassinated in April 1968, all of America mourned, black people because they had lost a hero and white people because they had lost a moderate leader who, more than anyone else, could prevent the country from being torn apart by racial strife.

Martin Luther King—Unsung Theologian

HERBERT

WARREN

RICHARDSON

ARTIN LUTHER KING was the most important theologian of our time not because of the plenitude of his literary production, but because of his creative proposals for dealing with the structure of evil generated by modern relativism, viz., ideological conflict. Over against this understanding of social evil, King created not only a new theology, but also new types of piety, new styles of Christian living.

Relativism is like gnosticism in that it affirms knowledge to be acquired only in a privileged way; but relativism is like scientific naturalism in that it claims the object of knowledge to be natural. The peculiar demonic tendency of relativism arises from the combination of these two factors. With respect to the fact that it affirms access to knowledge to be privileged and not public, relativism posits the same irrevocable and irreconcilable separation of the *cognoscenti* from outsiders that is found in gnosticism. But whereas the gnostic object of knowledge is supernatural, the relativistic object of knowledge is natural. Whereas gnosticism asserts an opposition between the natural and supernatural orders of reality, relativism asserts an opposition within a single natural order between those who truly understand the meaning of life and those who do not. In this way, modern relativism generates a unique institution: ritual ideological conflict. This conflict is undertaken both because of and in order to confirm ideological

REPRINTED BY PERMISSION OF COMMONWEAL PUBLISHING CO., INC.

commitments. It is not, in fact, conflict over particular problems; hence it is unresolvable in principle.

Modern relativism brings the dualism that is characteristic of religious gnosticism down into the natural order of time and space. In this situation there is inevitably conflict, for there is no basis for peaceful coexistence among parties that are ideologically opposed. Faced with the inevitability of ideological conflict, the relativists have replied that conflict, even war, is not only a necessary but also a valuable part of life. They say that it creates values rather than destroying them. Conflict not only encourages pluralism and diversity; it even creates or strengthens such values as justice, brotherhood and equality.

Relativism so pervades the world today that conflict, even violent conflict, is glorified not only by the extreme right and the extreme left; it has been increasingly structured into the whole fabric of modern culture. Faced with this demonic tendency, the Church must oppose relativism with a faith which will open it to a transcending redemptive reality.

Now, if we seek a conception of faith which is appropriately correlated with relativism, we shall understand faith as the power of reconciliation which works to unite the many relative perspectives and to thwart ideological conflict. In this context, faith is the commitment of man to oppose the separation of man from man. It is a commitment to struggle against attacks on the common good, against racism and segregation, and against the fragmentation of man's intellectual and spiritual life.

The most important proponent of a theology of reconciliation was Martin Luther King, who developed this theological principle into a new method for effecting social change. In his theology, therefore, faith affirms reconciliation in opposition to the relativism that denies its possibility. In intellectual discussion, faith hopes for agreement and not only dialogue. In war, faith expects and works for peace. In economic struggle, it calls for the common good. In the working together of churches, it anticipates ecumenical reunion. In all these acts, faith affirms something relativism cannot see, i.e., the power of divine unity working in all things to reconcile the ideological conflict generated by relativism itself. Quite concretely, too, faith as the affirmation of such a power of reconciliation also affirms that all those institutions and movements of our time which are working to overcome ideological conflicts are special instruments of redemptive power. One thinks immediately of King's support of the United Nations, of his development of the Southern Christian Leadership Conference, and of his concern for peace and ecumenism. These are the institutions where God is working in the world today. But only the eyes of faith can see it.

The struggle against ideological conflict anywhere in the world is the struggle for the unity of men living together in the world. Conversely, because the struggle against racism is really a struggle against ideological conflict, Martin Luther King recognized that he had to oppose this kind of conflict wherever it appears. He was, so to say, under this obligation *in principle*. Hence, King was the first of those who linked the civil rights struggle to opposition to the Vietnam war.

Civil Rights and Vietnam

It is instructive now to recall that many active supporters of King's civil rights program opposed his opposition to the Vietnam war. King, they said, was mixing up the civil rights movement with the problem of the war and this would weaken the struggle for integration. But these critics supposed that these were, in fact, two different problems rather than two manifestations of the same structure of evil: ideological conflict. By the very fact that King refused to separate these two issues, he showed the profundity of his theological insight into the nature of evil today. And who, today, would deny that what he first affirmed as a lone prophetic voice has now come to pass and been acknowledged by all among us as a basic social fact? Racial discrimination is but one form of the peculiar form of evil which characterizes our time—the presence of ideological hate within the world denies the possibility in principle of the unity of man with man.

King's perception of the human problem today as rooted in a certain structure of social evil led him to emphasize again and again that his struggle was directed against the forces, or structure, of evil itself rather than against the person or group who is doing the evil. Christian faith sees neither particular men nor particular groups as evil, but sees them trapped within a structure of ideological separation which makes ritual conflict inevitable. In order to overcome this kind of evil, faith does not attack the men who do evil, but the structure of evil which makes men act violently. Hence, there must be an *asymmetry* between the form in which evil manifests itself and the form of our opposition to evil. We should meet violence with non-violence. The philosophy of "black power" assumes that there must be a symmetry between the form in which evil manifests itself and the form of our opposition to it. But King saw that such a symmetrical response only perpetuates the structure of evil itself. In describing his work in the Montgomery bus boycott, King said:

"In my weekly remarks as president, I stressed that the use of violence in our struggle would be both impractical and immoral. To meet hate with retaliatory hate would do nothing but intensify the existence of evil in the universe. Hate begets hate; violence begets violence; toughness begets a greater toughness. We must meet the forces of hate with the power of love; we must meet physical force with soul force. Our aim must never be to defeat or humiliate the white man, but to win his friendship and understanding."

In this statement, the asymmetrical character of the struggle against evil is clearly noted and, as we have seen, the affirmation of the possibility of this asymmetry grows out of the vision that grounded King's theology. Face to face with the white man, bound, so to say, to the realm of relativism, to the order of visible differences and diverse histories, one can find no grounds for agreement, unity, or friendship. In such a realm, there are, as one theologian even today affirms, "only individuals and fights." But the vision of faith is that there is an invisible unity that makes the white and black man one in love, in holy communion, in common goal and good. But this realm of unity is seen only by faith, and the one who responds to evil asymmetrically, returning good for evil, is the man who lives by faith.

It should be noted that King did not argue for non-violence on a fideistic or confessional ground—as if hereby we are making an eschatological witness to the Lordship of Christ, a witness that

must, in our time, always be defeated. King argues that non-
violence is the sole *practical* way to struggle against evil because
it alone is based on a right understanding of reality itself. To
struggle against evil within the system of ideological conflict never
solves anything, but simply perpetuates the problem by confirming
the structure of evil itself. This is why so much concerned social
action is counter-effective—because one ideology lives off its opposition to another and thereby strengthens that which it opposes
in the very act of opposing it. King's profound understanding of
the way in which structures of evil in the world drive men to act
evilly, i.e., oppress men until they are sick and filled with hatred
and fear for all "outsiders," is what gave his theology a critical
focus that is duplicated nowhere else on the contemporary scene.

   Not only was King's understanding of the character of evil in
the modern world precise and relevant, but so too was his vision
of the goal of the struggle against evil and his understanding of
the relation of the two. King identified the goal of the struggle
against evil as the total interrelatedness of man with man, an
ability to live together with those who are different, even opposed.
We should not seek "to defeat or humiliate our opponent, but to
win his friendship and understanding." Note King's stress on
friendship as the ultimate value of human life. Protestant theology
has so neglected the development of an adequate value theory or
the idea of a chief good of life that we can scarcely understand
why King holds that friendship is this good, why it is the purpose
of all that we do. Protestants have, moreover, twisted the concept
of Christian love to the requirements of the doctrine of justification by faith, i.e., to the demands of Reformation dogma, affirming that Christian love is self-sacrificing agape—not personal
communion. To describe Christian love as self-sacrificing agape is
to put the cart before the horse. According to King, self-sacrificing
love grows naturally out of the love of friendship, out of the sense
of being in communion with the one to whom good is returned
for evil. Self-sacrifice cannot *establish* personal friendship, it can
only manifest it. If it does not manifest it, then this love is only
a more insidious form of evil, "the heaping of coals."

   Emphasis on Christian love as friendship involves an important
reversal of a pervasive Reformation error. Such a reversal could
come, I surmise, only from a perspective that was itself not wholly

at ease with the magisterial reformation, i.e., only from the "third wing," the spiritualists, the Baptists. One can understand today why Harvey Cox should say that the life and work of King make him proud to be a Baptist. And we should not forget this: that King's spiritualistic concern for the sanctification of the world and his vision of Christian love as friendship give his theological ethics a specificity that contrasts markedly with the other contemporary options.

We can understand the significance of King's insistence upon the unity of persons in friendship (brotherhood) as the goal of all life by contrasting it with an ethics that regards self-sacrificing agape (or the "faith" that receives it) as the chief good of human life. Such an ethics must regard evil as a necessary (even good) condition of human life. For in order for self-sacrifice to be possible, there must be an evil to be suffered. Self-sacrifice is good, therefore, not in itself, but because it deters or limits evil. In this framework, the fundamental fact of life is seen to be the ineradicability of evil—and by elevating self-sacrificial agape into the principal ethic, we know not the "essential good" but only the "deterrent good." In our own time, Reinhold Niebuhr reintroduced this Reformation, though semi-Manichean, understanding of evil back into American theology—and King's writings show a constant wrestling against him and the problem he raises. King's reply, his decisive repudiation of the Niebuhrian scheme, comes in his different, but more profound, understanding of evil as the structure that engenders ideological conflict, a structure that is to be opposed not by settling for proximate justice in the political order, and acknowledging the legitimacy of violent force to restrain evil, but by striving for a holy community of love in this world by the nonviolent striving to overcome evil with good.

King was regarded as a civil rights leader and as a man of extraordinary personal valor, but he has not been understood as a brilliant and mature theologian: the first two would, however, have been impossible without the third. It would be a tragedy, I believe, if we were to remember him only as hero and not as thinker—by still giving our minds over to the authors of ponderous tomes and the orators on prestigious lecture platforms while giving over only our hearts to him. He deserves our head as well as our heart. He is the theologian for our time.

James Baldwin

It is a terrible, an inexorable, law that one cannot deny
the humanity of another without diminishing one's own: in the
face of one's victim, one sees oneself. Walk through the streets of
Harlem and see what we, this nation, have become.

The Negro writer in America has been especially burdened by a conflict that confronts every modern author, the conflict between his role as an artist and his role as a man. His instinct is to express freely his every thought; the color of his skin prevents him from forgetting his social responsibility. He, struggles to be an artist, but he finds himself responding to social exigencies that ask him to speak as a man. Many Negro writers, from W. E. B. DuBois to Eldridge Cleaver, have been social leaders, and their art is often perilously and dramatically close to their lives. No Negro author of our time has been more troubled by his role as an artist and his role as a man than James Baldwin. No Negro author has spoken more eloquently or more perceptively about the conflict.

James Baldwin was born in New York on August 22, 1924, the first of nine children. Baldwin's early life was dominated by an authoritarian father who, as a minister in the church, insisted upon strict religious behavior in his family. Baldwin himself became a minister at the age of fourteen, but by the time of his graduation from high school in 1942, he had decided to leave the church, the community of Harlem, and his family. He traveled to Paris in 1948, seeking greater aesthetic distance from the racial problems that formed the substance of his early work. His expatriation lasted for almost ten years and during that period he published the novels *Go Tell It on the Mountain* (1952) and *Giovanni's Room* (1956) and the collection of essays *Notes of a Native Son* (1956).

Baldwin returned to America in 1958 and became a literary spokesman on Negro problems. His writing grew more militant and pugnacious, more directly tendentious. The essays of *Nobody Knows My Name* (1961) had been written over a five-year period and recall in mood and theme the earlier pieces in *Notes of a Native Son*; but in the 1960's Baldwin's point of view and style changed sharply. In 1962 he published his third novel, *Another Country*; in 1963, the long essay, *The Fire Next Time*; in 1964, the sociological drama, *Blues for Mr. Charlie*; in 1965, a collection of his stories, *Going to Meet the Man*; and in 1968, his most recent novel, *Tell Me How Long the Train's Been Gone*.

Baldwin is a representative black writer for many reasons. He has articulated the suffering of Negro people in a more cogent and persuasive manner than any other black essayist since World War II; he has informed his personal dilemmas with public significance, a characteristic common to the most effective and influential contemporary writers; and he has written of the central subject of our time—the conflict between love and power in American society. When this conflict is seen from the point of view of an articulate black man, as in the following essay, the result is a shock of recognition to the white man, for he recognizes that Baldwin has dramatically asserted a way of life that most Americans have only vaguely felt and understood.

Autobiographical Notes

JAMES

BALDWIN

I WAS BORN in Harlem thirty-one years ago.* I began plotting novels at about the time I learned to read. The story of my childhood is the usual bleak fantasy, and we can dismiss it with the restrained observation that I certainly would not consider living it again. In those days my mother was given to the exasperating and mysterious habit of having babies. As they were born, I took them over with one hand and held a book with the other. The children probably suffered, though they have since been kind enough to deny it, and in this way I read *Uncle Tom's Cabin* and A *Tale of Two Cities* over and over and over again; in this way, in fact, I read just about everything I could get my hands on—except the Bible, probably because it was the only book I was encouraged to read. I must also confess that I wrote— a great deal—and my first professional triumph, in any case, the first effort of mine to be seen in print, occurred at the age of twelve or thereabouts, when a short story I had written about the Spanish revolution won some sort of prize in an extremely short-lived church newspaper. I remember the story was censored by the lady editor, though I don't remember why, and I was outraged.

Also wrote plays, and songs, for one of which I received a letter of congratulations from Mayor La Guardia, and poetry, about which the less said, the better. My mother was delighted by all these goings-on, but my father wasn't; he wanted me to be a preacher. When I was fourteen I became a preacher, and when I was seventeen I stopped. Very shortly thereafter I left home. For

*Editor's note: This essay was published in 1955.
REPRINTED FROM Notes of a Native Son BY JAMES BALDWIN BY PERMISSION OF THE BEACON PRESS. COPYRIGHT © 1955 BY JAMES BALDWIN.

God knows how long I struggled with the world of commerce and industry—I guess they would say they struggled with *me*—and when I was about twenty-one I had enough done of a novel to get a Saxton Fellowship. When I was twenty-two the fellowship was over, the novel turned out to be unsaleable, and I started waiting on tables in a Village restaurant and writing book reviews—mostly, as it turned out, about the Negro problem, concerning which the color of my skin made me automatically an expert. Did another book, in company with photographer Theodore Pelatowski, about the store-front churches in Harlem. This book met exactly the same fate as my first—fellowship, but no sale. (It was a Rosenwald Fellowship.) By the time I was twenty-four I had decided to stop reviewing books about the Negro problem—which, by this time, was only slightly less horrible in print than it was in life—and I packed my bags and went to France, where I finished, God knows how, *Go Tell It on the Mountain*.

Any writer, I suppose, feels that the world into which he was born is nothing less than a conspiracy against the cultivation of his talent—which attitude certainly has a great deal to support it. On the other hand, it is only because the world looks on his talent with such a frightening indifference that the artist is compelled to make his talent important. So that any writer, looking back over even so short a span of time as I am here forced to assess, finds that the things which hurt him and the things which helped him cannot be divorced from each other; he could be helped in a certain way only because he was hurt in a certain way; and his help is simply to be enabled to move from one conundrum to the next—one is tempted to say that he moves from one disaster to the next. When one begins looking for influences one finds them by the score. I haven't thought much about my own, not enough anyway; I hazard that the King James Bible, the rhetoric of the store-front church, something ironic and violent and perpetually understated in Negro speech—and something of Dickens' love for bravura—have something to do with me today; but I wouldn't stake my life on it. Likewise, innumerable people have helped me in many ways; but finally, I suppose, the most difficult (and most rewarding) thing in my life has been the fact that I was born a Negro and was forced, therefore, to effect some kind of truce with this reality. (Truce, by the way, is the best one can hope for.)

One of the difficulties about being a Negro writer (and this is not special pleading, since I don't mean to suggest that he has it worse than anybody else) is that the Negro problem is written about so widely. The bookshelves groan under the weight of information, and everyone therefore considers himself informed. And this information, furthermore, operates usually (generally, popularly) to reinforce traditional attitudes. Of traditional attitudes there are only two—For or Against—and I, personally, find it difficult to say which attitude has caused me the most pain. I am speaking as a writer; from a social point of view I am perfectly aware that the change from ill-will to good-will, however motivated, however imperfect, however expressed, is better than no change at all.

But it is part of the business of the writer—as I see it—to examine attitudes, to go beneath the surface, to tap the source. From this point of view the Negro problem is nearly inaccessible. It is not only written about so widely; it is written about so badly. It is quite possible to say that the price a Negro pays for becoming articulate is to find himself, at length, with nothing to be articulate about. ("You taught me language," says Caliban to Prospero, "and my profit on't is I know how to curse.") Consider: the tremendous social activity that this problem generates imposes on whites and Negroes alike the necessity of looking forward, of working to bring about a better day. This is fine, it keeps the waters troubled; it is all, indeed, that has made possible the Negro's progress. Nevertheless, social affairs are not generally speaking the writer's prime concern, whether they ought to be or not; it is absolutely necessary that he establish between himself and these affairs a distance which will allow at least, for clarity, so that before he can look forward in any meaningful sense, he must first be allowed to take a long look back. In the context of the Negro problem neither whites nor blacks, for excellent reasons of their own, have the faintest desire to look back; but I think that the past is all that makes the present coherent, and further, that the past will remain horrible for exactly as long as we refuse to assess it honestly.

I know, in any case, that the most crucial time in my own development came when I was forced to recognize that I was a kind of bastard of the West; when I followed the line of my past I did not find myself in Europe but in Africa. And this meant that in some subtle way, in a really profound way, I brought to Shakespeare, Bach, Rembrandt, to the stones of Paris, to the cathedral at Chartres, and to the Empire State Building, a special attitude. These were not really my creations, they did not contain my history; I might search in them in vain forever for any reflection of myself. I was an interloper; this was not my heritage. At the same time I had no other heritage which I could possibly hope to use—I had certainly been unfitted for the jungle or the tribe. I would have to appropriate these white centuries, I would have to make them mine—I would have to accept my special attitude, my special place in this scheme—otherwise I would have no place in *any* scheme. What was the most difficult was the fact that I was forced to admit something I had always hidden from myself, which the American Negro has had to hide from himself as the price of his public progress; that I hated and feared white people. This did not mean that I loved black people; on the contrary, I despised them, possibly because they failed to produce Rembrandt. In effect, I hated and feared the world. And this meant, not only that I thus gave the world an altogether murderous power over me, but also that in such a self-destroying limbo I could never hope to write.

One writes out of one thing only—one's own experience. Everything depends on how relentlessly one forces from this experience the last drop, sweet or bitter, it can possibly give. This is the only real concern of the artist, to recreate out of the disorder of life that order which is art. The difficulty then, for me, of being a Negro writer was the fact that I was, in effect, prohibited from examining my own experience too closely by the tremendous demands and the very real dangers of my social situation.

I don't think the dilemma outlined above is uncommon. I do think, since writers work in the disastrously explicit medium of language, that it goes a little way towards explaining why, out of the enormous resources of Negro speech and life, and despite the example of Negro music, prose written by Negroes has been generally speaking so pallid and so harsh. I have not written about being a Negro at such length because I expect that to be my only subject, but only because it was the gate I had to unlock before I could hope to write about anything else. I don't think that the Negro problem in America can be even discussed coherently without bearing in mind its context; its context being the history, traditions, customs, the moral assumptions and preoccupations of the country; in short, the general social fabric. Appearances to the contrary, no one in America escapes its effects and everyone in America bears some responsibility for it. I believe this the more firmly because it is the overwhelming tendency to speak of this problem as though it were a thing apart. But in the work of Faulkner, in the general attitude and certain specific passages in Robert Penn Warren, and, most significantly, in the advent of Ralph Ellison, one sees the beginnings—at least—of a more genuinely penetrating search. Mr. Ellison, by the way, is the first Negro novelist I have ever read to utilize in language, and brilliantly, some of the ambiguity and irony of Negro life.

About my interests: I don't know if I have any, unless the morbid desire to own a sixteen-millimeter camera and make experimental movies can be so classified. Otherwise, I love to eat and drink—it's my melancholy conviction that I've scarcely ever had enough to eat (this is because it's *impossible* to eat enough if you're worried about the next meal)—and I love to argue with people who do not disagree with me too profoundly, and I love to laugh. I do *not* like bohemia, or bohemians, I do not like people whose principal aim is pleasure, and I do not like people who are *earnest* about anything. I don't like people who like me because I'm a Negro; neither do I like people who find in the same accident grounds for contempt. I love America more than any other country in the world, and, exactly for this reason, I insist on the right to criticize her perpetually. I think all theories are suspect, that the finest principles may have to be modified, or may even be pulverized by the demands of life, and that one must find, therefore, one's own moral center and move through the world hoping that this center will guide one aright. I consider that I have many responsibilities, but none greater than this: to last, as Hemingway says, and get my work done.

I want to be an honest man and a good writer.

Stokely Carmichael

*Black Power is a means for the black poor to get together, define
their needs and put people in power to achieve them.*

Black Power has assumed a most important dimension in
racial affairs today. As one of its most articulate as well as
militant spokesmen, Stokely Carmichael speaks for an increasing number of black people in America. He insists upon
"the coming-together of black people to elect representatives
and to *force those representatives to speak* to their needs. . . .
The power must be that of a community, and emanate from
there." More than any other political leader, Carmichael represents those who champion negritude and strong racial pride.

Stokely Carmichael was born in Trinidad on June 29,
1941, and was brought to Harlem when he was eleven. He
attended the Bronx High School of Science, where he was a
popular and successful student. In 1960 he grew intensely
conscious of the need for militancy. "When I first heard
about the Negroes sitting in at lunch counters down South,"
he has said, "I thought they were just a bunch of publicity
hounds. But one night when I saw those kids on TV, getting
back up on the lunch counter stools after being knocked
down, sugar in their eyes, catsup in their hair—well, something happened to me. Suddenly, I was burning. Then I
started picketing all over the place with a bunch of kids from
Core." Carmichael turned down scholarships to predomi-
nantly white universities and attended Howard University.

After his graduation from Howard University in 1964,
Carmichael rose to a position of influence very quickly, join-

ing the first Freedom Ride, Cambridge, and the Mississippi Summer Project. In May 1966, he was elected chairman of the Student Non-Violent Coordinating Committee and had a national platform from which he could advocate his view of negritude. Most of his ideas are recorded in *Black Power*, a manifesto which he wrote with the historian Charles Hamilton.

Black Power: Its Need and Substance

STOKELY
CARMICHAEL
and
CHARLES V.
HAMILTON

THE ADOPTION of the concept of Black Power is one of the most legitimate and healthy developments in American politics and race relations in our time. The concept of Black Power speaks to all the needs mentioned in this chapter. It is a call for black people in this country to unite, to recognize their heritage, to build a sense of community. It is a call for black people to begin to define their own goals, to lead their own organizations and to support those organizations. It is a call to reject the racist institutions and values of this society.

The concept of Black Power rests on a fundamental premise: *Before a group can enter the open society, it must first close ranks.* By this we mean that group solidarity is necessary before a group can operate effectively from a bargaining position of strength in a pluralistic society. Traditionally, each new ethnic group in this society has found the route to social and political viability through the organization of its own institutions with which to represent its needs within the larger society. Studies in voting behavior specifically, and political behavior generally, have made it clear that politically the American pot has not melted. Italians vote for

FROM *Black Power*, BY STOKELY CARMICHAEL AND CHARLES HAMILTON. © COPYRIGHT 1967 BY STOKELY CARMICHAEL AND CHARLES HAMILTON. REPRINTED BY PERMISSION OF RANDOM HOUSE, INC.

Rubino over O'Brien; Irish for Murphy over Goldberg, etc. This phenomenon may seem distasteful to some, but it has been and remains today a central fact of the American political system. There are other examples of ways in which groups in the society have remembered their roots and used this effectively in the political arena. Theodore Sorensen describes the politics of foreign aid during the Kennedy Administration in his book *Kennedy:*

> No powerful constituencies or interest groups backed foreign aid. The Marshall Plan at least had appealed to Americans who traced their roots to the Western European nations aided. But there were few voters who identified with India, Colombia or Tanganyika [p. 351].

The extent to which black Americans can and do "trace their roots" to Africa; to that extent will they be able to be more effective on the political scene.

A white reporter set forth this point in other terms when he made the following observation about white Mississippi's manipulation of the anti-poverty program:

> The war on poverty has been predicated on the notion that there is such a thing as a community which can be defined geographically and mobilized for a collective effort to help the poor. This theory has no relationship to reality in the deep South. In every Mississippi county there are two communities. Despite all the pious platitudes of the moderates on both sides, these two communities habitually see their interests in terms of conflict rather than cooperation. Only when the Negro community can muster enough political, economic and professional strength to compete on somewhat equal terms, will Negroes believe in the possibility of true cooperation and whites accept its necessity. En route to integration, the Negro community needs to develop a greater independence—a chance to run its own affairs and not cave in whenever "the man" barks—or so it seems to me, and to most of the knowledgeable people with whom I talked in Mississippi. To OEO, this judgment may sound like black nationalism. . . .[1]

1. Christopher Jencks, "Accommodating Whites: A New Look at Mississippi," *The New Republic* (April 16, 1966).

The point is obvious: black people must lead and run their own organizations. Only black people can convey the revolutionary idea—and it is a revolutionary idea—that black people are able to do things themselves. Only they can help create in the community an aroused and continuing black consciousness that will provide the basis for political strength. In the past, white allies have often furthered white supremacy without the whites involved realizing it, or even wanting to do so. Black people must come together and do things for themselves. They must achieve self-identity and self-determination in order to have their daily needs met.

Black Power means, for example, that in Lowndes County, Alabama, a black sheriff can end police brutality. A black tax assessor and tax collector and county board of revenue can lay, collect, and channel tax monies for the building of better roads and schools serving black people. In such areas as Lowndes, where black people have a majority, they will attempt to use power to exercise control. This is what they seek: control. When black people lack a majority, Black Power means proper representation and sharing of control. It means the creation of power bases, of strength, from which black people can press to change local or nation-wide patterns of oppression—instead of from weakness.

It does not mean *merely* putting black faces into office. Black visibility is not Black Power. Most of the black politicians around the country today are not examples of Black Power. The power must be that of a community, and emanate from there. The black politicians must start from there. The black politicians must stop being representatives of "downtown" machines, whatever the cost might be in terms of lost patronage and holiday handouts.

Black Power recognizes—it must recognize—the ethnic basis of American politics as well as the power-oriented nature of American politics. Black Power therefore calls for black people to consolidate behind their own, so that they can bargain from a position of strength. But while we endorse the *procedure* of group solidarity and identity for the purpose of attaining certain goals in the body politic, this does not mean that black people should strive for the same kind of rewards (i.e., end results) obtained by the white society. The ultimate values and goals are not domination or exploitation of other groups, but rather an effective share in the total power of the society.

Nevertheless, some observers have labeled those who advocate Black Power as racists; they have said that the call for self-identification and self-determination is "racism in reverse" or "black supremacy." This is a deliberate and absurd lie. There is no analogy—by any stretch of definition or imagination—between the advocates of Black Power and white racists. Racism is not merely exclusion on the basis of race but exclusion for the purpose of subjugating or maintaining subjugation. The goal of the racists is to keep black people on the bottom, arbitrarily and dictatorially, as they have done in this country for over three hundred years. The goal of black self-determination and black self-identity—Black Power—is full participation in the decision-making processes affecting the lives of black people, and recognition of the virtues in themselves as black people. The black people of this country have not lynched whites, bombed their churches, murdered their children and manipulated laws and institutions to maintain oppression. White racists have. Congressional laws, one after the other, have not been necessary to stop black people from oppressing others and denying others the full enjoyment of their rights. White racists have made such laws necessary. The goal of Black Power is positive and functional to a free and viable society. No white racist can make this claim.

A great deal of public attention and press space was devoted to the hysterical accusation of "black racism" when the call for Black Power was first sounded. A national committee of influential black churchmen affiliated with the National Council of Churches, despite their obvious respectability and responsibility, had to resort to a paid advertisement to articulate their position, while anyone yapping "black racism" made front-page news. In their statement, published in the *New York Times* of July 31, 1966, the churchmen said:

> We, an informal group of Negro churchmen in America, are deeply disturbed about the crisis brought upon our country by historic distortions of important human realities in the controversy about "black power." What we see shining through the variety of rhetoric

is not anything new but the same old problem of power and race which has faced our beloved country since 1619.

. . . The conscience of black men is corrupted because having no power to implement the demands of conscience, the concern for justice in the absence of justice becomes a chaotic self-surrender. Powerlessness breeds a race of beggars. We are faced with a situation where powerless conscience meets conscienceless power, threatening the very foundations of our Nation.

We deplore the overt violence of riots, but we feel it is more important to focus on the real sources of these eruptions. These sources may be abetted inside the Ghetto, but their basic cause lies in the silent and covert violence which white middle class America inflicts upon the victims of the inner city.

. . . In short, the failure of American leaders to use American power to create equal opportunity *in life* as well as *law*, this is the real problem and not the anguished cry for black power.

. . . Without the capacity to participate with power, i.e., to have some organized political and economic strength to really influence people with whom one interacts, integration is not meaningful.

. . . America has asked its Negro citizens to fight for opportunity as *individuals*, whereas at certain points in our history what we have needed most has been opportunity for the *whole group*, not just for selected and approved Negroes.

. . . We must not apologize for the existence of this form of group power, for we have been oppressed as a group and not as individuals. We will not find our way out of that oppression until both we and America accept the need for Negro Americans, as well as for Jews, Italians, Poles, and white Anglo-Saxon Protestants, among others, to have and to wield group power.

It is a commentary on the fundamentally racist nature of this society that the concept of group strength for black people must be articulated—not to mention defended. No other group would submit to being led by others. Italians do not run the Anti-Defamation League of B'nai B'rith. Irish do not chair Christopher Columbus Societies. Yet when black people call for black-run and all-black organizations, they are immediately classed in a category with the Ku Klux Klan. This is interesting and ironic, but by no means surprising: the society does not expect black people to be able to take care of their business, and there are many who prefer it precisely that way.

In the end, we cannot and shall not offer any guarantees that Black Power, if achieved, would be non-racist. No one can predict human behavior. Social change always has unanticipated consequences. If black racism is what the larger society fears, we cannot help them. We can only state what we hope will be the result, given the fact that the present situation is unacceptable and that we have no real alternative but to work for Black Power. The final truth is that the white society is not entitled to reassurances, even if it were possible to offer them.

We have outlined the meaning and goals of Black Power; we have also discussed one major thing which it is not. There are others of greater importance. The advocates of Black Power reject the old slogans and meaningless rhetoric of previous years in the civil rights struggle. The language of yesterday is indeed irrelevant: progress, non-violence, integration, fear of "white backlash," coalition. Let us look at the rhetoric and see why these terms must be set aside or redefined.

One of the tragedies of the struggle against racism is that up to this point there has been no national organization which could speak to the growing militancy of young black people in the urban ghettos and the black-belt South. There has been only a "civil rights" movement, whose tone of voice was adapted to an audience of middle-class whites. It served as a sort of buffer zone between that audience and angry young blacks. It claimed to speak for the needs of a community, but it did not speak in the tone of that community. None of its so-called leaders could go into a rioting community and be listened to. In a sense, the blame must be shared—along with the mass media—by those leaders for what happened in Watts, Harlem, Chicago, Cleveland and other places. Each time the black people in those cities saw Dr. Martin Luther King get slapped they became angry. When they saw little black girls bombed to death *in a church* and civil rights workers ambushed and murdered, they were angrier; and when nothing happened, they were steaming mad. We had nothing to offer that they could see, except to go out and be beaten again. We helped to build their frustration.

We had only the old language of love and suffering. And in most places—that is, from the liberals and middle class—we got back the old language of patience and progress. The civil rights leaders were saying to the country: "Look, you guys are supposed to be nice guys, and we are only going to do what we are supposed to do. Why do you beat us up? Why don't you give us what we ask? Why don't you straighten yourselves out?" For the masses of black people, this language resulted in virtually nothing. In fact, their objective day-to-day condition worsened. The unemployment rate among black people increased while that among whites declined. Housing conditions in the black communities deteriorated. Schools in the black ghettos continued to plod along on outmoded techniques, inadequate curricula, and with all too many tired and indifferent teachers. Meanwhile, the President picked up the refrain of "We Shall Overcome" while the Congress passed civil rights law after civil rights law, only to have them effectively nullified by deliberately weak enforcement. "Progress is being made," we were told.

Such language, along with admonitions to remain non-violent and fear the white backlash, convinced some that that course was the *only* course to follow. It misled some into believing that a black minority could bow its head and get whipped into a meaningful position of power. The very notion is absurd. The white society devised the language, adopted the rules and had the black community narcotized into believing that that language and those rules were, in fact, relevant. The black community was told time and again how *other* immigrants finally won *acceptance*: that is, by following the Protestant Ethic of Work and Achievement. They worked hard; therefore, they achieved. We were not told that it was by building Irish Power, Italian Power, Polish Power or Jewish Power that these groups got themselves together and operated from positions of strength. We were not told that "the American dream" wasn't designed for black people. That while today, to whites, the dream may *seem* to include black people, it cannot do so by the very nature of this nation's political and economic system, which imposes institutional racism on the black masses if not upon every individual black. A notable comment on that "dream" was made by Dr. Percy Julian, the black scientist and director of the Julian Research Institute in Chicago, a man for whom the dream seems to have come true. While not subscribing to "black power" as he understood it, Dr. Julian clearly understood the basis for it: "The false concept of basic Negro inferiority is one of the curses that still lingers. It is a problem created by the white man. Our children just no longer are going to accept the patience we were taught by our generation. We were taught a pretty little lie—excel and the whole world lies open before you. *I obeyed the injunction and found it to be wishful thinking.*" (Authors' italics)[2]

A key phrase in our buffer-zone days was non-violence. For years it has been thought that black people would not literally fight for their lives. Why this has been so is not entirely clear; neither the larger society nor black people are noted for passivity. The notion apparently stems from the years of marches and demonstrations and sit-ins where black people did not strike back and the violence always came from white mobs. There are many who still sincerely believe in that approach. From our viewpoint, rampaging white mobs and white night-riders must be made to understand that their days of free head-whipping are over. Black people should and must fight back. Nothing more quickly repels someone bent on destroying you than the unequivocal message: "O.K., fool, make your move, and run the same risk I run—of dying."

When the concept of Black Power is set forth, many people immediately conjure up notions of violence. The country's reaction to the Deacons for Defense and Justice, which originated in Louisiana, is instructive. Here is a group which realized that the "law" and law enforcement agencies would not protect people, so they had to do it themselves. If a nation fails to protect its citizens, then that nation cannot condemn those who take up the task themselves. The Deacons and all other blacks who resort to self-defense represent a simple answer to a simple question: what man would not defend his family and home from attack?

But this frightened some white people, because they knew that

2. *The New York Times* (April 30, 1967), p. 30.

black people would now fight back. They knew that this was precisely what *they* would have long since done if *they* were subjected to the injustices and oppression heaped on blacks. Those
of us who advocate Black Power are quite clear in our own minds
that a "non-violent" approach to civil rights is an approach black
people cannot afford and a luxury white people do not deserve. It
is crystal clear to us—and it must become so with the white
society—*that there can be no social order without social justice.*
White people must be made to understand that they must stop
messing with black people, or the blacks *will* fight back!

Next, we must deal with the term "integration." According to
its advocates, social justice will be accomplished by "integrating
the Negro into the mainstream institutions of the society from
which he has been traditionally excluded." This concept is based
on the assumption that there is nothing of value in the black
community and that little of value could be created among black
people. The thing to do is siphon off the "acceptable" black people
into the surrounding middle-class white community.

The goals of integrationists are middle-class goals, articulated
primarily by a small group of Negroes with middle-class aspirations or status. Their kind of integration has meant that a few
blacks "make it," leaving the black community, sapping it of
leadership potential and know-how. As we noted in Chapter I,
those token Negroes—absorbed into a white mass—are of no value
to the remaining black masses. They become meaningless show-
pieces for a conscience-soothed white society. Such people will
state that they would prefer to be treated "only as individuals,
not as Negroes"; that they "are not and should not be preoccupied
with race." This is a totally unrealistic position. In the first place,
black people have not suffered as individuals but as members of a
group; therefore, their liberation lies in group action. This is why
SNCC—and the concept of Black Power—affirms that helping
individual black people to solve their problems on an *individual*
basis does little to alleviate the mass of black people. Secondly,
while color blindness *may* be a sound goal ultimately, we must
realize that race is an overwhelming fact of life in this historical
period. There is no black man in this country who can live "simply
as a man." His blackness is an ever-present fact of this racist

society, whether he recognizes it or not. It is unlikely that this or the next generation will witness the time when race will no longer be relevant in the conduct of public affairs and in public policy decision-making. To realize this and to attempt to deal with it does not make one a racist or overly preoccupied with race; it puts one in the forefront of a significant *struggle*. If there is no intense struggle today, there will be no meaningful results tomorrow.

"Integration" as a goal today speaks to the problem of blackness not only in an unrealistic way but also in a despicable way. It is based on complete acceptance of the fact that in order to have a decent house or education, black people must move into a white neighborhood or send their children to a white school. This reinforces, among both black and white, the idea that "white" is automatically superior and "black" is by definition inferior. For this reason, "integration" is a subterfuge for the maintenance of white supremacy. It allows the nation to focus on a handful of Southern black children who get into white schools at a great price, and to ignore the ninety-four percent who are left in unimproved all-black schools. Such situations will not change until black people become equal in a way that means something, and integration ceases to be a one-way street. Then integration does not mean draining skills and energies from the black ghetto into white neighborhoods. To sprinkle black children among white pupils in outlying schools is at best a stop-gap measure. The goal is not to take black children out of the black community and expose them to white middle-class values; the goal is to build and strengthen the black community.

"Integration" also means that black people must give up their identity, deny their heritage. We recall the conclusion of Killian and Grigg: "At the present time, integration as a solution to the race problem demands that the Negro foreswear his identity as a Negro." The fact is that integration, as traditionally articulated, would abolish the black community. The fact is that what must be abolished is not the black community, but the dependent colonial status that has been inflicted upon it.

The racial and cultural personality of the black community must be preserved and that community must win its freedom while preserving its cultural integrity. Integrity includes a pride—in the sense of self-acceptance, not chauvinism—in being black, in the historical attainments and contributions of black people. No person can be healthy, complete and mature if he must deny a part of himself; this is what "integration" has required thus far. This is the essential difference between integration as it is currently practiced and the concept of Black Power.

The idea of cultural integrity is so obvious that it seems almost simple-minded to spell things out at this length. Yet millions of Americans resist such truths when they are applied to black people. Again, that resistance is a comment on the fundamental racism in the society. Irish Catholics took care of their own first without a lot of apology for doing so, without any dubious language from timid leadership about guarding against "backlash." Everyone understood it to be a perfectly legitimate procedure. Of course, there would be "backlash." Organization begets counter-organization, but this was no reason to defer.

The so-called white backlash against black people is something else: the embedded traditions of institutional racism being brought into the open and calling forth overt manifestations of individual racism. In the summer of 1966, when the protest marches into Cicero, Illinois, began, the black people knew they were not allowed to live in Cicero and the white people knew it. When blacks began to demand the right to live in homes in that town, the white simply reminded them of the status quo. Some people called this "backlash." It was, in fact, racism defending itself. In the black community, this is called "White folks showing their color." It is ludicrous to blame black people for what is simply an overt manifestation of white racism. Dr. Martin Luther King stated clearly that the protest marches were not the cause of the racism but merely exposed a long-term cancerous condition in the society.

Eldridge Cleaver

That is why I started to write. To save myself.

The current author of significance in the tradition of black militancy is Eldridge Cleaver. His books, *Soul on Ice* (1968) and *Eldridge Cleaver* (1969), which are collections of essays first published in *Ramparts, Esquire,* and other magazines, achieve their particular authority through their intimate candor. Like Jean Genêt, the French dramatist who has influenced him, Cleaver is his own creation, a man whose writings cannot be divorced from his life.

Born in Little Rock, Arkansas, in 1935, Cleaver grew up in the Negro ghetto of Los Angeles. He has spent time at San Quentin, Folsom, and Soledad prisons for reasons ranging from rape to theft. He has also been the Minister of Information for the Black Panther Party and its nominee for President of the United States in 1968.

"The heroes aren't Timothy Leary and Allen Ginsberg anymore," Jeff Shero, the editor of a New York underground paper, claims; "they're Che Guevara and Eldridge Cleaver." If this statement is even partially true, the following essay suggests why. Cleaver's argument is a good example of how traditional heroes of America can be seen in a revealing way—when the perspective is that of an American, a native son, who feels no kinship whatsoever with that American tradition.

White people cannot, in the generality, be taken as models

of how to live. Rather, the white man is himself in sore need

of new standards, which will release him from his confusion and place

him once again in fruitful communion with the depths

of his own being.

—JAMES BALDWIN, The Fire Next Time

The White Race
and Its Heroes

ELDRIDGE

CLEAVER

RIGHT FROM THE GO, let me make one thing absolutely clear: I am not now, nor have I ever been, a white man. Nor, I hasten to add, am I now a Black Muslim—although I used to be. But I *am* an Ofay Watcher, a member of that unchartered, amorphous league which has members on all continents and the islands of the seas. Ofay Watchers Anonymous, we might be called, because we exist concealed in the shadows wherever colored people have known oppression by whites, by white enslavers, colonizers, imperialists, and neo-colonialists.

Did it irritate you, compatriot, for me to string those epithets out like that? Tolerate me. My intention was not necessarily to sprinkle salt over anyone's wounds. I did it primarily to relieve a certain pressure on my brain. Do you cop that? If not, then we're in trouble, because we Ofay Watchers have a pronounced tendency to slip into that mood. If it is bothersome to you, it is quite a task for me because not too long ago it was my way of life to

REPRINTED FROM *Soul on Ice* BY ELDRIDGE CLEAVER. COPYRIGHT © 1968 BY ELDRIDGE CLEAVER. USED BY PERMISSION OF MCGRAW-HILL BOOK COMPANY.

preach, as ardently as I could, that the white race is a race of devils, created by their maker to do evil, and make evil appear as good; that the white race is the natural, unchangeable enemy of the black man, who is the original man, owner, maker, cream of the planet Earth; that the white race was soon to be destroyed by Allah, and that the black man would then inherit the earth, which has always, in fact, been his.

I have, so to speak, washed my hands in the blood of the martyr, Malcolm X, whose retreat from the precipice of madness created new room for others to turn about in, and I am now caught up in that tiny space, attempting a maneuver of my own. Having renounced the teachings of Elijah Muhammad, I find that a rebirth does not follow automatically, of its own accord, that a void is left in one's vision, and this void seeks constantly to obliterate itself by pulling one back to one's former outlook. I have tried a tentative compromise by adopting a select vocabulary, so that now when I see the whites of *their* eyes, instead of saying "devil" or "beast" I say "imperialist" or "colonialist," and everyone seems to be happier.

In silence, we have spent our years watching the ofays, trying to understand them, on the principle that you have a better chance coping with the known than with the unknown. Some of us have been, and some still are, interested in learning whether it is *ultimately* possible to live in the same territory with people who seem so disagreeable to live with; still others want to get as far away from ofays as possible. What we share in common is the desire to break the ofays' power over us.

At times of fundamental social change, such as the era in which we live, it is easy to be deceived by the onrush of events, beguiled by the craving for social stability into mistaking transitory phenomena for enduring reality. The strength and permanence of "white backlash" in America is just such an illusion. However much this rear-guard action might seem to grow in strength, the initiative, and the future, rest with those whites and blacks who have liberated themselves from the master/slave syndrome. And these are to be found mainly among the youth.

Over the past twelve years there has surfaced a political conflict between the generations that is deeper, even, than the struggle between the races. Its first dramatic manifestation was within the ranks of the Negro people, when college students in the South, fed up with Uncle Tom's hat-in-hand approach to revolution, threw off the yoke of the NAACP. When these students initiated the first sit-ins, their spirit spread like a raging fire across the nation, and the technique of non-violent direct action, constantly refined and honed into a sharp cutting tool, swiftly matured. The older Negro "leaders," who are now all die-hard advocates of this tactic, scolded the students for sitting-in. The students rained down contempt upon their hoary heads. In the pre-sit-in days, these conservative leaders had always succeeded in putting down insurgent elements among the Negro people. (A measure of their power, prior to the students' rebellion, is shown by their success in isolating such great black men as the late W. E. B. DuBois and Paul Robeson, when these stalwarts, refusing to bite their tongues, lost favor with the U.S. government by their unstinting efforts to link up the Negro revolution with national liberation movements around the world.)

The "Negro leaders," and the whites who depended upon them to control their people, were outraged by the impudence of the students. Calling for a moratorium on student initiative, they were greeted instead by an encore of sit-ins, and retired to their ivory towers to contemplate the new phenomenon. Others, less prudent because held on a tighter leash by the whites, had their careers brought to an abrupt end because they thought they could lead a black/white backlash against the students, only to find themselves in a kind of Bay of Pigs. Negro college presidents, who expelled students from all-Negro colleges in an attempt to quash the demonstrations, ended up losing their jobs; the victorious students would no longer allow them to preside over the campuses. The spontaneous protests on southern campuses over the repressive measures of their college administrations were an earnest of the Free Speech upheaval which years later was to shake the UC campus at Berkeley. In countless ways, the rebellion of the black students served as catalyst for the brewing revolt of the whites.

What has suddenly happened is that the white race has lost its heroes. Worse, its heroes have been revealed as villains and its greatest heroes as the arch-villains. The new generations of whites, appalled by the sanguine and despicable record carved over the face of the globe by their race in the last five hundred years, are rejecting the panoply of white heroes, whose heroism consisted in erecting the inglorious edifice of colonialism and imperialism; heroes whose careers rested on a system of foreign and domestic exploitation, rooted in the myth of white supremacy and the manifest destiny of the white race. The emerging shape of a new world order, and the requisites for survival in such a world, are fostering in young whites a new outlook. They recoil in shame from the spectacle of cowboys and pioneers—their heroic fore-fathers whose exploits filled earlier generations with pride—galloping across a movie screen shooting down Indians like Coke bottles. Even Winston Churchill, who is looked upon by older whites as perhaps the greatest hero of the twentieth century—even he, because of the system of which he was a creature and which he served, is an arch-villain in the eyes of the young white rebels.

At the close of World War Two, national liberation movements in the colonized world picked up new momentum and audacity, seeking to cash in on the democratic promises made by the Allies during the war. The Atlantic Charter, signed by President Roosevelt and Prime Minister Churchill in 1941, affirming "the right of all people to choose the form of government under which they may live," established the principle, although it took years of postwar struggle to give this piece of rhetoric even the appearance of reality. And just as world revolution has prompted the oppressed to re-evaluate their self-image in terms of the changing conditions, to slough off the servile attitudes inculcated by long years of subordination, the same dynamics of change have prompted the white people of the world to re-evaluate their self-image as well, to disabuse themselves of the Master Race psychology developed over centuries of imperial hegemony.

It is among the white youth of the world that the greatest change is taking place. It is they who are experiencing the great psychic pain of waking into consciousness to find their inherited heroes turned by events into villains. Communication and understanding between the older and younger generations of whites has entered a crisis. The elders, who, in the tradition of privileged classes or races, genuinely do not understand the youth, trapped by old ways of thinking and blind to the future, have only just begun to be vexed—because the youth have only just begun to rebel. So thoroughgoing is the revolution in the psyches of white youth that the traditional tolerance which every older generation has found it necessary to display is quickly exhausted, leaving a gulf of fear, hostility, mutual misunderstanding, and contempt.

The rebellion of the oppressed peoples of the world, along with the Negro revolution in America, have opened the way to a new evaluation of history, a re-examination of the role played by the white race since the beginning of European expansion. The positive achievements are also there in the record, and future generations will applaud them. But there can be no applause now, not while the master still holds the whip in his hand! Not even the master's own children can find it possible to applaud him—he cannot even applaud himself! The negative rings too loudly. Slave-catchers, slave owners, murderers, butchers, invaders, oppressors—the white heroes have acquired new names. The great white statesmen whom school children are taught to revere are revealed as the architects of systems of human exploitation and slavery. Religious leaders are exposed as condoners and justifiers of all these evil deeds. Schoolteachers and college professors are seen as a clique of brainwashers and whitewashers.

The white youth of today are coming to see, intuitively, that to escape the onus of the history their fathers made they must face and admit the moral truth concerning the works of their fathers. That such venerated figures as George Washington and Thomas Jefferson owned hundreds of black slaves, that all of the Presidents up to Lincoln presided over a slave state, and that every President since Lincoln connived politically and cynically with the issues affecting the human rights and general welfare of the broad masses of the American people—these facts weigh heavily upon the hearts of these young people.

The elders do not like to give these youngsters credit for being able to understand what is going on and what has gone on. When speaking of juvenile delinquency, or the rebellious attitude of to-day's youth, the elders employ a glib rhetoric. They speak of the "alienation of youth," the desire of the young to be independent,

the problems of "the father image" and "the mother image" and
their effect upon growing children who lack sound models upon
which to pattern themselves. But they consider it bad form to
connect the problems of the youth with the central event of our
era—the national liberation movements abroad and the Negro
revolution at home. The foundations of authority have been blasted
to bits in America because the whole society has been indicted,
tried, and convicted of injustice. To the youth, the elders are Ugly
Americans; to the elders, the youth have gone mad.

The rebellion of the white youth has gone through four
broadly discernible stages. First there was an initial recoiling away,
a rejection of the conformity which America expected, and had always received sooner or later, from its youth. The disaffected
youth were refusing to participate in the system, having discovered
that America, far from helping the underdog, was up to its ears
in the mud trying to hold the dog down. Because of the publicity
and self-advertisements of the more vocal rebels, this period has
come to be known as the beatnik era, although not all of the
youth affected by these changes thought of themselves as beatniks.
The howl of the beatniks and their scathing, outraged denunciation of the system—characterized by Ginsberg as Moloch, a
bloodthirsty Semitic deity to which the ancient tribes sacrificed
their firstborn children—was a serious, irrevocable declaration of
war. It is revealing that the elders looked upon the beatniks as
mere obscene misfits who were too lazy to take baths and too
stingy to buy a haircut. The elders had eyes but couldn't see, ears
but couldn't hear—not even when the message came through as
clearly as in this remarkable passage from Jack Kerouac's *On
the Road:*

At lilac evening I walked with every muscle aching among the
lights of 27th and Welton in the Denver colored section, wishing I
were a Negro, feeling that the best the white world had offered was
not enough ecstasy for me, not enough life, joy, kicks, darkness, music,
not enough night. I wished I were a Denver Mexican, or even a poor
overworkd Jap, anything but what I so drearily was, a "white man"
disillusioned. All my life I'd had white ambitions. . . . I passed the
dark porches of Mexican and Negro homes; soft voices were there,

occasionally the dusky knee of some mysterious sensuous gal; the dark faces of the men behind rose arbors. Little children sat like sages in ancient rocking chairs.

The second stage arrived when these young people, having decided emphatically that 'the world, and particularly the U.S.A., was unacceptable to them in its present form, began an active search for roles they could play in changing the society. If many of these young people were content to lay up in their cool beat pads, smoking pot and listening to jazz in a perpetual orgy of esoteric bliss, there were others, less crushed by the system, who recognized the need for positive action. Moloch could not ask for anything more than to have its disaffected victims withdraw into safe, passive, apolitical little nonparticipatory islands, in an economy less and less able to provide jobs for the growing pool of unemployed. If all the unemployed had followed the lead of the beatniks, Moloch would gladly have legalized the use of euphoric drugs and marijuana, passed out free jazz albums and sleeping bags, to all those willing to sign affidavits promising to remain "beat." The non-beat disenchanted white youth were attracted magnetically to the Negro revolution, which had begun to take on a mass, insurrectionary tone. But they had difficulty understanding their relationship to the Negro, and what role "whites" could play in a "Negro revolution." For the time being they watched the Negro activities from afar.

The third stage, which is rapidly drawing to a close, emerged when white youth started joining Negro demonstrations in large numbers. The presence of whites among the demonstrators emboldened the Negro leaders and allowed them to use tactics they never would have been able to employ with all-black troops. The racist conscience of America is such that murder does not register as murder, really, unless the victim is white. And it was only when the newspapers and magazines started carrying pictures and stories of white demonstrators being beaten and maimed by mobs and police that the public began to protest. Negroes have become so used to this double standard that they, too, react differently to the death of a white. When white freedom riders were brutalized along with blacks, a sigh of relief went up from the black masses, because the blacks knew that white blood is the coin of freedom in a land where for four hundred years black blood has been shed unremarked and with impunity. America has never truly been outraged by the murder of a black man, woman, or child. White politicians may, if Negroes are aroused by a particular murder, say with their lips what they know with their minds they should feel with their hearts—but don't.

It is a measure of what the Negro feels that when the two white and one black civil rights workers were murdered in Mississippi in 1964, the event was welcomed by Negroes on a level of understanding beyond and deeper than the grief they felt for the victims and their families. This welcoming of violence and death to whites can almost be heard—indeed it can be heard—in the inevitable words, oft repeated by Negroes, that those whites, and blacks, do not die in vain. So it was with Mrs. Viola Liuzzo. And much of the anger which Negroes felt toward Martin Luther King during the Battle of Selma stemmed from the fact that he denied history a great moment, never to be recaptured, when he turned tail on the Edmund Pettus Bridge and refused to all those whites behind him what they had traveled thousands of miles to receive. If the police had turned them back by force, all those nuns, priests, rabbis, preachers, and distinguished ladies and gentlemen old and young—as they had done the Negroes a week earlier—the violence and brutality of the system would have been ruthlessly exposed. Or if, seeing King determined to lead them on to Montgomery, the troopers had stepped aside to avoid precisely the confrontation that Washington would not have tolerated, it would have signaled the capitulation of the militant white South. As it turned out, the March on Montgomery was a show of somewhat dim luster, stage-managed by the Establishment. But by this time the young whites were already active participants in the Negro revolution. In fact they had begun to transform it into something broader, with the potential of encompassing the whole of America in a radical reordering of society.

The fourth stage, now in its infancy, sees these white youth taking the initiative, using techniques learned in the Negro struggle to attack problems in the general society. The classic example of this new energy in action was the student battle on the UC campus at Berkeley, California—the Free Speech Movement. Leading the revolt were veterans of the civil rights movement, some of whom spent time on the firing line in the wilderness of Mississippi/Alabama. Flowing from the same momentum were student demonstrations against U.S. interference in the internal affairs of Vietnam, Cuba, the Dominican Republic, and the Congo and U.S. aid to apartheid in South Africa. The students even aroused the intellectual community to actions and positions unthinkable a few years ago: witness the teach-ins. But their revolt is deeper than single-issue protest. The characteristics of the white rebels which most alarm their elders—the long hair, the new dances, their love for Negro music, their use of marijuana, their mystical attitude toward sex—are all tools of their rebellion. They have turned these tools against the totalitarian fabric of American society—and they mean to change it.

From the beginning, America has been a schizophrenic nation. Its two conflicting images of itself were never reconciled because never before has the survival of its most cherished myths made a reconciliation mandatory. Once before, during the bitter struggle between North and South climaxed by the Civil War, the two images of America came into conflict, although whites North and South scarcely understood it. The image of America held by its most alienated citizens was advanced neither by the North nor by the South; it was perhaps best expressed by Frederick Douglass, who was born into slavery in 1817, escaped to the North, and became the greatest leader-spokesman for the blacks of his era. In words that can still, years later, arouse an audience of black Americans, Frederick Douglass delivered, in 1852, a scorching indictment in his Fourth of July oration in Rochester:

What to the American slave is your Fourth of July? I answer: a day that reveals to him, more than all other days in the year, the gross injustice and cruelty to which he is the constant victim. To him your celebration is a sham; your boasted liberty, an unholy licence; your national greatness, swelling vanity; your sounds of rejoicing are empty and heartless; your denunciation of tyrants, brass-fronted impudence; your shouts of liberty and equality, hollow mockery; your prayers and hymns, your sermons and thanksgivings, with all your religious parade and solemnity are, to him, more bombast, fraud, deception, impiety and hypocrisy—a thin veil to cover up crimes which would disgrace a nation of savages. . . .

You boasted of your love of liberty, your superior civilization, and your pure Christianity, while the whole political power of the nation (as embodied in the two great political parties) is solemnly pledged to support and perpetuate the enslavement of three millions of your countrymen. You hurl your anathemas at the crown-headed tyrants of Russia and Austria and pride yourselves on your democratic institutions, while you yourselves consent to be the mere *tools* and *bodyguards* of the tyrants of Virginia and Carolina.

You invite to your shores fugitives of oppression from abroad, honor them with banquets, greet them with ovations, cheer them, toast them, salute them, protect them, and pour out your money to them like water; but the fugitive from your own land you advertise, hunt, arrest, shoot, and kill. You glory in your refinement and your universal education; yet you maintain a system as barbarous and dreadful as ever stained the character of a nation—a system begun in avarice, supported in pride, and perpetuated in cruelty.

You shed tears over fallen Hungary, and make the sad story of her wrongs the theme of your poets, statesmen and orators, till your gallant sons are ready to fly to arms to vindicate her cause against the oppressor; but, in regard to the ten thousand wrongs of the American slave, you would enforce the strictest silence, and would hail him as an enemy of the nation who dares to make these wrongs the subject of public discourse!

This most alienated view of America was preached by the Abolitionists, and by Harriet Beecher Stowe in her *Uncle Tom's Cabin*. But such a view of America was too distasteful to receive wide attention, and serious debate about America's image and her reality was engaged in only on the fringes of society. Even when confronted with overwhelming evidence to the contrary, most white Americans have found it possible, after steadying their rattled nerves, to settle comfortably back into their vaunted belief that America is dedicated to the proposition that all men are created equal and endowed by their Creator with certain inalienable rights—life, liberty and the pursuit of happiness. With the Constitution for a rudder and the Declaration of Independence as its guiding star, the ship of state is sailing always toward a brighter vision of freedom and justice for all.

Because there is no common ground between these two contradictory images of America, they had to be kept apart. But the moment the blacks were let into the white world—let out of the voiceless and faceless cages of their ghettos, singing, walking, talking, dancing, writing, and orating *their* image of America and of Americans—the white world was suddenly challenged to match its practice to its preachments. And this is why those whites who abandon the *white* image of America and adopt the *black* are greeted with such unmitigated hostility by their elders.

For all these years whites have been taught to believe in the myth they preached, while Negroes have had to face the bitter reality of what America practiced. But without the lies and distortions, white Americans would not have been able to do the things they have done. When whites are forced to look honestly upon the objective proof of their deeds, the cement of mendacity holding white society together swiftly disintegrates. On the other hand, the core of the black world's vision remains intact, and in fact begins to expand and spread into the psychological territory vacated by the non-viable white lies, i.e., into the minds of young whites. It is remarkable how the system worked for so many years, how the majority of whites remained effectively unaware of any contradiction between their view of the world and that world itself. The mechanism by which this was rendered possible requires examination at this point.

Let us recall that the white man, in order to justify slavery and, later on, to justify segregation, elaborated a complex, all-pervasive myth which at one time classified the black man as a subhuman beast of burden. The myth was progressively modified, gradually elevating the blacks on the scale of evolution, following their slowly changing status, until the plateau of separate-but-equal was reached at the close of the nineteenth century. During slavery, the black was seen as a mindless Supermasculine Menial. Forced to do the backbreaking work, he was conceived in terms of his ability to do such work—"field niggers," etc. The white man administered the plantation, doing all the thinking, exercising omnipotent power over the slaves. He had little difficulty dissociating himself from the black slaves, and he could not conceive of their positions being reversed or even reversible.

Blacks and whites being conceived as mutually exclusive types, those attributes imputed to the blacks could not also be imputed to the whites—at least not in equal degree—without blurring the line separating the races. These images were based upon the social function of the two races, the work they performed. The ideal white man was one who knew how to use his head, who knew how to manage and control things and get things done. Those whites who were not in a position to perform these functions nevertheless aspired to them. The ideal black man was one who did exactly as he was told, and did it efficiently and cheerfully. "Slaves," said Frederick Douglass, "are generally expected to sing as well as to work." As the black man's position and function became more varied, the images of white and black, having become stereotypes, lagged behind.

The separate-but-equal doctrine was promulgated by the Supreme Court in 1896. It had the same purpose domestically as the Open Door Policy toward China in the international arena: to stabilize a situation and subordinate a non-white population so that racist exploiters could manipulate those people according to their own selfish interests. These doctrines were foisted off as *the epitome of enlightened justice, the highest expression of morality.* Sanctified by religion, justified by philosophy and legalized by the Supreme Court, separate-but-equal was enforced by day by agencies of the law, and by the KKK & Co. under cover of night. Booker T. Washington, the Martin Luther King of his day, accepted separate-but-equal in the name of all Negroes. W. E. B. DuBois denounced it.

Separate-but-equal marked the last stage of the white man's flight into cultural neurosis, and the beginning of the black man's frantic striving to assert his humanity and equalize his position with the white. Blacks ventured into all fields of endeavor to which they could gain entrance. Their goal was to present in all fields a performance that would equal or surpass that of the whites. It was long axiomatic among blacks that a black had to be twice as competent as a white in any field in order to win grudging recognition from the whites. This produced a pathological motivation in the blacks to equal or surpass the whites, and a pathological motivation in the whites to maintain a distance from the blacks. This is the rack on which black and white Americans receive their delicious torture! At first there was the color bar, flatly denying the blacks entrance to certain spheres of activity. When this no longer worked, and blacks invaded sector after sector of American life and economy, the whites evolved other methods of keeping their distance. The illusion of the Negro's inferior nature had to be maintained.

One device evolved by the whites was to tab whatever the blacks did with the prefix "Negro." We had *Negro* literature, *Negro* athletes, *Negro* music, *Negro* doctors, *Negro* politicians, *Negro* workers. The malignant ingeniousness of this device is that although it accurately describes an objective biological fact—or, at least, a sociological fact in America—it concealed the paramount psychological fact: that to the white mind, prefixing anything with "Negro" automatically consigned it to an inferior category. A well-known example of the white necessity to deny due credit to blacks is in the realm of music. White musicians were famous for going to Harlem and other Negro cultural centers literally to steal the black man's music, carrying it back across the color line into the Great White World and passing off the watered-down loot as their own original creations. Blacks, meanwhile, were ridiculed as *Negro* musicians playing inferior coon music.

The Negro revolution at home and national liberation movements abroad have unceremoniously shattered the world of fantasy in which the whites have been living. It is painful that many do not yet see that their fantasy world has been rendered uninhabitable in the last half of the twentieth century. But it is away from this world that the white youth of today are turning. The "paper tiger" hero, James Bond, offering the whites a triumphant image of themselves, is saying what many whites want desperately to

hear reaffirmed: *I am still the White Man, lord of the land, licensed to kill, and the world is still an empire at my feet.* James
Bond feeds on that secret little anxiety, the psychological white
backlash, felt in some degree by most whites alive. It is exasperating to see little brown men and little yellow men from the
mysterious Orient, and the opaque black men of Africa (to say
nothing of these impudent American Negroes!) who come to the
UN and talk smart to us, who are scurrying all over *our* globe in
their strange modes of dress—much as if they were new, unpleasant arrivals from another planet. Many whites believe in their
ulcers that it is only a matter of time before the Marines get the
signal to round up these truants and put them back securely in
their cages. But it is away from this fantasy world that the white
youth of today are turning.

In the world revolution now under way, the initiative rests
with people of color. That growing numbers of white youth are
repudiating their heritage of blood and taking people of color as
their heroes and models is a tribute not only to their insight but
to the resilience of the human spirit. For today the heroes of the
initiative are people not usually thought of as white: Fidel Castro,
Che Guevara, Kwame Nkrumah, Mao Tse-tung, Gamal Abdel
Nasser, Robert F. Williams, Malcolm X, Ben Bella, John Lewis,
Martin Luther King, Jr., Robert Parris Moses, Ho Chi Minh,
Stokeley Carmichael, W. E. B. DuBois, James Forman, Chou
En-lai.

The white youth of today have begun to react to the fact
that the "American Way of Life" is a fossil of history. What do
they care if their old baldheaded and crew-cut elders don't dig
their caveman mops? They couldn't care less about the old,
stiffassed honkies who don't like their new dances: Frug, Monkey,
Jerk, Swim, Watusi. All they know is that it feels good to swing
to way-out body-rhythms instead of dragassing across the dance
floor like zombies to the dead beat of mind-smothered Mickey
Mouse music. Is it any wonder that the youth have lost all
respect for their elders, for law and order, when for as long as
they can remember all they've witnessed is a monumental bicker-
ing over the Negro's place in American society and the right of

people around the world to be left alone by outside powers? They have witnessed the law, both domestic and international, being spat upon by those who do not like its terms. Is it any wonder, then, that they feel justified, by sitting-in and freedom riding, in breaking laws made by lawless men? Old funny-styled, zipper-mouthed political night riders know nothing but to haul out an investigating committee *to look into the disturbance* to find the cause of the unrest among the youth. Look into a mirror! The cause is you, Mr. and Mrs. Yesterday, you with your forked tongues.

A young white today cannot help but recoil from the base deeds of his people. On every side, on every continent, he sees racial arrogance, savage brutality toward the conquered and subjugated people, genocide; he sees the human cargo of the slave trade; he sees the systematic extermination of American Indians; he sees the civilized nations of Europe fighting in imperial depravity over the lands of other people—and over possession of the very people themselves. There seems to be no end to the ghastly deeds of which his people are guilty. *GUILTY.* The slaughter of the Jews by the Germans, the dropping of atomic bombs on the Japanese people—these deeds weigh heavily upon the prostrate souls and tumultuous consciences of the white youth. The white heroes, their hands dripping with blood, are dead.

The young whites know that the colored people of the world, Afro-American included, do not seek revenge for their suffering. They seek the same things the white rebel wants: an end to war and exploitation. Black and white, the young rebels are free people, free in a way that Americans have never been before in the history of their country. And they are outraged.

There is in America today a generation of white youth that is truly worthy of a black man's respect, and this is a rare event in the foul annals of American history. From the beginning of the contact between blacks and whites, there has been very little reason for a black man to respect a white, with such exceptions as John Brown and others lesser known. But respect commands itself and it can neither be given nor withheld when it is due. If a man like Malcolm X could change and repudiate racism, if I myself and other former Muslims can change, if young whites can change, then there is hope for America. It was certainly strange to find myself, while steeped in the doctrine that all whites were devils by nature, commanded by the heart to applaud and acknowledge respect for these young whites—despite the fact that they are descendants of the masters and I the descendant of slaves. The sins of the fathers are visited upon the heads of the children— but only if the children continue in the evil deeds of the fathers.

V
Literature

☐ The literature of a country is one of its most accurate metaphors. When we wish to discover the spirit of a former civilization, we read its works of art so as to understand those literary heroes who represent their age. In American literature the hero has been of particular importance. The pious man of the Puritan age yields to the practical hero in the works of Benjamin Franklin. Toward the end of the eighteenth century, in the Revolutionary period, he assumes epic proportions, as writers like Freneau and Barlow, Dwight and Crèvecoeur seek to define "the American, this new man." In the nineteenth century the hero tends to be the self-reliant hero of Emerson's essays and Whitman's poetry, although his self-reliance can be viewed with skepticism by authors like Hawthorne, Melville, and James. In the twentieth century Hemingway, Fitzgerald, and Faulkner create heroes who find it increasingly difficult to believe in the concept of heroism that they have inherited from a former age.

☐ One does not meet the Romantic hero in American literature after World War II, nor does one witness the disenchanted hero of Hemingway, Fitzgerald, Eliot, and Faulkner. New heroes emerge who are at times more comic, affirmative, and idealistic; or, especially in the poetry of the period, more private and confessional. Saul Bellow, Philip Roth, Bernard Malamud, Joseph Heller, John Barth, and Bruce Jay Friedman create comic heroes who must laugh at themselves in order to believe in themselves. William Styron, Truman Capote, Carson McCullers, Flannery O'Connor, Kenneth Purdy, and Ralph Ellison describe Gothic heroes who find the authority of America so terrifying that they often must retreat into a private world of their own. Poets like W. D. Snodgrass, Sylvia Plath, Anna Sexton, and Elizabeth Bishop have written of very serious, personal, emotional experiences largely absent from poetry before the 1950's.

☐ Norman Mailer, J. D. Salinger, Robert Lowell, Allen Ginsberg, and Edward Albee clearly represent the comic,

Gothic, and confessional moods of contemporary American literature. Each of them, in his own style and from his own point of view, has been particularly concerned with the central issue of our time: the conflict between human possibility and institutional power, between hope and violence, between idealism and authority. Self-reliance assumes the practical function of self-survival in their work. Dogmatic, nihilistic answers turn into uncertainties, tentative explorations of the self. The figure in the carpet now becomes a question mark, and the ceaseless inquiries into the reality of twentieth-century man take on a desperate character: How does one survive war and its effects without remaining so bitter that life loses meaning? How does one carve out a life of self-regard in the face of collective power and authority? How can one live without absurdity when one considers life philosophically absurd? How can one care about a private idealism when public authority becomes overwhelming? How does one believe in one's self? How does one believe in the hero if one can no longer believe in heroism?

☐ The figure who emerges in the work of the modern American author seems hardly a hero—Ihab Hassan's term, the rebel-victim, would appear to be an apposite description of him. But he becomes in time more than rebellious, more than a victim; for all of his eccentricities and excesses, his private meditations and revelations, he develops into a genuine hero who refuses to accept the absolute decline of idealism. He may be excessively egocentric like Norman Mailer of *Advertisements for Myself* or mock-heroic like the Mailer of *The Armies of the Night*; he may be incredibly saintlike—this is Salinger's Seymour; he may seem momentarily fragile, like Robert Lowell, or irresponsibly Romantic, like Allen Ginsberg. Whatever the inward convolutions of his character and however unlikely he sometimes appears as a candidate for heroism, the contemporary literary figure believes—or rather he needs to believe—in an heroic ideal. He cannot afford anything less.

Norman Mailer

One may not have written it well enough for others to know, but you're in love with the truth when you discover it at the point of a pencil. That, in and by itself, is one of the few rare pleasures in life.

When one looks for that author who has been most sensitive to the frenetic life of America since World War II, there is little question that he is Norman Mailer—not quite a hero, perhaps, but certainly a representative writer of our time. Scarcely an aspect of American life has escaped Mailer's scrutiny in his self-appointed role as analyst of the nation, and because he himself has sought to incarnate the myth of the American hero—our novelist, our social critic, our ad man, our murderer manqué, our war hero, our intellectual eccentric (and even clown), our TV debater, our politician manqué, our lover, our reporter, our rebel—he has scattered his talents shamelessly; but the diffusion of his effort, however we may lament it, is in itself representative of our time. Mailer has created his own myth, and though he looks a little scarred from his twenty-five year battle with America and himself, his myth is largely America's myth: few practicing authors possess Mailer's sensitivity to the rhythms of American life.

Born in Long Branch, New Jersey, in 1923, Mailer grew up in Brooklyn, graduating from Boys' High in 1939. He went to Harvard with the expectation of becoming an aeronautical engineer, but he soon turned to the writing of short stories; in 1941 "The Greatest Thing in the World" won *Story* magazine's college writing contest. Mailer graduated from Harvard in 1944 and served as a rifleman in Leyte, Luzon, and Japan during World War II. His experiences helped him to write *The Naked and the Dead* (1948), a war novel which immediately brought him wide recognition. His next two novels, *Barbary Shore* (1951) and *The Deer Park* (1955) dealt with socialism and the movie industry; in 1967 *The Deer Park*, which in one form or another concerned Mailer for more than fifteen years, was turned into a play. There have been scattered portions of projected novels in his other books, but the two completed novels of the 1960's are *An American Dream* (1965) and *Why Are We in Vietnam* (1967).

Mailer has all the qualities necessary for an important novelist—stylistic facility, perception into character, an attention to details, wit, and the ability to sense and record the mood of his time. Yet he has not written the kind of fiction one would expect from an author of his talents. "I have a feeling I've got to come to grips with myself, with my talent, with what I've made of it and what I've spoiled of it," he said of himself in 1963. "I've got to find out whether I really can write a large novel or not." He has not been able to accomplish that longer work; his "ambition for guruhood, prophetic status, has run up against his violent need for immediate action," as Richard Gilman points out in the following essay. Still he has discovered a form particularly suited to his novelistic gifts—the social commentary. Mailer has taken to recording public events like political conventions and peace marches as well as analyzing some of the heroes of contemporary America. He views his subjects from the creative stance of the novelist and informs them with stylistic flair, wit, and acumen. These articles vary in quality, but *Advertisements for Myself* (1959), *The Presidential Papers* (1963), *Cannibals and Christians* (1966), *The Armies of the Night* (1968), and *Miami and the Siege of Chicago* (1968) contain essays that have become documents of our time—public journals, confessions, interviews—and have, as a consequence, taken on permanent value.

Mailer's work is too complex to assess in this brief space, but one central issue should be noted. Mailer has fixed his attention on those totalitarian aspects of American life that form the subject of many contemporary writers; he deplores the "fall from individual man to mass man" that has characterized twentieth-century American life and insists that we reassert "the dynamic myth of Renaissance, that every man [is] extraordinary."

What Mailer Has Done

RICHARD

GILMAN

I N Norman Mailer's hyperbolic world it will no doubt seem
like a putdown to say that his new book is a fine, exciting piece
of work, flawed but immensely interesting, a literary act whose
significance is certain to grow. Mailer never lets us forget that he
wants it all: all the kudos, all the marbles, honorary degrees in
every field, a status that can best be described in a phrase from
the adolescence he has never wholly shaken off: King of the Hill.
All estimation of him is affected by his having always wanted, in
the worst way, to *count*, the ferocity with which he attacks everything that stands in the way of his being seen to count having
its roots in the fact that, as he says in this book, "the one personality he finds absolutely insupportable [is] the nice Jewish
boy from Brooklyn."

That a nice Jewish boy from Brooklyn simply can't be a
representative American figure, much less a mover and shaker, is
the principle of much of Mailer's acrobatics and histrionic movements. He has willed himself into pertinence and power, and it
is one of the most fascinating and instructive episodes of our
recent cultural history. More than any other of our writers Mailer
has intervened in the age so that he has come to count, more
securely as times goes on, and if it isn't exactly in the way he
wants, if it still seems ridiculous to call him the *best* American
writer, he nevertheless matters in a way that only a man with so
mighty and precarious an ego as his could find disappointing. He
long ago made it out of niceness and Jewishness and Brooklyn;
with this book he makes it into a central area of the American

REPRINTED FROM THE NOVEMBER 1, 1968, ISSUE BY PERMISSION OF *The
New Republic*, © 1968, HARRISON-BLAINE OF NEW JERSEY, INC.

present, where all the rough force of his imagination, his brilliant gifts of observation, his ravishing if often calculated honesty, his daring and his *chutzpah* are able to flourish on the steady ground of a newly coherent subject and theme and to issue in a work more fully *in our interests* than any he has ever done.

Mailer's subject, as it has always been in some measure, is himself, but this time a self balanced between objective events and private consciousness in a riper way than ever before. And his theme is just that relation of antipathy but also fertile interdependence between the self and history, the ego and actuality, which he has always strenuously sought—with greater suggestiveness than substance it's often seemed—to make the arena and justification of his work. In writing about his participation in the anti-Vietnam demonstrations in Washington last October (most particularly the march on the Pentagon), Mailer has finally succeeded in laying hands on the novelistic character he has never quite been master of before, and at the same time succeeded in finding a superbly viable form for his scattered, imperfect and often greatly discordant gifts.

I don't think it's been clearly enough seen how Mailer's talents and strengths have for the most part been disjunctive if not wholly contradictory. Such contradiction may be a mainstay of his energy, but it's also an element of his fretful anarchy. His rather old-fashioned novelist's inquisitiveness about the behavior of men in society has, for example, often been diverted by his utopianism, his extra-literary hunger for things to change and change *now*, in palpable ways rather than in the imaginary, alternative ways, in which most artist-novelists deal. His ambition for guruhood, prophetic status, has run up against his violent need for immediate action. His reportorial gifts have been charged with novelistic daring but also corrupted by novelistic license. And his sense of writing as the expression and progress of personality, less a rigorous art than a style of public appearance, a way of counting, has kept him from achieving the full mastery of language, the hardwon grace of a conquest by which previously nonexistent realities are brought into being, that we associate with writers we call great.

In *The Armies of the Night* Mailer's talents come more than ever into working agreement and, moreover, move to ameliorate his deficiencies. Antinomies are resolved: the artist who has to invent and the observer who has to prey on facts merge into the same person; the transcendencies of art and the imminences of action move toward each other's replenishment; the excesses of personality find a new and strangely valuable use in the face of the opaque excesses (and history has come to be almost nothing but excesses) of our public days and years.

This is the central, rather wonderful achievement of the book, that in it history and personality confront each other with a new sense of liberation. By introducing his ego more directly into history than he ever has before, by taking events which were fast disappearing under the perversions and omissions of ordinary journalism as well as through the inertia we all feel in the face of what is *over with*, by taking these events and revivifying them, reinstating them in the present, Mailer has opened up new possibilities for the literary imagination and new room for us to breathe in the crush of actuality.

I don't think anyone who is more purely an artist than Mailer could have brought this off; but neither could any kind of journalist, no matter how superior. This is the conjunction of Mailer's special being—half artist-half activist, half inventor-half borrower—with what the times require: an end, for certain purposes, of literary aloofness on the one hand and of the myth of "objective" description on the other. With a speed approaching light's, history thrusts itself upon us, no longer the special province of "history-making" people, no longer the mysterious work of blind forces or, alternatively, of scientifically ascertainable "laws." History is indeed what we make it, and Mailer, by making himself the chief character of a "novel" whose truth doesn't have to be invented and by making history reveal an "esthetic" dimension has helped bridge gaps of long standing, has brought some ordinarily sundered things together in a revelatory book whose nearest counterpart in our literature, for all the obvious differences, is Henry Adams' *Education*.

How well Mailer's ego serves him now! He begins his education and the book with an account of his reluctant agreement to participate in the demonstrations. In these pages, the notorious literary personality, with its disarming shifts between megalomania and self-deprecation, is fully on display. He speaks (in the third person, as he does throughout the book) of the "living tomb of his legend," tells how "he hated to put in time with losers," writes grandly of how the "architecture of his personality bore resemblance to some provincial cathedral which warring orders of the church might have designed separately over several centuries," reveals that "a party lacked flavor for him unless someone very rich or social was present," and tells us about his "illusion of genius," the "wild man in himself," the "absolute egomaniac" and the "snob of the worst sort."

All this has two functions: to "humanize" the character who is going to participate in history, and to push his sense of self to its limits, so that history will have the most formidable, because most representative opponent. Much of Mailer's appeal has always lain in his stance vis-à-vis the powers that be; the Jimmy Cagney of literature, he has especially been a model for youth, who have always admired him perhaps more for being a welterweight taking on heavies than for being a heavyweight himself. And as Mailer moves on into the actual events of those four days in Washington this cocky stance—the self as the equal of all large intimidating public opponents, yet also the self aware of its small size and internal divisions—becomes a representative posture for all of us. More than ever, Mailer's embattled ego is seen to be the troubled, sacrificial, rash and unconquerable champion for all of ours.

The ego fluctuates wildly. He arrives in Washington in a sober mood: "Like most New Yorkers he usually felt small in Washington. The capital invariably seemed to take the measure of men like him." But the "wild man" he harbors pushes forward and takes over. At a party given by a liberal academic couple, in whose home he smells "the scent of the void which comes off a Xerox copy," he manages to affront his hostess. At a rally later at the Ambassador theatre he outrages nearly everybody by what is to be reported in the press as his drunken behavior. He is indeed somewhat drunk, but not without wit or point to his actions, and his account of the evening is a sustained triumph of autobiographical writing.

But autobiography of a particularly intense and unconventional kind. Into this report of a public meeting, his part in which had months before been corrupted into "history" by *Time* magazine and the daily press, Mailer introduces the most personal matters: his having missed the urinal in a dark men's room; his resentment at having been replaced as M. C., his strongly ambivalent attitude towards the audience. And into this candid and irreverent autobiography he sweeps the other participants—Paul Goodman, Dwight Macdonald, Robert Lowell—writing about them in a form of high and liberating gossip, infusing particularity and personality and queer informing detail into their remote public biographies, their status as names.

Macdonald, "the operative definition of the gregarious," "gesticulated awkwardly, squinted at his text, laughed at his own jokes, looked like a giant stork, whinnied, shrilled and was often inaudible." Lowell, towards whom Mailer positions himself through much of the book in a remarkably frank species of testing, a weighing of their very different personalities and backgrounds, stands "with a glint of the oldest Yankee light winging off like a mad laser from his eye," gives off "at times the unwilling haunted saintliness of a man who was repaying the moral debts of ten generations of ancestors," moves with a slouch the "languid grandeurs" of which testify to generations of primacy in Boston and at Harvard, and provides Mailer with one of the book's central themes and preoccupations.

For in seeking a shape for the relationship of the self to the historical events of that weekend in Washington, and to the historical realities that had led up to it, Mailer has understood how his own self has to be employed as both battleground and partial perspective, how other selves such as Lowell's, products of an almost wholly different background from his, an America of complex traditions, austere moralities, rooted political conscience, elegance, personal diffidence combined with patrician standards for public behavior—the textbook older American *style*—have to be taken into the picture so that it might be seen what a confluence of varied egos and personalities occurred at that point in

Washington, within history, facing it and making it. Lowell (the New England style), Paul Goodman (the wholly liberated urban Jewish style) and the multifarious styles of the older liberals and young dissidents and radicals who made up the bulk of the demonstrators: something congruent and crucial to our American understanding rose from their incongruity and widely separated motives, their having come from so many starting-points to that time and place.

As the demonstrators gather for the march on the Pentagon, Mailer moves brilliantly between analyses of his own immediate feelings, descriptions of the look and feel of the crowd, and a grand, lyrical sociology. As the tension rises he finds himself going beyond the play-acting which has subtly characterized his participation up to now, "as if some final cherished rare innocence of childhood still preserved intact in him was brought finally to the surface and there expired, so he lost at that instant the last secret delight in life as a game where finally you never got hurt if you played the game well enough."

He looks at the young rebels, who have started from points well beyond his own romantic and fundamentally "cultured" view:

A generation of the American young had come along different from five previous generations of the middle class. The new generation believed in technology, more than any before it, but the generation also believed in LSD, in witches, in tribal knowledge, in orgy and revolution. It had no respect whatsoever for the unassailable knowledge of the next step; belief was reserved for the revelatory mystery of the happening where you did not know what was going to happen next; that was what was good about it. Their radicalism was in their hate for the authority—the authority was the manifest of evil to this generation. It was the authority who had covered the land with those suburbs where they stifled as children while watching the adventures of the West in the movies, while looking at the guardians of dull genial celebrity on television; they had had their minds jabbed, poked and twitched and probed and finally galvanized into surrealistic modes of response by commercials cutting into dramatic narratives, and parents flipping from network to network—they were forced willy-nilly to build their idea of the space-time continuum (and therefore their nervous system) on the jumps and cracks and leaps and breaks which every phenomenon from the medium seemed to contain within it.

The balance he maintains, the breadth of his vision here, his capacity to see history whole while being immersed in its unfolding and while in the act of *rewriting* it (always a keen temptation to tendentiousness)—these, I think, are the result of his novelist's patience and sophistication holding his ideological horses in check. The young are "villains" too:

Mailer was haunted by the nightmare that the evils of the present not only exploited the present, but consumed the past, and gave every promise of demolishing whole territories of the future. The same villains who, promiscuously, wantonly, heedlessly, had gorged on LSD and consumed God knows what essential marrows of history, wearing indeed the history of all eras on their back as trophies of this gluttony, were now going forth (conscience-struck?) to make war on those other villains, corporation-land villains, who were destroying the promise of the present in their self-righteousness and greed and secret lust (often unknown in themselves) for some sexotechnological variety of neofascism. Mailer's final allegiance, however, was to the villains who were hippies.

The March proceeds. In a superb passage, one in which all the strands of personality and public stance, self and community, politics and feeling are brought reinforcingly together, Mailer moves to appropriate and give utterance to a passionate, coherent moment within the chaos and cross-purposes of life in this country in our time:

. . . the sense of America divided on this day now liberated some undiscovered patriotism in Mailer so that he felt a sharp searing love for his country in this moment and on this day, crossing some divide in his own mind wider than the Potomac, a love so lacerated he felt as if a marriage were being torn and children lost—never does one love so much as then, obviously, then,—and an odor of wood smoke, from where you knew not, was also in the air, a smoke of dignity and some calm heroism. . . . Mailer knew for the first time why men in the front line of a battle are almost always ready to die: there is a promise of some swift transit—one's soul feels clean . . . walking with

Lowell and Macdonald, he felt as if he stepped through some crossing in the reaches of space between this moment, the French Revolution, and the Civil War, as if the ghosts of the Union Dead accompanied them now to the Bastille. . . .

And now, as culmination:

. . . he was arrested, he had succeeded in that, and without a club on his head, the mountain air in his lungs as thin and fierce as smoke, yes, the livid air of tension on this livid side promised a few events of more interest than the routine wait to be free, yes he was more than a visitor, he was in the land of the enemy now, he would get to see their face.

From this point, about half way through, the intensity slackens somewhat, the writing growing rather more abstract, the thought more general. "Prisoner of his own egotism, some large part of the March had ended for him with his own arrest." Yet the book remains steadily interesting. Into the account of his two days in jail Mailer inserts passages of political and intellectual autobiography, opinions on many social matters, a theory and position paper on the Vietnam war (together with a remarkable, bold insight into how this most "obscene" of wars has paradoxically provided him and countless other Americans with "new energy"), obiter dicta on American phenomena, all of which are sustained and given resonance by the foundation of extraordinary pertinence and the atmosphere of intimate, incorruptible dialogue that have been established.

In the last quarter of the book Mailer turns from "History as a Novel" to "The Novel as History." What he means by these phrases isn't always clear, nor are his claims for what he's done convincing in the way he intends. In dividing his book this way— the first long section composing a history in the form of fiction, that is to say as a true "tale" with characters, a plot, a narrative, etc., the second making up a novel in the form of history, i.e. actual events treated as though they exemplify fictional structures and procedures, an "esthetic," as Mailer says—he hasn't succeeded in nailing down the distinctions he's after. One senses something only half right in his argument that only "the instincts of the novelist" can get at the "mystery" of such historical events as the Washington demonstration and in his proposition that because such history is so largely "interior" the "novel must replace history at precisely that point where experience is sufficiently emotional, spiritual, psychical, moral, existential, or supernatural to expose the fact that the historian in pursuing the experience would be obliged to quit the clearly demarcated limits of historical inquiry."

The trouble lies in Mailer's notion of "novel" and "novelist." The idea has always ruled him—and is, I think, the source of his erratic and inconclusive performance as an imaginative writer—of the novelist as someone whose gifts of intuition and prophecy enable him to see more deeply than other men into society or human organizations. From this follows the notion that novels are superior reports on social or psychic or moral phenomena and that fiction is therefore a superior way of agitating for change and helping bring it about. I think this a rather outdated conception of fiction and that his possession of it, along with his retention of the Hemingwayian policy of style as performance, has kept Mailer on certain wrong, if for him inevitable, tracks. Novels, the best ones, have very little to do anymore with such uses (what they once had to do with them was, for that matter, largely in the realm of pretext); novelists who are artists expect nothing to change, do not imagine that their work can safeguard or resurrect men, have no interest in being *acknowledged* legislators. The novel remains, through all its present travail, a medium for the creation of new kinds of truth and pleasure.

What Mailer has done is not to have written a novel in the form of history or history in the form of a novel, not to have produced any startlingly new forms, but to have rescued history from abstraction and aridity by approaching it with certain "novelistic" instruments at the ready and in a certain large, general "novelistic" spirit. They are rather old-fashioned things, constituents of an older idea of fiction, the kind of qualities we associate with Balzac and Zola and Maugham and textbook notions of the novel. A more advanced novelist than Mailer, one less interested in getting at social or political reality, wouldn't have been able to bring it off; that Mailer is only imperfectly a novelist, that his passion for moving and shaking the actual has prevented him from fully inhabiting imaginary kingdoms, is the underlying, paradoxical strength of this book.

The important thing is that Mailer has refused to leave history, actuality, to historians and journalists. Writing *as he can*, as part-inventor, part-observer, part-intervener, writing with gusto and vigor and an almost unprecedented kind of honesty, writing very badly at times (among dozens of examples, these: "they sensed quickly that they now shared one enclave to the hilt"; "On the *a fortiori* evidence, then, they were young men with souls of interesting dimension"; "psychedelic newspapers consider themselves removed from any fetish with factology") but writing always with a steady aim: to do for our present situation and, by implication, all our communal pasts and futures, what our traditional instrumentalities of knowledge and transcription haven't been able to do—place our public acts and lives in a human context—Mailer has put us all in his debt. In the light of that, whether or not he's the best writer in America, the best novelist or the best journalist would seem to be considerations out of a different sort of game.

J. D. Salinger

I'm just sick of ego, ego, ego. My own and everybody else's.
I'm sick of everybody that wants to get somewhere, do something
distinguished and all, be somebody interesting. It's disgusting—
*it is, it is. I don't care what anybody says.—*Franny

From 1948 until the mid-sixties, J. D. Salinger was no doubt the most popular writer among young people in America. He was, in Norman Mailer's words, "everyone's favorite . . . the most gifted minor writer in America . . . Salinger has been the most important writer in America for a generation of adolescents and college students. He was their leader in exile."

As a consequence of its popularity, Salinger's work received the kind of close reading and vehement discussion only accorded fiction which personally matters. *The Catcher in the Rye* reflected the disenchantment of adolescence and the insistence on absolute integrity in human relationships; the word *phony*, used by the young narrator of the novel as a kind of verbal shield against the world, became the byword of a suspicious younger generation. Salinger's stories—"A Perfect Day for Bananafish," "Uncle Wiggily in Connecticut," "For Esmé—With Love and Squalor," "Franny," "Zooey," and "Raise High the Roof Beam, Carpenters"—are among the finest fiction since the war, betraying a wit and feeling for the actual speech of people that is indeed rare in contemporary American literature. Although Salinger's production is not great, his writing is unique. No romantic writer like Byron, Hemingway, or Fitzgerald, Salinger represented those people of the fifties and the early sixties who were more private,

227

introspective, and quixotic: for them he became a kind of inverse cult hero. When young people took a more aggressive attitude toward their immediate world and began to protest the hypocrisies of the society in a communal fashion, Salinger seemed less relevant. Yet even today, despite his crotchety mannerisms and the infrequency of his publications, Salinger is the one American writer whose works most students know intimately.

The available facts of Salinger's life are brief because he has chosen for so long a time to isolate himself from society. "I live in Westport with my dog," he wrote on the jacket cover of *Franny and Zooey*; in actuality he had not lived in Westport or owned a dog for some time. Salinger's devious relationship with the outside world is one way of his retaining privacy. Born in New York in 1919, Salinger was the son of a Jewish father and a Christian mother. He grew up on the Upper West Side of New York, attended the McBurney School, which he left after a year, and the Valley Forge Military Academy, from which he graduated. He spent some time at New York University and Columbia University, where he took a course in the short story under Whit Burnett, the editor of *Story* magazine. In 1942 he was drafted, and he stayed in the army until 1945; his most poignant story, "For Esmé: With Love and Squalor," is based on his experiences as a lonely soldier in a small town in Wales.

Upon his return to New York, Salinger began to write the short stories which were soon to compose the famous Glass legend. The first significant story, "A Perfect Day for Bananafish," appeared in *The New Yorker* in 1948, and "Uncle Wiggily in Connecticut," "Down at the Dinghy," and other stories followed in the 1950's. In 1951 Salinger published *The Catcher in the Rye*, which spoke for a generation of young people as a confession of alienation from all forms of authority; in 1952, *Nine Stories* appeared. Salinger's other works include *Franny and Zooey* (1961); *Raise High the Roof Beam, Carpenters* and *Seymour, an Introduction* (1963); and *Hapworth 16, 1924* (which was published in *The New Yorker* in 1964). Salinger finally moved from Westport, Connecticut, to Cornish, New Hampshire, where he has continued to live in relative obscurity.

J. D. Salinger: Suicide and Survival in the Modern World

THEODORE L.

GROSS

ALINGER was the most gifted minor writer in America," Norman Mailer tells us in his requiem on Salinger's career, "the finest writer *The New Yorker* ever produced, but profoundly minor. . . . The Glass stories are not literature, but television. And Salinger's work since *The Catcher in the Rye* is part of his long retreat from what is substantial, agonizing, uproarious, or close to awe and terror. *The Catcher in the Rye* was able to change people's lives. The new books aren't even likely to improve the conversation in college dormitories."

We have heard the lament before, in a variety of voices, until it has become a cliché of contemporary criticism. But Mailer, like so many others, has not really explored those reasons for Salinger's popularity that lie beyond the superficial charms and at times irritations of his craft. It is easy enough to catalogue Salinger's faults —few important writers are more vulnerable than he; but the more relevant task would seem to be a consideration of why he has interested and often obsessed more readers than any other serious American author since the Second World War, why he has been, as Mailer himself admits, "everybody's favorite."

We might begin by citing Salinger's compassion for the victims and fallen figures of an urban America; his self-conscious, chastening wit; or his remarkable ability to illuminate character through the finest detail. But the deeper, more permanent attraction of Salinger's work must have something to do with his treatment of suicide and survival, his attempt to suggest a mode of survival in this world that is not without meaning and a little dignity. Suicide, we realize, as we trace the development of Salinger's fiction from "A Perfect Day for Bananafish" to *Seymour, an Introduction* and *Hapworth 16, 1924,* haunts his characters; and it becomes more self-conscious, more present, as he draws increasingly closer to Seymour Glass, signifying, in the case of the Glass family, not only the tragic death of an ideal man but the suicide of the poet and the consequent failure of art to survive in the modern world. The act of suicide—at times it seems the *only* act in all of Salinger's fiction—occurs in 1948, when Salinger first begins to write with a clarity of focus and with real efficacy; the rest is a painstaking and elaborate account of how individuals seek to forsake madness by understanding death and suicide, how they manage to survive in the world without yielding to an ultimate act of despair and yet, as Buddy Glass puts it, without "going astray in any cheap way." Whatever else we may say of him, Seymour Glass is a hero tenaciously committed to the ideal of art—he is the artist as hero. Apparently he could not modify his idealism when the authority of the real world encroached; suicide tore him away from the unbearable. But Seymour's suicide has allowed the other Glass children—particularly Buddy Glass—to survive; and in that sense it has not been without purpose.

In Salinger's fiction one feels a persistent idealism despite the profound distrust of all those forms of authority that contribute to conformity of mind and spirit. Indeed the struggle between idealism and authority causes the special tension of Salinger's work; it is a struggle that drives the hero to the point of madness and suicide. These concerns are evident in Salinger's early work as the idealist searches for a form of compassion that is all but impossible to realize, as his sanity is threatened by the trivial vanities of other people. *The Catcher in the Rye,* as Holden Caulfield tells us, is "about this madman stuff that happened to me around last Christmas just before I got pretty run-down and had to come out here [to a sanitarium] and take it easy." Holden discovers compassion only through his sister—for her he commits his one act of heroism, for her alone is he able to express his idealism by erasing an obscene word from her innocent eyes. The boy cannot adjust, as we say, to the deceit of his society—all of his action, or inaction as it were, is modified by his self-abasement, his tendency toward morbidity, even his potential madness; he creates an ideal world in his mind, filled with children whose innocence he will protect, that expresses his fear of experience. There is no resolution in *The Catcher in the Rye*; the entire book is the depiction of a morbid state of mind, one that reveals Holden in a hostile relationship toward all authority—"This is a people-shooting hat," he remarks about his hunting cap, "I shoot people in this hat"— and only his self-honesty, the knowledge that he is weak and irresponsible, romantic and craven, prevents him from absolute despair.

In the tales that Salinger reprinted in *Nine Stories*, the victimized figures are at times filled with an anxiety that approaches madness, or, at other times, are driven to suicide itself. "A Perfect Day for Bananafish" sets the mood of the collection and introduces Seymour Glass, the central character of Salinger's fiction, committing the central act of that fiction. His suicide in the story stems from a conflict with his vapid wife that comes at the climax, as we see in his later appearances, of an ideological conflict with a world in which his extraordinary, poetic, and ideal character can find no suitable place. In "A Perfect Day for Bananafish," poetry assumes only a suggestive form in the myth of the bananafish that Seymour tells to the girl on the beach; the power of the story, nevertheless, resides in the implied collision of the poet and the actual world. Seymour's suicide initiates the morbid tone of *Nine Stories:* "Uncle Wiggily in Connecticut," "For Esmé—with Love and Squalor," and "Teddy" share its mood of anxiety and terror, its sense of proximate madness; other stories—"Just Before the War with the Eskimos" and "Pretty Mouth and Green My Eyes" —also treat of aberration and neurosis. But it is not really until the publication of *Franny and Zooey* that Salinger's central ideas assume a clear pattern and that Salinger begins an elaborate, painstaking examination of the conflict between art and life, between the poetic vision and the vanity of existence, a conflict which Seymour himself could not resolve but which the other creative members of the Glass family—writers, actors, entertainers—grow to understand as they explore the meaning of Seymour's ideas and, ultimately, of Seymour's suicide.

The tension in *Franny and Zooey* is between the idealism of

Franny, expressed through the book of mysticism that she is reading, and the vulgarity of the outside world, represented in the first story by Lane Coutell and in "Zooey" by the Fat Lady. Franny rejects the reality of her particular world, those small-minded academicians who have forgotten that "knowledge *should* lead to *wisdom*" and who breed small-minded students in the form of Franny's lover, Lane Coutell. "You don't face any facts," Zooey criticizes her, and the degree to which she cannot accept the actual world, filled with people who want "to *get* somewhere, do something distinguished and all, be somebody interesting" is the degree to which she is losing her mind. Like Salinger's other characters she shuns the real world for the ideal one in her mind, represented in Franny's case by the memory of her eldest brother, Seymour.

Ultimately Franny retains her balance and achieves transcendence by referring her problem to Seymour. When Zooey despairs of helping his sister, he suggests that they try to speak to Buddy, but Franny tells him that she wants "to talk to Seymour," who of course has been dead for almost a decade and who in any case was eighteen years her senior and can now be only a dim, distorted image to her. Unable to receive direct advice from the one man who has seemed wise to her, she is nevertheless saved by Seymour through Zooey's parable of the Fat Lady. Seymour's former insistence that Zooey shine his shoes and that Franny smile for the Fat Lady—Salinger's gross symbol of humanity, suffering from boredom and cancer of the flesh and spirit—is his metaphoric way of saying that Zooey and Franny must obey the ideal in their own minds; for if the Fat Lady is Christ himself, suffering in her coarse and helpless way, and if Franny and Zooey must bring her their own finest selves, bound to the concept she embodies in whatever tenuous way, they are finally obeying the ironic name of their radio program—"It Takes a Wise Child"—by exhibiting wisdom, by coming to understand the suffering audience that they entertain. Wisdom is what Franny wishes, not "knowledge for knowledge's sake," and wisdom she attains, even though it appears years after she has abandoned her small role as "a wise child" and after her saintly brother has died.

Buddy Glass, who is the narrator of "Zooey," claims that his "current offering isn't a mystical story, or a religiously mystifying story, at all. *I* say it's a compound, or multiple, love story, pure and complicated." Which is not wholly true. "Zooey," as well as "Franny," is first of all a love story—a story of the love that Franny discovers for human nature; but it is also mystical, if not a religiously mystifying story, for it speaks of the Real as opposed to the Understanding (in Emersonian terms), Wisdom as opposed to Knowledge, Love as opposed to Lust. In these two stories, the transcendental has been grafted onto the realistic in a rather dissatisfying way, but our dissatisfaction stems perhaps from the embarrassment of making an affirmative statement in the contemporary world: what seemed natural in Emerson seems factitious in Salinger.

But in *Franny and Zooey*—and the same may be said of *Raise High the Roof Beam, Carpenters* (1955), published in the same year as *Franny*—our dissatisfaction is not fundamental: it is more annoyance at the crotchety mannerisms that stem from Salinger's awkward, straining, self-conscious affirmation. The difficult juxtaposition of the real and the ideal becomes a greater literary problem, however, in Salinger's last two stories—*Seymour, an Introduction* and *Hapworth 16, 1924*—as he concentrates exclusively on Seymour Glass, as he struggles to make the idealist a man with distinct human features. So long as Seymour serves as a moral frame of reference for Franny, Zooey, and Buddy, he can effectively illuminate their lives; but as Salinger avoids any account of the terrifying authority of the outside world and writes only of an inward idealism and affirmation, he loses the implied tension in all of his best work.

Seymour, an Introduction is difficult to read because it functions exclusively through indirection, as if Salinger does not quite see his hero clearly—the parts of Seymour's personality never quite mesh coherently. Still, as a narrative, *Seymour, an Introduction* is more significant thematically than any of Salinger's other works and it is, after all, only an introduction to Seymour. However much Salinger has sacrificed the actual world in *Seymour, an Introduction* (or in its successor, *Hapworth 16, 1924*), however much he has conceived of Seymour as joyful and saintly, precocious and prophetic, we know that this man will finally take his own life—his suicide is a response to the outside world, and though we do not yet know the full terms of that response, it nevertheless conditions Seymour's former affirmation and makes that affirmation macabre and less conclusive, less authoritative. Rarely has a writer's works been so dependent on one another as Salinger's: "A Perfect Day for Bananafish"; *Raise High the Roof Beam, Carpenters*; *Seymour, an Introduction*; and *Hapworth 16, 1924* are frustrating because they are incomplete, fragments of a mosaic that cannot really be persuasive until Salinger moves toward the eye of the tragedy itself—Seymour's suicide.

Evil, so vivid a force in Salinger's early work, is almost wholly absent from the formal texture of *Seymour, an Introduction* and *Hapworth 16, 1924*, although Salinger provides us with hints, as in Seymour's uncanny ability to suspend pain and suffering by a trick of the mind, a trick that the boy has learned by the age of seven but one that obviously will not work for all his later experiences. These torpid narratives strike us, for the most part, as clumsy temporizing before the central problem that Salinger has set for himself: the failure of the poet to survive in the modern world. As Buddy Glass warns us, in *Raise High the Roof Beam, Carpenters*, "not one goddamn person, of all the patronizing, fourth-rate critics and column writers, had ever seen him [Seymour] for what he really was. A poet for God's sake. And I mean a *poet*." And in *Seymour, an Introduction*, Salinger begins to explore the place of the poet in a world comprised of "middle-aged hot-rodders who insist on zooming us to the moon, the Dharma Bums, the makers of cigarette filters for thinking men, the Beat and the Sloppy and the Petulant, the chosen cultists, all the lofty experts who know so well what we should or shouldn't do with our poor little sex organs, all the bearded, proud, unlettered young men and unskilled guitarists and Zen-killers and incorporated Teddy boys who look down their thoroughly unenlightened noses at this splendid planet where (please don't shut me up) Kilroy, Christ, and Shakespeare all stopped."

Seymour is, as Buddy Glass confesses, also a sick man—one of Buddy's most traumatic moments occurred when he "was eleven years old and watched the artist and Sick Man I've loved most in this world, then still in knee pants, being examined by a reputable

group of professional Freudians for six hours and forty-five minutes." Buddy admits that "by every logical definition, he *was* an
unhealthy specimen, he *did* on his worst nights and late afternoons
give out not only cries of pain but cries for help, and when
nominal help arrived, he *did* decline to say in perfectly intelligible
language where it hurt." But Seymour was also a poet and therefore, in Salinger's terms, a seer; unlike the critics and scholars who
"don't listen properly to cries of pain when they come," Buddy
knows that "the bulk . . . of pain really come[s] from the heart.
However contradictory the coroner's report—whether he pronounces Consumption or Loneliness or Suicide to be the cause of
death—isn't it plain how the artist-seer actually dies? I say . . .
that the true artist-seer, the heavenly fool who can and does produce beauty, is mainly dazzled to death by his own scruples, the
blinding shapes and colors of his own sacred human conscience."

   Seymour, an Introduction is as unsatisfactory to Buddy Glass
as it is to the reader, for if Seymour is the hero and poet—a "full
Dichter," an artist-seer—then we must know the particular qualities that will induce our admiration; Buddy knows this, but he
claims that Seymour is "the one person who was always much,
much too large to fit on ordinary typewriter paper—any typewriter
paper of mine anyway." Seymour's poems are of little help, moreover, for "the more personal Seymour's poems appear to be, or
are, the less revealing the content is of any known details of his
actual daily life in this Western World"; and the physical descriptions only frustrate Buddy and the reader—"Hurrah," he confides
after attempting to describe Seymour's nose, "the nose is over.
I'm going to bed"—because they do not illuminate the man. Although the intention of the Glass stories is ultimately to explain
the meaning of Seymour's suicide—the details of which, as Buddy
Glass remarks, the narrator doesn't expect to examine "for several
more years"—Buddy can scarcely introduce his brother, no less
write about him in detail, because he exists as an ideal in his mind.
"I'm writing about the only person," he tells us, "I've ever known
whom, on my own terms, I considered really large, and the only
person of *any* considerable dimensions I've ever known who never
gave me a moment's suspicion that he kept, on the sly, a whole
closetful of naughty, tiresome, little vanities."

If Seymour represents the ideal that haunts each member of the Glass family, it is because the essence of his character is selflessness, the denial of personal pride. As the ideal poet he has transcended the real world—therein lies Buddy's difficulty in fixing him on the printed page; and, as the poet who finally rejects what the real world offers, he moves inexorably toward suicide. As Seymour himself writes, in *Hapworth 16, 1924,* surely the most precocious letter ever written by a seven-year-old child, "Unfortunately, here [in Hapworth], as elsewhere on this touching planet, imitation is the watchword and prestige the highest ambition. . . . Close on the heels of kindness, originality is one of the most thrilling things in the world, also the most rare." Seymour is painfully conscious of his precocity, and the burden of his youth, as revealed in *Hapworth 16, 1924,* is his attempt to find a *modus vivendi,* a "course of action" that is "both humane and acceptable." He cannot, of course, and the significance of his suicide is the inability of the extraordinary person to exist in contemporary America. "You are in a much stabler position to dislike heroes and heroism utterly," Seymour writes his parents, "if you yourself are quite equipped to do something heroic." Seymour does not have the heroism necessary to survive; the other Glasses are not heroic, either, although they manage to survive through the lesson of Seymour's life: "If you are not equipped to do anything heroic," Seymour continues, "you may still enter the discussion honorably, but with terrible caution and reasonableness, very deliberately and painstakingly turning on every single light in your body, also perhaps re-doubling your fervent prayers to God not to go astray in any cheap way." This is precisely the way of Buddy Glass, the family chronicler, who has now become fused indistinguishably with Salinger himself, and the suggested way of the Glass family in general.

"Seymour once said that all we do our whole lives is go from one little piece of Holy Ground to the next. Is he *never* wrong?" So Buddy Glass concludes *Seymour, an Introduction,* and thus suggests how he will escape the suicide of his brother. By accepting his students, by confessing that "There's no place I'd really rather go right now than into Room 307 [his college classroom]," Buddy Glass has made his separate peace with the world. There is an element of factitious emotion when he claims that "There isn't one girl in there, including the Terrible Miss Zabel, who is not as much my sister as Boo Boo or Franny," just as there is a false note of acceptance when Zooey reveals the meaning of Seymour's Fat Lady to Franny: these gestures represent Salinger's attempt to transcend the self-love of the Glass family and to express compassion for all people, to love the world even if he cannot completely understand it. And in his attempt, which becomes increasingly didactic with each new story, is a lesson for our time. So much in our America forces us to question if not satirize the idealistic statement, as everything within Salinger must contradict and doubt and suspect idealism (for how could he write the tortured prose that burdens *Seymour, an Introduction,* if he were not scarred by self-doubt), but his affirmation seems as far as a responsible person and an artist can take himself today—not the pretentious affirmation of Zooey, who substitutes a parable of idealism for genuine suffering, but the quiet acceptance of Buddy Glass, Salinger's true fiction self, who knows—"not always," as he says, "but he knows"—"There is no single thing I do that is more important than going into that awful Room 307." That perception, which stems from his life as a member of the Glass family and his role as Seymour's disciple, is the perception of an ordinary man who has witnessed the heroism of the artist. Acceptance of oneself, of one's occupation, is finally the acceptance of dull students—and the heroic brilliance of one's brother; of survival—and the madness of one's brother; of life—and the suicide of one's extraordinary brother; of all that lies outside oneself and one's family.

Finally, of course, it is not the affirmative statement that compels us to recognize Salinger as one of the few genuine American writers since the Second World War; it is the struggle toward the statement that is filled with the awe and terror of significant fiction. If Salinger is everybody's favorite, as Norman Mailer has claimed, he is for reasons other than craft or ingeniousness—although let us not minimize the achievement of our "most gifted minor writer," he has written the finest short stories of contemporary American literature. Salinger touches upon our collective desire and need to salvage whatever idealism we can in a country increasingly dominated by authority. As each member of the Glass family seeks to avoid Seymour's suicide, which is the fate of the exceptional man, of the artist-seer, so Salinger's readers seek a survival that is not altogether one that compromises ideals, one that does not "go astray in any cheap way." And Buddy Glass's resolution to accept his dual role as teacher and writer, learned from his ideal elder brother, who was in his turn a teacher and a poet and— unlike Buddy—a hero, seems a convincing resolution, after all. The relationship between the artist and the world is always a precarious one, at best; in Salinger's fiction it leads to a suicide that serves as edification. Seymour withdraws completely—the hero martyrs himself in the name of his ideals; but Buddy's withdrawal is never quite absolute, for he still maintains his telephone in New York and he has, more significantly, all those "twenty-four young ladies" waiting for him in Room 307. He has them as nourishment, bland as that nourishment may sometimes be, to feed his own frail idealism.

Robert Lowell

Almost the whole problem of writing poetry is to bring it back to what you feel, and that takes an awful lot of maneuvering.

"Our modern American poetry has a snarl on its hands," Robert Lowell has observed. "Something earth-shaking was started about fifty years ago by the generation of Eliot, Frost and William Carlos Williams. We have had a run of poetry as inspired, and perhaps as important and sadly brief as that of Baudelaire and his successors, or that of the dying Roman Republic and early Empire. Two poetries are now competing, a cooked and a raw. The cooked, marvellously expert, often seems laboriously concocted to be tasted and digested by a graduate seminar. The raw, huge blood-dripping gobbets of unseasoned experience are dished up for midnight listeners. There is a poetry that can only be studied, and a poetry that can only be declaimed, a poetry of pedantry, and a poetry of scandal."

If Allen Ginsberg, Geoffrey Corso, and Lawrence Ferlinghetti have tended to write a poetry of declamation—or what is familiarly known as "beat" poetry—another less volatile but equally intense school of poets has become popular since World War II. Commonly characterized as "confessional," it includes W. D. Snodgrass, Sylvia Plath, Anne Sexton, Elizabeth Bishop, and Lowell himself. These poets record serious, emotional, personal experiences which have previously not been so prominently exhibited in poetry; they admit their private crises in the most intimate fashion, believing, in Elizabeth Bishop's words, that "we live in a horrible and terrifying world, and the worst moments of horrible and terrifying lives use an allegory of the world."

The acknowledged leader of "confessional" poetry is

Robert Lowell, who was born on March 1, 1917, in Boston, Massachusetts. Lowell was the son of R. T. S. Lowell, a Commander in the Navy, and Charlotte Winslow, a descendant of Edward Winslow, one of the Pilgrim fathers. The Lowell family had been illustrious during the nineteenth and early twentieth centuries. One ancestor was president of Harvard; another was James Russell Lowell, the poet; still another was the Imagist poet, Amy Lowell. Educated at St. Marks Prep School and Harvard, Robert Lowell had a tense relationship with his parents, which is reflected in much of his poetry. He felt that his father was excessively weak and that his mother was stern and overbearing. He left Harvard after his freshman year and went to Kenyon College, where he fell under the influence of well-known poets such as John Crowe Ransom and Randall Jarrell. After graduating from Kenyon College with the highest honors, Lowell married the novelist Jean Stafford and converted to Catholicism. During World War II he attempted to enlist in the armed forces, but was rejected. A few years later, when he failed to obey the Selective Service Act, he was sentenced to a year and a day in federal prison; he was released after serving a sentence of five months. Lowell's first books of poems—*Land of Unlikeness* (1944) and *Lord Weary's Castle* (1946), which won the Pulitzer Prize—reflect his rejection of the Protestant tradition in America and his strong attraction to Roman Catholicism; his extreme seriousness and his personal suffering; and his lament that man has become alienated from God.

In 1948 Lowell was divorced; a year later he married the critic Elizabeth Hardwick. Within a short time he renounced Roman Catholicism. His reputation was not enhanced by the publication of *The Miller of the Kavanaughs* in 1951, which critics found too mannered and academic; but *Life Studies* (1959) was highly praised and became the first important and influential volume in the new tradition of confessional poetry. "These are the tranquillized Fifties,/and I am forty," wrote

Lowell, setting the mood for his book of poems, the sense of personal revelation in an historical setting. In *Life Studies* Lowell creates moving poems about his experiences in prison, the lives and deaths of his parents, and his own mental illness. *Life Studies* and his subsequent poetry of the sixties—*Imitations* (1961), *For the Union Dead* (1964), and *Near the Ocean* (1967)—mix details of his personal life with the poet's keen sensitivity to the heritage of America and its present moral condition.

"There is a poetry that can only be studied, and a poetry that can only be declaimed, a poetry of pedantry, and a poetry of scandal." Lowell's own work, as a recent critic has remarked, "fits into neither of these categories; neither 'academic' nor 'beat,' it is both learned and savage."

Robert Lowell and the Poetry of Confession

M. L. ROSENTHAL

RELUCTANCE to destroy himself any more rapidly than he was already doing may have been one of the causes of Dylan Thomas's refusal to look steadily into the abyss in his poetry. But in the most powerful work of the modern period the great push is often precisely in that direction. Eliot's interest in the "inexpressibly horrible," Pound's violence, Crane's suicidal symbolism, and the psychological self-probings of younger poets all point the same way. "I get the feeling," one of them has written me, "that the madhouse is not far away from many poets writing now. I think there is something wrong in both my feeling that this should become accepted as part of the state of affairs and my feeling that this should be countered consciously and fiercely. . . . I think too that this kind of writing . . . will hurl poetry up a tree it can't descend from. . . . Where will it go? *Can* it make a 'return,' can it reaccept the culture that after all fed it and flung it on its way?"

No one can really answer these questions, although my correspondent supplied *his* answer to the last of them: "No." Emily Dickinson once called publication "the auction of the mind," but today many of our writers seem to regard it as soul's therapy. We are now far from the great Romantics who, it is true, spoke directly of their emotions but did not give the game away even to themselves. They found, instead, cosmic equations and symbols, transcendental reconciliations with "this lime-tree bower my prison," or titanic melancholia in the course of which, merging a sense of

FROM *The Modern Poets: A Critical Introduction* BY M. L. ROSENTHAL. COPYRIGHT © 1960 BY M. L. ROSENTHAL. REPRINTED BY PERMISSION OF OXFORD UNIVERSITY PRESS, INC.

tragic fatality with the evocations of the nightingale's song, the poet lost his personal complaint in the music of universal forlorn-ness. Later, Whitman took American poetry to the very edge of the confessional in his *Calamus* poems and in the quivering avowal of his helplessness before the seductions of "blind loving wrestling touch, sheath'd hooded sharp-tooth'd touch." More recently, under the influence of the Symbolists, Eliot and Pound brought us into the forbidden realm itself, although a certain indirection in their work masks the poet's actual face and psyche from greedy eyes.

Robert Lowell's poetry has been a long struggle to remove the mask, to make his speaker unequivocally himself. As with Thomas, whose style Lowell's sometimes (especially in a few earlier poems) resembles, his chief mask has been that of the "crucified" man, overwhelmed by compassion and at the same time a boisterous participant in the human ordeal. He departs from Thomas in the specific meaning of the mask: for him it is a mask of moral guilt, like Eliot's, for the present decadence of values and the crash of a great tradition. He is after all a *Lowell*, and he charges him-self with all the meanness of contemporary New England as he sees it—sunken in commercialist degradation, the net result of the nastiness behind its long history going back to the repressive Puritanism and to the heartless extermination of the Indians. A Catholic convert for a number of years, Lowell worked this per-spective into his poetry as Eliot has done with his Anglicanism, but with a "jackhammer" passion (to use a figure from his savagely depressed poem "Colloquy in Black Rock"). He is also a social critic as uncompromising in his strictures as any Marxist. So his mask is a composite one, as his "Children of Light" shows:

> Our fathers wrung their bread from stocks and stones
> And fenced their gardens with the Redman's bones;
> Embarking from the Nether Land of Holland,
> Pilgrims unhoused by Geneva's night,
> They planted here the serpent's seeds of light;
> And here the pivoting searchlights probe to shock
> The riotous glass houses built on rock,
> And candles gutter by an empty altar,

> And light is where the landless blood of Cain
> Is burning, burning the unburied gain.

The driving rhymes and indignant irony in this poem and such others as "The Drunken Fisherman" and "As a Plane Tree by the Water" demonstrate Lowell's power even while they induce certain reservations. The feeling is genuine; it smashes home. And there is no question of its moral bearing. But in these poems from *Lord Weary's Castle* (1946), as in many of the pieces comprising Lowell's first volume, *Land of Unlikeness* (1944), the emotion is stronger and more immediate than the literal content. The level of *thought*, as opposed to that of *feeling* and *statement*, is a bit stale —even juvenile. He is shocked to realize what "our fathers" did to the Indians and embittered by the unconscious hypocrisy of Puritanism and its historical results. While Lowell handles these set themes beautifully, we have here an instance of the problem Eliot long ago raised of finding an objective correlative for an emotion not directly expressible, an emotion "in *excess* of the facts as they appear." Lines 4 and 5 of "Children of Light" will illustrate:

> Pilgrims unhoused by Geneva's night,
> They planted here the serpent's seeds of light . . .

As an intellectual proposition these lines are merely a hedging comment on a knotty point of doctrine of little interest to anyone now except theological apologists or historians. On the other hand, if we inquire into the emotional connotations of that paradoxical image "the serpent's seeds of light" we find that again and again in his writings Lowell uses snake and serpent images to suggest sly and furtive guilt, evil that *will* assert itself, and very often guilt or evil of a sexual character. The related meaning of "seeds" is obvious, and "light" suggests, if only ironically, that something not only desirable but valuable is associated with the guilt of the serpent's seeds. These implications are fully worked out in other poems. In "Between the Porch and the Altar," two guilty lovers, an unfaithful husband and his mistress, *become* snakes (in the husband's eyes) whenever they gratify themselves in the way that means "light" for them:

> . . . When we try to kiss,
> Our eyes are slits and cringing, and we hiss;
> Scales glitter on our bodies as we fall. . . .

If Lowell's lovers were not so oppressed by guilt, this would be exactly like the hissing end of Lawrence's "River Roses":

> . . . We whispered: "No one knows us.
> Let it be as the snake disposes
> Here in this simmering marsh."

"Between the Porch and the Altar" helped prepare the way for the maskless confessions of his most recent poems. Its adulterous, mother-dominated hero is first described in the third person, and its serpent imagery helps us see his pathological state:

> Meeting his mother makes him lose ten years,
> Or is it twenty? Time, no doubt, has ears
> That listen to the swallowed serpent, wound
> Into its bowels, but he thinks no sound
> Is possible before her, he thinks the past
> Is settled. . . .
>   Nothing shames
> Him more than this uncoiling, counterfeit
> Body presented as an idol. . . .

Throughout "Between the Porch and the Altar" the sense of sin, rather than sin itself, is clearly the protagonist's main problem. He is sick with the burden of his mother and of the crushing family traditions and "New England Conscience" associated with her, and he must throw the burden off even if it means, as his equally guilt-ridden sweetheart puts it, to "ruin" his two children and his wife. The Roman Catholic framework hardly solves the moral problems behind all this, but poetically it separates the protagonist's viewpoint sufficiently from that of the poem as a whole to enable us to see the difference. The speaker in Lowell's poems needs most of all the strength to "cast off remorse," as Yeats demanded. "Between the Porch and the Altar" begins to get at this need, and away from the half-relevant abstractions of other poems. Even "The Dead in Europe," with its picture of the bombed civilians who fell "hugger-mugger in the jellied fire," is marred by arbitrary and generalized religious rhetoric (whereas the later "A Mad Negro Soldier Confined at Munich" is not), and the magnificent elegy "The Quaker Graveyard in Nantucket" is almost betrayed by it. What saves the latter poem is the least pretentious thing about it, the crowded, sensuous concreteness of its description:

> A brackish reach of shoal off Madaket,—
> The sea was still breaking violently and night
> Had steamed into our North Atlantic Fleet,
> When the drowned sailor clutched the drag-net. Light
> Flashed from his matted head and marble feet,
> He grappled at the net
> With the coiled, hurdling muscles of his thighs. . . .

and

> . . . Sea-gulls blink their heavy lids
> Seaward. The winds' wings beat upon the stones,
> Cousin, and scream for you and the claws rush
> At the sea's throat and wring it in the slush
> Of this old Quaker Graveyard. . . .

or

> . . . a gaff
> Bobs on the untimely stroke
> Of the greased wash exploding on a shoal-bell
> In the old mouth of the Atlantic. It's well;
> Atlantic, you are fouled with the blue sailors. . . .

Lowell introduces into this elegy for his drowned cousin, Warren Winslow, motifs from *Moby Dick* and from Christian worship. (Section VI, entitled "Our Lady of Walsingham," is intended to suggest the ultimate calm confidence of true faith; the statue of Our Lady, "Expressionless, expresses God.") These motifs swell the organ music of the poem, enabling the poet to identify the death of young Winslow with that of Ahab and the *Pequod*'s crew and providing a specific religious and literary context for his contemplation of the ironies and the intransigence of existence, of "IS, the whited monster." Though Lowell relates them skillfully to his theme of one specific death and to his sea music, they are never-theless extraneous to the essential elegy. For this reason the poem lacks the piercing emotional authority of "Between the Porch and the Altar" and of some less elaborate poems (for instance, "The Slough of Despond," "The Death of the Sheriff," and "Rebel-lion"). Nor does it convey the terror of "is" as effectively as the less expansive "After the Surprising Conversions," "Mr. Edwards and the Spider," "Colloquy in Black Rock," and "The Ghost" (adapted from Propertius).

Lowell's 1951 volume, *The Mills of the Kavanaughs*, moves into the foreground themes more or less suppressed previously. In these poems, Lowell gives freer play to his driving motives of dis-torted and blocked love, mental exacerbation verging into insanity, and symbolic and actual homicide and suicide. The title sequence takes us into the mind of an elderly woman remembering her im-poverished and loveless childhood and compensatory self-love, her unsatisfactory marriage and the later breakdown of her husband, a wartime naval officer, his homicidal jealousy after his return, and her own burning but unsatisfied sexual need. She thinks of her-self in terms of the myth of Persephone, as one who has given "whatever brought me gladness" to death and the grave. "Her Dead Brother," with its theme of incest, and "Thanksgiving's Over," with its sexual cruelty, would-be suicide, and madness, and other poems in this volume show how Lowell is approaching the revolutionary breakthrough of *Life Studies*.

In this book he rips off the mask entirely. *The Mills of the Kavanaughs* had one ludicrous aspect, the circumstances of the protagonists cumbersomely devised to account for their pressing psychological despair. In most of *Life Studies* there is one pro-tagonist only—Robert Lowell. Through what he has to say about himself we discover the real, essential bearing of most of the earlier work. As a result, it is hard not to think of *Life Studies* as a series of personal confidences, rather shameful, that one is honor-bound not to reveal. About half the book, the prose section called "91 Revere Street," is essentially a public discrediting of his father's manliness and character, as well as of the family and social milieu of his childhood. Another section, the concluding sequence of poems grouped under the heading "Life Studies," reinforces and even repeats these motifs, bringing them to bear on the poet's psychological problems as an adult. The father, naval officer *manqué* and then businessman and speculator *manqué*, becomes a humiliating symbol of the failure of a class and of a kind of personality. Lowell's contempt for him is at last mitigated by adult compassion, though I wonder if a man can allow himself this kind of operation on his father without doing his own spirit incalculable damage. But the damage has clearly been in the making a long time, and Lowell knows very well that he is doing violence to himself most of all:

> . . . I hear
> my ill-spirit sob in each blood cell,
> as if my hand were at its throat. . . .
> ("Skunk Hour")

He does not spare himself in these poems, at least two of which have to do with sojourns in mental hospitals and his return home from them. We have grotesque glimpses into his marital life. "Man and Wife," for instance, begins: "Tamed by *Miltown*, we lie on Mother's bed." It later tells how

> All night I've held your hand,
> as if you had
> a fourth time faced the kingdom of the mad—
> its hackneyed speech, its homicidal eye—

"My mind's not right," says the speaker in "Skunk Hour," the poem which ends the book. It is partly Lowell's apology for what he has been saying in these pieces, like Gerontion's mumbling that he is only "an old man, a dull head among windy spaces." And it is partly his assertion that he cannot breathe without these confessions, however rank they may be, and that the things he has been talking about are too stubbornly alive to be ignored:

> I stand on top
> of our back steps and breathe the rich air—
> a mother skunk with her column of kittens swills the
> garbage pail.
> She jabs her wedge-head in a cup

of sour cream, drops her ostrich tail,
and will not scare.

It will be clear that the first impression given by *Life Studies* is that it is impure art, magnificently stated but unpleasantly ego-centric, somehow resembling the triumph of the skunks over the garbage cans. Since its self-therapeutic motive is so obvious and persistent, something of this impression sticks all the way. But as the whole work floods into view the balance shifts decisively. Lowell is still the wonderful poet of "The Quaker Graveyard in Nantucket," the poet of power and passion whose driving aesthetic of anguish belies the "frizzled, stale and small" condition he attributes to himself. He may be wrong in believing that what has happened to New England's elite is necessarily an embodiment of the state of American culture, the whole maggoty character of which he feels he carries about in his own person. But he is not wrong in looking at the culture through the window of psycho-logical breakdown. Too many other American poets, no matter what their social class and family history, have reached the same point in recent years. Lowell is foremost among them in the energy of his uncompromising honesty.

Furthermore, *Life Studies* is not merely a collection of small moment-by-moment victories over hysteria and self-concealment. It is also a beautifully articulated sequence. I say "articulated," but the impact of the sequence is of four intensifying waves of move-ment that smash at the reader's feelings and break repeatedly over his mind. The poems that make up the opening movement are not personal in the sense of the rest of the book. They are poems of violent contradiction, a historical overture to define the disintegra-tion of a world. In the first a train journeys from Rome to Paris at mid-century. The "querulous hush-hush" of its wheels passes over the Alps and beyond them, but nowhere in the altitudes to which it rises does it touch the sanely brilliant heights of ancient myth and thought. For its riders there are, at one terminal, the hysteria of *bella Roma*, where "the crowds at San Pietro screamed *Papa*" at the pronouncement of the dogma of Mary's assumption and where "the Duce's lynched, bare, booted skull still spoke"; and at the other terminal, the self-destructive freedom of "Paris,

our black classic." The next poem reaches far enough back in time
to reveal the welter of grossly sensual, mindlessly grasping egotism
that attended the birth of the modern age. Marie de Medici, "the
banker's daughter," soliloquizes about "blood and pastime," the
struggle between monarchy and the "pilfering, pillaging democracies," the assassination of her husband. The third poem returns
from modern Europe and its bloody beginnings to our own American moment. All that turbulence of recent centuries now seems
frozen into intellectual and moral death:

> Ice, ice. Our wheels no longer move.
> Look, the fixed stars, all just alike
> as lack-land atoms, split apart,
> and the Republic summons Ike,
> the mausoleum in her heart.

But then the fourth poem hurls at us the monologue of a mad
Negro soldier confined at Munich. Here the wit, the audacious
intimacy, the acutely bizarre tragic sense of Lowell's language take
on jet speed. In this monologue the collapse of traditional meaning and cultural distinctions is dramatized in the frenzy of one
contemporary figure. Thus Lowell begins to zero in on his main
target, himself as the damned speaking-sensibility of his world.
The humiliated, homicidal fury of the Negro soldier throws its
premonitory shadow over the disturbed "comedy" of "91 Revere
Street" which follows. It helps us to see, beneath the "Jamesian"
nuances of relationship in a society of ritual pretensions but no
center of gravity, how anguished is this prose section's murderous
dissection of the poet's parents and its complaint against a childhood gone awry. In this way it prepares us for the personal horrors
with which the book closes.

But before that long, devastating final wave of poems, there is
a smaller one, corresponding in gathering force with the first
group. This third wave is again made up of four poems, each of
them about a modern writer with whom Lowell feels kinship as an
embattled and alienated spirit. Following hard upon the prose,
these poems clearly say: "This is what the predatory centuries, and
the soul-devouring world in which I walked the maze of my childhood, have done to man's creativity." Lowell first portrays Ford

Madox Ford, the "mammoth mumbler" cheated out of his earned
rewards, scratching along in America, sick and "gagged for air."
Then, dear to Lowell's heart, the self-exiled Santayana looms before us, "free-thinking Catholic infidel." The third poem recreates
with sentimental bitterness a winter Lowell and Delmore Schwartz
spent at Harvard in 1946. Nothing could be more pathetically open
about Lowell's state of mind concerning himself and his art than
the parts of their conversation he chooses to record and even to
italicize:

> . . . "Let Joyce and Freud,
> the Masters of Joy,
> be our guests here," you said. The room was filled
> with cigarette smoke circling the paranoid,
> inert gaze of Coleridge, back
> from Malta—his eyes lost in flesh, lips baked and black. . . .
> You said:
> *"We poets in our youth begin in sadness;*
> *thereof in the end come despondency and madness;*
> Stalin has had two cerebral hemorrhages!"

The ironic facetiousness that so often marks Schwartz's writing
and conversation is here absorbed by Lowell into a vision of un-
relieved breakdown centered on the image of Coleridge's "paranoid gaze" in the picture. That image, together with the mocking
allusion to Stalin as one of "we poets" who come at last to madness, brings past and present, and all political and psychological
realities, into a single focus of defeat. Then in the fourth poem,
"Words for Hart Crane," the group comes to a climax paralleling
that of "A Mad Negro Soldier" in the first group. Crane's brief,
self-destructive career is seen as the demand of the creative spirit,
deliberately wearing the most loathsome mask it can find, for unquestioning love from the culture that has rejected it. Here, just
before he plunges back into his major theme, the "life studies" of
himself and his family, Lowell again, at the most savagely committed pitch he can command, presents the monologue of a dramatically suffering figure whose predicament has crucial bearing
on his own situation.

In large part, the fourteen poems of the final section echo the prose of "91 Revere Street." But they echo it as a storm echoes the foreboding sultriness of a threatening spell of weather before it. Apart from the obvious differences that verse makes, they break out of the cocoon of childhood mentality that somehow envelops "91 Revere Street" despite its more sophisticated aspects. Lowell, like Yeats and Thomas, casts over his autobiographical prose a certain whimsey (though often morbid) and childlike half-awareness. But the poems are overborne by sadness first and then by the crash of disaster. Side by side Lowell places memories of his confinement in mental hospitals and a denigration of his great act of defiance as a conscientious objector in World War II which led to his imprisonment for a year:

> I was a fire-breathing Catholic C.O.,
> and made my manic statement,
> telling off the state and president. . . .

The only poem of this group in which he does not talk in his own person, " 'To Speak of Woe That Is in Marriage,' " is a monologue by the wife of a lecherous, "hopped-up" drunkard. It is placed strategically just before the last poem "Skunk Hour," and after "Man and Wife," in which Lowell makes certain we know he is discussing his own marriage, and it is a deliberate plunge into the depths of the theme of degradation at all but the last moment. Finally, "Skunk Hour," full of indirections and nuances that bring the sickness of our world as a whole back into the scene to restore a more universal vision, reaches a climax of self-contempt and of pure symbol-making. This is Lowell's fantastic, terrifying skunk image for the secret self's inescapable drive to assure itself of continued life:

> I myself am hell;
> nobody's here—
>
> only skunks, that search
> in the moonlight for a bite to eat.
> They march on their soles up Main Street:
> white stripes, moonstruck eyes' red fire
> under the chalk-dry and spar spire
> of the Trinitarian Church

Life Studies brings to culmination one line of development in our poetry of the utmost importance. Technically, it is an experiment in the form of the poetic sequence looser than but comparable to *Mauberley* and *The Bridge*. To build a great poem out of the predicament and horror of the lost Self has been the recurrent effort of the most ambitious poetry of the last century. Lowell's effort is a natural outgrowth of the modern emphasis on the "I" as the crucial poetic symbol, and of the self-analytical monologues of the sensibility which have helped define that emphasis from "The Love Song of J. Alfred Prufrock" to Miss Rukeyser's *Elegies*. It is also an outgrowth of the social criticism that has marked almost the whole sweep of poetry in this century. Thus, Lowell's poems carry the burden of the age within them. From this fact they derive (given Lowell's abilities) an authority not quite present in the post-Byronics of *The True Confession of George Barker*,* or in other works in which the speaker thrusts himself to the fore mainly as an *interesting* person.

* George Barker, *The True Confession of George Barker*, Alan Swallow, Denver, 1950.

Allen Ginsberg

*Sometimes I feel in command when I'm writing. When I'm in
the heat of some truthful tears, yes. Then, complete command.
Other times—most of the time not. Just diddling away, woodcarving,
getting a pretty shape; like most of my poetry. There's only a few
times when I reach a state of complete command . . . a sense of
being self-prophetic master of the universe.*

America has not been a country in which serious poets have
enjoyed wide popularity. They have often associated themselves with universities or, like T. S. Eliot and Ezra Pound,
they have become expatriates from a country which has failed
to nourish their creativity. In America popular poets have
usually been bad poets, although there have been occasional
exceptions, like Robert Frost and Carl Sandburg. At times a
poet such as Walt Whitman self-consciously seeks to reach
the common man, but ironically Whitman's work has been
largely required reading for students in college and the
average American scarcely knows his work. But a curious
phenomenon has occurred within the past decade. A bardic,
oral poetry has become popular which is directly in the tradition of Whitman. Indeed the man who has received the
greatest degree of recognition—and at times notoriety—is
someone who has adopted Walt Whitman's distinctive style,
traveling with his satchel from Paterson, New Jersey, to
Columbia College and San Francisco, from London to Havana, from Calcutta to Prague and the other cities of the
world. The bearded Allen Ginsberg preaches sexual liberty as
Whitman did in *Song of Myself*, and the *Calamus* and *Chil-*

dren of Adam poems; and Ginsberg has extended Whitman's argument into the twentieth century to include other forms of behavior that are censured by society.

Born on June 3, 1926, in Paterson, New Jersey, Allen Ginsberg is the son of a poet and schoolteacher, Louis Ginsberg. After graduating from high school in 1944, Ginsberg entered Columbia College. In 1945 he was suspended by the dean for scrawling an obscenity on the dusty dormitory window; but he was later reinstated and in 1948 he was graduated. After college, Ginsberg held a wide variety of jobs: dishwasher, night porter, market researcher, and book reviewer. In 1953, at the age of twenty-seven, Ginsberg took a letter of recommendation from William Carlos Williams and went to San Francisco to meet Kenneth Rexroth, who introduced him to other poets. Soon Ginsberg was writing extensively and becoming known as a leader of the Beat Generation of poets. His first important poem was *Howl*, published in 1956. *Empty Mirror* and *Kaddish* appeared in 1960 and *Reality Sandwiches* in 1963. In the past few years, Ginsberg has associated himself with the drug movement—he has been characterized affectionately as the "Pied Piper of the drug movement"— and with efforts to change the laws regarding obscenity and sexual behavior.

I am the man,

I suffered,

I was there.

—WALT WHITMAN

Allen Ginsberg: Artist as Apostle, Poet as Preacher

RICHARD

KOSTELANETZ

Qui generis, one of a kind—that Latinism is perhaps the only phrase that can adequately encapsulate Allen Ginsberg; he is such an incredible human being, so unlike any other in the world, that if he did not exist in life, he would scarcely be credible in fantastic fiction. Among other identities, he is a prominent American poet, a prophet, a political persuader, a publicist, a personable performer, a public presence, an apostolic pot-head, a pederast; and because he is such an original and such an activist, he combines several roles in his bearded, smallish, instantaneously identifiable figure, as well as coalescing a number of growing cultural tendencies. Though not an organizer, he is a leader, with several distinct armies of followers; though lacking any formal organization, he can still personally organize the sympathies, if not the actions, of thousands of people. In literature, for instance, he was the major figure in the "beat" revolution in the middle fifties that decisively changed the complexion of American poetry; and to this day, at bookstores catering to the young, as one manager in England told me and another in America confirmed, "More Ginsberg mysteriously disappears than anything else." In the increasingly populous "underground" society, he was an early

REPRINTED BY PERMISSION OF THE AUTHOR.

advocate of marijuana, LSD, rock music and other mind-blowing experiences; young people the world over regard him as an apostle of the disaffiliated life in a contagiously affiliating society. Needless to say, no other poet in the western world can draw such large crowds to a public reading; and no other has read to appreciative audiences at as many of the world's universities. . . .

In his hirsute flesh, Ginsberg stands five feet eight inches, weighs about one hundred fifty pounds, and looks considerably less than his forty-plus years, despite the fact that he is, but for a few strands, completely bald on top. A mass of luxuriant, shoulder-length dark-brown curls hang from a horseshoe-shaped fringe, while his face supports an untrimmed, thick, grey-streaked black beard that runs from just below his eyes to his button-down shirt. Behind horn-rimmed glasses are small dark eyes which stare directly, if not penetratingly, at whomever Ginsberg is addressing, hardly blinking and rarely suffering distraction. His skin is pale and relatively unlined, his teeth stained from the cigarettes he constantly smokes, his lips full, and his mannerisms generally masculine; and whether in khakis or a suit, his clothes are invariably styleless, informal and rumpled. His demeanor is lively, his face animated; and particularly when he chants or sings, his head and hair turn and shake in a manner at once beautiful and and grotesque. His voice is a resonant bass, able to command a live audience or sustain a droning Oriental tune; his diction has the clarity of one accustomed to public speaking. In many ways, he looks and sounds, one cannot help but think, like a Hasidic rabbi chanting not *mantras* but Hebrew prayers; his religion, by his own description, is that of a "Buddhist Jew."

Part of his international popularity stems from his command personality; like many leaders-without-organization, he possesses that quality Max Weber once defined as "charisma"—the capacity to establish confidence by sheer presence. He is innately bright, alert, energetic, straightforward, gregarious and generous with his time; and not only will he eagerly reply to familiar questions but he speaks with enviable frankness of his own experience and opinions and desires (though his elliptical syntax is at times befuddling); for instance, he has no qualms about closing a public reading with, "I'm lonesome here. Would someone please take me home," merely, as he explained to me, "making articulate what every poet feels before an audience of beautiful young people." Nonetheless, because his friendliness and tenderness are at best a bit indiscriminate, if not impersonal, he often drops a curtain, makes a testy remark or fires a criticism that surprises, or shocks, the person to whom he is talking; and if the other is visibly up-set (and Ginsberg has the time or inclination), he will apologize and attempt, usually in vain, to re-establish the original com-radely spirit. Similarly, though he lacks any impulse to con or deceive, his unbounded enthusiasm sometimes produces self-deceptions, if not outright contradictions.

Precisely because he has overcome self-consciousness of his unconventionality, he handles himself politely and confidently, endeavoring to speak directly to people (always looking at them eye-to-eye); and always gutsy in ominous situations, he is par-ticularly adept at disarming possible antagonists. It was largely Ginsberg who persuaded California's notorious Hell's Angels to protect the protesting hippies and pacifists, rather than attack them. (As an Angels' spokesman reportedly declared, "For a guy that ain't straight at all, he's the straightest son of a bitch I've ever seen.") And he got the motorcycle gang to be guardian angels at the first great San Francisco Be-In, early in 1967, which Ginsberg regards as one of the great, prophetic events of recent years. "Allen's humanity, his unqualified humanity, his almost Franciscan view of things," writes Barry Farrell in *Life*, "has won him a genuine influence he never quite achieved in his old Beat days." Indeed, it may be unnatural, if not impossible, for anyone over fourteen or under fifty to address him as "Mr. Ginsberg," rather than "Allen."

Though his appearance, frankness and self-confidence are all a bit intimidating, making even the most eccentric of us seem ir-reparably square, he tries to get through to audiences. "The problem," he told me, "is to learn how to communicate without frightening people. Some mode of affectionate reassurance will give people a feeling of safety when they move their awareness out to a new place, so they need not fear their being is destroyed." He is enviably able to treat as equals students young enough to be his children; and at a Congressional hearing on narcotics legislation, he opened by declaring, "I hope that whatever prejudgment you may have of me or my bearded image you can suspend so that we can talk together as fellow-beings in the same room of Now, trying to come to some harmony and peacefulness between us." Then he cordially began to describe, in an enticing way, his own experiences with various hallucinogens, particularly how during a recent trip on LSD he lost his antagonism for President Johnson, instead praying for his health. Then too, at major radical-hippy events, whether the San Francisco Be-In, the Chicago demonstrations at the Democratic National Convention (where he chanted *mantras* to cool off the overheated crowd), a discotheque fundraising benefit in New York City, or the conference on the Dialectics of Liberation in London, Ginsberg is nearly always there. Whether with establishment politicians or students, he has the instincts less of a lecturer than a seminar-leader, listening attentively, remembering new names, replying quickly, keeping the dialogue moving, and trying to coin aphorisms that extract the gist of a discussion. Ideally, he would like to teach in a university, but few have dared offer him a position; nor does he think any university would tolerate him. "I'd want to smoke pot in class and sleep with my students," he explained succinctly. "Besides, I teach all the time right now."

He has lived for many years in New York City, in a succession of small, well-cleaned slummy apartments in the eastern East Village. The place where we talked in 1968 is east of Avenue C, on the hot top floor of a smelly walk-up tenement across from a new housing project. The door opens into the side of a kitchen, sparsely equipped with nondescript utensils; the hallway leads past the bathroom into a small room with a white-top dining table and a window onto an air-shaft on one side and, on the other, a piece of plywood laid across some files, on top of which are a tall stack of *New York Times,* and some bookshelves (including one largely of poetry in the late Poundian tradition). Another bookcase, reaching to the ceiling of the adjoining wall and covered with clear plastic, is filled exclusively with books and magazines containing his own work. Through glass doors is a small front room with a few more bookshelves and a double bed on the floor; and just off this is an even smaller room, which like the bedroom also looks out onto the street. At one point after midnight, the telephone rang, causing Ginsberg to spring up from the dining table into the front room; and in reply to an apparent request, he said politely, "I wish I could, but I'm not that well organized."

In recent years, he has found the air in New York dustier, the smells and noise more grating, the garbage on the neighborhood streets more pervasive; and after itemizing their probable effects on his physiognomy, he dramatically ran his hand across the plywood table to show how much dirt had accumulated since he cleaned it the day before. "The ecological situation is terrible. I don't think its livable here any more," he declared through a haze of cigarette smoke, adding, "If you can't see the stars, how do you know you're on this planet, rather than Mars? Riots in the cities have a lot more to do with physical surroundings than Riot Commissions realize." So, since 1967 or so, Ginsberg and Peter Ganesh Orlovsky, since 1953 his "common law wife" (to whom he is not entirely faithful), have been spending much of their time on a small farm in upstate New York, actually owned by the non-profit Committee on Poetry, Inc., where various vegetables are grown, mostly for the occupants' own consumption; and even though the metropolis is the major subject and perhaps an inspiration of his poetry, Ginsberg finds himself retreating to the country whenever possible. . . .

Although Ginsberg has been publicly cast in a number of unflattering images, ranging from clown to exhibitionist, the dominant impression conveyed in conversation holds that he is, and has always been, primarily a poet. His formal education at Columbia College was mostly in English literature, and, within that turf, largely in poetry; and he can be as disappointed as Lionel Trilling to discover someone has not read Blake or Wordsworth. In London, he proposed we meet in a bookshop, where he had already made the acquaintance of the manager and clerk and where I found him browsing in the poetry section. He relates to poets, living and dead, far more closely than to other public and historical figures (and rock singers next best after them); and he knows thoroughly the traditions informing his own work and ambitions, including such varied and, only a few years ago, unusual sources for his prosody as "[Hart] Crane's *Atlantis,* Lorca's *Poet in NY,* Biblical structures, psalms and lamentations, Shelley's high buildups, Apollinaire, Artaud, Myakovsky, Pound, Williams & American metrical tradition, the new tradition of measure. And Christopher Smart's *Lamb.* And Melville's prose-poem *Pierre.* And finally the spirit and illumination of Rimbaud." Similarly, he can also elaborately explain how his Tibetan *mantras* represent an attempt, out of poetry, to communicate without syntax, if not without language—a preoccupation he eagerly relates to Alfred Lord Tennyson's attempt to obliterate linguistic consciousness by repeating his full name over and over again, or some of Gertrude Stein's experimental prose, which he regards as "a form of Buddhist meditation."

Unlike any other American poet of note, Ginsberg is of a species more common in England and Europe than here—the son of a poet, Louis Ginsberg, a high-school teacher by trade (recently retired), whose writings were perhaps more admired in the thirties than now; and Ginsberg has since admitted that the comparatively restrictive, impersonal quality of his earliest work was due to his fear of his father's disapproval. . . . Not only have the two Ginsbergs, in recent years, given public readings together, but Allen's conversation portrays his father as his favorite "square" antagonist. Though he has as varied a collection of acquaintances as any eminent, well-traveled man, those he calls his "best friends" are all writers—William Burroughs, Jack Kerouac, Gregory Corso, Gary Snyder, Peter Orlovsky, Herbert Huncke, Ed Sanders. Beyond that, he takes especial pride in connecting poets with publishers, at times even agenting their manuscripts (at no cost to them, of course); and by gathering scraps written by William Burroughs into *Naked Lunch,* he played, as Leslie A. Fiedler ironically quipped, "the Ezra Pound to Burroughs' T. S. Eliot, collating and editing what the madness of another had created but could not organize."

Born in Newark, New Jersey, in 1926, Ginsberg went to high school in nearby Paterson, "where I thought of myself as a creep, a mystical creep. I had a good time, was lonesome; but I first read Whitman there." Though the great doctor-poet William Carlos Williams lived nearby in Rutherford, New Jersey, Ginsberg never had the courage to approach him until after he went to college, first to interview him for a local newspaper and then to make the elder poet's friendship. "He was physically slight of build," Williams wrote a decade later, "and mentally much disturbed by life which he had encountered about him." Williams was one of the young poet's earliest major influences, and it was Williams who wrote the polemical introduction to Ginsberg's *Howl and Other Poems* (1956) and even incorporated, anonymously, the younger poet's personal letters into his own long poem, *Paterson* (1946–58).

At seventeen, Ginsberg entered Columbia College, where he attended classes taught by such eminent professors as Meyer Schapiro, Mark Van Doren and Lionel Trilling. He became a member of the debating team, editor of the *Columbia Review*, president of the Philolexian Society (for word-lovers). Majoring in English, he attained an A-minus average and won several prizes for poems which he now places as stylistically "after Wyatt and the silver poets." He remembers Columbia as a dreary place, where "almost nothing of importance was taught"; yet he regards the late Raymond Weaver, Melville's early biographer and the discoverer of the manuscript of *Billy Budd,* as "one of the few true teachers there. He was using Zen Koans as a method for awakening the student's mind in a course called 'Communications.' "

It was during his years at Columbia that he first met William Burroughs, who lived several blocks south of the campus and was then addicted to heroin and living off a family trust fund. In our conversation, Ginsberg characterized Burroughs as "my greatest teacher at that time. He put me onto Spengler, Yeats, Rimbaud, Korzybski, Proust and Celine. Burroughs educated me more than Columbia, really." There and then too, he encountered Jack Kerouac, who came to Columbia as a football player, quit the sport, lost his football scholarship, and was subsequently dismissed from Columbia for not paying his refectory bills. "Hanging around with Kerouac" was one of the reasons for Ginsberg's own dismissal in 1945. The other reason was two obscenities atop a skull and crossbones, which Ginsberg drew in the dust of his dormitory window. . . . The critic and Columbia-wife Diana Trilling, in a controversial essay called "The Other Night at Columbia," has since interpreted the remark (which was an obscenity attacking the Jews) as symbolizing Ginsberg's rejection of middle-class Judaism; but the poet insists that there was no motive beyond shocking an anti-Semitic Irish cleaning lady who worked in the dormitories. The domestic was, in fact, offended; and she reported the scribble to the straight-laced dean who, likewise outraged, found a second cause to expel Ginsberg, with the parting admonition, "I hope you realize the enormity of what you have done."

After his expulsion, he hung around Columbia, mopping floors in a nearby Bickford's, working in a succession of factories and then shipping out as a messboy on a tanker; and he was later re-admitted to graduate with a B.A. in 1948. That same year Ginsberg had another sort of experience which, like his acquaintance with Burroughs, had a greater effect upon his later life than academic matters: "a vision in which I heard Blake's voice, experienced a sense of lightness of my body and a spiritual illumination of the entire universe as the Great Live Self of the Creator." Since then, he has been an avid admirer of Blake's work; and during that stay in London, he acquired a special pass to see Blake's illuminated manuscripts in the British Museum. At Cambridge, he spent one morning studiously admiring the Blake manuscripts in the Fitzwilliam Library; but in the afternoon, after the midday closing, so the attendant there told me, Ginsberg was all giddy and difficult. "He must have had something for lunch," was the librarian's uncomprehending explanation. More recently, the poet has been picking out on a harmonium musical settings to Blake's poems—compositions he hopes his rock-singer friends will perform.

Early in 1948, he applied to Columbia for both a graduate fellowship and a teaching position, suffering a double rejection. "I was respected at Columbia as a wild poet who smoked pot and had gotten kicked out of school under extremely glamorous circumstances," he told *The New Yorker* reporter Jane Kramer, "but as far as giving me a job—nobody wanted that kind of responsibility." He passed through a variety of positions—dishwasher at Bickford's again, reporter for a labor newspaper in Newark, market-researcher, book reviewer for one summertime at *Newsweek*, and so forth. He also got arrested in the company of real criminals and had his picture splashed on the front page of the *Daily News*, "as a brilliant student who was like plotting out big criminal scenes." His former English teachers at Columbia, shocked at first, came to the rescue with a law professor who advised Ginsberg to plead himself into a mental home, the highly selective New York Psychiatric Institute; and here he had the good fortune of meeting Gerd Stern, a poet who has since become a founding member of the artists' collective USCO, and the legendary Carl Solomon, to whom *Howl* was eventually dedicated. The oft-repeated story goes that Solomon, already an inmate, asked the newcomer, "Who are *you?*" "I'm Myshkin," Ginsberg said. "I'm Kirilov," was Solomon's reply. It was Solomon who turned Ginsberg onto Antonin Artaud and other writers not taught at Columbia; and together they questioned the conventional conceptions of sanity and reality. In retrospect, this sojourn seems the first step in Ginsberg's self-transformation from a neurotic, clumsy, slightly interminable Columbia alumnus to one of the most vivacious personalities of our time.

Particularly in the late forties and early fifties, Ginsberg was, as he later wrote, working largely under "ideas of measure of American speech picked up from W. C. Williams' Imagist Preoccupations." But in 1955, "I suddenly turned aside in San Francisco, while enjoying unemployment compensation leisure, to follow my romantic inspiration—Hebraic bardic breath. I thought I wouldn't write a *poem*, but just write what I wanted to without fear, let my imagination go, open secrecy, and scribble magic lines from my real mind—sum up my life." Perhaps the mixture was spiced by a dash of Walt Whitman too, for the results included "Howl," the poem whose long lines first established Ginsberg's poetic presence; "The Supermarket in California," which records the poet's actual vision of Whitman's return to a contemporary setting; and "America," which concludes with that fantastic line, "America, I'm putting my queer shoulder to the wheel." As early as 1955, Ginsberg was declaiming "Howl" to small gatherings, mostly on the West Coast; but not until October, 1956, did San Francisco's City Lights Books, run by the poet Lawrence Ferlinghetti, issue *Howl and Other Poems.*

Reactions were immediate and nation-wide, including polemical reviews for or against the poet and/or his poems, a number of slick-magazine pieces on Ginsberg and his colorful colleagues, and a San Francisco "obscenity" trial that implicitly afforded "Howl" the best publicity; and by the late fifties, the world of American poetry had polarized into two camps at war over the significance of the "beats"—in particular, over Ginsberg's almost systematic rejection of the guiding poetic canons (ironic, non-urban, impersonal, mythic, etc.) of the post-T. S. Eliot academic establishment. Turned bitter by the attacks of conservatives, most of them resident in the universities, Ginsberg wrote in 1959, "A word on the Academies: poetry has been attacked by an ignorant and frightened bunch of bores who don't understand how it's made, and the trouble with these creeps is they wouldn't know poetry if it came up and buggered them in broad daylight." Nonetheless, perhaps because Ginsberg was the sole potentially great poet in his band, the only one to author widely memorable poems, his leadership coalesced a number of disparate talents— with Kerouac, Ferlinghetti, and Gregory Corso at the vortex; indeed, without him there might well not have been any "beat" movement at all. Within a dozen years, the City Lights edition alone went through twenty printings and over one hundred fifty thousand copies; and not only do nearly all the anthologies and college surveys of modern poetry by now include samples of Ginsberg's work, but the doggedly anti-academic poet of a decade ago has become a regular lecturer on the university circuits.

In the years since the opening salvos, most of the critics and poet-critics who objected to Ginsberg's work have made peace with him, a few even admitting outright in his presence that "I was wrong in 1956," another few even rejecting the ironic, formalist mode for Ginsberg's freer, more personal style; and his poetry alone places him among the dozen major American writers of the post-1945 period. As, in Karl Shapiro's phrase, "not a poet but an overthrower of poets," Ginsberg single-handedly changed American poetry and the appearance of American poets (many of whom now sport full-faced beards); and not only did he overthrow the restrictions against the use of four-letter words, in both poetry itself and the public speech of poets, but his impact has also removed from common discourse about poetry such fifties epithets as "art," "critical," "successful," "strict," and "intricate." As Leslie Fiedler put it, "He has not destroyed a world, but displaced a tired style; has not created a new heaven and a new earth, but only made a school." Since 1957 too, City Lights has been his primary publisher, issuing *Kaddish and Other Poems* (1961), collecting the work of 1958–60; *Reality Sandwiches* (1963), which contains miscellaneous pieces written between 1953 and 1960; and the recent *Planet News* (1968), which collects 1961–7, in addition to a book of epistolary remarks on hallucinogens in South America written in collaboration with William Burroughs, *The Yage Letters* (1963). [Another Book, *Empty Mirror* (1961), collected his earliest poems, those written prior to 1953; *Airplane Dream* (1968) contains a short story and three poems not collected elsewhere; while two recent limited editions—*Wichita Vortex Sutra* (1966), *T. V. Baby Poems* (1968)—both contain material incorporated into *Planet News*.] In line with his autobiographical processes, in these books, as elsewhere, Ginsberg insists upon the precise dating of his poems; and the forthcoming Anglo-American edition of his complete poems will, at his insistence, print all his work in chronological order. His poems have also been translated into Italian, German, French, Spanish, Bengali, Russian, Czech, Japanese, Hindu, etc.; and although other poets may have greater reputations at home, to the world at large Ginsberg is the most famous and most admired of contemporary American poets.

Over the years, his poetry has ranged in style from conventionally rhymed lyrics to the freest of poetic structures. "Trouble with conventional form (fixed line count and stanza form) is," he wrote in a published extract from his journal, "it's too symmetrical, geometrical, numbered and pre-fixed—unlike my own mind which has no beginning and end, nor fixed measure of thought (or speech—or writing) other than its own cornerless mystery." In purpose, the poems range from meditation to remembrance to polemic, in tone from Apollinairean surrealism to uncompromising negation to anarchic humor, and in stance from narrative factual statements to the hysterical personal confession of "Kaddish," the lament for his dead mother which is probably his best single work. The whole of Ginsberg's work, however, is uneven in quality, full of confused, flaccid, impenetrable or outright bad poems, that, as he knows quite well, probably should have remained in the notebooks; yet like Whitman before him, Ginsberg is a poet of the great line and the sustained vision, social resonance and open-ended energy. "He is a sort of Theodore Dreiser of American poetry," writes the critic Stephen Stepanchev, "He is awkward in phrase and ungainly in manner as that novelist often was. His poems find their shape only after fighting almost insuperable obstacles in rhythm, grammar, and diction." Nonetheless, the measure of a poet's reputation is ultimately not his worst work but his best; and among the masterpieces most critics (as well as myself) would nominate "Howl," "A Supermarket in California," "In the Baggage Room at Greyhound," "America" (all included in *Howl and Other Poem*), "Kaddish," "Aether," "Wichita Vortex Sutra"—a selection that more or less agrees with Ginsberg's own evaluation of his works.

More important perhaps is Ginsberg's indubitable success at becoming the truly popular poet that Whitman only imagined himself to be—the author of lines that have the status of scripture, that live in the minds of the literary young in America and, increasingly, in Europe and the Orient:

I saw the best minds of my generation destroyed by madness, starving, hysterical naked,
dragging themselves through the negro streets at dawn looking for an angry fix, . . .
who bared their brains to Heaven under the El and saw Mohammedan angels staggering on tenement roofs illuminated, . . .
who chained themselves to subways for the endless ride from Battery to holy Bronx on benzedrine until the noise of wheels and children brought them down shuddering mouth-wracked and battered bleak of brain all drained of brilliance in the drear light of Zoo, . . .
who talked continuously seventy hours from park to pad to bar to Bellevue to museum to the Brooklyn Bridge, . . .
who lit cigarettes in boxcars boxcars boxcars racketing through snow toward lonesome farms in grandfather night, . . .
and who were given instead the concrete void of insulin metasol

electricity hydrotherapy psychotherapy occupational therapy ping-pong & amnesia. . . .

And anyone who has ever heard Ginsberg read aloud these lines from "Howl," whether live or on record—he does not mind reciting the same poem over and over again—will not forget their distinct cadences, the sound of their images or the inimitably cigaretty, yet youthful, timbre of Ginsberg's voice. Indeed, few contemporary poets can declaim their own work so well—as the poet-critic Tom Clark put it, "He seemed to enter each of his poems emotionally while reading them." Or as Paul Carroll movingly wrote of a later performance of "Wichita Vortex Sutra":

Here was an American poet calling—for the first time in our literature perhaps and certainly for the first time since Whitman—for the possibility of the existence of the ancient verities in the life of these States. Ginsberg was calling for communion with the gods and for release of love and peace in the souls of Americans. He was calling, in truth, for the realization of himself and by all of us that the Kingdom of God is within everybody.

This is the kind of power, of words and person, that has made Ginsberg, in Leslie Fiedler's words, "the nearest thing to a best-selling poet we have had since Frost (though his audience consists of bad boys rather than good ones)."

The corpus of Ginsberg's poetry divides into a succession of periods, each of which represents a slightly different way of working with the materials of his art. The earliest era was at Columbia, where his poems, as noted before, were very much in the pre-Elizabethan, Renaissance mode. The next was closer to the idiomatic, perceptual short-line verse of William Carlos Williams. A poem written early in 1953, "My Alba," opens with the following circumspect lines:

> Now that I've wasted
> five years in Manhattan
> life decaying
> talent a blank

By the following year, however, in a poem like "Siesta in Xblaba," the line has become longer, the imagination more exotic, the cadences more various. "I became more worldly skilled," he explained to me, "at the question of finding form to articulate aweful perceptions." By "Howl," written in 1955–6, the visionary sensibility fused with a sense of social commentary and, as Ginsberg characterizes it, "hallucinogenic terror rhetoric" that eventually fed into "Kaddish," which is, in contrast, however, a searingly intense and courageous personal poem.

In the sixties, Ginsberg's best poetry turned outward, commenting upon the world situation and the milieus through which he traveled. "Television Was a Baby Crawling Toward that Death Chamber," written in the winter of 1961, is, as its title suggests, an attack on the electronic world. "The Change" (1963), which Ginsberg considers a crucially important poem, was written just after his sojourn in India; "Kral Mayales," as noted before, was composed on the plane out of Prague; "I Am A Victim of Telephone" (1964) is about the interruptions of a typical day at home in New York. "City Midnight Junk Strains" (1966), written for Frank O'Hara just after his death, reveals that kind of bitter, penetrating criticism that Ginsberg previously directed upon society, rather than individuals, living or dead:

> and I stare into my head   & look for your/   broken roman nose
> your wet mouth-smell of martinis
> & a big artistic tipsy kiss.

Throughout the sixties, Ginsberg has been moving toward a more immediate, if not instantaneous, poetry; and once Bob Dylan gave him a high-class tape recorder for Christmas, 1965, he began to dictate poems, rather than scribble them into his notebook. The magnificent "Wichita Vortex Sutra" was created, in the spring of 1966, out of words observed or sprung into his head during eighteen hours of traveling through the Middle West. "This poem," he wrote in a letter that Paul Carroll reprints in *The Poem and Its Skin* (1968), "is a collage of news radio optical phenomena observed & noted in a field of vision outside car window, at stops, etc. + fantasy + imagination, memory of history, desire, etc." Particularly brilliant at evoking the contraries and space of the American landscape, and at dealing with the magical properties of mundane language, "Wichita Vortex Sutra" is the first of a projected cycle of poems Ginsberg plans to call "These States." (A contrary recent poem has been "Wales Visitation," which is about communing with the English earth and the tradition of English nature poetry while high on LSD in Wales; and he told me that this poem, which cracked *The New Yorker*, went through more revisions than is usual for his poetry, partly because he wanted the poem "to exist simultaneously or identically in acid consciousness and normal consciousness and mediate between them.")

The personal, if not confessional, character of his poetry stems partly from several experiences with psychoanalysis, which left him skeptical about Freudian methodology and more sure of the analysis's value as a human relationship. The first of his many analyses was with William Burroughs, on a couch in the latter's living room, back in the Columbia days. The second, for three months, with "a Reichian who is no longer a Reichian." The third, for eight months, with "dreary Freudians" at the New York State Psychiatric Institute; the fourth, for two and one-half years, with a doctor formerly attached to the Institute. Then, "In 1955, in San Francisco, I did a year with a good doctor from the Washington School—you know, Harry Stack Sullivan's—he was the best," and it was this doctor, I later found out, who urged Ginsberg to abandon the square life of a market researcher for Peter, poetry and pleasure. After pausing to light another cigarette, he summarized, "If an analyst is a good man, then the analysis will be good. Dig? What's necessary is tender communication between two people—in analysis or life." So, his outlook remains closer to that of Martin Buber and Hasidism than to the Jewish rationalistic tradition exemplified by Freud.

Ginsberg would like to think of himself as espousing a message above earthly politics, as consciousness stands above society. "We're in science fiction now. All the revolutions and the old methods and techniques for changing consciousness are bankrupt, like the Democratic Party. We're back to magic, to psychic life. Like the civil-rights movement hasn't succeeded in altering the fear consciousness of the white Southern middle-class, but the

hippies might." And he said in 1968 that his current politics derived largely from a book on top of his plywood table, Mircea
Eliade's esoteric study of *Shamanism*. Nonetheless, over the years
he has signed advertisements in support of the pro-Castro Fair
Play for Cuba Committee (only to be expelled from Cuba), and
petitions against American involvement in Vietnam (and yet been
expelled from Czechoslovakia as well); and he has continually
brought ecological problems, particularly the poisoning of food
and air, to the attention of anyone who will listen, including the
late Senator Robert F. Kennedy, with whom the poet spoke
early in 1968. More recently, his experiences at the Chicago Democratic Convention, as well as persistent harassment by narcotics
authorities (largely in response to his pro-pot publicity), persuade
Ginsberg to regard America as an incipient police state; and he
fears that unless people wake up to the threat, there will be a
series of paramilitaristic *putsches* across America.

In all, he is less anti-American than, as an anarchist by temper
and persuasion, opposed to certain forces and ideas in both super-
powers. "America," he explained to me, "is one of the main
Judases of the contemporary world. As things are going now, it
seems to me that dogmatic cold-war types in the U.S. and the
Socialist countries are mirror-images of each other and are bent on
world destruction. Everything the Communists say about the U.S.
is right; everything we say about the Communists is right, too,
give or take a little bit of inaccurate reporting here and there.
Everybody's bankrupt except for the long-haired young and the
peaceful old." Inevitably, when Czechoslovakian authorities, in
inviting him to Prague, expected him to make statements critical
of America, Ginsberg, the truest of anarchists, surprised them
by making anti-Communist ones too; and few can testify from
personal authority to the similarity of police-state methods in
Havana, Prague and Chicago, all directed against him, as he
puts it, for "the same sort of thing—performing an exorcism at
the wrong time."

Another of Ginsberg's major interests has been the politics of
pot; and here as elsewhere, he is the best publicist for his own
passions. He discovered early in life that drugs afforded a means
of experimenting with consciousness; and always willing to be the

courageous guinea pig of persuasive ideas, he has since experimented with practically everything, typically remembering which drug inspired which poem. Throughout the sixties, he has been an active participant at pro-pot demonstrations, as well as a witness at Congressional hearings, and the author of one of the most comprehensive and elegantly written pro-pot polemics in print, "The Great Marijuana Hoax," submitted to several magazines before it appeared in the *Atlantic Monthly* and since reprinted in *The Marijuana Papers* (1966). Here he argued, as "a mature middle-aged gentlemen, the holder at present of a Guggenheim Fellowship," that pot is less deleterious than alcohol, that it is not habit-forming, that it does not necessarily lead to habit-forming drugs, that a huge, pernicious and self-seeking law-enforcement bureaucracy has grown around the idea of marijuana as a "menace," that millions of respectable Americans were smoking pot (and therefore disobeying the law), that pot is a legitimate pleasure in respectable circles around the world, that most disorders following marijuana usage were due to fear of arrest, and, in conclusion, "that it is time to end Prohibition again. And with it put an end to the gangsterism, police mania, hypocrisy, anxiety, and national stupidity generated by administrative abuse of the Marijuana Tax Act of 1937." As sophisticated as ever, he is also toying with a suit claiming the existing anti-marijuana laws violate the artist's right to the materials of his trade.

Back in the middle fifties, Ginsberg became a public issue whom nearly all self-styled decent men found objectionable; but by the late sixties, he has become an established cultural figure, a friend of the eminent, a success with an upper-middle class income, who has posed for respectful profiles in *Life*, *The New York Times Magazine*, *The New Yorker* and other square periodicals. He has received a listing in *Who's Who* (whose publisher bowdlerized his common-law marriage, as well as other unusual details), as well as a Guggenheim Fellowship and a prize from the National Council on the Arts, among other cultural honors. (All that awaits him in this sweepstakes is initiation into the august National Institute of Arts and Letters and perhaps the cover of *Time*.) A poster of him dressed in the costume of Uncle Sam was a best-seller in 1966, and from time to time there is talk of run-

ning him for President—not only the first Jew, but the first bi-
sexual and the first pot-head. Nearly every campus in America is
open to him—exceptions being Catholic colleges, where the students who invite him invariably protest the administration's ban;
and he even got onto the floor of the 1968 Chicago Democratic
Convention as a reporter for Hearst's *Eye* magazine, only to perform in the balcony a public exorcism while a priest was uttering a
benediction and then be hustled out of the auditorium by the
Secret Service. Regarding his own celebrity, he told me in 1965,
"It's a Kafkian situation, like a repetition of consciousness. If one
takes one's identity from a vague idea of oneself, fame can cause
confusion of identity. If one takes one's identity from one's desire and the feelings of desire in the body, then one is stabilized."
He stopped for a moment, fumbled for words. "If your soul is
your belly, nobody can drive you out of your skull." At the time
I asked him about a decade hence. "I'll be living in a little cottage
in the country," he declared, "with a wife and twelve children."
He paused, then added, "I'll be scribbling poems." However,
though he often speaks of wanting to propagate, he has yet to
take a female wife.

Around the world, Ginsberg is also, it seems, the most widely
acclaimed unofficial American cultural ambassador, hailed particularly by the young, which is to say the Future; and at times
I suspect that in a decade perhaps he will be a permanent, but
uncompromised, employee of the State Department. For one
thing, his presence abroad symbolizes persuasively the genuine
variousness and tolerance of America, as well as contradicting the
common images of both native totalitarianism, suggested by certain anti-American propaganda, and the endless, mindless vulgar
suburb that our movies present to Europe and too many of our
official representatives confirm. In America, too, Ginsberg particularly appeals to that element of the younger generation with
values and aspirations different from their elders'; and not only
do they take sides, rather than offense, with the poet when the
established authorities restrict or condemn him, but unlike, say,
Paul Goodman, who does not say yes to everything, Ginsberg
condones, or encourages, nearly the entire gamut of youthful, anti-
social behavior. By doing and saying publicly what many of the

world's young do and say privately, he becomes their spokesman; and as perhaps the only major cultural figure to successfully make the transition from Beat to Hip, he has miraculously managed to influence, by now, several generations of the young. Fulfilling Whitman's dream, he is, like his friend, Yevgeny Yevtushenko, a public poet whose best lines have infiltrated the public consciousness, who has attained a cultural importance beyond the merit of his poetry. "There is no way," writes the Canadian poet Irving Layton, inadvertently speaking of Ginsberg, "for the poet to avoid misunderstanding, even abuse, when he follows his prophetic vocation to lead his fellowmen toward sanity and light." As a truthteller, and author of some of the greatest lines of our time, Ginsberg ought to become the first American poet to win the Nobel Prize. As a prophet for youth and other avant-garde minorities, he is also one of Shelley's "unacknowledged legislators" or a harbinger of a new kind of existence in an age of cybernation and increased leisure, when many more people will be able to devote a larger portion of their lives, as Ginsberg does, not only to poetry and the arts but also to the cultivation of an uninhibited variety of possible pleasures.

Arthur Miller

*I have, so to speak, a psychic investment in the continuity of life.
I couldn't ever write a totally nihilistic work.*

"Yes, it's got so we've lost the technique of grappling with the world that Homer had," Arthur Miller has recently observed, "that Aeschylus had, that Euripides had. And Shakespeare. How amazing it is that people who adore the Greek drama fail to see that these great works are works of a man confronting his society, the illusions of the society, the faiths of the society. They're social documents, not little piddling private conversations." Miller, who has been writing successful plays for more than two decades, has devoted himself almost exclusively to social and political drama. His concern with the themes of ambition, responsibility, and justice is conveyed in familiar dramatic terms—he forgoes the radical form and style of many new playwrights—and functions as an overt critic of the society in which he lives. Deeply aware of the great dramas that have preceded his own writing, Miller has attempted to create tragedies that are a reflection and an interpretation of modern American life.

Arthur Miller was born on October 17, 1915, in New York City. He attended the University of Michigan, where he won several dramatic awards which gave him the confidence to continue writing. After graduating from college, Miller returned to New York to write radio scripts and a novel, *Focus*, which became a best seller in 1945. He then turned to drama and wrote *All My Sons*, which won the New York Drama Critics' Award in 1947. Miller's most famous play, *Death of a Salesman*, appeared in 1949 and was awarded the

Critics' Circle Award and the Pulitzer Prize for Drama. Other plays enhanced his reputation: *The Crucible* (1953), *A View from the Bridge* (1955), *After the Fall* (1963), *Incident at Vichy* (1964), and *The Price* (1968). Miller also adapted his story "The Misfits" (1960) into a film which starred his second wife, Marilyn Monroe, and published a collection of his stories, *I Don't Need You Any More* (1967).

For Arthur Miller tragedy seemed to be "the only form [of drama] there was. The rest of it was all either attempts at it, or escapes from it. But tragedy was the basic pillar." Miller has struggled in his various plays to create a modern form of tragedy. He claims that it is impossible to make an absolute comparison "between any contemporary work and the classic tragedies . . . because of the question of religion and power, which was taken for granted and is an a priori consideration in any classic tragedy." Thus Miller has dealt with tragic themes as they pertain to modern situations rather than create tragedy in formal and traditional terms. The hero obsessed by one idea (like Willy Loman and his need to be successful) or capable of great sacrifice (like Victor Franz in *The Price*) or possessed with power he does not wholly understand (as in *Incident at Vichy*)—these are some of the themes of Miller's plays. The dramas are not about princes or kings, the royalty of classic tragedy; but they are concerned with heroes who have a deep purpose in life, experience intense passion, and gain some kind of perception.

Introduction to Collected Plays

ARTHUR

MILLER

THE PLAY [*Death of a Salesman*] was always heroic to me, and in later years the academy's charge that Willy lacked the "stature" for the tragic hero seemed incredible to me. I had not understood that these matters are measured by Greco-Elizabethan paragraphs which hold no mention of insurance payments, front porches, refrigerator fan belts, steering knuckles, Chevrolets, and visions seen not through the portals of Delphi but in the blue flame of the hot-water heater. How could "Tragedy" make people weep, of all things?

I set out not to "write a tragedy" in this play, but to show the truth as I saw it. However, some of the attacks upon it as a pseudo-tragedy contain ideas so misleading, and in some cases so laughable, that it might be in place here to deal with a few of them.

Aristotle having spoken of a fall from the heights, it goes without saying that someone of the common mold cannot be a fit tragic hero. It is now many centuries since Aristotle lived. There is no more reason for falling down in a faint before his *Poetics* than before Euclid's geometry, which has been amended numerous times by men with new insights; nor, for that matter, would I choose to have my illnesses diagnosed by Hippocrates rather than the most ordinary graduate of an American medical school, despite the Greek's genius. Things do change, and even a genius is limited by his time and the nature of his society.

I would deny, on grounds of simple logic, this one of Aristotle's contentions if only because he lived in a slave society. When a vast number of people are divested of alternatives, as slaves are, it is rather inevitable that one will not be able to imagine drama, let alone tragedy, as being possible for any but the higher ranks of society. There is a legitimate question of stature here, but none of rank, which is so often confused with it. So long as the hero may be said to have had alternatives of a magnitude to have materially changed the course of his life, it seems to me that in this respect at least, he cannot be debarred from the heroic role.

The question of rank is significant to me only as it reflects the question of the social application of the hero's career. There is no doubt that if a character is shown on the stage who goes through the most ordinary actions, and is suddenly revealed to be the President of the United States, his actions immediately assume a much greater magnitude, and pose the possibilities of much greater meaning, than if he is the corner grocer. But at the same time, his stature as a hero is not so utterly dependent upon his rank that the corner grocer cannot outdistance him as a tragic figure—providing, of course, that the grocer's career engages the issues of, for instance, the survival of the race, the relationships of man to God —the questions, in short, whose answers define humanity and the right way to live so that the world is a home, instead of a battleground or a fog in which disembodied spirits pass each other in an endless twilight.

In this respect *Death of a Salesman* is a slippery play to categorize because nobody in it stops to make a speech objectively stating the great issues which I believe it embodies. If it were a worse play, less closely articulating its meanings with its actions, I think it would have more quickly satisfied a certain kind of criticism. But it was meant to be less a play than a fact; it refused admission to its author's opinions and opened itself to a revelation of process and the operations of an ethic, of social laws of action no less powerful in their effects upon individuals than any tribal law administered by gods with names. I need not claim that this play is a genuine solid gold tragedy for my opinions on tragedy to be held valid. My purpose here is simply to point out a historical fact which must be taken into account in any consideration of tragedy, and it is the sharp alteration in the meaning of rank in society between the present time and the distant past. More important to me is the fact that this particular kind of argument obscures much more relevant considerations.

One of these is the question of intensity. It matters not at all whether a modern play concerns itself with a grocer or a president if the intensity of the hero's commitment to his course is less than the maximum possible. It matters not at all whether the hero falls from a great height or a small one, whether he is highly conscious or only dimly aware of what is happening, whether his pride brings the fall or an unseen pattern written behind clouds; if the intensity, the human passion to surpass his given bounds, the fanatic insistence upon his self-conceived role—if these are not present there can only be an outline of tragedy but no living thing. I believe, for myself, that the lasting appeal of tragedy is due to our need to face the fact of death in order to strengthen ourselves for life, and that over and above this function of the tragic viewpoint there are and will be a great number of formal variations which no single definition will ever embrace.

Another issue worth considering is the so-called tragic victory, a question closely related to the consciousness of the hero. One makes nonsense of this if a "victory" means that the hero makes us feel some certain joy when, for instance, he sacrifices himself for a "cause," and unhappy and morose because he dies without one. To begin at the bottom, a man's death is and ought to be an essentially terrifying thing and ought to make nobody happy. But in a great variety of ways even death, the ultimate negative, can be, and appear to be, an assertion of bravery, and can serve to separate the death of man from the death of animals; and I think it is this distinction which underlies any conception of a victory in death. For a society of faith, the nature of the death can prove the existence of the spirit, and posit its immortality. For a secular society it is perhaps more difficult for such a victory to document itself and to make itself felt, but, conversely, the need to offer greater proofs of the humanity of man can make that victory more real. It goes without saying that in a society where there is basic disagreement as to the right way to live, there can hardly be agreement as to the right way to die, and both life and death must be heavily weighted with meaningless futility.

It was not out of any deference to a tragic definition that Willy

Loman is filled with a joy, however broken-hearted, as he approaches his end, but simply that my sense of his character dictated his joy, and even what I felt was an exultation. In terms of his character, he has achieved a very powerful piece of knowledge, which is that he is loved by his son and has been embraced by him and forgiven. In this he is given his existence, so to speak—his fatherhood, for which he has always striven and which until now he could not achieve. That he is unable to take this victory thoroughly to his heart, that it closes the circle for him and propels him to his death, is the wage of his sin, which was to have committed himself so completely to the counterfeits of dignity and the false coinage embodied in his idea of success that he can prove his existence only by bestowing "power" on his posterity, a power deriving from the sale of his last asset, himself, for the price of his insurance policy.

I must confess here to a miscalculation, however. I did not realize while writing the play that so many people in the world do not see as clearly, or would not admit, as I thought they must, how futile most lives are; so there could be no hope of consoling the audience for the death of this man. I did not realize either how few would be impressed by the fact that this man is actually a very brave spirit who cannot settle for half but must pursue his dream of himself to the end. Finally, I thought it must be clear, even obvious, that this was no dumb brute heading mindlessly to his catastrophe.

I have no need to be Willy's advocate before the jury which decides who is and who is not a tragic hero. I am merely noting that the lingering ponderousness of so many ancient definitions has blinded students and critics to the facts before them, and not only in regard to this play. Had Willy been unaware of his separation from values that endure he would have died contentedly while polishing his car, probably on a Sunday afternoon with the ball game coming over the radio. But he was agonized by his awareness of being in a false position, so constantly haunted by the hollowness of all he had placed his faith in, so aware, in short, that he must somehow be filled in his spirit or fly apart, that he staked his very life on the ultimate assertion. That he had not the intellectual fluency to verbalize his situation is not the same thing as saying that he lacked awareness, even an overly intensified consciousness that the life he had made was without form and inner meaning.

To be sure, had he been able to know that he was as much the victim of his beliefs as their defeated exemplar, had he known how much of guilt he ought to bear and how much to shed from his soul, he would be more conscious. But it seems to me that there is of necessity a severe limitation of self-awareness in any character, even the most knowing, which serves to define him as a character, and more, that this very limit serves to complete the tragedy and, indeed, to make it at all possible. Complete consciousness is possible only in a play about forces, like *Prometheus*, but not in a play about people. I think that the point is whether there is a sufficient awareness in the hero's career to make the audience supply the rest. Had Oedipus, for instance, been more conscious and more aware of the forces at work upon him he must surely have said that he was not really to blame for having cohabited with his mother since neither he nor anyone else knew she was his mother. He must surely decide to divorce her, provide for their children, firmly resolve to investigate the family background of his next wife, and thus deprive us of a very fine play and the name for a famous neurosis. But he is conscious only up to a point, the point at which guilt begins. Now he is inconsolable and must tear out his eyes. What is tragic about this? Why is it not even ridiculous? How can we respect a man who goes to such extremities over something he could in no way help or prevent? The answer, I think, is not that we respect the man, but that we respect the Law he has so completely broken, wittingly or not, for it is that Law which, we believe, defines us as men. The confusion of some critics viewing *Death of a Salesman* in this regard is that they do not see that Willy Loman has broken a law without whose protection life is insupportable if not incomprehensible to him and to many others; it is the law which says that a failure in society and in business has no right to live. Unlike the law against incest, the law of success is not administered by statute or church, but it is very nearly as powerful in its grip upon men. The confusion increases because, while it is a law, it is by no means a wholly agreeable one even as it is slavishly obeyed, for to fail is no longer to belong to society, in his estimate. Therefore, the path is opened for those who wish to call Willy merely a foolish man even as they themselves are living in obedience to the same law that killed him. Equally, the fact that Willy's law—the belief, in other words, which administers guilt to him—is not a civilizing statute whose destruction menaces us all; it is, rather, a deeply believed and deeply suspect "good" which, when questioned as to its value, as it is in this play, serves more to raise our anxieties than to reassure us of the existence of an unseen but humane metaphysical system in the world. My attempt in the play was to counter this anxiety with an opposing system which, so to speak, is in a race for Willy's faith, and it is the system of love which is the opposite of the law of success. It is embodied in Biff Loman, but by the time Willy can perceive his love it can serve only as an ironic comment upon the life he sacrificed for power and for success and its tokens.

Edward Albee

We must try to claw our way into compassion.

America has produced few important dramatists. Eugene O'Neill, Arthur Miller, and Tennessee Williams have written impressively, but even they have created only several plays that can be considered of permanent value. Since the late 1950's, the only new American dramatist who has written widely and effectively has been Edward Albee. Although he has not yet produced a body of drama equal to that of O'Neill, Miller, or Williams, Albee continues to write the most interesting and representative plays in America.

Born on March 12, 1928, in Washington, D.C., Albee was adopted by Reed and Frances Albee, people connected with the theater; Reed Albee worked in his father's Keith-Albee theater circuit. Young Albee was never attracted to school—as he said, he did not write *The Catcher in the Rye*, he lived it—and he went from the Lawrenceville School in New Jersey to Valley Forge Military Academy in Wayne, Pennsylvania, finally graduating from the Choate School in 1946. Albee studied at Trinity College for a year and a half but was dismissed for having cut classes and chapel. He went to New York City and began to write poetry and novels as well as continuity for a radio program; but these forms were not compatible to his talent and he turned to drama. In 1959 his first play, *The Zoo Story*, was produced in Berlin and on January 14, 1960, at the Provincetown Playhouse on Cape Cod. Albee's other early drama began to appear frequently on off-Broadway: *The Sandbox* (1960), *Fam and Yam* (1960), *The Death of Bessie Smith* (1961), and *The Ameri-*

can Dream (1961). *Who's Afraid of Virginia Woolf?*, produced on Broadway on October 13, 1962, was his first full-length play and its success on the stage and screen gained him national recognition. Since then Albee has been prolific, adapting the prose works of others—Carson McCullers' *The Ballad of the Sad Cafe* (1963) and James Purdy's *Malcolm* (1965)—as well as creating his own plays, *Tiny Alice* (1964) and *A Delicate Balance* (1966).

The quality that distinguishes Albee's early work from that of O'Neill, Miller, and Williams is its harsh cynicism. However despairing the old playwrights may be, there is a romanticism that colors their work and humanizes their characters. In *The Zoo Story*, *The Death of Bessie Smith*, *The American Dream*, and *The Sandbox*, the characters are presented in terms of extreme and at times abnormal behavior. As Albee has developed, his plays have explored character more traditionally, but even in *A Delicate Balance* there is a bitter wit and an irony that lends the play its particularly contemporary tone.

Edward *Albee: Conflict of* Tradition

HENRY
KNEPLER

I N THE INTRODUCTION to his excellent collection *American Playwrights on Drama* Horst Frenz remarks, axiomatically, that "O'Neill never founded a school." He is right, of course, if one considers school to refer to the usual stylistic or structural elements of drama. In the Marlovian or Racinian sense O'Neill did not found a school. In the sense in which his work has become engrained in the American dramatic tradition, however, he did. I do not mean the rather facile, negative sense which Professor Frenz refers to in the same sentence: "O'Neill never founded a school, and the constant experimenting and frequent change of style, which are so noticeable in his work, characterize the work of other American dramatists as well." Mere eclecticism of theatrical modes is not the cohering element of a school or a tradition.

Nor has the American drama "sprung full-grown from the imagination of Eugene O'Neill" as it seems to Robert Brustein. Somewhere between these poles lies the meeting ground of O'Neill's talent and the cultural forces through which the drama in America developed into a reasonably coherent literary tradition. That this tradition has a strong affinity for psychological or psychiatric or psycho-analytic modes needs no particularly extended rehearsal. But, again, these modes are not what gives American dramatic literature its particular cohesive quality. The Freudian couch which hovers, Chagall-like, over the American drama, is not of itself a tradition, only a manifestation of it. Rather, the same forces which spread the psycho-analytic interest until it

REPRINTED FROM *Modern Drama*, VOL. X, NO. 3 (DECEMBER 1967).

pervaded much of American intellectual life, also underlie the tradition.

Perhaps unawares himself, Arthur Miller characterizes its source: "... by force of circumstance I came early and unawares to be fascinated by sheer process itself. How things connected. How the native personality of man was changed by his world, and the harder question, how he in turn could change the world." The key word is repeated in the passage: how. How to build a better mousetrap. How to fix our cities, our youth, our wars, our world, our inner and outer selves. The interest in psycho-analysis is therefore part of a montage made up of, among other things, urban renewal, Dale Carnegie, prohibition, mass education, and what Theodore H. White calls the action-intellectuals. This is said in all seriousness; the American willingness to change things, from cars to countries, is no laughing matter. This leaves man a world in the process of amending itself to which he must make a running adjustment as best he can, his radar spinning away, in David Riesman's analogy, in search of other friendly bleeps in the void.

Eugene O'Neill, transforming personal necessity into brilliant drama, not so much established the tradition as translated it from the larger scene to the stage. In the context of the drama that world view had of course to be made explicit in terms of conflict: this explains not so much the attention as the kind of attention paid to sex and to the family: in the American tradition they do not merely become opponents in a tug of war; the pervasive concern with understanding, explaining and amending them makes them roadstations on the Calvary of change. They are of course also the factors, or reputed to be so, which send American man to the psychiatrist, thereby providing the obverse of the coin: Our fascination with process sends us to the repairshop. And it also gives us the idea that all things can be fixed, if we try hard enough. At this junction of consequence and desire resides the American dream.

In the plays which Edward Albee has written so far the conflict between two traditions, the American and the Absurd, is fierce, because they are intellectually incompatible and because he attempts to use both simultaneously. The American prescribes that man must attempt to make sense of his environment and, moreover, that someday, somehow, he will. The Absurd, as stated by Martin Esslin (and quoted, with disapproval, by Albee) "attempts to make [man] face up to the human condition as it really is, to free him from illusions that are bound to cause constant maladjustment and disappointment . . . For the dignity of man lies in his ability to face reality in all its senselessness." Albee fights that senselessness with all the brilliance of his characterization, his dialogue and his symbols, while at the same time using the modes and theatrical elements of the Absurd: the disembodied static situation; the hints of other dimensions beyond the real or visible; the allegorical maze; and so on. He uses the means or themes of the Absurd to portray the human condition: isolation; repetition; illusion. But he uses them in the American manner: isolation is very conscious and involuntary; repetition is guiltily self-imposed and recognized; and illusion is hallucinatory, mad, *i.e.*, a clinical matter. And he puts it all in the sexual, familial context of O'Neill, Miller, Williams and Inge. This paper attempts to single out some of the results in Albee's work of the conflict between the two traditions. It does not give an over-all evaluation of his work; it merely tries to describe a sub-surface conflict creating surface dramatic problems which, moreover, Albee seems to be resolving. His latest play, A *Delicate Balance*, veers rather strongly back to the tradition of O'Neill.

In his two earliest plays, *The Zoo Story* and *The Death of Bessie Smith*, Albee handles the familial, sexual causality directly. As Jerry tells it in *The Zoo Story* ". . . good old Mom walked out on good old Pop when I was ten and a half years old; she embarked on an adulterous turn of our southern states . . ." The second scene of *Bessie Smith* shows the dominance of the Nurse over the would-be invalid father, and their hate for each other, which in turn underlies her domination of her would-be lover, the Intern, and of the Orderly, a Negro, and in turn is vaguely made to underlie not only her racism but all racism. This causal element is of course only one aspect of a series of subtle and complex relationships. The point about this element is, however, that it stands out in both plays and serves, especially in *The Zoo Story*, as an almost gratuitous addition to a wealth of other material characterizing

Jerry and his position. It stands out, I am inclined to think, as if Albee had felt that, without this bit of Freudian byplay, Jerry or even the Nurse would have been incomplete.

Albee's next play, *The American Dream*, with its satellite, *The Sandbox*, need only be compared to Ionesco's *Bald Soprano* and Pinter's *Collection* to show the familial, always heavily sensual, as the burial ground of the human condition. Mommy and Daddy are as desiccated as Mr. and Mrs. Smith in Ionesco's play or the couple in Pinter's, but their condition differs. Mr. and Mrs. Smith show, perhaps, the aimless boredom of middle class existence, the Pinter couple displays the cruelty of replacement and renewal, but Mommy and Daddy are held together by the perdurable hoops of steel made of impotence and guilt, the chief fixings of all couch-based fixes.

In Albee's first full-length play, *Who's Afraid of Virginia Woolf?* Mommy moves toward reality and becomes Martha, the castrating wife, in a three-hour running battle all in the family. In *The Ballad of the Sad Cafe*, an adaptation of Carson McCullers' novella, Miss Amelia's marriage to Marvin Macy is a necessary part of her Calvary. In *Tiny Alice*, Miss Alice's marriage to Julian is part of his Calvary—and a very explicit Calvary at that. Mommy and Daddy reappear in *A Delicate Balance*—softened, more rounded and more realistic, tending toward Inge rather than Ionesco, beset by friends fleeing from a nameless threat, by a daughter back from her third or fourth divorce, and an alcoholic sister as the commentator character. Divorce and alcoholism, like impotence, homosexuality, and loss of religious faith, underlie the variations, presented with often great subtlety, of man's isolation without and within himself.

To seal this isolation Albee uses a psychological variant of a device which James O'Neill, Eugene's father, would have remembered well. In nineteenth century drama it was known as the Pathetic Child. With Albee it becomes the would-be child, ranging from the symbolically emasculated young man in *The American Dream* to the alienated divorcee in *A Delicate Balance*. The phantom child in *Virginia Woolf* is the most interesting. Martha and George have invented a child for themselves; it is a secret between them, whose disclosure to visitors leads to George's "killing" him, by means of a fictitious telegram about a car accident at his fictitious college. I was struck by the parallel to Salinger's story "Uncle Wiggily in Connecticut": there, a small girl, alone and alienated from her mother, invents a playmate for herself. When the mother tells a friend about that phantom playmate, the little girl has him killed in a car accident, and calmly invents another. The same air of contamination pervades the story as the play. In *Virginia Woolf* George and Martha are really children in a statement on arrested development which corresponds to Freudian theory. The variations continue: Miss Amelia, in the *Sad Cafe*, adapts rather than adopts the little hunchback Cousin Lymon as one would a child; she loses him when he runs off with her would-be husband Marvin Macy, to whom she refused to bear a child. The most complicated man-child relationship is in Albee's most equivocal play, *Tiny Alice*. In different ways the play deals with two children. Brother Julian, the protagonist, in his morning-glory freshness and honesty, is the innocent fallen among the thieves. The other child is part-object of a story he himself tells. An inmate of a mental hospital believes herself to be with child; a medical examination discloses that she has a fatal cancer of the womb. The edifice of symbols surrounding this simple event is a fretwork of mirrors of illusions: the woman believes that she is the Virgin Mary; Julian committed himself to the mental hospital in which she was a patient because of his loss of religious faith which was accompanied by hallucinations. Because of these hallucinations he is not sure if he did or did not have intercourse with the woman. The whole structure of illusion therefore has a medical bent which is also noticeable in other Albee plays. The imaginary child in *Virginia Woolf* is an indication of his parents' sickness, just as the emasculated and therefore perfect American Dreamboat is of the sickness of society. The *Delicate Balance* is the one between sanity and insanity, or what we believe these two states to be. The guests who foist themselves upon Agnes and Tobias in that play are driven from their home by an undescribed, hallucinatory experience. Albee, though he may not have intended this, cannot rid his plays of the idea that illusion is sick, or at least a matter of clinical concern. The prevalence of would-be children whether as phantoms, like in *Tiny*

Alice and *Virginia Woolf*, or as seemingly grown up, like in *The American Dream* and *The Ballad of the Sad Cafe*, has therefore a double function: isolation and illusion. Except for a few culture heroes like Grandma (*The American Dream*) and Martha's father (*Virginia Woolf*) men and women are seen as children and therefore given to illusions. The child-man relationship is not Wordsworthian, however; it is a case of arrested development, of stunted growth or maturity, according to psycho-analytic principles. The trap of human illusion which is sprung for us in *The Caretaker* or *Waiting for Godot* has no such causes, nor could it have.

Repetition, the third major element singled out here, is a central aspect of the Absurd drama. *The Bald Soprano* is a *perpetuum mobile*, ending with the same lines as the opening. *The Balcony* has its variations of a theme in the brothel; repetition is the point in *The Collection; The Dumb Waiter* has its hired killers doing just another job; and so on. Repetition serves Albee in the same manner, but it also gets in his way at times. As we watch *Who's Afraid of Virginia Woolf?*, we find that Nick and Honey are not the first victims drawn and quartered on the battle-ground of Martha and George. The battle is permanent which would make it a condition rather than a process. So Albee contradicts and weakens his impact in several ways: at the end of the play the phantom child has been liquidated, and the ground rules of battle are changed thereby. And Honey, who was afraid of childbirth before, leaves the inferno wanting a child. (She has just one line, one moment, to indicate that, which makes it appear more like the old crime movie where the last sixty seconds show that crime, so lovingly portrayed for eighty-nine minutes, does not pay.)

In *Tiny Alice* the trouble is exactly the opposite: the uniqueness of the situation, so obviously desired for Julian, is undermined by symbols and conversation until one gets a kind of *déjà vu* effect, as if Miss Alice and her crew were quite used to swatting such flies as Julian. Repetition and illusion are closely linked in Albee's work. There is comfort in repetition and pattern, comfort for children to witness expected and expectable events, comfort for all ages, if we can see that terrifying constant process

of change somehow patterned; comfort especially if we remember
that the kindly clinician needs to be able to find the pattern in
order to cure. That, perhaps, accounts for the occurrence of symbols in circular patterns, often great swaths of interlocking circles.
In *Virginia Woolf*, for example, George tells Nick the story of a
prep school friend who advertently-inadvertently killed his parents,
later ran his car into a tree, and ended his days in a mental
institution. The story reappears as George's own, though we cannot be sure of that, and also as a novel he wrote, which was suppressed by his formidable father-in-law, the president of the college. In the end George reports that the death of the phantom
son occurred in the same way as the suicide attempt of the prep
school boy.

At times, these great swaths of symbols look most like the
creations of a talented, malicious child who wants to provide
happy hunting grounds for English teachers. My favorite is the
commingling of blood and wine, semen and blood, stringing
together a great edifice of sex and faith in *Tiny Alice*. In the end
blood turns back to wine, the bottles of the magnificent wine
cellar, poorly tended, are popping the rotting corks; especially of
a superb Mouton Rothschild—Blood of the Lamb indeed!

A *New Yorker* cartoon not long ago depicts a group of men
and women on folding chairs around a table, on a stage: a first
reading of a play. One man is up, talking, his foot on his chair:
the director. The caption says: "Now, the first thing we have to
get straight is what exactly Aristophanes was trying to say." Albee
plays on our culturally conditioned desire to get behind things, to
see, in Arthur Miller's phrase, "how things connect." With
O'Neill this was legitimate, so to speak, a genuine desire caused
by a genuine anguish. With Albee it seems to be a structure
consciously made up of rewards and punishments for the audience,
which perhaps makes him a Pavlovian rather than a Freudian in
the American theatrical tradition. He challenges us deliberately,
he dares us to look behind what he says. He does it brilliantly,
with a wealth of talent in construction, in dialog, in imagery.
Perhaps he is both admired and disliked because his now-you-see-
it-now-you-don't view of the human condition gives us the kind
of inside dope we currently deserve.

VI
Film

☐ "There is no world so but it has its heroes," F. Scott Fitzgerald wrote in *The Last Tycoon*, "and Stahr was the hero. Most of these men had been here a long time—through the beginnings and the great upset, when sound came, and the three years of depression, he had seen that no harm came to them. The old loyalties were trembling now, there were clay feet everywhere; but still he was their man, the last of the princes."

☐ Monroe Stahr, who is modeled after Irving Thalberg, is a brilliant Hollywood producer in Fitzgerald's novel. He has risen to his high position through hard work, keen intelligence, and inner discipline—he is Fitzgerald's sophisticated version of the twentieth-century Horatio Alger, "the last of the princes"; and he feels that, with equal determination, others can also be successful. Unlike most of the Hollywood executives, Monroe Stahr remains compassionate toward his subordinates and they respond with respect, affection, and loyalty. Stahr also believes that the making of films is a creative act, and though he is sharply aware of the practical restrictions on this mass medium, he sees it in imaginative terms and views himself primarily as an artist. "Stahr like Lincoln was a leader carrying on a long war on many fronts; almost single-handed he had moved pictures sharply forward through a decade, to a point where the content of the 'A productions' was wider and richer than that of the stage. Stahr was an artist only, as Mr. Lincoln was a general, perforce and as a layman." Stahr battles against the business officials of the Hollywood studios, but it is clear that he will not be pragmatically successful. Hollywood, in the 1930's, was already developing into a vast industry in which the respect for creative direction or distinctive acting had surrendered to the desire for mass appeal.

☐ Few men in Hollywood have triumphed over the commercialization of the film medium. D. W. Griffith, Mack Sennett, Erich von Stroheim, Ernst Lubitsch, and John Ford have succeeded in directing highly imaginative motion pictures.

Charlie Chaplin, Buster Keaton, the Marx Brothers, and
Greta Garbo have created unique images as independent stars.
But there have been no producers of the Stahr-Thalberg type,
and producers like Louis B. Mayer, Harry Cohn, Samuel Gold-
wyn, Walter Wanger, and Darryl F. Zanuck have dominated
the industry.

□ Hollywood has traditionally frustrated actors with long-
term contracts, a production code, and an ostensible desire
for films to remain a *kitsch* art form. In the 1950's and 1960's,
however, American movies have been influenced by other art
forms and by some of the great European film directors; they
have become more adventurous, sexually explicit, and intellectually mature. The development of Mike Nichols as a
director, Elizabeth Taylor as an actress, and Sidney Poitier as
an actor attests to the increasing subtlety of contemporary
films. As three representative figures of the movies, they suggest the candor and intelligence that have recently characterized some American movies.

Mike Nichols

*I often can't think of anything I'd rather do than make movies—
you can go anywhere with it.*

It is a commonplace to speak of movies as a director's
medium, and yet we identify most motion pictures by their
leading actors and actresses or, in the idiom of the industry,
their "stars." We think of European directors like Bergman,
Fellini, Antonioni, Truffaut, and others as having produced
oeuvres, and we estimate them in terms of their masterpieces
and their failures, their development as artists who have a
singular vision of the world. America is the country of the
movie star—directors like Hitchcock or Ford who can boast
of reputations independent of particular actors or actresses
are indeed rare. In the sixties the director who has attracted
widest popularity and admiration—from those actors he has
directed as well as from audiences—is Mike Nichols, and the
movie that has proved to be his greatest success is *The Graduate*.

Mike Nichols was born in Berlin, Germany, in 1931, the
son of a Russian-Jewish physician who fled Nazi Germany
with his family and settled in New York City. Nichols, who
was seven years old when his father brought him to America,
attended the Dalton School in New York, the Cherry Lane
School in Darien, Connecticut, and Walden High School in
New York. He went on to the University of Chicago and
began as a premed student, hoping eventually to become a
psychiatrist. Soon, however, he grew interested in acting and
left the university after two years, returning to New York to
study with Lee Strasberg at the Actors Studio. In Chicago,

Nichols joined Elaine May, whom he had met in college, as part of six performers called The Compass. In 1957, Nichols and Miss May established an act of their own and began to do improvisations in nightclubs and on records. Their humor was mixed with perceptive and caustic social satire, and they quickly became national celebrities. The success of the team culminated in *An Evening with Mike Nichols and Elaine May*, which opened on Broadway on October 8, 1960, and closed on July 1, 1961.

Since 1961, Nichols has become an increasingly well-known director. Every play and movie he has directed has become a success: *Barefoot in the Park, Luv, The Odd Couple, The Apple Tree, Who's Afraid of Virginia Woolf?*, the revival of *The Little Foxes*, and *Catch 22*. These plays and movies are comedies, and Nichols has brought his own wit, his unaffected intelligence, and sure sense of timing to an understanding of them. As one observer has commented, "Nichols today is one of those absolute American success stories—a fellow who is recompensed enormously for being himself." His special talent is well-exhibited in *The Graduate*, a movie that has had enormous success and that well may realize the prediction of its producer and become "the highest-grossing film in motion-picture history."

The popularity of *The Graduate* depends, as Jacob Brackman points out in the following essay, on its perception into youth. "Isolated and starved by the culture," Brackman writes, youth "face a crisis of imagination." When Benjamin's father asks him, "What do you want," and Benjamin answers, "I don't know," we begin to realize the degree to which the younger generation has been emotionally and ethically starved. Mike Nichols has successfully captured the vacillations of youth, their lack of any moral direction, the so-called "generation gap" between parents and children, and the vapidity of so much life in America.

Onward and Upward with the Arts: "The Graduate"

JACOB

BRACKMAN

THOUGH we all identify European movies by naming their directors, film buffs who refer to American movies that way have seemed a little pedantic. Familiar though we are with the axiom that European *auteurs* produce unmistakably personal visions, we have seen Hollywood movies, even the movies of our most "distinctive" directors, as committee efforts. "Who's Afraid of Virginia Woolf?" was the Burton-Taylor movie or, in certain circles, the Albee movie. But "The Graduate" is, definitively, the Mike Nichols movie. In fact, it has given everybody the chance to be a movie buff; that is, to talk about the *director*. Even its actors, in interviews, have tried to turn attention away from themselves toward Nichols. The critics—including some who usually scorn *auteur* notions—tended overwhelmingly to speak of "The Graduate's" success in terms of Nichols' success. Many of them called him a genius. The New York Film Critics and the Motion Picture Academy elected "In the Heat of the Night" Best Picture, but both groups chose Nichols over Norman Jewison (and Arthur Penn) as Best Director. The Directors' Guild of America also gave Nichols its annual award. John Allen wrote in the *Christian Science Monitor*, "The director . . . has [hereby] announced his candidacy for election to the upper chamber of filmmakers now occupied by Fellini, Truffaut, Antonioni, and others of their calibre. Mr. Nichols, as a director whose sure control shapes and colors every frame of film with a distinctive, recognizable style, is almost sure of election. . . . Mr. Nichols is everywhere, blending, coloring, illuminating. He gives to 'The Graduate' that special brilliance that occurs when all the right lights are filtered through the proper prism: his touch as a director is a veritable chandelier of finely cut crystal." Will Jones wrote more or less the same thing in the Minneapolis *Tribune*: "Everybody asks why the Americans don't make movies the way Europeans do, right? Okay, buddies, here's European moviemaking done right in the heart of American movieville. Hey, there, Schlesinger, Richardson, Antonioni, Truffaut . . . can little Mikey Nichols come play with your gang? You bet." Nichols said recently, rather as if biting the hands that had fed him so generously, "Critics are like eunuchs watching a gang-bang. They must truly be ignored." The fact is that critical hungers have been working in Nichols' favor. Americans want to feel good about what is being produced here. In the early nineteenth century, when Continental literati scoffed, "Who ever read an American book?," our critics often fell into a similar aesthetic chauvinism; this or that new author was always promising to take his place beside the European masters. A century later, when American movie pioneers set the pace for the international field, the heirs of those critics were quick to claim cinema as a fully legitimate medium for art. But its rapid industrialization—the demand for "something for everyone," to insure maximum returns on huge production investments—soon dictated a cinema not of truth or beauty but of wish fulfillment: of prosperity, romance, and moral simplicity. At least since the end of the Second World War, with the flourishing of Italian neo-realism and, later, the French *nouvelle vague*, American entertainment has been forced back into the shadow of European art. Our cultural insecurity vis-à-vis the Old World is at work again. Oppressed by the confusions of the times, we look for the film genius who will do for us what Rossellini, Visconti, De Sica, Fellini, Antonioni, and Olmi have done for the Italians. It is an immense task, granted, but we cannot afford to accept less from our first mid-century genius. He must give this frazzled country some feeling for itself, for its contradictions and despairs, even as it goes through changes that make the job almost impossible.

Not altogether unlike Benjamin, Nichols has long existed on
the verge, in a portentous condition of promise. He had a way of
shrugging off his unbroken string of successes (five stage and two
Hollywood hits out of seven tries) which made them appear play-
ful warmups for some grand feat of art. Because his mastery
over "unworthy vehicles" seemed consummate—because, in other
words, he had attempted nothing in the theatre that strained at
the limits of his talent—people considered him "better" than
anything he had done showed him to be. Nearly every artist
secretly thinks of himself in this way, but Nichols' recent public
statements suggest that critical overestimations of "The Graduate"
may have momentarily beguiled him into presuming that the
quality we are willing to attribute to *him* can already be found in
his work.

Nichols has provided his film with the texture, if not the substance, of contemporaneity. Like "Blow-Up," and more than any
other recent American film, "The Graduate" has the *look* of today.
The Berkeley students look like Berkeley students—not like
Berkeley students of a dozen years ago, or like a middle-aged conservative's nightmare of Berkeley students, or like a pop huckster's
souped-up Berkeley students. (Nichols is reported to have salted
his crowd with casting-agency hippies. He evidently has an exceptional eye for extras.) Similarly, his camera has captured the exact
appearance of a contingent of senior citizens, a *nouveau-riche*
poolside lawn party, a Berkeley student boarding house, an Ivy
League-type locker room, a suburban Los Angeles den. The care
that Nichols has devoted to surface reality infuses into familiar
personalities and their backgrounds a recognizability uncommon in
American films (and virtually nonexistent on television). There's
something thrilling in that accomplishment—something rather
like the strange excitement of overhearing one's name mentioned
—but his ability to capture our surroundings gives him an authority he does not merit on the subject of the feelings we experience in them.

Nichols also seems determined to weaken the impact of his
settings with an almost random series of cinematic tricks. Unusual
ways of photographing the details of physical reality—the simple
fact of things—are supposed to comment upon the camera's ob-

jects, upon what is really there. Presumably, a director uses the perspectives of his camera (its lens distortions, its angle of vision, its filter coloration, its distance, the suddenness of its attention) to indicate the proper attitude toward the visual facts, more or less as a writer chooses between words to suggest his own viewpoint. The way it works out most often in movies, of course, is that a director tosses off variations in perspective in a spirit of arbitrary virtuosity, confusing us or distracting us from his text, in the manner of a poet whose rhyme and metre bear no more than an incidental relation to the sense they serve. Many critics and moviegoers imagine that intrusive alterations of perspective are the "mark" of a film director, much as readers once believed that similes and conceits were the mark of a writer. We now understand that good writing can exist quite independent of such conventions—that, in fact, a careless, eclectic use of them results in bad writing. Nichols approaches his visual arrangements like a young writer stuffing incongruous stylisms of Dickens, Joyce, Faulkner, and Hemingway—and some good schtik from Salinger, Mailer, and Bruce Jay Friedman as well—into his prose. In reading, we have a clear view of how disastrously this subverts what reality of his own a writer manages to bring to his material, but we are not so wary of the non-integral perspectives of the motion-picture camera.

Nichols may be somewhat proud of his artful photography, for he has apparently authorized as the film's advertising emblem a composition that he employs twice, ostentatiously, in the film: Benjamin (in the ad he is decked in ceremonial cap and gown) framed by the bare, curvaceous leg of Mrs. Robinson. Nichols goes in for this sort of camerawork throughout the movie. What's the point?

"Well, to take this particular issue, the shot of Benjamin through Mrs. R.'s leg as she fiddles with her stockings is intended to fill our field of vision, like Benjamin's, with brassy sexuality."

"Well, then, why are we looking *through* the leg *at* Benjamin, instead of at the leg as if through Benjamin's eyes?"

"Well, this way we get to see Benjamin's reacting as well as what he's reacting to."

"Well, why don't they just show the leg from Benjamin's

shoulder and then right away show us him reacting in a closeup, because we get distracted from him by that *leg* in the foreground anyway."

"Well, this way you get the whole idea instantaneously, in a single shot."

Clearly, the argument can continue on both sides, and over each jarring cinematic change: Is this new perspective justified at this moment by what is happening in the movie? Does it work here? Though unusual perspectives are often assumed to be self-justifying, they tend to make us aware of ourselves as an audience —to insist upon the urgency of our being entertained, or else to give us the uneasy feeling that the director is providing insights we aren't absorbing. Like a child who has been given a great many presents at once, Nichols seems to have just discovered that the camera will do all sorts of remarkable stunts at his bidding. Now he has it crouching low to peer up into a dazzling blur of sunlight. Now staring wide-eyed into the headlights of oncoming cars so that the beams bounce from the lens, creating floating discs in the night. Now jumping into a swimming pool to catch the swirly patterns of air bubbles in moving water. Now snuggling in a closet corner and ogling out past the hangers, now squinting through a fish tank, now gazing at reflections in a polished tabletop. Now it's barrelling low along a bumpy highway, now jogging on some unseen shoulder, lending a "documentary" quality by cutting off the tops of people's heads for cruel, open-pore closeups. Now its lens is foreshortening, now it is wide-angle, now telescopic, now looking to one side so that the main image is way off center. Nichols' devices keep elbowing us nervously in the ribs, as if without them our attention might stray: anticipated-sound cuts, with dialogue from a new scene beginning while the image of the previous one still lingers on the screen; dizzying fast cutting back and forth between Benjamin and Mrs. Robinson when she first offers herself to him, turning her naked body into a blur of flesh; a painful sequence photographed through the distorting glass of a scuba mask; a pullback to a bird's-eye shot of Benjamin sitting in a deserted Berkeley plaza, which dissolves, to suggest the passage of time, into a shot of Benjamin in precisely the same posture but with the light brighter and the plaza filled with bustling students;

a phantasmagoric series of cuts, beginning with the affair proper, that include shots of Benjamin being borne by his raft in the pool and by Mrs. Robinson's body in bed, Benjamin having breakfast with his parents, then watching TV at home and watching TV in the hotel room.

Nichols' cameraman, Robert Surtees, has been quoted as saying, "I needed everything I learned in the past thirty years to shoot 'The Graduate,' " as if this were automatically to be taken as testimony to Nichols' directorial brilliance. Ideally, of course, a director's style should emerge organically from his over-all conception of the material. A cohesive point of view should lead to a legible plan that relates each shot to the film in its entirety— or, failing that, at least to the surrounding shots, to whole scenes. Nichols, fairly bursting with ambitious ideas, seems to have been squeamish about giving any of them up. His apparent compulsion to retain each distinct evidence of his "creativity" unhooks scenes from one another, and even produces a disjointed quality within individual scenes, as though he intended, instead of a narrative, a series of vignettes. Denied the cabaret option of discretionary blackouts, Nichols is frequently at a loss for some means of proceeding gracefully from one cut to the next. Often, he ducks out of his dilemma with facile irony. He caps a tense family scene at the breakfast table with a cheap guffaw: browned slices pop providentially from a toaster—punctuation of the sort that kept viewers chuckling over the "Dick Van Dyke Show." When Elaine goes off with Carl at the San Francisco Zoo, Benjamin is left alone in front of the monkey cage. Nichols lingers on the inevitable mugging chimps, granting us also a glimpse of the over-appropriate sign "Do Not Tease."

How are we to account for these lapses? Once a writer has embarked upon the act of composition, he must put all the fine prose he has read out of his mind, and I suspect that a film-maker, at some juncture—if not while shooting, then in the cutting room —must do the same with all the movie footage he has viewed admiringly. Nichols seems to assume naïvely that shots that looked good in someone else's movie will look good in his own. The framing thing, for example, used to be a fad in still photography—we recall the Armistice Day parade viewed through an amputee's

crutch and remaining leg, or the tennis player framed in the
netting of his opponent's racket—but since it failed to tell as much
as it promised, its interest soon waned. So it goes with Nichols'
devices. They send us scurrying in search of absent meanings. To
complicate matters, we recognize certain types of shots from other
films, and tend to associate them with certain directors—to consider them, in fact, the substance of a particular director's style.
And a number of Nichols' imitative shots are so strikingly reminiscent of their originals that they compound our distraction by
calling us back into a previous film experience. The huge, beauty-
parlored faces frozen in artificial hilarities which so impinge upon
Benjamin's fragile homecoming sensibilities dance before the
camera just like party faces from "8½" or "Juliet of the Spirits."
Fellini's camera catches more of the truth about those who impose
their presences upon the distraught Mastroianni: they are terrible
harpies, but, even so, something is to be learned, not merely endured, from observing them. The startling zoom-back shot of
Mrs. Robinson leaning rain-drenched against a blank wall—an
image so drained of color as to appear virtually black-and-white—
evokes a shot from Antonioni's "La Notte." Its main effect here,
however, is unintended. It strikes us with the depths of Anne
Bancroft's sudden ugliness, and the image is affecting not because
of what has befallen an unsavory character but because the spectacle of an unsparingly photographed woman star has an overwhelming poignance. In the face of Miss Bancroft's professional
courage, we are ashamed to have doubted the honesty of the enterprise for which she abases herself. Again the mind has been
drawn in an undesirable direction. Astonishingly, Nichols seems
to miss the point at times. Much of the business involved in Benjamin's wait for Mrs. Robinson in the hotel room recalls a similar
scene in Truffaut's "The Soft Skin." Here the effect of Benjamin's
flicking the trysting-room lights on and off is largely dissipated
because the camera is so close in on him; we get little sense of
Benjamin in the whole room as it flips between light and darkness.

When critics speak at all of this sort of directorial borrowing,
they tend to talk, with absurd politeness, about "influence." Thus,
in his review of "The Graduate" Stanley Kauffmann writes, "In
'Virginia Woolf' I thought I saw some influence of Kurosawa; I

think so again here," or speaks of a "Godardian irony through objects." (Irony is irony; Kauffmann means to draw our attention to specific methods that Godard has fathered—lingering on props to comment upon the action, or juxtaposing shots of characters with shots of things that supposedly illuminate character.) Again, in noticing the "aged, uncomprehending passengers" who turn to stare at Benjamin and Elaine on the bus, he writes, "One last reminder!—of Lester's old-folks chorus in 'The Knack.' " This critical approach implies that a director somehow absorbs the craft of his mentors, which gives his work additional resonance. But a conscious artist is rarely influenced in any such abstruse way. Nearly every great director, writer, composer, or painter plagiarizes his forebears' craft—especially early in his career, before he has fully worked out his own thing. He learns, as Archibald MacLeish has put it, "the way a boy learns from an apple orchard—by stealing what he has a taste for and can carry off." To speak of this imitation as "influence" falsely implies unawareness. Obviously, Nichols isn't trying to sneak anything past us; he has sufficient ingenuity to disguise his borrowings better, if he cared to.

Nichols (and Webb before him) clearly aimed at that comedy which arises naturally out of a scrupulous observation of life— that vision of human frustration and inadequacy which is devastatingly true yet devoutly compassionate. This is probably the highest form of comedy and, at its most successful, the funniest. It is the comedy of Chekhov, of some Mark Twain stories and some of Chaplin's movies, of Lenny Bruce, of Salinger—the wise laughter rising above apparent tragedy. Now, there can also be a certain condemnation in such laughter, but never so much as to overwhelm charity with contempt. The song that Simon and Garfunkel do on the sound track after Benjamin flees from Mrs. Robinson's cops suggests its temper: "And here's to you, Mrs. Robinson, Jesus loves you more than you will know." Great comedy is naturally subversive, by virtue of its accuracy, but it is never venomous. It may give exquisite pleasure over long periods without making us laugh out loud. Then, when the sidesplitters do come, they have a quality almost of spiritual purgation. Nichols would have liked, one imagines, to make "The Graduate" this sort of comedy, but he was trained in a theatre—cabaret and Broadway—where comedy's success is meter-measured: How many in the audience laugh? How often and how loud? Nichols seems to care about getting the laughs, even easy ones; he doesn't particularly care who it is he's laughing at, and he apparently believes that a laugh is as good a way out of an artistic problem as any other.

An odd change occurs in Nichols' point of view at the beginning of the middle section of the film (when Benjamin telephones Mrs. Robinson) and persists until the end of that section (when Benjamin realizes he loves Elaine): Benjamin himself becomes the butt of the jokes. In the first part of the film, adults seemed laughable, or pitiable, yet basically well intentioned. Here they seem wicked (Mrs. Robinson) or dangerously insensitive (Benjamin's parents). Having become sinister, the grownups no longer seem fit objects for comedy. Nonetheless, this middle section of "The Graduate" is the most comically intended of the three, and, to judge by the reactions of the audience, it is the most comically successful. Benjamin turns into a victim here—not only a victim of Mrs. Robinson's wiles but a victim of his own ineptitude. It is the second victim, in particular, that we are meant to laugh at. Nichols has filled the section with the sort of broad funny business he polished in staging Neil Simon's comedies on Broadway. Benjamin should be uncomfortable with Mrs. Robinson partly because of his naïveté but more because he understands that she can have no real place in the scheme of his life. Nichols, however, exaggerates the naïveté until it becomes farcical. About fifteen minutes of running time elapses, for example, between the time Benjamin telephones Mrs. Robinson and the time they hit the hotel bed together—fifteen minutes of sight and sound gags on the theme of nervousness. Benjamin fumbles through the arrangements for their rendezvous—nodding maniacally, scratching, wheezing from deep in his throat, like a frightened animal—as though he expected a vice squad to descend on him at any instant. In some business with the room clerk that centers on his having no luggage, Benjamin loses his cool completely. The single, frenetic joke—the ninny doesn't know what he's doing—continues after Mrs. Robinson gets up to the bed-

room: Benjamin kisses her just after she has inhaled smoke from
a cigarette, so she must hold the smoke in until the kiss is over;
Benjamin tries to bring her a wooden hanger for her dress, but it's
attached to the closet rod; and so forth. We quickly exhaust our
ways of receiving the joke, and our laughter becomes similarly
frenetic.

Critics have remarked that the excruciating exchanges between
Benjamin and Mrs. Robinson are reminiscent of some of the bits
that Nichols used to do with Elaine May. Their work together
often portrayed men and women coming on with each other, and
Nichols and May were particularly sharp at skewering common
dishonesties, egotistical little games, and ulterior desperation. Yet
the one scene in "The Graduate" in which Benjamin lets his hair
down to Elaine ("I feel like I'm playing this game somebody else
made up the rules to . . .") is closer to a Nichols and May routine
than any conversation with Mrs. Robinson—though heaven forbid
we should laugh at it. Their comedy almost never took sides—
one of them didn't become the other's butt. Nichols' character
was just as derisible as May's, and neither used gag lines to make
us laugh; instead, each tried to express himself with the utmost
seriousness and wound up—partly to our embarrassment, because
each said things that any of us might hear ourselves saying—
fatuous. In "The Graduate," Nichols treats as revelation the kind
of material he would once have used for his comedy, and makes
comedy out of the kind of material that would once have been
beneath him. When Benjamin first arrives at the hotel, he does a
double take when the clerk asks him, "Are you here for an affair?"
Soon we are asked to laugh at every hint of his anguish. Mrs.
Robinson becomes more than a domineering female. The traditional sexual roles are reversed: she clearly wants nothing more
than a good time in bed, and Benjamin, like a Vassar girl, keeps
working the conversation around to his misgivings about not having a "meaningful relationship." Her frank, predatory sexuality
begins to look like derision of Benjamin. His compliance begins to
suggest that he must despise himself. Had Nichols made a more
substantial case against Benjamin's surroundings—had that issue
survived the first third of the film—his self-degradation would have

made sense, at least dramatically; he might have felt so sullied by his inability to break connections with society that he could not foresee ever feeling pride in himself.

After the surprising credibility of the first third, the tight structure of plot and character begin falling to pieces. We are assaulted by a series of unbelievable details. Presumably vital questions of plot become irrelevant, because of incredible elements within the plot. Is Benjamin a virgin or isn't he? After the first hotel-room scene with Mrs. Robinson, we could equally well decide either way. Since Benjamin's entire motivation in the scene hinges upon the "true" answer, we may assume that Nichols at least whispered it in Dustin Hoffman's ear, and, without very much extra effort, could have tipped off the audience. If Benjamin *is* a virgin, we may chalk up most of his terrible distress to first-time jitters. (Many of the critics made exactly this assumption, and consequently took Benjamin's sexual initiation, or "coming of age," to be the major theme of the film.) If he is not, we must look for more interesting and disturbing causes. Having read the book, as John Lennon says, I can report that although the Benjamin of the film usually acts as though he'd never even seen *Playboy*, the Benjamin of the novel is not a virgin. Ten pages are devoted to his departure for and return from three weeks on the road, undertaken, after graduation, to relieve his metaphysical distress, and he informs his father afterward, "There were a few whores included in the tour." Nor is there any indication that they were Benjamin's first. Just as Nichols has declined to let us know about Benjamin's previous sexual experience, he has left out the trip altogether, even though many of its incidents might have had tremendous cinematic potential. Benjamin tells his father of fighting a forest fire in Shasta country, of hitching rides from common folk, of sex in "a cow pasture, Dad," going on to say of this, "It was about three in the morning and there was ice in the grass and cows walking around us." And he asks, rhetorically, "Have you ever had a queer Indian approach you while you're trying to keep your clothes from burning up?" The stuff a Dylan song is made of! Yet Nichols omits the whole diminished *Bildungsroman*, possibly because it so forcefully underscores the proper problem of "The

Graduate"; it shows beyond doubt that Benjamin is desperately in earnest about trying to determine what sort of life he wants to construct for himself. By concealing Benjamin's sexual experience from us, Nichols is able to get mileage out of the boy's naïveté and ineptitude. We could not laugh in quite the same way if we knew that Benjamin had just returned from sleeping with prostitutes on the road; we would have to treat him more seriously. We would have to interpret his reluctance to embark upon an affair with Mrs. Robinson as more sensible and telling.

The virginity question is just one example of what happens as "The Graduate" veers from its early course. As soon as Nichols starts fudging on his material, he gets caught up in a web of implausibilities. First we have the B.M.O.C. Benjamin—evidently head of the debating club, campus editor, captain of the cross-country team, social chairman of his house—transformed into a somnambulistic, clowny schlepp, and, again, into an aggressive tiger. It's natural for a guy to manifest different aspects of his personality with different girls, but the "cool" Benjamin, in shades, who knows his way around tough Sunset Strip burlesque joints simply cannot be the shook-up fellow with the big-eyed stare who assures Mrs. Robinson as he prepares to grant her fondest wish, "I want you to know how much I appreciate this." Next, Mrs. Robinson—a handsome, worldly, unhappily married woman—is transformed first into a businesslike mistress and then into a hell-hound. Nichols seems on the verge of making her human in the fight after Benjamin pleads, of their affair, "Couldn't we liven this up with a little conversation?" For a moment, he allows us to realize that the young man has the position of strength in a liaison of this kind, and that the older woman—worn out, fearful about wrinkles and flab and her waning capacity for arousing desire or affection—is the one who is truly vulnerable. Just as we begin to feel some sympathy for this wretched woman, Nichols snaps the witch mask back on her. The remarkable thing is that there is not the slightest necessity for either of these sequences of transformation. Nothing essential to the story requires that Benjamin ever be less than bright and competent. Nor does anything demand Mrs. Robinson's consummate villainy; the wooing of a girl after an affair with her mother would by itself present a hero with plenty of obstacles—especially once the father-husband found out. So Nichols has introduced these two distortions of personality as though to help captivate us away from our initial focus, and from them spring a litter of false bits. Benjamin would not continue to call Mrs. Robinson by her surname after they have been sleeping together for weeks. He would not make such an idiot of himself over retrieving his toothbrush from his car. He would not drive his car literally off the road at Elaine's casual mention of the hotel where he and Mrs. Robinson have been trysting. Mrs. Robinson would not be so insanely touchy on the subject of her daughter. She would not perpetually address Benjamin in that excessively clear tone one reserves for small children. She would not lean over indifferently to rub out a smudge on her slip when Benjamin puts a hand on her brassiered breast—her hungers could not be so cold. She would not be so ready to tell Elaine of the affair, nor would Benjamin—they would not race each other home to break the news. She would not then invent a preposterous story about Benjamin's getting her drunk and raping her—stab him in the back and then try to hang him on a concealed-weapons rap—and if she did, neither her daughter nor her husband would believe her, because they could not live twenty years with such a woman and know nothing of her treachery. Indeed, Mrs. Robinson becomes so impossible that her machinations have to take place offscreen for almost the last hour of the movie, except for a two-minute confrontation with Benjamin when he appears searching for Elaine, and a one-line appearance in the wedding finale. With Mrs. Robinson out of the way, Elaine must share the burden of uncertain characterization. She falls for the rape story completely and dismisses Benjamin for good, then immediately believes his denial and falls in love with him. We might make allowances for that much, but suddenly she becomes inexplicably flighty; her feelings seem to be serving some unfathomable higher demands— the director's, we cannot help suspecting. Precisely when the course of the film hinges upon her response to Benjamin, she grows so wildly fickle that even the conventions of "femininity" will not excuse her. For no apparent reason, she shatters our picture of the obstacles arising from a misguided adult world.

Much of the excitement surrounding "The Graduate" has stemmed from the proposition that, in *Glamour's* words, it "gets to the very heart of what youth is about," and is also a superbly "adult" movie. (Very few children's movies come out of Hollywood anymore, but producers still reserve the term "adult" for films they regard as uncommonly truthful.) Critics who previously had only scorn for film renderings of Youth hail "The Graduate" as the first American motion picture to deal authentically with today's much discussed generation gap. Yet in representing the gap between contemporary adults and youth the film unwittingly calls urgent attention to the gap between the America of today and the America of ten years ago, from which its generational vision might more credibly have emerged.

"The Graduate" hinges upon Benjamin's *interestingness*, and it is an interestingness not so much portrayed as established by a tautological convention: People who don't say much and who look pained in frequent closeups are deep and interesting because why else would they be pictured that way? Carl Smith is introduced and limned to underscore our impression of Benjamin. Carl is the Lane Coutell figure—tweedy, suave, "giving the impression of having at least three lighted cigarettes in each hand." His fraternity brothers, naturally, refer to him as "the make-out king." But what, after all, does the contrast between Carl and Benjamin amount to? I asked a number of people who saw the movie. Most of them, in fascinating departures from the text, immediately replied that the two were as different as Jacob and Esau, and went on to paint subjective portraits of Carl as an unfeeling square and Benjamin as a sort of radical-hippie—a logical extension of his "interestingness." But an interesting young man of the late fifties transplanted into the America of 1968 would be barely conscious. Ten years ago, a primitive rejection of adult emptiness and hypocrisy was a sufficient condition for interestingness. Today, by itself, it isn't nearly enough. It may not even be necessary.

On the basis of all we can learn directly from the film, the differences between Carl and Benjamin are these: Benjamin is the sloppier dresser, the more awkward, the more sour, the more confused, and—almost logically—the more interesting. But isn't he, really, awfully straight arrow? Poor Carl, like the President, is condemned for his idiom. (He proposes to Elaine by saying, "I think we'd make a pretty good team.") He sees the course of his life stretching clearly ahead of him and prepares to traverse it without ambivalence, confident in the relevance of his past (primarily, we assume, his studies) to his business in the world. He carries himself in a way that suggests he envisions not so much a future as a beneficent destiny. Benjamin, on the contrary, lacks the pleasant conviction of progress. By common definitions, he has already proved he can succeed, but he is unable to gain any satisfaction from that excellence. He finds himself unexpectedly disenchanted with award-winning and aunt-kissing, and he regards his education as useless, but nothing that looks like an option has presented itself to him. Webb's novel continually emphasizes these points:

". . . I'm finished with schools, Dad." A section of grapefruit fell off his spoon and onto the table. "I never want to see another school again. I never want to see another educated person again in my life."

"Come on, Ben."

"Come on!" Benjamin said, standing up. "Now I have wasted twenty-one years of my life. As of yesterday. And that is a hell of a lot to waste."

"Sit down."

"Dad," Benjamin said, "for twenty-one years I have been shuffling back and forth between classrooms and libraries. Now you tell me what the hell it's got me."

"A damn fine education."

"Are you kidding me?"

"No."

"You call me educated?"

"I do."

"Well, I don't," Benjamin said, sitting down again. "Because if that's what it means to be educated then the hell with it."

"Ben?" his mother said. "What are you talking about."

"I am trying to tell you," Benjamin said, "I'm trying to tell you that I am through with all this."

"All what."

"All this!" he said, holding his arms out beside him. "I don't know what it is but I'm sick of it. I want something else."

"What do you want."

"I don't know."

Now, for a man to be twenty-one years old in America today, for a man to have grown up around Los Angeles and have been through four years at the nerve center of an Eastern college, and for him suddenly to wrestle with dissatisfactions so unfamiliar to him that their articulation is as primitive as this—and it is *more* primitive in the movie—can only be a sign of some serious retardation. Such a man is "interesting" only insofar as we might marvel at how soundly he has slept through the life that was going on around him, at how thoroughly he has managed to avoid exposure to a dozen explanations for his malaise. Yet the movie's importance rests upon our assumption that Benjamin represents the best, the vanguard, of his generation. Nichols cannot be permitted the line of defense divined by those polls that are forever showing comfortable majorities of students supporting the war, abhorring drugs, and so forth—polls that never point out that at Harvard, for example, six per cent of the students support the war, a quarter have indicated they will go into exile or prison rather than submit to the draft, and fewer than half have never turned on. Benjamin is not supposed to be a "typical" collegian. (He doesn't wear a "STATE" sweater.) He is supposed to be pointing toward the future—showing us which way the wind is blowing. Even in the late fifties any harbinger would have had much clearer ideas about what he was rejecting. (There were beatniks then, after all, issuing position papers on American society.) The true Benjamin of Eisenhower America would have spoken to his father more in this vein: "Dad, you're worried about my 'negative attitude.' But I can't see keeping on with the scramble anymore. Don't take this personally, but you and your friends look dead to me. The system is a trap, huh? It whooshes you along in frantic, meaningless patterns—college, mixers, grad school. And then the whole Good Life in America syndrome—career, tony wife, kids in good schools, Martinis, intelligent friends, two-week vacations, *Newsweek* . . .

No adventure, no honesty, no *breakthrough*. Well, I see how impoverished my ambitions have been so far." Vanguard youth went on like that in the fifties; they accepted the seriousness of their parents' beliefs and life styles, and could therefore address themselves to adult society in the manner of prosecuting attorneys. In the sixties, a paradigmatic father-and-son conversation would begin just where Webb's conversation ends:

"What do you want."

"I don't know."

And that would probably be the whole of the conversation, because one or both of them would then get up and leave the room, weary of preaching to the wind, racked (or delighted) by the impossibility of saving the other, no longer caring. When the Benjamin of the fifties finally said "I don't know," he had run out of ways to explain himself but he still believed in the possibility of explanation, if he were but a little more articulate, his parents a little more sensitive. The Benjamin of today would say "I don't know" right at the start because he wouldn't consider explanation pertinent, or even feasible. The very language given him by the adult world, he would feel, leads perniciously, inexorably back into that world. "So you've got no *respect!*" a father accuses, and as soon as the son tries to redefine the word his case is lost. Instead of the old heated philosophical debates, almost grown children now simply attempt to humor or manipulate their parents— ideally, creating the impression that they are allowing themselves to be manipulated. Indeed, many young people have made this faculty a criterion of being grown: When you finally understand where it's at, you abandon fruitless argument.

Twenty-year-olds today can dismiss their parents' vision without a lot of agonizing partly because they have the sense of being into much that their parents can't even know about. Some adults continue to maintain that Blind Youth always suffers from this delusion: "You'll look back in ten years and realize how right I was." But those who have paid closer attention to their children perhaps have felt more deeply put down than any generation of parents in history. For the first time, parents have taken to heart the feedback they got from their kids, have come to suspect they may be leading pointless lives and have thereby been rendered unable to take pride in what they have achieved. Properly, the Braddocks display no such defensive doubts in relation to their son: Benjamin cannot even begin to formulate precisely what it is that's wrong. More critically, his "rebellion" seems to arise, unprompted, from a *tabula rasa* of experience; he sees into *less*, not more, than his parents, and he has little appreciation of their needs and binds. He is unable to lie to them, let alone manipulate them. He gives the impression of having investigated little and "been through" even less. Has Benjamin already checked out psychedelics, heavy sex, solitude, S.D.S., mysticism, and so on? Unaccountably, a number of people I spoke with guessed that he had, even though there is no evidence for it in the film, nor does anything in his personality, as it comes across on the screen, give the "feel" of such experience. Eisenhower America: In the late fifties, a young man could leap directly from a normal middle-class scene into this paralyzing condition of being altogether lost. The culture had not prepared him for the violence of his disillusionment, nor had it offered him a series of seductive alternate routes. "The Graduate" is largely the work of people who experienced some version of this dilemma a decade ago. They've now apparently decided that America is ready to be told—told not that her very best youth despairs for her but that some eccentric few are having unspecified "misgivings."

The people at Embassy Pictures suggested that I might like to accompany Dustin Hoffman on trips around Long Island and to Washington, D.C., where he was to address "bodies of educators" on the subject of Youth Today. I thanked them and declined. The movies co-opt our intelligences; remarkably, we look to them for truths that stalk us every day. Mr. Hoffman, who has received a quarter of a million dollars for his second movie, is over thirty and has been a professional actor for a dozen years. He has been quoted as saying that Benjamin is like an exaggeration of himself ten years ago, and although he has made the part eminently "his own"—the charming gestures, mannerisms, and postures of this kid in the movie surely reflect as much Dustin Hoffman as Benjamin Braddock—one still gets the feeling that a youthful-looking thirty-year-old is playing an ironic memory of himself at twenty-one. I asked a man at Embassy Pictures what, besides a movie role, qualified Hoffman as an expert on Youth Today. "A lot of the young people are turning to him," the man replied. "The Graduate" appears to be a most "liberal" film. It sympathizes with Benjamin's disgust at adult things; it seems to condone some fairly taboo sexual behavior; it makes one feel "good" about this younger generation everyone has been fretting about. In fact, it is a kind of propaganda of desperation. Sophisticated movie audiences fall prey to its snow jobs no less than unsophisticated ones. The latter don't yearn for "honesty" and so don't search for traces of it; the former react too hungrily when traces reveal themselves. "The Graduate" concedes that upper-middle-class life is not as golden as Hollywood once cracked it up to be, and even so slight an admission leaves moviegoers breathless with surprise and gratitude. Mike Nichols has claimed as a theme "the Los Angelesization of the world . . . in which *things* take over a person's life." Yet shortly after he suggests this theme, he begins, as if he had quickly discovered that it wasn't all that compelling, to shrug it off.

In admitting the Eisenhower secret, "The Graduate" obfuscates the truth about Johnson America, which is that hardly *any* of its most interesting young men looks forward to "making it" in our present society. Popular art has helped us sustain a preposterous myth about how it feels to grow up in this country. A young man who tries to reject the cant and depersonalization that threaten to drain him is generally—as he appears to us in films, television, and magazine articles—a problem-ridden case. He may, of course, engage our sympathy with his basic goodness, his sensitivity, or his personal charm, but the central point about him remains his maladjustment—he needs "straightening out." We still seem willing to believe that adjustment is the proper object of growth—that the closer one comes to "being adjusted," the more mature one is. Naturally, the definition acts as a defense for all that is most repressive in society. When the protagonist of a film is a murderous young hoodlum, for example, the deep social problems he may represent become subordinate to the film's theme —society's inexorable crusade to get hold of the kid and "rehabilitate" him, or, at least, eliminate him from the scene by imprisoning or killing him.

Moviegoers are desperately starved for cinematic truth about what it is like to live in America at this moment in history. Twenty years ago, Robert Warshow wrote a piece about gangster movies in which he talked of maintaining public morale as the principal responsibility of mass culture: "At a time when the normal condition of the citizen is a state of anxiety, euphoria spreads over our culture like the broad smile of an idiot." The anxiety of the populace has by now grown so acute that even responsible statesmen have voiced warnings of an internal crisis to match the Civil War or the Great Depression—a kind of national nervous breakdown. And by now the organs of mass culture—especially the movies—have been forced to develop more sophisticated techniques of allaying, or disguising, our trauma. The whole idea of maladjustment, for one, has become a nice vehicle for dealing with confused or unhappy protagonists. (Movies are not, of course, the only contemporary art that uses "dealing with" to mean "getting rid of the problem of.") In this period, when the "sensitive" individual is supposed to feel so profoundly helpless to alter horrible trends, American movies are insisting more strongly than ever upon the power of a single fine person to transform an entire bad scene. Two of the most successful films of the past year —"To Sir, with Love" and "Up the Down Staircase"—left us with this optimistic moral. People dimly sensed that "Bonnie and Clyde" suggests more about our present lives than most pictures with contemporary settings do. They talked on about our sense of ambient violence, and so forth (several *Village Voice* readers who responded to a Ten Best Movies poll pencilled "Why are we in Vietnam?" next to their votes for "Bonnie and Clyde"), but its relevance perhaps has more to do with the doom that stalks its two central characters relentlessly from the beginning. Both are beings with no possibility of anything but drab, impoverished lives. The thematic force of the movie lies in our understanding that their fate is never substantially altered; they are simply doomed to a more precipitate and compelling bad end. We are protected from the metaphor of their hopeless lives by distance and by disguise. They lived in a bad place during a bad time. And gang-

sters can't make it. We have not yet made our move. We are still
lying low, figuring the angles, plotting our breakthrough. Yet we
suspect that our distinction between legal and criminal is a quib-
ble, that any shortcut toward making it will be seen as an aggression: you cannot bust magnificently out of the game. "Bonnie and Clyde" seems to argue, with Bob Dylan, that we live
"Where the executioner's face is always well hidden . . . Where
black is the color, where none is the number," where kamikaze
assault is the only alternative to diminished existence. Despite the
largely fixed, nearly classic dramatic patterns of "Bonnie and
Clyde," its hard authenticities draw us close to the transgressor-
victims, and lay claim to our feelings of desperation and inescapable failure.

"The Graduate" also progresses through the traditional patterns of a classic genre—the initiation story with romantic triangle
—and so goes further than previous films of its genre toward making "alienation" understandable. But movies like "The Graduate,"
however much they "criticize" society, must ultimately affirm the
possibility of individual liberation. The tragic conception of
American life has found expression in films that are—almost
without exception—about criminals. We have had a tradition of
"serious" movies, too, which have shown that success isn't *that*
easy—have seemed to cry out against a too cheerful Americanism.
Yet even the suffering, failure, and deaths in these movies have led
us toward an irresistible, transcendent optimism; since they make
concessions to a bleak conception of our lives along the way, they
give us fewer grounds for finally rejecting their overriding vision.
Still, American directors cannot be said to have done their affirming in bad faith. If the sailor's girl in "The Best Years of Our
Lives" had found that she could not, after all, spend her life with
a man who had hooks instead of hands, and if Brando in "On the
Waterfront" had been thrown unconscious into the river after
being beaten by Lee J. Cobb's thugs instead of rising to lead the
magically rebellious longshoremen back to work, neither movie
would have been satisfying emotionally—*or* artistically. Movies
have created for themselves a peremptory demand—that criminals
never succeed or good Americans fail. If twenty adults had laid
hands on Benjamin in the church and held him for the paddy

wagon while Elaine drove off with Carl for their honeymoon (as would probably have happened in life), we would leave the theatre feeling cheated and lied to. The thoughtful moment on the bus, the absence of a clinch at the curtain—this is the maximum pessimism we can bear, though I notice that most of the audience, anticipating the extent of Nichols' "seriousness," got up to leave the theatre as soon as Benjamin and Elaine climb aboard the bus. Should the "optimism" of the ending be undercut by what we have already glimpsed of society? Benjamin's slipping away without ever adequately defining his relation to it makes the question unanswerable. From time to time, Nichols breaks out of the affirmative mood, but he is forever reintegrating his material into protective conventions: misunderstood youth, love conquering obstacles, vigor and persistence rewarded.

Since it is so hard to end an American movie with the defeat of a good man, directors inform their work with seriousness by being "negative" along the way—by acknowledging that problems do exist. Some war veterans face difficulties of readjustment; some union leaders exploit and intimidate workers; some parents threaten the happiness of their children. Mindless optimism having become nearly a convention of the American cinema, a little pessimism—even if it is no better thought through, and therefore no truer, than the buoyant vision it is meant to supplant— goes a long way in advancing the director's reputation. The more negative his vision appears to be, short of causing him to neglect his civic duty—the closer he can "cut it"—the more likely an educated audience is to call him a genius. Because American films straggle so far behind literature and European films in reflecting the actual quality of modern life, rudimentary negativism can easily be taken for truthfulness, and a decade-old vision can appear to be "ahead of its time."

To the extent that we learn about the life around us through art, we are often learning what life was like ten or more years ago. The literature of generation gap that has abounded in the last year or so, particularly on and off Broadway, has been conceived either from an adult point of view, which implicitly regards the generation gap as a comfortably perennial problem, or, in the more significant instances, from youth's point of view—at least, as well as it can be recollected—which vaguely senses an unprecedented wide breach. Since the authors of these pieces are now, at the youngest, pushing thirty, the general public has only lately become conscious of a species of generation gap—dolled up with a contemporary vocabulary and milieu—that existed in the fifties, when cool Berkeley coeds could get engaged to guys like Carl, and vague mutterings of discontent still had a radical ring.

One of "The Graduate's" falsehoods in the light of contemporary experience arises from the supposed "strangeness" of Benjamin's condition. Isolating him so (isolating him by his *vision* of things, for in his outward aspect he is the perfect teacher's pet) seems meant to frighten potential malcontents into adjustment. In life, of course, Benjamin would have met hundreds of his peers—heads, revolutionaries, and some who would not fall so easily into categories—who shared his sense of America's disorder, and he would have already begun to work with them on new conceptions of community, and of sanity. At the very least, he would have had a friend who felt as he did. Likewise, if he were a real boy returning home, none of the people around him would be totally surprised at his behavior; they would quickly understand him in terms of what they had already learned of alienated youth. "Thinking of dropping *out*, Benjamin?" his father would ask, with a nervous chuckle, as he passed his son in the pool for the sixteenth straight afternoon. "Benjamin's starting to act like a *hippie* or something," Mrs. Braddock would complain. Their friends and neighbors might still clutch at him, but it would be because here he was, practically the *only* great kid around not yet acting all crazy about his future and the lives of his elders. And then, when Benjamin started to exhibit his malaise more openly, or when they caught on to his new feelings, they might not understand the whole thing but they would recognize the symptoms. And not of some rare disease but of an epidemic. A friend might come over and say, "Braddock, my kid in law school wrote me the same kind of nutty stuff last week, and my fifteen-year-old daughter is threatening to run away to some damn commune in Big Sur. What the hell is going on, Braddock?"

Responsive parents have come to realize that something more momentous than the perennial rift between children and the adult world is now in the air. The rebellious youth of the fifties—of which Benjamin may be considered a not particularly precocious example—rejected a number of life styles within the system but never deeply questioned the necessity of the system itself. Like Benjamin, they didn't know what they wanted to do—only that they didn't want to punch a clock, or spend Saturday afternoon with a beer and a ball game. Yet even their negations orbited in one or another epicycle of the adults' neat Ptolemaic system. They believed in intelligent compromise. Whereas Eisenhower youths were forever finding poignant contradictions in the lives of their parents, Johnson youths have found mostly irrelevance. Eisenhower youths tried to reëducate their families, sometimes at a traumatic cost—to get them to *understand*. Johnson youths, in the realization that only those who have ears to hear will hear, have tried to minimize hassle. Young people no longer simply inherit attitudes; many of them have tuned in to the outside world. Parents are hard pressed to believe that, beyond an early age, they no longer play terribly important roles in their children's psychic lives. Permissiveness, far from being responsible for youth's new attitudes, may be the most genuine and most fitting response to them. It takes seriously the feeling that significant points of alignment have vanished. For a time, parents appeal to all sorts of motives that they feel *must* reside within their kid—his desire, for example, to live up to their expectations, to "make something of himself." But these motives derive from their vision of the world, and reside, *ipso facto*, only within that vision. Permissiveness, when it is practiced, testifies to the uselessness of traditional devices. The kid is not rebelling; he hasn't oriented himself in relation to his parents' lives at all. Therefore, nothing they can say or do will bring him into line.

Benjamin's malaise is so impossibly vague, then, that the Braddock family's generation gap can be no more than a convention. What meaning it has arises not from anything that Benjamin says or does but from the artful observation that Nichols lavishes upon the moral ugliness of an environment. His fidelity of observation, however, awakens our appetite for further honesties. Because he has given us the visual reality, we expect some measure of reality beneath the surface. If the whole suburban scene had

been pictured by the usual Hollywood camera—if it had been a
Saturday Evening Post suburb, or the Anderson suburb of television's "Father Knows Best"—then it would never have occurred
to us that the "problem" of the movie might be larger than
Benjamin's problem of adjustment. His "identity crisis" would
have seemed to have nothing to do with the times; he would
have been merely a talented young man who must, upon graduation, abandon his fantasy of limitless possibilities—who must
realize that he could not be a lawyer and a scientist and an artist
all at once. His paralysis would have suggested a young adult's
agony of decision over what he must give up. But the perspectives
of Nichols' camera are so slanted toward Benjamin's vision as to
warrant his malaise. If things look generally good to us, Benjamin's
course of resolution is clear: he just has to work things out (in
his own head) and get on with it. This is the perspective we
would expect from his parents. If things look bad to us, however,
the entire message of the film is transformed: Benjamin's problem
is objective and terrible, the course of its resolution not at all
apparent. If things look bad, it means that Benjamin is the only
person in the movie who has any idea what is happening; everybody's else's life is delusion. His anomie becomes reasonable, and
his "brilliant future" an empty concept. If Nichols had only
carried this single insight through to its conclusion, it would
scarcely matter that Benjamin is not haunted, as so many of his
peers are, by the war, the blacks, the poor—mysteriously, not
even by the draft. We would need no apocalyptic consciousness
from him, no sense of a culture unravelling. Born to the "best"
that American society can offer, Benjamin could represent—simply
by his decent, tormented stolidity—something of the difficulty
of living in America at this time. Benjamin is at loose ends.
Perhaps he is not strong enough to forge a new life style. But he
will never pursue his parents' kind of life, or, if he does, he will
never be free from inner agitation. Our understanding should not
be that next week he will settle on law school or the Peace Corps
and everything will be right. His ends must be looser, and deeper,
than that.

    Dropping out is not so much an activity as a sensibility. One directly engages the relevant, but one cannot rebel against an irrelevance; one drops out of it. Underground propaganda has made us think of dropping out as a rather bold, active stroke. It is more often a paralyzed sabbatical that spontaneously interrupts an "upward climb" with doubts so urgent as to short-circuit away all energy. Abulia, a total failure of alternatives that makes all courses of "positive action" appear equal evasions, is attacking not simply the crazies who spring to mind at the label "drop-out" but alarming proportions of our most splendid young men. We have come to think of them with a certain shame, partly because their example seems to express too much disapproval of America but more because their failure of direction, their shiftless gloom or joy, itself seems somehow un-American. The media, whose understanding of alienation is rooted in the fifties, have used "dropping out" to describe something that hippies do—something exploratory, and, in that sense, temporary, traditional, and safe. Even comparatively young writers speak anachronistically of things like "hippies' condemnation of middle-class society." Beatniks condemned things, defined themselves as opposite to "the square world," and derived their meaning from acts of flouting. Dropping out, in whatever costume, happens inside one's head and may be, to an important degree, irrevocable. And what else is all Benjamin's "drifting" about?

A few transformative years witnessed—not fortuitously—dramatic shifts in the administration of government (from Eisenhower to Kennedy and then to Johnson), a new consciousness of domestic deprivation, the beginnings of racial militancy, a new obsession with international morality and the advent of psychedelic substance and the intense eclectic spiritualism that grew up around them. The direction of American youth during the past decade has been bound to politics and to drugs as the subgenerations got shot at in Mississippi, organized for student power and for the grape strikers at Berkeley, and grooved to the Airplane at the Avalon Ballroom on a thousand Owsley micrograms. During the four and a half years between the Kennedy assassinations, unprecedented numbers of young people awakened to the propor-

tions of America's imperfection. Those to whom John Kennedy
held out a promise had graduated when the Johnson mandate
began to sour. But the postwar babies didn't feel betrayed. They
had never known the promise—the strong pride in America. They
doubted if it was *ever* more than a dream. Many of them grew
up hard and cynical, or simply aloof from the abyss of American
problems. Though drugs form the actual focus only of the hippie
scene, they have become an integral part of the daily environment
in almost every sphere that young people influence. Yet if one of
Nichols' Berkeley extras had lit up a joint in the background, the
effect would be shocking; it would suddenly place Benjamin in a
different time setting altogether.

In one sense, Nichols cannot be faulted for choosing to ignore
protest and pot and the evangelism of individual and com-
munitarian consciousness—any more than for not allowing a
single black to pass more than fleetingly before his camera and for
not mentioning the war in Vietnam. Yet in another sense what
Nichols is talking about is precisely these things, for which the
suburban void is no metaphor at all. He had not simply denied
attention to drugs or politics; he has created a world in which they
play no part, a world still obsessed with that old hangup sex. "The
Graduate" has to do with an outstanding young man who finds
himself turned off by the society he has been preparing to
ensconce himself in. Yet all the readily available images to justify
a turn-off far more compelling than Benjamin's have been declined. Nichols has depicted Benjamin's milieu as dishearteningly
barren, but beyond showing its implicit conspiracy against everything that is seemly in his protagonist he has not begun to hint
at why its barrenness may now be dangerous. When Benjamin's
landlord accuses him of being an outside agitator, the slight jest
at the expense of right-wing Californians fails to draw any resonance from life; there is, for example, no trace of the compulsive
political and cultural polarizations in that state, or of Berkeley's
significance as a New Left citadel, or of our myth that agitation,
in the universities or the ghettos, wings in from "outside." Nichols
has made a film about growing up that is really about growing
down, the lowering of consciousness; a film about dropping out
that is really about working in; a film about alienated youth that

refuses to acknowledge the momentous sources of alienation. "The Graduate" treats the question of alienation with an easy familiarity. It makes alienation seem to spring from unreasonable idealism, from overreaction to the harmless vulgarity of plenty. A disaffection more extreme than Benjamin's—more in line with the disaffection of his actual generation—would have seemed disproportionate to the innocuous "evils" that Nichols has depicted.

We have grown quick to regard citizens exhibiting signs of disaffection as neurotic, delinquent, or "confused"—as members of a vaguely inferior minority whose discontent rests largely upon the fictions of disturbed imaginations. The President of the United States, in his State of the Union Message, makes get-tough asides about draft-card burners, marijuana smokers, and LSD takers. His listeners, his applauders immediately conjure up a picture of scruffy, nihilistic hooligans. Yet the President may be talking about some of the most promising young men on the campuses at Berkeley, Chicago, Harvard, and Yale—young men who, like Benjamin, are the sons of our best-educated and most privileged class, and should, by tradition, inherit the country.

The Benjamin of the fifties—the Benjamin of the movie—makes trouble for a while, but pretty soon he comes around. In a lecture, Nichols informed an audience of Brandeis students that Benjamin would end up like his parents. Although this remains unsaid in the film—young audiences would find it unbearably offensive—it functions perpetually to integrate Benjamin's flirtation with dropping out into a reassuring psychological tag, "the difficult phase." "The Graduate" offers youth a subversive message: You cannot sustain an opposition to America; find someone to submit with, if you can. It seems unaware that history has upped the price of submission. In the fifties, "conformity" was the dragon against which valedictorians tilted their earnest lances. The trap of the sixties is complicity. The Benjamin that contemporary reality suggests could no longer imagine a life of quiet desperation in a social vacuum. He would begin to formulate definitions of "making it" all his own. He would concern himself with getting off, not with getting on. He might be driven by the need to change the system or to take revenge upon it. He might care only to ignore it or take it for a ride. But he would not still interpret himself in its terms. He would perceive his role with a certain detached irony, recognizing himself to be a particular person—with a birth, some years in the world, a death—whose "business" had not yet become the business of being alive, and was colored with absurdity.

There are now a million such Benjamins, with visions of a healthier culture. At this moment, young people in the vanguard of change feel little hope for their chances. Many are possessed by paranoid visions of our collective future; thrown into relief by the reassurances of our official culture, they appear deranged. Indeed, by refusing to explore the terrible tension with which young Americans now experience their relation to America, and by suggesting the patterns of dissidence in figures as unpersuasive as Benjamin, the culture insists upon their derangement. If television, magazines, or at least a serious film like "The Graduate" reflected how grievously expectations for America have shrunk, a great many more young people would begin to discover one another. They would come to recognize the sudden prevalence of their own response and to believe more deeply in its aptness. The true Benjamins—those who feel themselves isolated, suspended in limbo between Lyndon Johnson and Ken Kesey, between acquiescence and domestic guerrillahood—would come to understand the depths of their fellowship and their strength.

I suggested earlier that the principal reason Benjamin couldn't look forward to becoming an adult was that his environment had offered him no viable ideal of adulthood. He had to imagine for himself what a creditable grown-up life might look like, and he failed to come up with much of a picture. It's unlikely that the efforts of others to conceive and test out new life styles would escape a person of Benjamin's particular background. (Think of it: the new politics, the new bohemia, student power, the sexual revolution, acid, rock, the underground press—all germinated on his home turf. Where was he?) Yet such efforts cannot directly reach large numbers of young people who are removed from the heartlands of changing social consciousness. These people *are* still like the Benjamin of the movie—put off, ready to pass up the fruits of their preparation, but wholly uncertain as to their options. Isolated and starved by the culture, they face a crisis of imagination. They can learn of their peers' experiments only through the fun-house mirrors of the news media. Movies, the obvious source of help, have not begun to depict adult lives that thoughtful young people might admire or imitate; nor have they begun to examine, with any respect, young people going about the adult business of trying to find something propitious in their lives and their country. "The Graduate" has been accorded a reception like that of "The Catcher in the Rye," even though it scarcely elaborates on the attitudes of adolescent discontent that Salinger's book helped to reveal, and create, seventeen years ago. If we give unreserved praise to our cultural leaders for a vision of youth that ignores a generation's worth of change, we must expect them to remain as barren of relevance as our political leaders. "The Graduate," which in the end only quickens our perception of dead-end alternatives, begins with the radical intimation that there is some choice to be made on the threshold of adulthood— some yes-or-no decision about one's future in American society. A film artist with the intelligence and the tremendous prestige of Mike Nichols should now begin to lay bare the nature of that choice, if it still exists.

Sidney Poitier

I don't want to die as the most successful Negro actor.

It will have circumscribed me terribly.

Sidney Poitier is now considered one of the most popular and accomplished actors in America. In most of his roles he portrays the professional man who is tough-minded but tender, the middle-class individual who wishes to rise but who is careful not to be ruthless. Poitier's career as an actor is complicated by his position as one of the few well-known black movie stars. Because of his sensitive role as the representative Negro performer in America, he chooses his parts with great care. "Years ago," he has said, "long before I was an actor, I became terribly embarrassed whenever I saw a black on the screen. He or she was always devoid of dignity: a funny butler or a comic maid, someone like that. . . . So since I've been in a position to do so, I've tried to play parts that make a positive contribution to the image of black people."

Sidney Poitier was born in Miami, Florida, in 1924 and taken as a child to the Bahama Islands. He was educated by private tutors, but during the depression his father suffered financial reverses and the boy returned to Miami to work. He came to Harlem with $1.50 in his pocket and took menial jobs in order to live. After serving in the army, he returned to Harlem and tried to establish himself as an actor. At the outset he experienced considerable difficulty because of his strong West Indian accent; but he trained his voice by listening to formal English spoken on the radio, and in time he was accepted into the American Negro Theater. His first important movie was *Cry, the Beloved Country* (1952). His other movies include *The Blackboard Jungle* (1955); *Something of Value* (1957); *The Defiant Ones* (1958); *A Raisin in the Sun* (1960), which was originally a play also starring Poitier; *Lilies of the Field* (1964), for which he won an Oscar award; and *To Sir, with Love* (1967).

"The American form of recognition, fame and money, can be the most devastating penalty" for artists, writes James Baldwin in the following essay. The popular movie star who wishes to be an actor is confronted by this problem: his own desire to develop his ability is often frustrated by the demand that he repeat the same role which originally led to his popularity. Poitier has the added difficulty of trying to avoid the restraints of his color. "I don't want to die as the most successful Negro actor," he has remarked, and in recent years he has played in movies whose central theme is not racial. The future of his career—his ability to act in roles which realistically explore human complexity—will be one measure of the maturity of Hollywood motion pictures.

Sidney Poitier

JAMES
BALDWIN

THE first time I met Sidney, I walked up to him at an airport. He didn't know me, but I admired him very much, and I told him so. I've never done that with anyone, before or since, and Sidney looked at me as though he thought I was crazy, but he was very nice about it. Some years later, I really met him. We were both in Philadelphia. He was doing *A Raisin in the Sun*, and I was working with Kazan in *Sweet Bird of Youth*, and we hit it off.

Then, of course, years passed. Things happened to Sidney; things happened to me. All artists who are friends have a strange relationship to each other; each knows what the other is going through, even though you may see each other only briefly, at functions, at benefits, at airports; and this is especially true, I think, for black artists in this country, and especially over the last several years. It's ironical indeed, but it's only the black artists in this country—and it's only beginning to change now—who have been called upon to fulfill their responsibilities as artists and, at the same time, insist on their responsibilities as citizens. As Ruby Dee once said to me, when we were working on the Christmas boycott campaign following the murder of the four little girls in Birmingham, "Soon, there won't be enough colored people to go around." She wasn't joking—I might add that that statement has, today, a rather sinister ring.

As the years passed, and given the system in which all American artists, and especially all American actors, work, I began to

REPRINTED FROM Look MAGAZINE, JULY 23, 1968. REPRINTED BY PERMISSION OF ROBERT LANTZ-CANDIDA DONADIO LITERARY AGENCY, INC. COPYRIGHT © 1968 BY COWLES COMMUNICATIONS, INC.

tremble for Sidney. I must state candidly that I think most Hollywood movies are a thunderous waste of time, talent and money, and I rarely see them. For example, I didn't think *Blackboard Jungle* was much of a movie—I know much more than *that* about the public-school system of New York—but I thought that Sidney was beautiful, vivid and truthful in it. He somehow escaped the film's framework, so much so that until today, his is the only performance I remember. Nor was I overwhelmed by *Cry, the Beloved Country*, but Sidney's portrait, brief as it was, of the young priest, was a moving miracle of indignation. That was the young Sidney, and I sensed that I was going to miss him, in exactly the same way I will always miss the young Marlon of *Truckline Cafe* and *Streetcar Named Desire*. But then, I miss the young Jimmy Baldwin too.

All careers, if they are real careers—and there are not as many of these occurring as one might like to think—are stormy and dangerous, with turning points as swift and dizzying as hairbreadth curves on mountain roads. And I think that America may be the most dangerous country in the world for artists—whatever creative form they may choose. That would be all right if it were also exhilarating, but most of the time, it isn't. It's mostly sweat and terror. This is because the nature of the society isolates its artists so severely for their vision; penalizes them so mercilessly for their vision and endeavor; and the American form of recognition, fame and money, can be the most devastating penalty of all. This is not the artist's fault, though I think that the artist will have to take the lead in changing this state of affairs.

The isolation that menaces all American artists is multiplied a thousand times, and becomes absolutely crucial and dangerous for all black artists. "Know whence you came," Sidney once said to me, and Sidney, his detractors to the contrary, *does* know whence he came. But it can become very difficult to remain in touch with all that nourishes you when you have arrived at Sidney's eminence and are in the interesting, delicate and terrifying position of being part of a system that you know you have to change.

Let me put it another way: I wish that both Marlon and Sidney would return to the stage, but I can certainly see why they don't. Broadway is almost as expensive as Hollywood, is even more hazardous, is at least as incompetent, and the scripts, God knows, aren't any better. Yet I can't but feel that this is a great loss, both for the actor and the audience.

I will always remember seeing Sidney in A *Raisin in the Sun*. It says a great deal about Sidney, and it also says, negatively, a great deal about the regime under which American artists work, that that play would almost certainly never have been done if Sidney had not agreed to appear in it. Sidney has a fantastic presence on the stage, a dangerous electricity that is rare indeed and lights up everything for miles around. It was a tremendous thing to watch and to be made a part of. And one of the things that made it so tremendous was the audience. Not since I was a kid in Harlem, in the days of the Lafayette Theatre, had I seen so many black people in the theater. And they were there because the life on that stage said something to them concerning their own lives. The communion between the actors and the audience was a real thing; they nourished and recreated each other. This hardly ever happens in the American theater. And this is a much more sinister fact than we would like to think. For one thing, the reaction of that audience to Sidney and to that play says a great deal about the continuing and accumulating despair of the black people in this country, who find nowhere any faint reflection of the lives they actually lead. And it is for this reason that every Negro celebrity is regarded with some distrust by black people, who have every reason in the world to feel themselves abandoned.

I ought to add, for this also affects any estimate of any black star, that the popular culture certainly does not reflect the truth concerning the lives led by white people either; but white Americans appears to be under the compulsion to dream, whereas black Americans are under the compulsion to awaken. And this fact is also sinister.

I am not a television fan either, and I very much doubt that future generations will be vastly edified by what goes on on the American television screen. TV commercials drive me up the wall. And yet, as long as there is *that screen* and there are *those commercials*, it is important to hip the American people to the fact that black people also brush their teeth and shave and drink beer and smoke cigarettes—though it may take a little more time for the American people to recognize that we also shampoo our hair. It is of the utmost importance that a black child see on that screen *someone who looks like him.* Our children have been suffering from the lack of identifiable images for as long as our children have been born.

Yet, there's a difficulty, there's a rub, and it's precisely the nature of this difficulty that has brought Sidney under attack. The industry is compelled, given the way it is built, to present to the American people a self-perpetuating fantasy of American life. It considers that its job is to entertain the American people. Their concept of entertainment is difficult to distinguish from the use of narcotics, and to watch the TV screen for any length of time is to learn some really frightening things about the American sense of reality. *And the black face, truthfully reflected, is not only no part of this dream, it is antithetical to it.* And this puts the black performer in a rather grim bind. He knows, on the one hand, that if the reality of a black man's life were on that screen, it would destroy the fantasy totally. And on the other hand, he really has no right *not* to appear, not only because he must work, but also for all those people who need to see him. By the use of his own person, he must smuggle in a reality that he knows is not in the script. A celebrated black TV actor once told me that he did an entire show for the sake of *one line.* He felt that he could convey something very important with that *one line.* Actors don't write their scripts, and they don't direct them. Black people have no power in this industry at all. Furthermore, the actor may be offered dozens of scripts before anything even remotely viable comes along.

Sidney is now a superstar. This must baffle a great many people, as, indeed, it must baffle Sidney. He is an extraordinary actor, as even his detractors must admit, but he's been that for a long time, and that doesn't really explain his eminence. He's also extraordinarily attractive and winning and virile, but that could just as easily have worked against him. It's something of a puzzle. Speaking now of the image and not of the man, it has to do with a quality of pain and danger and some fundamental impulse to decency that both titillates and reassures the white audience. For example, I'm glad I didn't write *The Defiant Ones,* but I liked

Sidney in it very much. And I suppose that his performance has
something to do with what I mean by smuggling in reality. I
remember one short scene, in close-up, when he's talking about his
wife, who wants him to "be nice." Sidney's face, when he says,
"She say, 'Be nice. Be nice,'" conveys a sorrow and humiliation
rarely to be seen on our screen. But white people took that film
far more seriously than black people did. When Sidney jumps off
the train at the end because he doesn't want to leave his buddy,
the white liberal people downtown were much relieved and joyful. But when black people saw him jump off the train, they
yelled, "Get back on the train, you fool!" That didn't mean that
they hated Sidney: They just weren't going for the okey-doke.
And if I point out that they were right, it doesn't mean that
Sidney was wrong. That film was made to say something to white
people. There was really nothing it *could* say to black people—
except for the authority of Sidney's performance.

Black people have been robbed of everything in this country,
and they don't want to be robbed of their artists. Black people
particularly disliked *Guess Who's Coming to Dinner*, which I
made a point of seeing, because they felt that Sidney was, in effect,
being used against them. I'm now on very delicate ground, and
I know it, but I can't really duck this issue—because it's been
raised so often. I can't pretend that the movie meant anything to
me. It seemed a glib, good-natured comedy in which a lot of able
people were being wasted. But, I told myself, this movie wasn't
made for *you*. And I really don't know the people for whom it
was made. I moved out of their world, insofar as this is ever possible, a long time ago. I remember the cheerful English lady in a
wineshop in London who had seen this movie and adored it and
adored the star. She was a nice lady, and certainly not a racist,
and it would simply have been an unjust waste of time to get
angry with her for knowing so little about black people. The
hard fact is that most people, of whatever color, don't know much
about each other because they don't care much about each other.
Would the image projected by Sidney cause that English lady
to be friendly to the next West Indian who walked into her
shop? Would it cause her to *think*, in any real way, of the *reality*,
the presence, the simple human *fact* of black people? Or was

Sidney's black face simply, now, a part of a fantasy—the fantasy of her life, precisely—which she would never understand? This is a question posed by the communications media of the 20th century, and it is not a question anyone can answer with authority. One is gambling on the human potential of an inarticulate and unknown consciousness—that of the people. This consciousness has never been of such crucial importance in the world before. But one knows that the work of the world gets itself done in very strange ways, by means of very strange instruments, and takes a very long time. And I also thought that *Guess Who's Coming to Dinner* may prove, in some bizarre way, to be a milestone, because it is really quite impossible to go any further in that particular direction. The next time, the kissing will have to start.

I thought of something else, something very difficult to convey. I remember a night in London, when Diana Sands was starring in *The Owl and the Pussycat*. There were about four or five of us, walking to some discotheque, and with us was a very angry, young, black cat. Across the street from us was Sidney's name in lights in some movie I've not seen. Now, I understand the angry, young, black cat, and he was right to be angry. He was not angry at Sidney, but at the world. But I knew there was no point in saying that at the time I was born, the success of a Sidney Poitier or a Diana Sands was not to be imagined. I don't mean to congratulate the American people on what they like to call progress, because it certainly isn't. The careers of all black artists in this country prove that. Time passes and phenomena occur in time. The *presence* of Sidney, the precedent set, is of tremendous importance for people coming afterward. And perhaps that's what it's really all about—just that.

Sidney, as a black artist, and a man, is also up against the infantile, furtive sexuality of this country. Both he and Harry Belafonte, for example, are sex symbols, though no one dares admit that, still less to use them as any of the Hollywood he-men are used. In spite of the fabulous myths proliferating in this country concerning the sexuality of black people, black men are still used, in the popular culture, as though they had no sexual equipment at all. This is what black men, and black women, too, deeply resent.

I think it's important to remember, in spite of the fact we've been around so long, that Sidney is younger than I, and I'm not an old man yet. It takes a long time in this business, if you survive in it at all, to reach the eminence that will give you the power to change things. Sidney has that power now, to the limited extent that *anyone* in this business has. It will be very interesting to see what he does with it. In my mind, there's no limit to what he might become.

But Sidney, like all of us, is caught in a storm. Let me tell you one thing about him, which has to do with how black artists particularly need each other. Sidney had read *Another Country* before it came out. He liked it, and he knew how frightened I was about the book's reception. I'd been in Europe, and I came back for the publication because I didn't want anyone to think I was afraid to be here. My publisher gave a party at Big Wilt's Smalls Paradise in Harlem. Sidney came very early. I was ready to meet the mob, but I was scared to death, and Sidney knew it, and he walked me around the block and talked to me and helped me get myself together. And then he walked me back, and the party was starting. And when he realized that I was all right, he split. And I realized for the first time that he had only come for that. He hadn't come for the party at all.

And the following may also make a small, malicious point. There's speculation that the central figure of my new novel, who is a black actor, is based on Sidney. Nothing could be further from the truth, but people naturally think that, because when they look around them, Sidney's the only black actor they see. Well, that fact says a great deal more about this country than it says about black actors, or Sidney, or me.

Elizabeth Taylor

Whatever it is I may have in acting—that part of me is minuscule—
it's not technique. It's instinct and a certain ability to concentrate.
. . . I would like to be able to say that I'm not a movie star, but an
actress. But that would be phony. It's very difficult once you've
become public domain to be taken seriously.

Few people in America are more rewarded—in terms of money, fame, and prestige—than the actor or actress. Photographed and analyzed, emulated and imitated, envied and criticized, the actor is the most glamorous incarnation of the cult hero, representing the fantasies of people who live less exciting lives than he. In twentieth-century America there has not been a rich tradition of acting; there has been no place in which to perfect the art, like the Royal Academy or the Moscow Art Theater or the Comédie Française, and contemporary Americans cannot point to great actors who have mastered their craft and performed in a variety of difficult roles. In the last forty years America has produced the movie star, not the actor: John Barrymore, Clark Gable, Katherine Hepburn, Gary Cooper, Marilyn Monroe, Cary Grant, and Grace Kelly. In the last ten years, the same principle has held true, and the actress who has loomed as more magnetic than any other has been Elizabeth Taylor.

Born in London, England, on February 27, 1932, of American parents, Elizabeth Taylor was sent to the United States at the beginning of World War II. She had studied ballet in England under the famous dancing teacher Vaccani, and in

America she was signed to a contract with Universal Studios and then with Metro-Goldwyn-Mayer. She went to the Hawthorne School in Beverly Hills and the M-G-M school, graduating from University High School in Hollywood in 1950. She had already established herself as a child actress in *Lassie Come Home* (1942), *The White Cliffs of Dover* (1943), and especially *National Velvet* (1944), a movie for which she qualified by eating and exercising so that she grew three inches within several months. Her emergence as an adult star began with *A Place in the Sun* (1951), the movie based on Dreiser's *An American Tragedy* and the first film in which, as she has said, she "was asked to do any *acting*." Her career continued to flower in a variety of other movies: *Cat on a Hot Tin Roof* and *Butterfield Eight* (1961), *Cleopatra* and *Who's Afraid of Virginia Woolf?* (1966), *Reflections in a Golden Eye* (1967), and *The Comedians* (1967).

Whatever criticism one may have of Elizabeth Taylor's acting—and unlike most of Hollywood's stars who are noted for their beauty she can perform in many different types of roles—there is little question that she is the most dynamic American actress on the screen today. Remarkably self-aware and candid, she has denied her own attractiveness: "I don't think I'm a great beauty," she has said. "I don't have a complex about my looks, but I'm too short of leg, too long in the arms, one too many chins, big feet, big hands, too fat. My best feature is my gray hairs." But clearly she can be so self-critical only because she possesses great beauty. Her charisma is also due to the publicity of her private life, the ostensible freedom with which she has acted, her willingness to do things others would not dare to do. She has been married five times: to Conrad Hilton, Michael Wilding, Mike Todd, Eddie Fisher, and Richard Burton. Her marriage to Burton caused a scandal in 1964, and, characteristically, she analyzed that love affair with perception, defining the reason for the popularity of Burton and herself: "Maybe Richard and I are sex symbols together because we suggest love. At first illicit love. . . . Our love is married love now. But there is still a suggestion, I suppose, of rampant sex on the wild." She knows that her "life has lacked dignity," but, as she facetiously remarks, "there's no deodorant like success." ⌐

The Rise and Fall and Rise of Elizabeth Taylor

A STUDY IN POP SOCIOLOGY: FROM
SNOW WHITE TO SCARLET WOMAN
TO MOTHER EARTH TO TOO MUCH

LEE
ISRAEL

To APPRECIATE the rise and fall and rise again of Elizabeth Taylor, it is necessary to understand the successful assumptions that the editors of fan magazines make about the taste, the values, the tolerance threshold, and the intellectual limitations of their readers. Contrary to expectations, fan-magazine stars are born and not manufactured. No editor in the world could have guessed in 1955, when *The Mickey Mouse Club* bowed on TV, that Baby Annette Funicello, pudgy and unformed, would strike a responsive kid-sister chord in a whole generation of readers. When Uncle Walt Disney reported that Baby had drawn more fan mail for him than any other luminary since Fess (Davy Crockett) Parker, the Club's ratings soared, and the magazines themselves were inundated with ballots marked "FAVORITE STAR: Annette." Only then did the editors know they had a live one. No one could have foreseen, two seasons ago, that *Big Valley*'s Lee Majors would emerge as the hot new brooding-young-man, that Patty Duke would make it from *The Miracle Worker* to *Go Go Teen*, that Dean Martin would return from the ashes as an older sex symbol, that they'd buy Connie Stevens rather than Dot Provine and buy Julie Christie not at all, despite her monumental success in the medium for which the fan magazines supposedly exist,

REPRINTED BY PERMISSION OF *Esquire Magazine*; © 1967 BY ESQUIRE, INC. FIRST PUBLISHED IN *Esquire Magazine*.

despite the fact that many misguided editors did *try* to sell her
to their readers.

But the cast of characters is about the only variable in the
whole business of turning out fan mags. All the rest is formula-
based bulk prepared for the appetites of the emotional shutins,
for the millions of personality worshipers among us—those who
lack the sophistication to understand, let alone sublimate their
need for symbolic archetypal heroes, friends, lovers, demons, and
parent-figures. Their letters and their consumer responses indicate
that they are either very young and at the mercy of some fearsome bodily changes, or older and at the mercy of almost anyone
who knows them well enough: rainmaker, demagogue or publisher. This older group comprises the loyal readership; they don't
outgrow their problems. Most of them are provincial, unlettered,
fundamentalist Americans who are likely to have written at least
one letter to a soap-opera star in which they confused the actor
with the part he plays. To the real pitchman, these marks are
not even a challenge. They wear their needs on their sleeves.

The editors, publishers, and writers of the various motion-
picture fan magazines are, therefore, a pretty phlegmatic lot.
They have, all but the brightest of them, reached a kind of peace
with themselves about what they do for a living. They take
special pleasure in the fact that even *Harper's Magazine* features
a misleading cover line every now and then, and they get really
mad only when *Time,* The Weekly Newsmagazine, gets on them
about Jackie Kennedy [Onassis]. Their business, having been reduced to a complex of dependable formulas, is surprisingly uneventful. Seldom are the presses stopped and only very rarely does news,
except when it involves the sudden death of a star, find them
unprepared. (I have been writing for these magazines on and off
for the past five years, and I do not recall one case of divorce or
separation not preceded by weeks or months of fully reported
harbingers. The fact of the matter is that this gossip is almost
invariably, Delphically correct.)

If their calm separates the fan-mag people from the journalistic
fraternity, it is, of course, because the fan-mag people are not,
nor did they ever intend to be, members of the journalistic fraternity. Theirs is a completely separate two-penny genre, a kind

of para-fiction. The "Elizabeth Taylor" mentioned here in the context of the movie mags is a para-fictive character, based on a real person in much the same way that the Madame Pompadour of an historical novel is based on the real Madame as she lived and breathed. Yet the character "Elizabeth Taylor" cannot move completely independent of the real Taylor. She cannot be born in a different year, go to Majorca when the real Taylor is in Rome, have a gratuitous divorce or appendicitis attack. It would be outlandish moreover for the fan magazines to risk monkeying with those basic facts, even if they could get away with it, since it is not the facts that matter, but the *interpretation* of them. It isn't the niggling complexities of journalism that sell movie books, but the gritty lessons of drama.

The jazzy cover lines which have aroused so much indignation and disgust among non-fans belie not only the content of the mags, but the spirit, the pace, the whole feeling inside—which is much closer to *As the World Turns* than to the *National Enquirer.* Each issue of each magazine is really like a chapter of a soap opera. The stars are continuing characters whose lives unfurl at an almost psychedelically slow tempo, each of their stories proving something about the advantaged life. The character Julie Andrews, an English movie star who made it very big very fast, was in the throes of a fictional dilemma that lasted for almost two years with not a jot of new fact added. The dilemma was a moral one involving the exigencies of her career as opposed to the value of her marriage to a scenic designer named Tony Walton. The story of Julie's moral bind, known in the trade as The Oscar versus Tony Tale, must have been told hundreds of times in the fan mags. A statement by the real-life Julie Andrews, in October, 1966, announcing her separation from Tony seemed dull, repetitious, anticlimactic, and not a little cheeky.

An elaborate system of labeling has been imposed upon the Hollywood scene by the editors of the fan magazines at the behest of their readers. The town is divided into Young Lovables (Annette Funicellos, The Lennon Sisters, Elvis "King" Presley, the A.I.P. Beach Crowd); Inner Peace People (John "Duke" Wayne, Barbara "Missy" Stanwyck, Cary Grant, Debbie Reynolds,

Paul Newman and Joanne Woodward); The Troubled Ones (Julie Andrews, Hedy "Ecstasy" Lamarr, David "Ilya" McCallum, Hayley Mills); The Gallivanters (Natalie Wood, Barbara Parkins, Michael Caine, Warren Beatty), etc. These are dramatic categories, far less basic than the Moral Classifications, of which there are only three in number: Saint, Sinner, and Victim—all of them applied to Elizabeth Taylor at one time or another.

Almost all of the fan-magazine characters fit into the category Victim. This by definition. To be over endowed with beauty, money, talent, wit, personality, or any combination thereof is to be victimized, cursed, vulnerable at all times to catastrophe. There is no tenet more basic to the fan-magazine mystique.

Elizabeth Taylor was not always the fiend of *Photoplay*. For years she appeared in the fan books as simply, typically a Hollywood Victim, and before that as a Baby Saint. Elizabeth (never Liz) was a rung above all the swell young contract players of her day in spirituality. An animal lover in a pantheistic era, the fourteen-year-old kid-star Elizabeth wrote a best-seller about her pet chipmunk, called *Nibbles and Me*. Spooky Margaret O'Brien adored her: "She is my ideal. When I grow up I am going to be a jockey exactly like her." *Photoplay* itself concluded a story about "Velvet Girl" thus: "And you may be sure that every night down beside her green chintz bed, Elizabeth and God are going into a huddle again." This prompted a loyal fan to remark, "Let's see your Peggy Ann Garner do that!"

Set up so high and mighty, she had to fall, a victim of her own blessings. She did so amenably soon after she passed her sixteenth birthday. There were men in Taylor's life. Nibbles was jettisoned for Glenn Davis and the deluge began. She was engaged twice and twice "the spell was broken." She married, divorced, married, divorced. She was the Nat Wood of her day, of whom the readers could say: "There, Harry, but for the grace of God goes me." The death of her third husband, Mike Todd, made Elizabeth Taylor victim extraordinaire. This was the man, they said posthumously, who could have made the difference. Yet Mike's death surprised none of the fan-magazine readers, conditioned as they are to umbrellas opened by graveside and the

sentiment that it is more difficult for a beautiful woman to enter
the kingdom of happiness than for a camel to pass through the
eye of a needle.

Photoplay began its death story with a quote from Elizabeth's
couturier: "I fixed her wedding veil and her gown when she
was a bride of eighteen. Elizabeth Taylor, the Girl Who Has
Everything, they called her."

At this point, and after a suitable period of mourning, Taylor
could have chosen to be the third party in any marriage in all of
Tinseltown and not too much would have been said. She might
have been scolded, exonerated, *understood*. But, alas, the man was
Eddie Fisher and his wife was Debbie Reynolds; Debbie, the
Annette Funicello of her day, bouncy, bright, not threateningly
pretty, a mother and a leader of Girl Scouts. Very bad for Taylor.
A brawl in a saloon is one thing, but when it breaks down the
nursery door, that's quite another. Taylor was moving gradually
from the category of Victim to that of Sinner.

Silver Screen pondered: Was Elizabeth Taylor really "the
callous adventuress . . . the home wrecker?" . . . Or was she "a
frail goddess, tortured and tormented by whirlwinds of emotions
she could not cope with nor easily control"? The evidence was
being considered carefully—"home wrecker" was beginning to
nose out "frail goddess" when Taylor got sick and almost died.
Eddie rushed to her side. John Wayne visited. The whole thing
read like a Ross Hunter scenario with Turner and Zimbalist, Jr.
Taylor was exonerated, of course. Death or nearness to it is the
great purifier. When Pat Neal recently suffered those multiple
strokes she became overnight a superstar heroine in the fan
mags. Dorothy Malone broke a blood vessel and became *Motion
Picture*'s Mother of the Year.

Taylor, because she had been abused and misjudged prior to
her illness, emerged from it with dimensions of greatness. *Modern
Screen*, in its "Tribute to Our Bravest Star," raved: "Unfair that
a girl who fought *that* hard, *that* bravely against years of agonizing
physical pain should now drown in a sea of mucus, tubes in her
lungs and her ankle, unable to talk, head throbbing, fighting no
more. Next issue we promise ourselves to print the longest, fullest,
most complete story of Elizabeth Taylor's life that anyone has

ever read anyplace. It's our way of thanking Liz for reminding us
to remember those we love *when* they're alive!"

They did and it was.

Then the Burton blitz began. Instead of coming back from
the valley of the shadow a resplendent penitent washed in the
blood of the lamb, Elizabeth Taylor went to Rome and did it
again. The fan magazines had themselves a live one. As stern as
they can be, there is an aura of New Testament in *Photoplay*, et
al., a generosity of spirit which compels a fan-magazine writer, after
painting a black and hopeless picture of somebody's human condition, to add: *We're sure that Natalie Wood will seek competent
professional help before it is too late,* or *Ann-Margret is no dummy.
She will, she must, awaken to the fact that this kind of behavior
is profiting her not one bit in the ledger marked happiness. We'll
pray for her. We only hope Roger Smith can wait that long.*
Redemption is usually a possibility, but not for Elizabeth Taylor.
They threw the Old Testament at her. She was recidivistic,
arrogant, beyond counsel, enormously evil. Having no choice, the
fan magazines pulled out the hoary sin-and-suffer bag that hadn't
been used since Ingrid Bergman left for Stromboli. If Taylor was
not to be smote in some way, the world made no sense at all; the
lives of the righteous were wasted. She must pay for her transgres-
sions in some important way; she must be got where she lived.
And all the sensational Liz-Burton stories reflected that imperative.

But the years passed. At the time in her life when Mrs.
Richard Burton should have been blind and crazy at least, she
was in her prime, exchanging lusty banter with the Welshman,
who was to have left her years ago for Sybil or Sue Lyon; enjoying
the hell out of her children, the ones who were going to be
taken from her or turn against her; feeling better than ever despite
the fact that she was living purportedly on borrowed time, inhabiting a body wrecked and rheumed by accidents, operations,
bronchitis, meningitis, sciatica, broken commandments; at the
top of her form artistically (for the first time an actress as opposed to a star) when emotional turmoil, high living, frightful
health, and a history of having copped one husband from Debbie
Reynolds as played by Janet Lennon and another from Sybil
Burton as played by Julie Andrews should have made her worse

not better. Taylor, no matter how you looked at it, wasn't suffering.]

Liz, the real Liz, started to loosen up and talk to the press, the real press. When she said "happy," "permanent," "love Richard," it sounded as though she really meant it. The prognosis was not a good one. Barring famine or disaster, it seemed she wasn't about to suffer either. Taylor and Burton were ecstatic. In all likelihood, they would stay married, grow fat together, and maybe open an acting school in St. Tropez. The fan mags simply couldn't go on predicting doom, yet they could not relinquish the sin-suffer syllogism either. Like our concept of justice, this one is indivisible. What they've been doing gradually, subtly, and perhaps unconsciously over the past eight or nine months is to posit a sinless Elizabeth Taylor. Sure all those who sin suffer, but what has that to do with Mrs. Richard Burton? She is obviously no longer suffering; ergo she must never have sinned. Her acts of defiance have been reinterpreted as courageous. The sly intimations of continuous post-marital problems on both sides have been eliminated entirely. It is no longer considered blasphemous for Elizabeth Taylor's name to be mentioned in the same breath with Jackie Kennedy [Onassis']. Liz and Dickie are quite legal now: in slippers and wedgies they wend their way to a charity performance at Oxford or Old Vic or City Center. They have become the Alfred and Lynn of the fan magazines, somewhat dull, almost stuffy. Although the new image still has not fully established itself and can be modified or reversed as fast as the editors can change their covers, Burton and Taylor are no longer superstars of *Photoplay*, *Motion Picture*, or *Modern Screen*, merely featured players. But that seems to be all right with everyone concerned.

"Elizabeth Taylor" has vindicated herself completely. Her case indicates that nothing much has changed in River City since the days when we were throwing witches into the water to judge them according to whether they sank or swam. Liz made it to shore.]

VII
The Arts

□ There is a popular tradition that speaks of America as fundamentally a materialistic nation, unconcerned if not antagonistic to the arts, indifferent to anything which does not serve a utilitarian purpose. The spokesmen and their specific quarrels with America have varied—Thoreau and the world outside of Walden pond; Mark Twain and the Gilded Age; the expatriates and the American "booboisie"; Sinclair Lewis and Babbitt—but the underlying theme has been similar: America has not been a country congenial to the artistic life. □ The conflict between the arts and society has not been resolved in America, nor will it probably ever be; but clearly it is not so intense as it once was. Never in the history of America has the serious artist been so drawn into the marketplace; never has he attracted so wide an audience of sophisticated people who have the patience and the willingness to attend to all the complexities of his work. The artist has been assimilated into the society to so remarkable an extent that one feels his presence in the university, where he is essentially subsidized to carry on his private work, and in the mass media, where he is paid handsomely for works that are often complex, contentious, and sharply critical of that very society which rewards him. From a commercial point of view, the serious artist has probably never enjoyed greater popularity and prestige than in contemporary America. One can argue the consequent dangers of assimilation—one can assert, for example, that art has simply become another product of a utilitarian society and is unhealthy for the creative man who needs, in Melville's words, to cry "No, in thunder"—but the range and diversity of art in America are greater now than ever before in our history and are richer than anywhere else in the world. □ In *The Two Worlds of American Art*, Barry Ulanov makes a useful distinction between the private artist "who communicates to one man at a time" and the popular artist, who seeks "the largest possible audience for his work." The private artist is represented in this section as well as in that devoted to literature; the popular artist finds his place in Part IX, "Popular Culture." Serious and popular art still remain in healthy contrast to one another, and the two kinds of art—the private and the popular—appeal inevitably to different audiences; but the very difficulty of categorizing the cult heroes of our time suggests the degree to which American culture has been democratized. Leonard Bernstein has composed several symphonies, but he has also written the music for *West Side Story*; Andrew Wyeth's paintings appear in *Life* and *Time* as well as in the Museum of Modern Art; Mailer, Bellow, and Salinger write for a sophisticated audience, and their books invariably appear on best-seller lists; Edward Albee's first plays were produced in an off-Broadway theater, but *Who's Afraid of Virginia Woolf?*—a play that does not pander to popular tastes—has received wide popularity as a movie directed by Mike Nichols, who was once connected only with light comedies, and performed by Elizabeth Taylor, who is the embodiment of the popular movie star.

□ The private and the popular arts in America are often difficult to distinguish from each other, and with the close association of academic life and the arts, the trend is likely to continue. More than half the population of America is below the age of twenty-five, and most young people will be learning of music and art, literature and dance, as part of their formal academic training. With this prospect in mind, the private arts will never be quite so private again; and the popular arts may become increasingly sophisticated and subtle.

Andrew Wyeth

I think that the really American thing
in my painting is movement.

In an age that has been dominated by great experimentation in art—from abstract to pop to op art—Andrew Wyeth seems old-fashioned. That is the view of contemporary artists like Larry Rivers, Jack Levine, and Robert Motherwell. But no painter of our time is better-known or more highly regarded by Americans, and for reasons that represent the society in which we live. "I think that the really American thing in my painting is movement," Wyeth has said. That spatial quality and the sense of nostalgia for a simple life which no longer exists and which seems irrecoverable has attracted wide audiences.

Wyeth learned the basic skills of painting from his father, who was a well-known illustrator. Born in 1918, the last of five children, Wyeth did not adapt well to school and studied with a tutor until he was sixteen years old. All of his life he has lived in Chadds Ford, Pennsylvania, near Philadelphia. His father's death in 1945 and a serious chest operation on himself had great effect on Wyeth and deepened his compassion for suffering, lonely people. Some of his most famous paintings—"Christina's World" (1948), "Chambered Nautilus" (1956), and "The Gentlemen" (1960)—reflect his quiet and restrained compassion. Other well-known paintings —"Wind from the Sea" (1947), "River Cove" (1958), "Ground Hog Day" (1959), and "Her Room" (1963)—depict scenes of Maine, where he has summered, and Pennsylvania, where he lives during the winter.

These paintings demonstrate Wyeth's most notable qualities: his appeal to the senses; his realistic attention to details; his love of nature; his nostalgia; his affirmation of life. As Fred E. H. Schroeder points out in the following essay, Wyeth is in the tradition of the American transcendentalists—a distinctly American artist who has created his work independent of momentary fashions in the art world.

Andrew Wyeth and the Transcendental Tradition

FRED E. H.

SCHROEDER

N THE LAST DAY of February, in 1860, Henry David Thoreau watched in amused and musing admiration a little boy wearing a woodchuck-skin cap. Remarking to the boy on the cap's warmth, Thoreau recorded how the boy's "black eyes sparkled, even as the woodchuck's might have done."[1] Some seventy-five years later one of Thoreau's disciples, the artist N. C. Wyeth, illustrated an edition of selections from Thoreau's journals, and chose this encounter as one of the scenes to recreate in oils.[2] Some sixteen years later his son, Andrew Wyeth, painted another picture, of another boy, his son, in another fur cap.[3] Each picture, from Thoreau's word-miniature to Andrew Wyeth's portrait of Jamie might be dismissed as quaint trivia of Americana were it not for Thoreau's observation that "Such should be the history of

1. *Men of Concord and Some Others as Portrayed in the Journal of Henry David Thoreau*, ed. Francis H. Allen, illustrated by N. C. Wyeth (Boston, 1936), p. 239.
2. *Ibid.*, plate X.
3. *Reader's Digest*, Jan. 1964, p. 168 (reprinted from *Woman's Day*, Aug. 1963). Other color reproductions of paintings referred to in this essay and the periodicals in which they appear are: *Horizon*, Sept. 1961, pp. 89–96, "Albert's Son," "Karl," "Tenant Farmer," "Ground Hog Day," "Nicky," "Young America" and "River Cove"; *Time*, Dec. 27, 1963, pp. 46–49, "Trodden Weed," "Northern Point," "Distant Thunder," "Christina's World"; *Art in America*, Winter 1958–59, p. 23, "Corner of the Woods"; *Studio*, Apr. 1959, p. 121, "Chambered Nautilus" (in black and white); *Studio*, Dec. 1960, p. 206, "Raccoon."

REPRINTED FROM *American Quarterly*, VOL. XVII (FALL 1965). COPYRIGHT, 1965, TRUSTEES OF THE UNIVERSITY OF PENNSYLVANIA.

every piece of clothing that we wear."[4] From woodchuck's garment to boy's fur cap was no great leap for Thoreau, so long as there were an honest and consistent continuity between the wild and the domestic; so long as there were unity of nature and man, the transcendental unity which becomes the "organic principle" in the design of Louis Sullivan, the architecture of Frank Lloyd Wright, the city planning theory of Lewis Mumford, the poetry of Walt Whitman and Robert Frost and the painting of Andrew Wyeth.

The fountainhead for this creative tradition is, of course, Ralph Waldo Emerson, whose abstract dicta provided the impetus for these Americans to look for inspiration in the natural objects and common men of America. The danger of misinterpretation and abusive application of the Emersonian principles appears right at the source, for it is not always easy for either artist or audience to distinguish between works which are quaint, picturesque, or even chauvinistic and sentimental, and those works which exemplify the paradoxical conjunction of analysis and synthesis, of the expression of wholeness by means of detail, which marks the transcendent achievement. Understandably, some will equate James Whitcomb Riley with Robert Frost, and Norman Rockwell with Andrew Wyeth. But from these superficial equations another paradox of the Emersonian tradition becomes apparent: the American artist must be a democrat. That is, his art must be "universally intelligible"[5] for the many, not privately abstruse for the few. Thus, in achieving popularity, the Emersonian artist has apparently fulfilled one of his primary functions. So, as *Self-Reliance* is probably still available in dime-stores as a gift book, and Robert Frost speaks at a presidential inauguration, Andrew Wyeth's pictures are available at supermarket check-out stands in *Woman's Day* and *Reader's Digest*.

Yet transcendentalism, like all brands of idealism, is one of the most difficult philosophies to understand, let alone to live by. The universal intelligibility of Emerson, Thoreau, Frost and Wyeth brings to mind the anecdote of the man who, upon looking at the eye-chart, says that he can read it, but he can't pronounce it. Anyone can read Wyeth's paintings, but few, if any, can really pro-

4. *Men of Concord*, p. 239.
5. "Art," *Emerson's Complete Works* (Boston, 1898), II, 333.

nounce them. Yet all these artists try to speak as plainly as they can. Thoreau apologized: "You will pardon some obscurities, for there are more secrets in my trade than in most men's, and not voluntarily kept, but inseparable from its very nature. I would gladly tell all that I know about it, and never paint 'No Admittance' on my gate.''[6]

Wyeth, who is conscious of an affinity with the literary artists of the Emersonian or transcendental creative tradition (I use the terms interchangeably), has no "No Admittance" sign on his gate, as the content of his remarks in several interviews attests.[7] He is quite willing to explain precisely what he is doing. But the more he tries, the vaguer, and more abstract, and more distant from the familiar detail of his paintings his remarks become. Robert Frost never had this problem, but then Robert Frost, an artist of language, never spoke an abstract word without attaching it to a natural symbol. Or without detaching it from the general and the vague. For example, when Robert Frost wants to tell us that "Men work together whether they work together or apart"—certainly a bodiless abstraction—he exemplifies the abstraction by attaching it to two natural symbols, a tuft of flowers and a butterfly, which he has detached from the confusion of nature in general.

Attachment and detachment. These words are keys to understanding both the purpose and technique of Andrew Wyeth's art. For the abstract principles of attachment and detachment, we must turn to Emerson, but first it would seem only just to explain the network of influences which legitimately places Andrew Wyeth in the Emersonian tradition. Wyeth is only casually acquainted with Emerson's essays, but he is steeped in Thoreau; both because of his father's enthusiasm and because of his own sincere faith in the basic simplicity of Thoreau. Further, Andrew Wyeth loves the poetry of Emily Dickinson, another follower of Emerson, and he is filled with limitless admiration for Robert Frost, which admiration was reciprocated.[8] Henry David Thoreau and Robert Frost

6. Henry D. Thoreau, "Walden" (Concord ed.; Boston, 1929), I, 18.
7. In *Horizon*, Sept. 1961; *Woman's Day*, Aug. 1963; *Time*, Nov. 2, 1962 and Dec. 27, 1963; *Atlantic Monthly*, June 1964.
8. The validity of these influences has been supported in a letter to the author from Mrs. Wyeth (Feb. 1, 1964) and acknowledged later in a letter from Andrew Wyeth (June 27, 1964).

were artists who searched for the Absolute in examination of the specific and the common. That is, they concentrated their attention on the trees to discover the essence of the forest. The problem which they encounter, as we've seen before, is that the detail, the realistic detail, can blind the audience, who may not see the forest for the trees. Nonetheless, the forest is there, greater, vaguer and harder to grip than the trees. Similarly, in the detailed works of the naturalists and the localists Thoreau and Frost, there remain the principles of the abstractionist Emerson. He who can read the artists right cannot but pronounce the philosopher. Thus, Andrew Wyeth has, I think, extracted Emersonian artistic theory from the practical manifestations of this theory in the works of his favorite authors, and for this reason it seems reasonable to use as touchstones some of Emerson's theoretical statements of the ideas which Mr. Wyeth is trying to communicate through naturalistic, representational painting.

"The virtue of art," Emerson wrote, "lies in detachment, in sequestering one object from the embarrassing variety. . . . For every object has its roots in central nature, and may of course be so exhibited to us as to represent the world."[9] Detachment is Wyeth's method of selection of subject. He detaches the subject from "embarrassing variety" frequently by placing the primary object against a neutral flat background. Thus "Karl" is seen from a very low viewpoint, so that the ceiling, broken only by two hooks and some plaster cracks, is the background. "Young America," again from a low perspective, has featureless gray sky—eighty per cent of the painting—and flat land as the background. A portrait of Mrs. Wyeth entitled "Corner of the Woods" shows her seated before a large gray tree-trunk which commands half the space. "Far Away," the portrait of young Jamie Wyeth in the fur cap, shows the boy seated against a hillside of dry grass. Yet another kind of detachment operates. Wyeth paints no group pictures. People are alone in his paintings, and where there are no people, then buildings, berry baskets or logs are alone. When he has two living things as subjects, they are psychologically isolated.

9. "Art," pp. 330–31.

In "Distant Thunder," the artist's wife lies with her face covered with a hat, while the dog's attention is focused on the thunder, not on its human companion. And in "Raccoon" three dogs are shown in three worlds: one, her chain drawn taut, facing left, one lost in repose in the center and one consumed in introspection. Detached. All Wyeth's subjects have an air of detachment which not only separates them from the other objects in the composition, but from artist and audience as well. Perhaps this is what prompts so many to compare Wyeth's portraits to those of Thomas Eakins. But Wyeth goes a step further, nearly always detaching the primary subject from *itself*. Human figures are ofttimes incomplete—"Trodden Weed," a portrait of Wyeth's boots striding on brown ground, is the most dramatic example—or they are turned away, their attention focused on something beyond our vision, as in "Nicky," where the boy has his back to us and his gaze turned indefinitely seaward; but Wyeth invests the inanimate, as well, with an air of detachment, by cutting the objects off from the whole. In "Northern Point," for example, the head of land is detached from real terra firma, the barn roof is detached from the building, and the sea, one might say, is detached from land and sky by a haze which obscures the horizon. In "Ground-Hog-Day" nothing is complete. The window is cut off, the table is cut off, the sunlight is cut off—even the place setting is cut off, there being only a knife beside the plate and cup and saucer!

Wyeth is often called a dramatic artist. Yet, nothing happens in his paintings, at least no action is taking place. But oddly, this air of detachment of his subjects is charged with drama. The drama is essentially that of tension. The inanimate "Ground-Hog-Day" is tense with the contrast of the sere and windy outdoors and the hope bespoken by the slant of sun on the warm yellow flowered wallpaper within, in addition to the unresolved chord of the incomplete place setting. This is the drama of Emily Dickinson's:

> There's a certain slant of light
> Winter afternoons
> That oppresses like the heft
> Of Cathedral Tunes . . . .

The composition of "Raccoon" evokes the dramatic tension in the chain which is pulled by a dog whose forelegs and head are off the panel, as well as in the detached air of the hound on the right, for Wyeth's introspective figures are only physically at rest. The artist's wife, in "Corner of the Woods," is not at ease. She is a portrait of a working mind; not a busy mind, but a working mind. Likewise, "Karl" is physically in one room, but his ear is drawn to another place. And the little boy in "Far Away" is aware of the presence of the artist, but he is yet far away. There is tension in being neither here nor there, but both at once.

These detached subjects, Emerson said, may "represent the world." Wyeth's portrait subjects, as we have seen, are worlds to themselves, in worlds of themselves. Two of Andrew Wyeth's most popular paintings spell out this conception more explicitly. "Chambered Nautilus," probably as close to genre painting as Wyeth ever got, depicts a convalescent girl seated in a tester bed in her bedchamber, thus doubly chambered. She looks out a closed window, and at the foot of the bed on a chest, lies a nautilus shell. This bed is her world, but there is a tension implied in the juxtaposition of her outward gaze and the pressure of the outside world on her bed curtains, which appear to be stirred by a breeze from another window. A treatment of the same subject, less explicit, but more dramatic is "Christina's World." In this painting the detachment of the primary objects from the "embarrassing variety" is quite pronounced: Christina is alone on a vast field, her body intent on the complement of buildings alone on the stark horizon. The featureless expanses of the composition are divided into two almost equal parts by the diagonal tension-line from Christina's feet to the house. Despite the aloneness and detachment of Christina, she dominates the composition. This is technically the result of perspective and color: the balance of empty expanse and primary subject is invariably as perfect in Wyeth's work as in Chinese painting; but the significance of Christina's dominance is important, particularly since the artist said eleven years later that he might have tried now to paint the field without Christina, so that one might "sense Christina."[10]

The mark of man on the land is a common theme in the tran-

10. *Horizon*, p. 100.

scendental creative tradition. Thoreau once pondered the death of a man, "and there is nothing but the mark of his cider-mill left."[11] Robert Frost's "The Wood-Pile" and "Ghost House" deal with similar themes. Thoreau, in a passage from the book which N. C. Wyeth was illustrating when Andrew was a boy of nineteen, described and analyzed a scene which embodies much of the drama, composition and significance of Andrew Wyeth's paintings. Thoreau had gone to Long Island to search for the "relics" of the famous woman transcendentalist Margaret Fuller, her husband and her child, who had been shipwrecked off Fire Island on their return from Italy. A body had been found the day before, and the site marked with a stick:

I expected that I should have to look very narrowly at the sand to find so small an object, but so completely smooth and bare was the beach—half a mile wide of sand—and so magnifying the mirage toward the sea that when I was half a mile distant the insignificant stick or sliver which marked the spot looked like a broken mast in the sand. As if there was no other object, this trifling sliver had puffed itself up to the vision to fill the void; and there lay the relics in a certain state, rendered perfectly inoffensive to both bodily and spiritual eye by the surrounding scenery. . . . It was as conspicuous on that sandy plain as if a generation had labored to pile up a cairn there. Where there were so few objects, the least was obvious as a mausoleum. It reigned over the shore. That dead body possessed the shore as no living one could. It showed a title to the sands which no living ruler could.[12]

Where man has passed, and left his mark, the sense of his presence is sovereign. Christina's world is the world which she has possessed; and so we can begin to understand how Wyeth might be tempted to paint Christina's world without Christina. As we shall see, his work has been coming closer to this achievement in past years.

Detachment, therefore, explains much of Wyeth's techniques of composition, but detachment alone is only a trick, albeit a

11. *Men of Concord*, p. 45.
12. *Ibid.*, p. 24.

worthy one. Attachment is equally important in the transcendental creative tradition, as we've casually observed in Robert Frost's "The Tuft of Flowers." Transcendental philosophy is basically monistic, believing in the unity of matter and spirit, and therefore the details of nature are important only as they exemplify the over-soul, the unifying principle. In his first essay, "Nature," Emerson stated that "Every natural fact is a symbol of some spiritual fact."[13] And in later works he asserted that the task of the poet, the artist, the seer, was to restore the beauty of the unity of natural fact and spiritual fact. He said, "For as it is dislocation and detachment from the life of God that makes things ugly, the poet, who re-attaches things to nature and the Whole—re-attaching even artificial things and violations of nature, to nature, by a deeper insight—disposes very easily of the most disagreeable facts."[14] It is here that Thoreau's observations about the woodchuck and the boy become clear. He is reattaching the natural fact, the woodchuck's unity with his skin, one might say, to the apparent violation of nature in the woodchuck skin's becoming an article of human clothing. The boy's warmth and his sparkling eyes make the displaced woodchuck-skin an object of beauty.

A recent Wyeth painting, "Tenant Farmer," shows an old red brick farm house with a barren weeping willow before it, and hanging from the willow, a deer. Of this painting, the artist said, "I kept seeing the deer swing around under the willow tree, and he seemed almost to have an affinity with the building, almost, well, as if he'd lived there. And it became more than a deer shot by some damn hunter. It became a symbol to me."[15] The house is "artificial," the slain deer a "violation of nature," but to the artist there is a consistency, a wholeness about the two. In composition, Wyeth succeeds in evoking a balanced whole despite the overwhelming weight of the color and mass of the house, which seems almost on the verge of devouring the deer, partly because the lacework of the willow tree holds in its interstices the gray sky, which characteristically in Wyeth's paintings is flat, neutral and blends

---

13. "Nature," *Complete Works of Ralph Waldo Emerson* (Centenary ed.; Boston, 1903), I, 26.
14. "The Poet," *Emerson's Complete Works* (Boston, 1898), III, 23.
15. *Horizon*, p. 88.

with the snow. In other words, although the house has all the weight, the deer and the tree command the natural background. But this does not make the deer live in the house. Two symbols do, however. In what is almost a Wyeth hallmark, a window is open and the curtain is blowing in. Like Frank Lloyd Wright's, and Thoreau's, for that matter, bringing the outdoors indoors, these windows and curtains join the outer natural world, whose sovereign in this picture is the hanging deer, to the man-made artificial interior.

For the second symbol, we must, like the artist, lean on the crutch of language. The painting is entitled "Tenant Farmer," and so we know that the violated creature of nature is not an urban trophy, but something which will be ingested and digested by the man who killed it. Man and deer will be one, as boy and woodchuck became one. One sidelight: a prospective buyer's wife asked that Mr. Wyeth paint the deer out of the picture,[16] doubtless because it was a "disagreeable fact." This may seem a prototype of philistinism, yet Thoreau had been bothered by somewhat the same problem as was this woman as he watched the savagery of a hen-hawk. He concluded, "What we call wildness is a civilization other than our own. . . . So any surpassing work of art is strange and wild to the mass of men, as is genius itself."[17]

One of the strangest and wildest and most abstract of Andrew Wyeth's paintings is "River Cove," which is composed of three triangular masses in the bottom four-fifths of the panel and two horizontal strips at the top, one dark and wide, one light and narrow. The lowest triangle, whose hypotenuse runs down from left to right is the shallow brown bottom of the river. The second triangle is a low peninsula of shell-littered gray mud. The third triangle is the reflected sky, the first strip the inverted reflection of dark evergreens on the bank and the highest strip is the other gray strand edging the pool. The only sign of an animal is three heron tracks. And the only man is the invisible artist through whose eyes we see. But in this rectangular composition are five depths of nature: bottom, beach, surface, sky and forest; and two

16. *Ibid.*, p. 99.

17. *The Journal of Henry David Thoreau*, eds. Bradford Torrey and Francis H. Allen (Boston, 1959), XI, 450.

depths of time, the static and eternal symbolized by the still water and air, and the transitory symbolized by the tracks of what has been and gone. The scene is a wild, disordered segment of nature, but the artist, by stratifying the forms, has reattached the apparently ugly variety of nature and in this case has come closer to a truly transcendent unity than in any of the other works discussed here. The disordered is ordered. The sweep of nature from submarine to stratosphere has been condensed—and with no abuse of epistemological accuracy—to one small rectangle of egg-tempera. Thoreau too finds Time in the strata of natural fact: "Time is but a stream I go a-fishing in. I drink of it; but while I drink I see the sandy bottom and detect how shallow it is. Its thin current slides away, but eternity remains. I would drink deeper; fish in the sky, whose bottom is pebbly with stars."[18] To reduce such abstractions as these to paint, to reattach man, nature and time to eternity, to show Christina's world without Christina; these are the tasks which Andrew Wyeth has set for himself, and with increasing sureness, he is succeeding, and drinking deeper as the stream flows past.

18. "Walden," p. 109.

Hans Hofmann

Space sways and resounds . . . [it is] filled with tensions and
functions . . . with life and rhythm and the dispositions of
sublime divinity. . . . The plane is the creative element. . . .
Out of a feeling of depth, a sense of movement develops itself.
. . . The effects potentize themselves. . . . Depth in a pictorial, plastic
sense, is not created by the arrangement of objects one after another
toward a vanishing point, in the sense of the Renaissance perspective,
but on the contrary (and in absolute denial of this doctrine) by
the creation of forces in the sense of push *and* pull.

The career of Hans Hofmann spans the first two-thirds of the twentieth-century, and in its development one can measure the many movements in modern art. Hofmann had deep faith in the worth of the individual and in painting as an expression of his poetic insight. Growing up before World War I, he did not find his idealism in conflict with world events. He was able to maintain his belief in creativity and the individual despite the fact that many artists, in the period between the world wars, expressed themselves in largely negative terms, viewing the individual as small, insignificant, and victimized. As head of his own art school in New York for more than forty years, Hofmann insisted upon permanent standards in a world that constantly threatened those standards; as an artist, he was a leader in the most important style of American painting since World War II—Abstract Expressionism. "The grand old man of American abstract painting," he has been called, a teacher and an artist of extraordinary dimensions.

Hans Hofmann was born in Weissenberg, Germany, on March 21, 1880. His family moved to Munich in 1886, where he attended the public schools and the Gymnasium. In 1898 Hofmann enrolled at Moritz Heymann's art school in Munich; from 1904 to 1914 he worked in Paris, supported by Phillip Freudenberg, who had been greatly impressed by his work. Hofmann was influenced by those artists who were leaders in the fauvist and cubist movements: Matisse, Picasso, Braque, and Robert Delaunay. After World War I, in which he did not fight because of a lung illness, he opened a school for modern art in a Munich suburb. The reputation of his school spread so that students came from everywhere in the world. In time, Hofmann was invited to teach in America, and in the fall of 1932 he opened the Hans Hofmann School of Fine Arts in New York. In the summer of 1934 he established a summer art school in Provincetown, Massachusetts. Combining the free use of color, which he had learned from Matisse, and cubist design, he created paintings like "Red Trickle" (1939) and "The Poet" (1940), which anticipated complete abstraction. In March 1944, Hofmann had his first New York showing. From that time until his death in 1966 his one-man showings appeared frequently.

At the center of Hofmann's art is the belief, as Harold Rosenberg points out, that "every technical concept must have its equivalent in feeling, or it will result in mere decoration." Rosenberg has been an important explicator of Hofmann's art, insisting that Hofmann was one of that small number of people who in the past thirty-five years have made the term " 'New York art world' mean something more than a mere exhibition center or marketplace."

Hans Hofmann: Nature into Action

HAROLD
ROSENBERG

O F ALL *liaisons dangereuses* none is considered more perilous to the artist than living with ideas. In that alliance, every passion is diluted by argument, every response of sensibility by examinations of purpose. The quiet exercise of talent is out of the question, and one may wake up any morning to discover that the conceptual bitch has run off with everything. For more than half a century Hans Hofmann has triumphantly survived this essentially young man's pastime, developing through it his power of inventiveness, vivacity, and assurance.

The canvases of Hofmann are demonstrations of concepts—and of getting away from them. A founder of automatism in American painting, he was led to his reflexes by theory and to the accidental by the recognition that the demands of consciousness can be too exacting for creation. Only a model of obedience to law could have been so insistent on acquiring for art the resources of chaos, or so alert to distinguish actual spontaneity from manneristic representations of the spontaneity formula. If in the act of painting Hofmann "wants not to know what I am doing" (as Elaine de Kooning quoted him as saying in an early article on him), it is not because he wishes to lay claim to revelation but because there is a not-knowing "element" in art that may be too far diminished by over-insistent intention. Hofmann's suspensions of thought are an homage to the immanent logic of the medium laid bare by his experiments. He is an Action Painter (not in all

REPRINTED BY PERMISSION OF THE PUBLISHER, HORIZON PRESS, FROM *The Anxious Object* BY HAROLD ROSENBERG. COPYRIGHT 1964, 1966.

his modes) to whom an action implies responsibility to the mind and to something beyond it.

I distinguish in Hofmann's paintings three (or four) major phases, each of which points to a different conception of the term "abstract" art—though Hofmann does not close them off from one another but goes back and forth among them.

In the first phase, the artist's primary interest is analytical study of "Nature," as interpreted in the metaphysical lingo that more than anything German has remained stuck to him.* Most deeply enmeshed in Hofmann's classroom labors, this "learning to see" period centers on a system for transforming visual experience into "plastic creation on a flat surface without destroying this flat surface." The union of brain and eye are saluted in his breeze-laden Cape Cod landscapes: "Truro River," 1937, and "Province-town Harbor," 1938, are built of ragged-edged rectangles of vivid oranges, blues, yellows, the "color-bearing planes" holding depth under control with the aid of flying scrawls still used to outline objects. Components of these landscapes, no longer harnessed to representations of water and rowboats but with their look retained, are recognizable in' differently specialized forms in the work of dozens of American contemporaries, including Hans Hofmann himself.

Still lifes of these years lack the strength and airiness of the landscapes. They incline towards crowding, even clutter, as if the artist's intellect had insisted that everything that presented itself ought to be taken care of esthetically and that no advantage needed to be gained through external economy. At this time Hofmann obviously requires the outdoors; he also seems freer of Matisse there. A dozen years later, with analysis of nature transcended by a succession of syntheses, the problem of How Much?

---

* Catalogues of Hofmann's shows have often contained explanatory theses bearing such titles as "The Resurrection of the Plastic Arts" or "The Color Problem in Pure Painting—Its Creative Origin." These how-to-do-it, or rather how-to-think-it, communications, whose point has often been left behind by the paintings being shown, are among the most congenial pleasantries of the contemporary art world. The last-named article, incidentally, begins: "The genuine value of a painting is greatly determined through its basic concept"—regardless of the growing irrationalism in his approach Hofmann has not neglected his courtesies to his mental partner.

has eliminated itself as Hofmann's interiors are swept clean by cerebral gusts.

In his later landscapes Hofmann continues to recall some of his early pictorial means, now transfigured by different aims. In "The Garden," '56, the rectangles of "Truro River," reduced to small slabs of pure color, have become a pavement of light through cliffs and jungles of fierce impasto; released from the dispositions of observed forms, they swirl in the rotating pull of massive discs long a feature of certain of Hofmann's paintings of the human figure (one might interpret them as "heads" launched in cosmic space). The circular movement engages itself in the substance of the heavy pigment in a manner different from Van Gogh's, a canvas like "Le Gilotin," '53, becoming a relief composed of hunks of charred velvet, strips of bluish silver elastic, clots of bituminized bananas.

Before such new "nature" could come into being the research into visual perception had to be superseded by another mode of imitation equally dissociated from copying. In Hofmann's second phase the dynamism of the picture takes precedence over the truth of the scene. Abstraction now results not from the translation of appearances into the alphabet of the medium but from the "automatic responses of the picture surface." The painter still starts with the model, but once his notations have begun working on each other the canvas is allowed to take over, the painter "thinks not" nor sets requirements but follows the intimations of the picture's brain with its dialectic of tensions and counter-tensions, Hofmann's "push and pull."

The effects of automatism depend of course on who is being automatic. Working at a speed that excludes meditation, Hofmann now seeks to be guided by the debate of pictorial knowledge with itself. The automatism is in the logic of the discourse: since this "plastic animation" has taken place, an opposing movement must reply to it . . . and so forth. When the painting quiets down Hofmann finds out what he has been thinking.

The tendency of this phase, very dominant in Hofmann's painting between 1947 and 1951, is towards constructions rigged of geometrical contours. These are at times effects of compositional intuitions ("Magenta And Blue"); or, seeming to originate apart from the visual world, they constitute emblems of psychic states or entities ("Perpetuita," "Germania," both 1951), like in impulse to, though not resembling, Kandinsky's later abstractions. "Ecstasy," 1947, an angular, machine-like projection of planes, and of lines employed as planes, is, in its kinship to metal and wire sculpture, rich in hints yet to be exploited: on the other hand, one is reminded of pre-dada analytical art—the "ecstasy" might have been that of one of Duchamp's bachelors.

With regard to the tensions it is capable of setting up in our bodies, the medium of any art is an extension of the physical world; a stroke of pigment, for example, "works" within us in the same way as a bridge across the Hudson. For the unseen universe that inhabits us, an accidental blot or splash of paint may thus assume an equivalence to the profoundest happening. It was not inconsistent with Hofmann's rigorous conception of nature that he early began the exploration of accident in painting. But his remark on "The Prey," 1956, a canvas which arouses in him the enthusiasm of an indescribable reminiscence, shows how profoundly he has weighed the gifts of chance in art: "for this," he said, "you need to be in the rarest states." It is, in other words, by the magic of spirit that one "earns" unexpected successes in art.

If the ultimate subject matter of all art is the artist's psychic state or tension (and this may be the case even in non-individualistic epochs), that state (e.g., grief) may be represented through an abstract sign. The innovation of Action Painting was to dispense with the representation of the state in favor of enacting it in the physical movement of painting. The action on the canvas became its own representation. This was possible because action which carries the psychic into the material world is by its nature sign-producing; it leaves the trace of a movement whose origin and character are not ever altogether revealed—for instance, the act of love results in a correlation of bodies which, as Freud pointed out, may be mistaken for murder. Yet, once accomplished, the action also exists in the thing which it has transformed as by a scratch on a cheek.

In turning to action, abstract art abandons its alliance with architecture, as painting had earlier broken with music and with the novel, and offers its hand to pantomime and dance. To this transformation of painting belong such Hofmann masterworks as "Burst Into Life," 1952, and "X," 1955. "Liebesbaum," 1955, is a tree danced—in the scent of one of Rilke's nymphs.

"Dance the orange. The warmer landscape, fling it out of you, that the ripe one be radiant in homeland breezes!"

In painting, the primary agency of physical motion (as distinct from the visual representation of motion, as in Delacroix or the Futurists) is *line*. As stroke or as figure (in the sense of figure skating) a line is the direct manifestation of an act, though of course it also has other functions in painting; for example, to define contours, to connect two points, to be a narrow plane between other planes. In its passage on the canvas each line establishes the actual movement of the artist's hand as an esthetic statement, and this is true whether it outlines a pony cart or belongs to the shading of a nose or is there without any external reference.

In Hofmann's Action Paintings, which include some of his most remarkable canvases, the strokes of color retain their separate identities within the picture situation and function as forces in conflict, instead of being changed by their width or length into mere relations of planes. . . . It is this that brings his Action Paintings into focus with those of Kline and de Kooning. Among the first to make compositional use of the free scrawl, Hofmann has not, in order to obtain linear momentum, turned himself over to calligraphy with its tendency toward monotony, but has known how to vary his line almost at will from wiry volutes to the broadest staccato jots. Nor has the immediacy made possible by Action Painting often seduced him into compulsiveness —nor into that depressing bogus decontrol fashionable in Europe. Weakness in Hofmann's painting occurs when the artist has moved so fast that the action on the canvas is finished before he has been able to get into it: compositions of this type lack development and turn into more or less lucky swipes of color. Weakness also appears when Hofmann loses his grip on the action and falls back on concept to bring the painting to completion: here the artist's undefined feelings are suppressed. The best Hofmanns hold the action from rhythm to rhythm in a superb synthesis of impulse and esthetic consciousness.

Action Painting restores art to an ethic beyond mass ideals and taste. The dialectics of Hofmann's morality balances on his struggle against the given, the struggle for the "creative" (his favorite word) as the sole reality—it involves putting into practice his fixed romantic assumption that painting must be constantly prevented from becoming the means by which the artist repeats himself. Beginning again is not only the rule for each new canvas; it is the inner process which gives meaning to the picture.

No American artist can mount a show of greater coherent variety than Hans Hofmann. Fed by his tireless consciousness, constantly growing more concrete and inwardly responsive, his originality suggests no limits. Besides the innovations flowing from his enveloping approach to art and experience, he has been able to derive novel conclusions from reflections of his thought sent back to him by artists whose inventions have been in debt to his teachings or to talk about them. This latter kind of originality is today more rare than original originality—it is more rare for a man to keep up a continuing communication with himself through others, as Hofmann has done, than to build a unique mouse trap in the desert.

Andy Warhol

I think everybody should be a machine. I think everybody should be like everybody. That seems to be what is happening now.

Pop art is a recent and unique reflection of contemporary America in that it uses commercial art for aesthetic purposes. In an age when billboards and posters, magazines, newspapers, and television have created a visual experience that constantly diverts the eye, one is not surprised to discover that artists seek to understand the meaning of that experience. Advertising dominates many aspects of American life, and pop artists have interpreted this commercial idiom for their viewers. Some of the more important pop artists in America are Jim Dine, Robert Indiana, Robert Rauschenberg, Roy Lichtenstein, George Segal, and Tom Wesselman. The most popular, experimental, and controversial of the group—"the true primitive of pop art"—is Andy Warhol.

Born on August 8, 1927, in Pittsburgh, Pennsylvania, Andy Warhol began his career as a commercial artist—he won the Art Director's Club Medal in 1957 for a giant shoe ad—but soon he turned to painting. "I used to have the same soup lunch every day for twenty years. So I painted soup cans." He also painted stacked brillo boxes, electric chairs, car crashes, and silk screens of Marilyn Monroe and Troy Donahue. The two types of paintings for which Warhol gained the greatest popularity were blow-ups of comic strips like "Dick Tracy" and "Nancy" and his silk screenings of "beautiful" people like Jacqueline Onassis, Elizabeth Taylor, and Marilyn Monroe. Recently he has turned to the creation of underground movies, and *Sleep; Eat; Kiss; Empire; The Chelsea Girls; I, A Man;*

and others have represented a logical extension of his realistic painting. In 1964, Warhol received the Film Culture Award and the Los Angeles Film Festival Award.

The contemporary artist has a role vis-à-vis society that is distinctly different from that of the traditional artist. As Mario Amaya points out in *Pop Art . . . and After:*

Traditionally the artist has been the ignored producer, appreciated when it was too late, misunderstood, isolated from his culture. Today's artist is "with it" not only in terms of his "popular" subject matter but by his new status in society as a celebrity figure, sought after, lionised, interviewed, photographed. His success is not so different from that of the movie star: he may be taken up or dropped at a moment's notice, he is subject to changing fashion, he must constantly be in the foreground and ahead of the game. This leads to a sort of performance-artist, who works in almost direct relationship to the commercial art world, who produces for exhibitions rather than for himself, who tries to anticipate the expectations of powerful critics and dealers, and who must create attention at all costs or perish in a sea of thousands of other artists, all fighting to reach the raft of success.

The pop artist confronts the facts of contemporary life realistically. In his art he mirrors the frenetic quality of urban life; he uses mechanical elements like a soup can or a tube of toothpaste directly, objectively, and with no inhibitions; he concerns himself with the commonplace, reflecting the world he knows with absolute fidelity; he heightens familiar objects by placing them in new contexts; and he views the relationship of cause and effect as an illusion "created by the mind through the channel of repetitive experience." These various characteristics are found in the work of Andy Warhol.

In the following essay Mario Amaya uses the term "Super Realism" as a synonym for Pop Art, believing that this new art form "alludes not only to a new type of realism which has nothing to do with that of the past, but to the super elements in our culture: the supermarket, supermen idols, the super-sales directive, the super-sophistication of a super-saturated society that values the new for its own sake."

Andy Warhol

MARIO

AMAYA

F ALL the New Super Realists, Andy Warhol is the most straightforward, and forces the issue of mechanical versus hand-made almost to the breaking point. His pictures allow little give and take: you either accept them as art or you don't; there is nothing in between. He avoids any reference to painting, either of the past or present, and he not only uses mechanical processes but even has assistants who do the work for him, thus removing us as far as possible from a fine art experience.

If, as it has been suggested, Abstract Expressionists have reduced to a minimum the difference between creator and creation, and Pop has reduced to a minimum the difference between ready-made and hand-made, then Warhol must be the new movement's perfect exponent.

Silk-screening photographic news images, or stencilling commercial labels in a sort of orgasm of aesthetic "delight," Warhol and his assistants turn out dozens of the same object, whether exact stencil replicas of *Brillo* crates which ironically were designed by Abstract Expressionist Jim Harvey (in solid and unfunctional form) or signed, real Campbell Soup tins. The silk screening and stencilling is done in varying sizes and degrees of intensity, and slight variations can occur from image to image. But these series of never-ending candid photos and brand labels run through our minds with a terrifying monotony that forces us to concentrate on the most minute changes in density, positioning and detail. Both High Camp and emotional *ennui* seem to be expressed in these forced experiences of pleasure in repetition; it is as if we were seeing a reflection of a feeling at the end of a camera lens.

One can find in Warhol's subject matter much to moralise upon, although this is certainly not a stated intention: Negro-hunts in Alabama, a waiting electric chair, Jackie Kennedy's horror-stricken face, Marilyn Monroe trapped in her own gilt-edged image, the "Disaster" series of deaths. But nothing is overtly stated except by repetition, and we are thrown into a confusion between reading the images in strip form as a "message" and appreciating the formal design effects for their own sake.

Some see Warhol as a great *faux naif* in the tradition of Douanier Rousseau (who also never objected to someone finishing his paintings). Others consider him a supra-intellectual, and still others think of him as a brilliant art director, organising his images with the timeliness and insight of a window display man.

Warhol himself wants to be a machine: "The things I want to show are mechanical. Machines have less problems." He further clarifies his position by stating, "I think somebody should be able to do all my paintings for me. I think it would be so great if more people took up silk screens so that no one would know whether my picture was mine or somebody else's." He predicts, "Some day everybody will think just what they want to think, and then every-body will probably be thinking alike."

Born in Pittsburgh in 1927, he started his career as commercial artist, doing shoe advertisements, greeting cards and window dis-plays. His blown-up comic strip paintings of Dick Tracy were used as a 1961 window display for Lord and Taylor's. It is rumoured that he "painted" his first stencil pictures of dollar bills around 1961 on the suggestion of a lady art dealer; when she asked him what was the most important thing in his life, his answer was, "Money." "Well, then," she reputedly advised, "paint it!" He began his Campbell Soup tin "paintings" because "I used to drink it. I used to have the same lunch every day, for twenty years, I guess; the same thing over and over again."

Boredom holds a particular fascination for Warhol, and he has experimented with the lengths to which one can go and still retain some thread of interest: like a gramophone needle stuck in a groove, the same thing repeats over and over, until it begins to assume a new rhythm and pattern of its own. In his experimental films he deals with subjects that test our ability to hold attention fixed on one image without shift in focus, angle or distance, for almost unendurable lengths of time. *Sleep* has a camera trained on a man sleeping for over six hours, *Empire* scrutinizes one façade of the Empire State Building for eight, and *Henry Geldzahler* shows a close-up of the Metropolitan Museum official smoking a cigar for ninety minutes. The magazine *Film Culture* finds in these films that "The world becomes transposed, intensified, electrified. We see it sharper than before . . . as pure as it is in itself; eating as eating, sleeping as sleeping, haircut as haircut."

Warhol's answers to questions by Geldzahler perhaps throw some light on his unique point of view about his art:

Geldzahler: Do you know what you are doing?

Warhol: No.

Geldzahler: Do you know what a "painting" is going to look like before you do it?

Warhol: Yes.

Geldzahler: Does it end up looking like you expect?

Warhol: No.

Geldzahler: Are you surprised?

Warhol: No.

Leonard Bernstein

A performer is a highly public figure whose whole compulsion is to get out there in front of people and let it out. Now, the creative person is a whole other guy. He has a complex inner life. His big relationship is with himself or his Muse, or his God, or his unconsciousness. Most people of the arts belong to one group or the other. My misfortune is to live in a schizophrenic world of both.

Serious music has never been so popular in America as it was from 1958 to 1969, when Leonard Bernstein was director of the New York Philharmonic. There has always been an unhealthy distance in America between the popular and the serious arts, and when Bernstein, who had already composed Broadway musicals like *On The Town* and *West Side Story*, came to the Philharmonic to conduct the music of great classical composers, he was regarded with suspicion. When he began to popularize the classics on television and on radio, he was accused of being an exhibitionist who lacked inner discipline and yielded to the effect of the moment. He has been called "an egoist with empathy," "an optimist with anxiety," "a professor who is never absent-minded." But in time it has become clear that this commentator and composer, professor and pianist, television music lecturer and conductor is an extraordinarily talented man whose versatility does not imply superficiality. "A showman who can speak the language and write the music of Broadway," a biographer remarks, "Bernstein is also an earnest, thoroughly trained musician."

Leonard Bernstein was born on August 25, 1918, in Lawrence, Massachusetts. He attended the Boston Latin School, Harvard University, and the Curtis Institute of Music, where he studied under Fritz Reiner and Mme. Vengerova. He went to the Berkshire Music Festival in 1940 and studied under Serge Koussevitsky, returning to graduate from the Curtis Institute in 1941. In the summer of 1942, Bernstein served as assistant conductor to Koussevitsky and in the 1943–44 season he was assistant conductor at the New York Philharmonic. The turning point of his career as a conductor was on November 14, when he substituted for Bruno Walter and gave a spectacular performance. Bernstein became the conductor of the New York City Symphony in 1945 and remained at that position until 1948. In the next ten years he was head conductor of the Berkshire Music Center (1954–1955), Professor of Music at Brandeis University (1951–1956), and conductor of The New York Philharmonic with Dimitri Mitropoulos in the 1957–1958 season. In 1958 he was appointed Musical Director of the New York Philharmonic and remained in that position until his retirement in 1969. Although Bernstein is best-known for his conducting, he has also composed a great deal of music. His classical work includes *The Clarinet Sonata* (1942); *Symphony No. 1* (*Jeremiah*, 1942); *Symphony No. 2* (*The Age of Anxiety*, 1949); and *Symphony No. 3* (*Kaddish*, 1963). His Broadway plays are *On The Town* (1944), *Wonderful Town* (1953), *Candide* (1956), and *West Side Story* (1957). He has also written a movie score (*On The Waterfront*, 1954), ballet (*Fancy Free*, 1944), incidental music (*Peter Pan*, 1950; *The Lark*, 1957), and a book (*The Joy of Music*, 1959). Upon his retirement from the New York Philharmonic, Bernstein was named New York Laureate Conductor so that he would be free to conduct the orchestra as well as broaden his other musical activities.

Bernstein has often spoken of the conflict between the inner life of the composer and the outer life of the conductor. Although he has spent most of his career in the glare of publicity and is the showman *extraordinaire*, he has a craving to retreat to a creative life which will permit him to compose both classical and popular music. One of Bernstein's favorite composers—the one whose music he conducts with particular sympathy—is Gustav Mahler. The observation made of the German applies equally well to Bernstein: "If half of him was a romantic, the other half was that characteristic twentieth-century figure: the restless seeker for the naked truth (whether 'beautiful' or 'ugly'), ridden with doubt and perplexity, ill-at-ease in an unfriendly cosmos."

The Blinding Facility of Leonard Bernstein

MARTIN

MAYER

Y PROBLEMS NOW are just what they were when I went to Harvard," said Leonard Bernstein one hot day last July, thinking ahead, perhaps, to the rainy day in November when he would announce an intention to retire in 1969 from his post as conductor of the New York Philharmonic. "That's a generation ago—at this moment, I'm a month short of my forty-eighth birthday. But if I were asked now what I want to be when I grow up, I would say just what I said when I was at Harvard—a musician. I think that's a noble word.

"And if anyone asked, 'What do you mean? What do you want to *do* in music?' I would still say, 'Anything I can.' "

He looked like a comfortable guru, protesting the weather in a sparkling and freshly pressed open-neck white shirt which hung outside equally sparkling white slacks, apparently of the same material. Both blinds and shades were drawn over the windows of the large square study in his Park Avenue penthouse. A diagonal half of the room was work area: big piano, with a comfortable chair and music rack nestled in the curve; and along the adjacent wall hanging bookshelves, with cabinets and jutting desk below. The other half was couches, rocking chair (of course), phonograph, huge square coffee table, glass over cane, and on the glass a litter of books and magazines—*The Nation, Saturday Review, Cue, Newsweek*, Arvin's *Melville*, Fall's *Viet-Nam Witness*, Hausner's *Justice in Jerusalem*. . . . Not music.

REPRINTED FROM *Esquire Magazine*, VOL. LXVII (FEB. 1967). REPRINTED BY PERMISSION OF CURTIS BROWN, LTD. COPYRIGHT © 1967 BY ESQUIRE, INC. FIRST PUBLISHED IN *Esquire Magazine*.

The room was specifically lit, brilliant pools over the piano and the desk, and as a result mostly dark; the furniture was primarily black lacquer with red lacquer touches, and there was a large porcelain cat: part Victorian, part *Chinois*. In the place of honor over the piano bench hung a framed parchment scroll, "To Maestro Leonard Bernstein with affection and admiration," signed by the cast of the Metropolitan Opera *Falstaff* of 1964, musically the greatest triumph of his quarter century as a conductor; and around it were some of Franco Zeffirelli's costume sketches for the production.

Bernstein was bone weary. In decency (and under union pressure), his New York Philharmonic had guaranteed its men a full year's pay and a full year's work. A hard season (including a long stretch in Vienna for another *Falstaff*, and recording sessions there) had therefore been followed by a Stravinsky Festival to employ the men, and then by a group of outdoor *stravaganze*. At this moment, he was freshly returned from Milwaukee, where he had led the Philharmonic in an outdoor concert sponsored by Schlitz, again an action dictated by decency, because Schlitz would pick up some of the bills for the orchestra's outdoor series in New York, and was entitled to a reward for its home folks. Meanwhile he had accepted a commission to compose a long "theatre piece" to occupy the opening evening at Kennedy Center in Washington. "I have a million librettos," he said rather gloomily, "which is the same as saying I have none."

Even the coming August could not really yield much rest, because there was a season with the Philharmonic to prepare—and it was going to be a hard season (though Bernstein at the time seemed remarkably unconscious of the problem), because the strings of the orchestra were to be led by a new concertmaster, David Nadien, who is a great violinist but almost totally inexperienced, not only at running a fiddle section, but at playing in a symphony orchestra. "I wake up at night thinking of Dave," said the concertmaster of another orchestra, "and that moment in the *Pathétique* when he realizes that he's responsible for what the Philharmonic fiddles are doing, and he barely knows his own part." Bernstein, for whom the stringed instruments are by no means a specialty (he plays none of them), would have to organize a solution.

What peace might have been gotten out of the dark room on a July afternoon was periodically shattered by the braying of the telephone (and, of course, by the presence of a reporter). There was work to be done on a new book to be made from his television scripts. There was advance planning for the orchestra's 125th anniversary season in 1967–68, for which Bernstein has "commissioned a whole raft of pieces, a range from Howard Hanson to Stockhausen, everything." The Vienna Opera was after him to come conduct *Rosenkavalier*. "They say, 'Then we will really hear *our Rosenkavalier*,'" he commented; "it's very flattering. And they call twice a week, like it was from Irvington, New Jersey." Beyond such serious concerns there were the duty calls, the recurrent, insistent demands for time which are the lot of the celebrity, the man who is "well-known," as Daniel Boorstin once put it, "for his well-knownness."

"You have to remember," says Carlos Moseley, the Philharmonic's manager (who first worked with Bernstein in 1941, when he was a student pianist and Bernstein a student conductor at Tanglewood, and they played the Brahms *B-Flat* together), "that Lenny is the symbol of music throughout the length and breadth of this land. Anybody who's building a school, or wants to bring business and music together, or education and music together, or just wants to raise money—he wants Bernstein. The quantity of this sort of thing is beyond belief."

The odd part of it is that so much of this sort of thing seems to amuse Bernstein. "He *must* be at the very peak of his capacity," an old friend said recently, rather puzzled at his own and Bernstein's belief that somewhere there are new heights he will scale. Even before his announcement that he would leave the Philharmonic there were rumors (firmly discouraged by their subject) that he would finally accept that non-job at Kennedy Center which the Kennedy family has been pushing at him since Congress first appropriated money for the building, that what he really wanted was the management of the Met on Rudolf Bing's retirement. (Indeed, it has been noted with interest that the time of his announced retirement from the Philharmonic coincides with the time when Bing has said he wanted to leave the Met.) The wise money has known for years that Bernstein was bored at the Philharmonic. ("During his first season," says an old acquaintance, "he came off stage at intermission and he was really shaking. He told me, 'All through the Brahms, I was going over my luncheon appointments for next week.' He didn't know what would happen to him if he couldn't keep burning all the time at a white heat.") It seems unlikely that Bernstein really was bored as ordinary mortals know boredom, because he can always retreat into an unusually well-furnished interior; but at forty-eight he is still openly afraid of being bored. It makes everybody more than a little nervous, including Bernstein.

The living symbol of music was born, oddly enough, in an unmusical home. Almost alone among the major musical talents of history, Bernstein was not a prodigy. The son of a Russian immigrant who had a barber-supply business in Boston, he never touched an instrument until he was ten years old, and through his years at the Boston Latin School and Harvard he had neither conservatory training nor significant teachers (except in composition, where the Harvard music department was strong). On the other hand, his schooling in the general academic subjects was about the best the nation offered.

During the years when ambition solidifies, Bernstein was spending most of his time as a budding intellectual with other budding intellectuals at Harvard. The literary interests acquired then show up in his work (nearly all his major compositions have involved a text) and in his conversation, which sparkles from the many facets of a huge and lovingly employed vocabulary. He cares about language. His intellectualism does not, of course, set him apart from the world of conductors—Steinberg, Leinsdorf and especially Szell are probably more profoundly educated, certainly more likely to spend their time with academicians, and better read in scholarly disciplines. (Where Bernstein will have read the newest well-regarded piece of history in the bookstores, Szell will be up on contemporary wrangles in historiography.) Though a good linguist, Bernstein does not shift comfortably from language to language, as the Central Europeans do, and tends to translate English words into the language he is speaking rather than make that remarkable adjustment of temperament and *Weltanschauung* that comes automatically to the man who is really at home in several tongues. For a Szell or a Steinberg or a Leinsdorf, however, intellectual life is a private business; while Bernstein, extrovert, lover of parties, of bull sessions, of word games and doggerel verse (which he writes on occasion), has made the play of his intelligence part of his public life, as though he had gone on from Harvard to be, say, Arthur Schlesinger, Jr. rather than Leonard Bernstein.

Once he found out about it, his life was full of music. He took piano lessons, even practiced a little, wrote a school song, played piano behind the Harvard Glee Club, staged a student performance of Marc Blitztein's deliberately naïve pop-opera *The Cradle Will Rock* (which he was to revive in New York in 1947, and stage again, in much sadder circumstances, in his touching memorial to Blitztein in 1965)—but all this was essentially fun and games. Not until he had been graduated from Harvard and moved on to Philadelphia's Curtis Institute, at the age of twenty-one, did he have to put up with the severity (and the nonsense) of professional discipline.

"You know, Lenny was a pupil of mine," said Fritz Reiner, greatest of all orchestral technicians, sitting over a drink at his Connecticut home half-a-dozen years ago. "At Curtis." There was a brief pause while Reiner took judicial notice of the fact that this information was not news to his interlocutor. "Then one day he came to me and told me he was going to Tanglewood for the summer. I said, 'Lenny, by all means go to Tanglewood, it's near your home. But don't come back here; the two schools don't mix.' He cried. He wrote me a letter eight pages long, on blue paper, it had tearstains in it—I show it to you. Also, he wrote to Mrs. Bok. So for one more year, I took him back, but then he had to go."

After a season in which he had played with Ormandy, Reiner and Szell, the pianist Leon Fleisher once said, "I have reunited the Austro-Hungarian Empire." Nobody, not even the ardent young Bernstein, could unite the machine-shop exactitudes of Reiner with the atelier sentiments of Boston's Koussevitzky, whose protégé Bernstein now became, both at Tanglewood and at home. Of all the major conductors of this century, Koussevitsky was technically the least accomplished: there was even at one point a silly rumor that he couldn't read a score. After a hard time at one of his rehearsals, the harpsichordist Yella Pessl once asked the English-horn player Louis Speyer, "When do you come in with this orchestra?" Speyer, after looking around to make sure nobody was in earshot, said, "When you *dare*." Koussevitzky at a concert gave his orchestra very few specific instructions, and those he gave were usually wrong. But at rehearsals he heard everything, and by a combination of cajoling and throwing temper tantrums he could get exquisite work from his men—and great loyalty, too (his was the last significant orchestra of the time to be organized by the American Federation of Musicians). To this school, Bernstein became an apprentice, making the necessary adaptation to his own personality. It was a short apprenticeship.

Like nobody else before or since, Bernstein made a habit of coming in at the top. The first orchestra he conducted as a professional rather than as a Tanglewood student was the New York Philharmonic; the first opera house he worked in was La Scala. His first large-scale work for orchestra, the *Jeremiah Symphony*, won the New York Music Critics Circle Award; his first Broadway musical, *On The Town*, ran more than a year and sold to M-G-M. At the age of twenty-seven, he had his own orchestra in New York —the ill-fated City Symphony, which Leopold Stokowski had founded the year before.

It is by no means without importance in Bernstein's history that on most occasions when he was playing a piece for the first time he has been before the most sophisticated publics of the world. He made no contact with that noodling over and improving of performances which established the security of the European conductors of the last generation—the first effort in Düsseldorf, brushed up in Riga, modified in Stuttgart and perfected in Dresden before any attempts in Berlin. As a result, he often feels that when he's played a piece once he's "done" it. This attitude couples easily with what associate conductor Martin Rich of the Metropolitan Opera calls Bernstein's "blinding facility." (Rich had to get the singers ready for Bernstein to take over in *Falstaff*, and couldn't make an appointment to see what Bernstein wanted; at one point, gloomily, Rich said, "Nobody has to worry; Lenny could probably learn even this score in three days if he had to.") The combination has given Bernstein what may be, weight for age, a world's record in total number of different pieces performed—but it also means that not everything he plays has securely emerged from the rehearsal phase.

At the New York City Symphony in the late Forties, Bernstein conducted without a baton, molding phrases and (worse) giving beats with his fingers, while the rest of his body danced around the podium. "You were all right in the orchestra," one of the men who played in it said recently in affectionate but cruel recollection, "so long as you didn't look up." Both by circumstance and by political choice, Bernstein was "Lenny" rather than "Maestro." Those were brave days, when the union spirit was strong (Bernstein had turned down a chance at a debut in Boston prior to his New York opportunity, because the American Federation of Musicians had declared a boycott on the then still-unorganized Boston Symphony). It suited both Bernstein and the men, many of whom were graduates of the old W.P.A.-sponsored music projects, that a conductor should be *primus inter pares.*

Still, there was a lot of showmanship on the podium, and musicians disliked the choreographic and sometimes effete platform mannerisms by which Bernstein would impose his conceptions of a piece more on the audience than on the men. The critic Virgil Thomson worried in print that "having to learn classical repertory the hard way, which is after fifteen, and in a hurry, he would throw his cultural beginnings away and build toward success on a sheer talent for animation and personal projection." Particularly annoying were the slow movements of symphonies, during which Bernstein would bow his head in loving contemplation; the orchestra's capacity for sustained tone was limited and at these romantic moments its conductor appeared not to be hearing what were some pretty awful performances. But mostly the orchestra gave Bernstein its very best, because the men liked him, and because his musicality deserved it. "The young Bernstein," Igor Stravinsky recently wrote, "was articulate and readily likable [he still is], and he obviously adored music [he still does]."

What Bernstein did well—at the age of twenty-seven, with virtually invisible background—he already did better than anybody else in the world. Even in his appearances as a substitute, critics had noted his extraordinary rhythmic sensitivity. In the backwash of Wagner, classical tonality had collapsed as a means of organizing large-scale pieces of music; and except for the Viennese twelve-tone school and a few French, the "dissonant" composers of the twentieth century placed rhythmic patterns in polyphonic texture at the center of their music—a condition that persisted through the long drift back toward tonality that characterized the Thirties. Bernstein's extraordinary security with complicated rhythms made him the interpreter of choice for most contemporary scores. In 1946 (for the benefit of those who came in late), Stravinsky was a few years younger than Aaron Copland is today; his music, and that of Bartok, Hindemith, even Prokofiev, was pretty violently contemporary. Bernstein showed that it was also eternal.

The New York City Symphony died in 1948, and Bernstein went guesting around the world. In 1951 he married, announced that he didn't want to conduct any more, took a professorship at Brandeis, composed. From the viewpoint of the professional musical world of New York, he was in the wilderness. The road back, it seems now, began in Milan in late 1953, when Bernstein made his professional debut as an opera conductor, his prima donna being no less than Maria Callas in her first year as a svelte and fashionable heroine. This tourist was in Milan later that season, and remembers Luigi Oldani, the unflappable working boss of La Scala, speaking with awe strange to American ears of Maestro Bernstein and his brilliance in Cherubini's *Medea*. By the time he returned to Scala in 1955, for Bellini's *Sonnambula*, Bernstein was back in the mainstream at home, too—though here the lift to his reputation was given by the bourgeois small beer of *Omnibus* rather than any stronger artistic draught. In 1958, he took on the Philharmonic—becoming, incidentally, the first American-born conductor to hold the post.

One day a few years back, Igor Markevitch and his wife were trying to explain to a third party what distinguishes the great conductor, and they decided that the most important quality was "*rayonnement*." There was a search for the English equivalent of this French expression (the dictionary definition is "radiance") before the third party, somewhat to the Markevitches' annoyance, came up with "projection." During the course of the search, Mme. Markevitch, looking adoringly at her husband, said, "Whatever it is, the man who had most of it in all the world was Jesus Christ."

Be that as it may, the man who has the most of it of anyone now among us is Leonard Bernstein. As a person, as an intelligence and as a musician, he projects beautifully—and projects, moreover, almost uniquely, as an American. The desire to be rich and famous is that of the American boy; so is the distrust of the hermetic and the need to explain it. American, too, is the long list of friends— real friends, as close as or closer than family—and the wish to function in the company as an equal, with dignity nourished a little, of course, but not protected. Bernstein is a gentleman: his manners are good everywhere. He gets on first-name terms almost instantly with almost everyone because he really does like people; as Carlos Moseley puts it, "No matter how crowded the room is, when he sees somebody he knows, there's a special ray of sunshine for that person." Though nobody who is part of a fashionable in-group ever entirely escapes its little contempts, Bernstein continues his friendship for (and often makes himself useful to) people who have for one reason or another been excluded from their former circles. He is surrounded by crowds not only because he is successful, but also because the radiance is honest.

This *rayonnement* and an almost instant sense of what is in a score for him are Bernstein's major assets as a conductor. "There's nobody in existence who has that kind of *eyes*," says Arnold Arnstein, who makes orchestral parts from composers' sometimes rough scores for virtually every significant composer in the East. "He sees things as fast as I can"—meaning that if a composer has, for example, written a transposing instrument as he wants it to sound rather than as the player should play it, Bernstein will spot the mistake at first glance. One of Bernstein's little trials at any rehearsal with any orchestra is that he sees instantly where he wants the men to pick up again (most conductors have to think about it for a perceptible second), and then he has to accept other men's need to find the place that is so apparent to him.

Bernstein communicates with an orchestra primarily through an unspoken current of musicality. Like all conductors, he sings (though not nearly so much as, say, Bruno Walter); he stresses a beat very hard at a trouble spot to make sure everybody knows which side of the beat he is working on; he suggests markings that would probably be meaningless to anybody who had not just sat through that moment in the rehearsal. But similar moments at a Reiner rehearsal gave observer and participant the notion that they had just learned something: that what Reiner wanted had a kind of logical coherence. What Bernstein wants is emotional, immediate, often without logic: either you get it or you don't. When everything works, the experience of getting it, of participating in this unique phenomenon of a perception that extends into the invisible spectra, is among the most exciting musical communications available to modern man. Unfortunately, it often seems less impressive in retrospect, especially to the men, because it does not leave behind that self-satisfaction which is the last residuum of learning.

Certainly, Bernstein's communication is no great shakes technically: often he cannot tell his men through conventional means precisely how to get the phrasing he wants. During the rehearsal of the *Boris Godunov* excerpts that opened this season, for example, he wanted from his fiddles in the haunting tune of *I Have Attained the Highest Power* something much lighter in texture than they were giving him. "Don't do a delicate thing like this down at the frog," he said, referring to the near end of the bow; "try it up top." Most of the men continued to use the bowings they had chosen originally—but they knew what he wanted now, and they gave it to him. Similarly, during the *Falstaff* rehearsals, he once rather shocked the Metropolitan Opera fiddles by asking them to play "down bow," with one stroke, a phrase that just could not be managed that way—but his musical desire was so clear (and once grasped, so persuasive) that union musicians spent their break in the rehearsal discussing how one could in fact get the effect Lenny wanted.

It is easy enough to compare Bernstein's inability to give specific instructions with the educational exactitudes of a Szell or an Ormandy—but the fact of the matter is that a first-rate orchestral musician, once he knows what the boss wants, may be able to find a better way to do it than the boss can know. Those who heard the performance will not soon forget the Metropolitan Opera Orchestra management of the marvelous little string tune that breaks in on the trombones at the end of Ford's jealous aria, announcing the arrival of a Falstaff bedecked for his appointment with Ford's wife. Bernstein got this effect from the men with one remark, at the second orchestral rehearsal. They lumbered into the passage, playing the notes, and he stopped them. "Gentlemen," he said rather softly, "this is the *divine* moment of this work. If you f - - - this up at the performance, so help me God, I'll murder you." After the uproar had ended, they played it precisely right. "That's *beautiful*," Bernstein said, and everyone glowed.

Most of any conductor's work is done, of course, at rehearsals— and sitting down, not striding the podium like a colossus. Bernstein has a remarkable stool, very sturdy on four widespread metal legs, which not only gives him a place to sit but also, by means of a platform about a third of the way up, a high place to stand when he absolutely has to stand. This gesture of rising to his feet substitutes more than adequately for the jumping at the orchestra which still expresses his *sforzando* at performances. But the fundament of the conductor's job at a rehearsal is not his gesturing or his speaking: it is his listening. Like any other creation or discovery, a musical performance is the result of a series of successive approximations; and it is only by knowing where things are now, and correcting for the next go-round, that a conductor can achieve what he finds in the score.

To attend a Szell or a Reiner or a Klemperer rehearsal is to learn how much more there is to hear in a piece you thought you knew. To attend a Bernstein rehearsal is to learn how much more *Bernstein* hears. The difference is, as the scientists say, nontrivial. Donald Francis Tovey wrote somewhere about the wonder of some lovely Haydn phrases that can't be heard in performance— like the medieval sculptures that were finished in back though they would stand against a wall, because God saw everywhere. Bernstein has none of that. His vision is sometimes supernaturally penetrating, but it is almost always narrowly focused: he listens for what he wants to hear. In John Briggs's biography of him, Bernstein is quoted as saying that "Only this morning, the leader of one of the sections told me, 'Lenny, I don't like the way my boys are playing this passage. Maybe you'd better speak to them about it.' The men take pride in themselves and their playing." The imagination boggles at the thought of a section leader telling, say, Reiner, that his boys were missing something: it was Reiner who heard what the men were doing wrong, and Reiner who chewed out the section leader.

A world-famous pianist says he resents playing concertos with Bernstein, "because he won't pay attention to anything that doesn't interest him." Nothing about Bernstein is more engaging —or more infuriating—then this utter reliance, in many parts of many pieces, on the fiduciary sense of the union musician. Often, by no means always, it turns out to be more responsibility than orchestral flesh and blood can carry. Wandering into Philharmonic Hall, one can often tell, simply from the sound of the orchestra in a brief passage, whether or not Bernstein cares for the work at hand.

At a performance, the conductor's central role—once the initial upbeat establishes the tempo—is to remind the men of what happened in the rehearsals. (At a concert last October, Bernstein gave a charming display of how peripheral a conductor's contribution *can* be at a performance. Expansively signaling an entry to pianist Wilhelm Kempff in the last movement of the Beethoven *Third Concerto*, he whipped his stick into the railing around the podium —and the performance continued unaffected for a minute or so while he stopped conducting and solicitously examined his baton.) For such reminder purposes, Bernstein has written, "The conductor always has to be at least a beat or two ahead of the orchestra." This necessity to be always preparing is what Richard Strauss was driving at with his famous aphorism that the conductor should never sweat; only the audience gets warm. Bernstein's physical response to the music he is hearing clashes with his need to stay ahead. A violinist complains that Bernstein conducts like a pianist, keeping his own secrets until he is about to hit the keys. Though they almost always come out right, there is an element of brinkmanship about the Philharmonic's *ritardandos* and *accelerandos*. At a break in a *Falstaff* rehearsal, Bernstein spoke with awed delight of the flexibility of the Metropolitan Opera Orchestra: "They can follow *any* rubato, instantly." The

soprano Regina Resnik replied, "Sure. They play for singers." And
Bernstein nodded reflectively.

What Bernstein's executant critics say is that he is not a professional: he came to professional training too late to acquire the
taste for a routine job perfectly done. No man is so likely as a
conductor to be a hero to the populace and something less to his
valet. Audiences do not know when conductors make mistakes
("Did you ever hear a wrong note on a conductor's stick? *Never!*"
says a wind player); while the men know when a conductor is
given credit for something they have done themselves. Bernstein,
partly for his inattention to detail, partly for the glamour-puss
aspects of his life, partly for insouciance at serious moments, has
been especially abused: "Among musicians," says Stefan Bauer-
Mengelberg, the new head of New York's Mannes College of
Music, "he is the most underestimated conductor of our time."

Few of Bernstein's friends are musicians, and his intelligence
and taste are mostly literary and theatrical. "I don't think of myself," he says, "and I never have thought of myself as having a
career." As a result, he demands excitement: "I used to think,"
says someone who worked closely with him some years ago, "that
he really was beset with all those problems. Then I found he
wanted it that way; he never wanted anything resolved. That way
you have a perpetual series of opening nights."

After 1969, when he becomes a guest conductor at the Philharmonic and elsewhere, Bernstein will have many more opening
nights, which may be all to the good. Working only where he
wants on what he wants to do, the electricity of his musicianship
moving with less loss from the resistance of familiarity, he may
win more often that massive, instinctive acceptance of his phras-
ings that made the Metropolitan Opera Orchestra's *Falstaff* so
transcendent an experience. What would be caviar to lesser talents
is meat and drink to Bernstein.

Opening night, of course, is where the fashionable people are;
and the disturbing criticism of Bernstein is that he persists in being fashionable—as a conductor, as an intellectual, even as a
society figure. He picks up the "fun" thing almost automatically:
for all the burdens he was carrying, he found time last fall to catch
Timothy Leary's psychedelic spook show. Even in areas where he

must know better, he will operate as fashionable people do. "One year," he says, "four of us bought a box at the Met—the Liebersons [president of Columbia Records], the Bernsteins, the Avedons [photographer], the Adolph Greens [Broadway]. That was quite a box. We thought it would be great fun to get dressed up, have a good dinner, go to the opera. The first night we lasted through it, wilting as we went along. The second one we lasted through the second act. The third one we didn't all show up. The Met's so *boring*—the level is so mediocre." The difficulty with this story was once phrased by Molière as "*Mais que diable allait-il faire dans cette galère?*" (What the hell was he doing on that ship?) Bernstein has no need to buy subscriptions: his position is such that tickets can be found for him even at the Met for anything he wants to hear. No subscription series is going to yield winners all the time (not even a Philharmonic subscription), and if Bernstein wanted to hear good opera he just had to drop word at the Met that he would like to be called when they had something special on the way. In fact, of course, he wasn't very interested in the opera; he was interested in the experience of taking a box, which is expensive, fashionable and fun.

Shortly after accepting the direction of the Philharmonic, Bernstein announced that he would do no more guest conducting. The rule was broken on occasion (especially for first performances of his own works); I was in Copenhagen the day after Bernstein had conducted the local orchestra in a Nielsen Symphony as part of Denmark's Nielsen Festival—to such effect that the story was the banner head on every morning paper. But after turning down almost everybody, Bernstein accepted an invitation to conduct the second-rate Monte Carlo Symphony—because he had "promised Princess Grace."

More serious has been the refusal to use his position with the Philharmonic polemically—to promote styles of American music in which he believes, to make the careers of individual composers. He sometimes seems to be uncritically "for" contemporary American music the way the audience is against it. By devoting a dozen evenings to an unfortunate assortment of the clever-clever avant-garde (clearly on the grounds that they had a right to be heard; his distaste for most of what he played was apparent), Bernstein

may even have harmed the cause. Whatever its problems, contemporary American composition is musically better organized and
more secure than the stuff Bernstein played in 1963–64. Neither
in his writing nor in his performing has Bernstein made any consistent assertion of personal taste. His improvisations are original
(sometimes, especially in Bach and Handel, unfortunately so); his
studied reactions are predictable. It is almost as if, like a boy, he
were afraid of being wrong about something important.

"Lenny's talent is so great it frightens me," says Isaac Stern,
who is no mean talent, himself, and not easily frightened. That
bountiful a talent, backed by that considerable an intelligence, has
better employment than whipping up excitement for whatever is
afoot. Still, the excitement itself is real. If Bernstein never acquired
the professional's solidity or artistic convictions, he also avoided
the professional's contempt for his own métier. In a work which
commands both his sympathy and his interest—an Ives *Third*, a
Stravinsky ballet, a Mahler *Second*, a Nielsen *Third*, a Hindemith
Violin Concerto, anything American and almost anything French
from this century—he will give you a performance which against
all logic makes the symphony orchestra immensely vital as a
musical institution. Given his intense theatricality, and the impossible challenge of the form, he would probably do it every time
in an opera pit. And now he will have more time for opera.

In 1964–65, Bernstein took a full year's sabbatical not only
from the Philharmonic but from all conducting, in the hope of
producing a significant composition. "I did not get the piece [a
musical treatment of *The Skin of Our Teeth*] I had set my heart
on writing," he said a year later, not bitter, "though I did write
Chichester Psalms, which I'm very fond of." For all his labors as
a conductor, Bernstein presents himself to posterity (and to those
among today's musicians who consider themselves surrogates for
posterity) primarily as a composer. He is an able composer, too,
recently praised in so austere and avant-garde a publication as
Perspectives of New Music (in an issue which also contains a discussion of a Stockhausen score, beginning with the immortal line,
"The music is read from left to right"). Like *Chichester Psalms*,

which is a good summation of his work to date, all his pieces have moments that are pretty as can be, and sometimes something more; but this listener, trying hard, happened to put a recording of Aaron Copland on the phonograph between bouts with the Bernstein *oeuvre*, and the cat was quickly out of the bag. There is a difference not of degree but of kind between master and pupil: Copland is a great composer, and Bernstein is not. His work should not, I think, be mentioned in the same breath with that of an Elliott Carter, a Leon Kirchner or a Lukas Foss—to take only Americans of roughly the same age, give or take ten years. As a writer of musical comedy, too, Bernstein is skilled and pleasant, but surely not the equal of a Gershwin or a Porter. Such comparisons hold him to high standards—but no higher than the standards he meets as a conductor.

By 1966, after almost a decade of the discipline of the Philharmonic, Bernstein's reputation among people whose good opinion is worth having was independent of his qualities as a personality and firmly based on musical assessments. Though he still gave himself the (unfortunately obvious) pleasure of talking to his admirers about why they ought to like music too, he no longer scripted his actual concerts, as he did on Thursday nights when new to the Philharmonic. (He also tried to costume his men for these occasions in rehearsal jackets modeled after Bruno Walter's, but musicians are more comfortable in tails. Bernstein himself, incidentally wears a custom-made dress shirt of his own design.) Nor would he tell an audience today, as he did one incredible Friday afternoon, that they were about to hear a bad performance of a Brahms Concerto, because he and the soloist Glenn Gould had disagreed about how the piece ought to go. The range of music Bernstein plays well has expanded year by year—he recently recorded quite straightforward performances of Beethoven's *Eroica* and the Brahms *Third*, works he once twisted all out of shape, stressing individual phrases at the expense of architecture, to keep himself interested.

Much of the Lenny syndrome has vanished from musical conversation: New Yorkers have, at last, begun to take Bernstein seriously. How much Bernstein's decision to leave the Philharmonic reflects a fear of being taken seriously, of being regarded as an established and completed artist, nobody can know: it is the worrisome question.

Certainly, he had a good supply of other reasons to lay this burden down. The extension of the season and the retirement of concertmaster John Corigliano had made the Philharmonic job, always difficult, a much more tiring business to live through; and presumably Bernstein's standards for his own performances were rising: no significant artist can function on any other basis. This fall, he allowed himself unusual moments of impatience: when the winds didn't give him the phrasing he wanted at a moment in Schönberg's *Survivor From Warsaw,* he actually stopped a public performance and had them try again. To reach his rising standards week after week at the Philharmonic, he probably would have had to drop everything else.

Bernstein greatly wished to clear time to go to Vienna for *Rosenkavalier,* and elsewhere for other things. He said last summer that his discovery of the previous season was how long he'd been away from Europe and how much he enjoyed working there. Most important, he hoped to compose more when conducting less. Though Chicago's Jean Martinon manages to couple the two, and the conductor who was *not* a composer was a rarity until this century, modern musicians have mostly found the double harness too heavy. George Szell, whose music was played all over Germany before he was out of his teens, gave up composing completely; Stanislaw Skrowaczewski, who was regarded as one of the most important young composing talents in postwar Poland, has found that the attitudes and requirements of the Minneapolis Symphony make it impossible for him to write. For someone like Bernstein, who wants above all things to be a melodist (he has written amusingly and masochistically about his problems), there must be a special menace in keeping one's head stuffed with other people's tunes.

Anyway, he hasn't been composing much. He still owes a number of commissions (including one to his own orchestra, a *Festival Overture,* which was to be ready for the opening of Philharmonic Hall in 1962). During the break in one of the first rehearsals of this season, in response to a question about whether he was going to be able to go to Vienna for *Rosenkavalier,* he hooked all his future plans to the progress of his piece for Kennedy Center. He was committed to the proposition that this would be a significant piece; and with his mind on Philharmonic problems he couldn't find ideas for it that pleased him.

Still, like it or not (and often he doesn't much), Bernstein's significant contribution to the musical life of his time has been as a conductor of other men's music; and his retirement from the direction of the Philharmonic does not, as he pointed out in his press conference, mean a retirement from conducting. Indeed, the end of administrative responsibilities (and of the need to make programs with an eye to an entire season) will free him to conduct more orchestras and especially more operas. Few musicians other than Bernstein himself are concerned about what he will do when he grows up: he will be a great conductor. When he grows up. Maybe sooner.

VIII
Science

□ Ours is an age of science. With the exception of actual policy makers, scientists are the most influential men in American society. Their great discoveries—the atomic and hydrogen bombs; exploratory rockets; birth control devices; and antibiotics—have affected every man and have resulted in the most complex of political problems. The association between government and the scientific community has grown extremely close within the past ten years, and the scientist, in addition to carrying on his own teaching or research, may now be an adviser to the president; a member of the Atomic Energy Commission; and a consultant to innumerable corporations. So intimate has the relationship between politics and science become that Don K. Price, an important political scientist, felt it necessary to warn both the politician and the scientist that "The union between political and scientific estates is not like a partnership but a marriage. It will not be improved if the two become like each other, but only if they respect each other's quite different needs and purposes."

□ Before the 1960's science was a specialized area of human knowledge which few people understood. There were, to use C. P. Snow's term, "two cultures"—a culture of science and a culture of the arts. General awareness of the physical and biological sciences depended upon either the scientists themselves or upon sympathetic observers who tended to celebrate if not glorify the scientific way of life. But the practical impact of scientific research soon provoked curiosity in the layman, and the science writer emerged to interpret the meaning of science to the average man and to analyze—sometimes to censure— the actual life of the scientist. Young people, who thought of becoming scientists, read more realistic accounts of science than had been written before and they discovered, in the universities of the sixties, a fascinating but complicated and sometimes depressing world of scientific investigation.

□ In the universities, where the scientists are trained, there is a value system. The highest status is accorded to those who receive their Ph.D.'s and conduct independent research; these men are, in many ways, the intellectual aristocrats of the society. But most science-engineering graduates, as Spencer Klaw suggests in *The New Brahmins* (1968), never receive their Ph.D.'s and enter industry, where they "become part of an intellectual proletariat." Often "the average industrial researcher has little more choice about what he does to earn a living than a worker on an assembly line." The ideal image of the scientist who pursues truth selflessly has been tarnished by recent accounts of the industrialization, unhealthy competitiveness, and militarization of the physical and biological sciences. Young people sense that the scientific life can often be a dull existence in some corporation or a fiercely competitive career in a university; they also associate science with much of the destruction that has occurred in their own lifetime. These and other reasons have resulted in the disenchantment with science on the part of many young people.

□ Yet the essential excitement and creative possibilities of science are too compelling not to attract the youth of America. In *The Scientific Life* (1962), Theodore Berland interviewed nine well-known scientists and commented upon "the magnificent compulsion" that is central to the scientist's existence and that will always provoke the interest of students. He noted that these men have great internal drive and intellectual curiosity; they care deeply about education and the world which they affect so much; they are well-informed, humanitarian men who travel widely, work with government, and have a hunger for knowledge and truth. "The life of science, in short, is a life of compulsion to discover. It is a magnificent compulsion. No other words sum up so well the personality of the scientist of the 1960's [and 1970's], the man whose work will so influence our lives, the man we must come to know better."

Murray Gell-Mann and Richard Feynman

. . . And, Dr. Gell-Mann, why are you a scientist?

Because I goddamn well want to know what makes things tick.

Period. And I care in all subjects. I don't care only in physics. I care

in archaeology. I care in psychology, and I care in economics and

in geology and in astrophysics and in any field. I want to know what

makes the damn thing tick, whether it's a society or a star or a galaxy

or a universe or an elementary particle or a planet or whatever

it is. I think it's interesting. I think it's as worthwhile an activity as

human beings have ever come across. It's satisfying and ennobling,

in the same way as art is.

"I am over and again appalled by how ignorant, how incredibly ignorant of the most rudimentary things about my subject [science] are my fellows the historians, my acquaintances the statesmen, my friends the men of affairs. They have no notion of what cooks in any other science." These words, spoken by Robert Oppenheimer, have been echoed by many other scientists and humanists since World War II. In an age when physical scientists create atomic and hydrogen bombs and advise political leaders on the most critical issues; when biological scientists invent polio vaccines, penicillin, and other antibiotics; and when social scientists present statistics which, as Philip Hauser has remarked, "have become the guide for decision making"—in this age a knowledge of scientific work, at least in elementary terms, has become a practical necessity as well as a cultural imperative. Two of the most creative physicists of contemporary America are Murray Gell-Mann and Richard P. Feynman.

Murray Gell-Mann was born in New York City on September 15, 1929, the son of Austrian immigrants. His father, a man of varied intellectual interests, recognized the boy's precociousness and transferred him to a school for the intellectually gifted. Gell-Mann entered Yale University at the age of fifteen and graduated with a B.S. degree in physics in 1948. He then studied at Massachusetts Institute of Technology, receiving his Ph.D. degree in January 1951, for research on the intermediate coupling problem. After a period at the Institute for Advanced Study at Princeton, he became an instructor of physics at the University of Chicago's Institute for Nuclear Studies in 1952, where he met Willard F. Libby, Harold C. Urey, and Enrico Fermi. After teaching at Columbia University and the Institute for Advanced Study at Princeton, Gell-Mann went to the California Institute of Technology where he was appointed to the rank of full professor.

Gell-Mann's chief interest has been the understanding and classification of elementary particles. In 1953 he developed what he called "The Strangeness Theory" and in 1963 the "Eightfold Way," "which probes the mystery of the atomic nucleus by describing particles in terms of eight quantum numbers that enable them to be grouped into a few distinct families."

Richard P. Feynman was born on May 11, 1918, in New York City. He took his B.A. from M.I.T. in 1939 and his Ph.D. from Princeton in 1942. Feynman was a member of the atomic bomb project at Princeton from 1942–1943 and at Los Alamos from 1943–1945. He has taught at Cornell and California Institute of Technology. In 1965 he received the Nobel Prize in physics. Feynman has contributed a theory of quantum electrodynamics, beta decay, and liquid helium.

Both of these physicists presently teach and do research

at California Institute of Technology. They have worked on various problems together, and their personalities, as Lee Edson points out in the following essay, complement each other. Gell-Mann himself has spoken eloquently of the scientific spirit, of scientific inquiry, and of his work with Richard P. Feynman.

There were a lot of experiments on the weak interaction. And some of the experiments seemed to contradict others. Probably some of them were wrong. It was possible, perhaps, to construct a theory which would incorporate most of the existing experiments, but it would be very ugly. And we concluded, therefore, that such a theory was not right, because it would be ugly. We proposed, instead, a very beautiful one. We and certain other people proposed a very beautiful one which contradicted most of the experiments. Now there is clearly something there besides science. In a sense it's an old idea that hypotheses should be simple. But still it's a slight extension of that idea, it's using an essentially aesthetic criterion: that a natural law at a fundamental level must be simple. This doesn't apply to biology. But at the level of elementary particle physics there is a principle about principles, namely that they are simple. There's something to be learned from that. It keeps happening. On a fundamental level nature expresses herself in a very simple way, but you have to search for the simplicity, you have to find the right way of looking at things before the simplicity strikes you.

Two Men in Search of the Quark

LEE
EDSON

I N THE LAST couple of years an intensive hunt has been going on
all over the world for an elusive quarry known as the quark. This
is no Alice-in-Wonderland adventure; far from it. The hunters
are some of the world's leading physicists. The hunting grounds:
almost anywhere from the high atmosphere to the bottom of the
sea to the inside of the latest atom smashers. One enthusiastic
researcher at the University of Michigan even has been grinding up
oysters on the theory that an oyster eats almost anything—so
why not a quark?

Despite this painstaking search, the quark so far has remained
as hard to track down as Lewis Carroll's Snark.* There is an excellent reason. According to modern theoretical physicists, the

---

*". . . the Snark is at hand, let me tell you again!
    'Tis your glorious duty to seek it!
"To seek it with thimbles, to seek it with care;
    To pursue it with forks and hope;
To threaten its life with a railway-share;
    To charm it with smiles and soap!
"For the Snark's a peculiar creature, that won't
    Be caught in a commonplace way.
Do all that you know, and try all that you don't:
    Not a chance must be wasted today! . . .
" 'But oh, beamish nephew, beware of the day,
    If your Snark be a Boojum! For then
You will softly and suddenly vanish away,
    And never be met with again!' . . ."
                —"The Hunting of the Snark."

FROM THE OCTOBER 8, 1967 ISSUE OF *The New York Times Magazine*.
REPRINTED BY PERMISSION OF THE AUTHOR.

quark, if it exists at all, is the simplest particle in the universe, out of which almost everything else is made.

Capturing this incredibly wraith-like substance may not help us produce superbombs—the implications of gaining new elementary facts about nature depend on how man uses them, whether for war or for peace, and are not ascertainable for years, anyway. But to physicists, the excitement in confronting the quark is something more sublime than the discovery of a new application to everyday life. It is the immediate realization that through it we may uncover the missing linkage to our understanding of the structure of matter throughout the universe.

The men largely responsible for sending scientists on this wild quark chase are two California Institute of Technology physicists named Murray Gell-Mann and Richard Feynman. Each has won a fistful of high honors. In 1965, Feynman shared the Nobel Prize for his achievements in explaining some of the abstruse mechanisms in the subatomic world. Many physicists think Gell-Mann is next. One California scientist calls the two men "the hottest properties in theoretical physics today."

What makes them radiate so fiercely on the high-energy physics circuit is a fine blend of showmanship and brilliance. Take the quark hunt, for instance. "Dick and I were batting around some aspects of theoretical physics," Gell-Mann recalls. "We started to get excited about a new theory and threw out words for our ideas. There have been some crazy ones in physics lately. The theory depended on a triplet of particles, with the right characteristics, and we needed a word for it. I started to say 'squeak,' 'skuark,' and it came out 'quark.' We loved the word as soon as it was uttered. Much to my surprise, I found the line 'Three quarks for Muster Mark' in James Joyce's 'Finnegans Wake.' Nothing could have fitted better."†

Of course, both men could have rejected the word for some-

---

† The line in "Finnegans Wake" actually refers to the cuckolding of King Mark in the medieval legend of Tristan and Isolde. And in German the word *Quark*, which means literally "cream cheese," conveys the colloquial impact of "Baloney!" One must assume that Gell-Mann, like Joyce, was working a multilingual joke.

thing sane and august and ending with "on" like "electron" or "neutron," or even used "ace, deuce, trey" as later suggested by physicist George Zweig of Cal Tech, who came to a similar conclusion about the nature of the fundamental particle, but Gell-Mann admits to a certain puckishness in accepting and publicizing the quark. "Maybe it will help C. P. Snow to bridge his two cultures," he says with a smile.

Gell-Mann and Feynman—who claim they work together separately—are nearly unique in modern physics. In a field noted for quiet introversion, they generate a kind of charisma which draws students and faculty members to Cal Tech to an extent that had not been seen on the campus since the days of Robert Oppenheimer. The lectures of both men play to S.R.O. audiences. When Feynman won the Nobel Prize, one blasphemous sophomore admirer celebrated by slipping his picture into a plaque of the Last Supper in place of Jesus.

Although they have comparable intellectual impact, Feynman and Gell-Mann create their sparks in entirely different ways. Feynman, a lean, intense, dark-haired man of 49 who is beginning to fear that he may soon be regarded as a premature elder statesman, is a natural showman, full of exuberance for his subject. His lectures are couched in pithy, often rough-cut phrases—"I always try to say things differently," he says—and he uses hand gestures and intonations the way Billy Rose used beautiful women on the stage spectacularly but with grace.

Occasionally he sets the stage. In one popular lecture on color vision, for instance, Feynman flooded the entire stage with a rainbow of light. "Why use a tiny prism on a small table, which people have to strain to see?" he says. "Nature is too interesting to stick in a corner." But generally he needs no such props. The subject matter to him is so glorious that it is only necessary to see it honestly, as it really is, for everyone to respond to his fervor. "I always come to Feynman's lectures," says an old-time faculty member, "because I am sure there will be at least one good surprise."

Gell-Mann is less flamboyant but equally compelling on the platform. Eleven years Feynman's junior, he is roundfaced and bespectacled, and looks somewhat like a jovial neighborhood storekeeper. In the classroom, his lectures are clear, smooth and amusing, and draw upon an extraordinary erudition. But he really excels among small groups. If Feynman can be compared to a star who basks in the warmth of large audiences, Gell-Mann seems to enjoy the give-and-take intimacy of a seminar of bright, articulate graduate students. Like Oppenheimer, he prefers a small but devoted following—and, indeed, he has declared often that a teacher lecturing in front of a class represents a primitive form of education.

Despite this personality difference, the two men work well together—which means, according to a friend, that they argue continuously and loudly but, after a few moments, come to an understanding and move forward rapidly. This rapport was almost interrupted a few years ago when Gell-Mann for several reasons thought seriously of leaving Feynman and switching to Harvard. He decided not to, according to gossip among physicists, when he found that Harvard was willing to meet all his demands except one—changing its name to Gell-Mann Institute.

Since that time, the two men have mellowed, but an undercurrent of rivalry occasionally crops up. "Dick is always calling up to see whether Murray is working," says Mrs. Margaret Gell-Mann, an attractive blonde from Birmingham, England. "If I say he's in the garden, Dick is happy for the rest of the day. But if I tell him Murray is doing physics, then Dick gets nervous and immediately wants to come over."

When Dick married an English girl a few years ago (his third wife), he made a point of calling Murray and saying: "I looked around to see what you and I didn't have in common. I saw that you had an English wife and a brown dog, so I went out and got both."

One quality both men do have in common is an extraordinary capacity to make physics lucid and highly romantic. In part, the romance is made easy by the nature of the world of physicists. In the pecking order of this society, the theoretical physicist is the glamour boy. After him comes the experimentalist, the fellow in the laboratory, and then the engineers and applied physicists who make such things as sonar, rockets and hydrogen bombs.

Right now, the theoretical physicists have captured the front and center of scientific interest because they seem to be on the threshold of answering a long-asked, almost child-like question: What are things really made of? Have we at last come down to the last foundation stone from which we can build anything: a table, a human being, or a universe? Or must we go on looking at smaller and smaller pieces, and going deeper and deeper into a bottomless pit?

To answer these questions, one has to remember that from the very start of civilization philosophers have wanted to find a simple idea that would unite everything we experience in the world around us. So there has always been a search for the building block, like the cell or gene in biology. The fifth-century B.C. Greek Democritus receives the honor of declaring that the simplest thing out of which everything else is made is an atom (*atomos* means "uncut"), and this idea sufficed for 2,000 years.

In the 19th century scientists came to realize that the atom was not the ultimate particle after all. Inside the atom was a nucleus, with electrons orbiting around it like the planets around the sun. Then, in the 20th century, scientists began to concentrate on the nucleus, and saw that this was no simple item either. It contained smaller things, such as neutrons and protons, which must be held together by a very strong force, perhaps the strongest in the universe. So the question for years was: What was this "strong interaction," this glue that held the nucleus together?

In 1935, a Japanese physicist named Hideki Yukawa provided the first educated guess. He theorized that there was another particle in the nucleus, which he called a meson. It would act as a carrier of force between the proton and the neutron, so that energy would be exchanged among the particles pretty much as a football is passed between players in a game. Two years later Dr. Carl Anderson of Cal Tech discovered a particle that he thought might be Yukawa's carrier. Physicists exulted. Things seemed neat again—until it was found that the new particle failed to obey predictions expected from the laws of physics, and indeed created such a mess in attempts to relate theory and experience that Columbia's I. I. Rabi threw up his hands and said: "Who needs it?" It took five years for physicists to realize that the new particle was not the Yukawa meson, but an unrelated particle known as a muon. After the war, as bigger and more powerful atom smashers appeared, a number of mesons were discovered, including the one suggested by Yukawa. This constituted a major advance in understanding the strong interaction— the interaction which is known to us in everyday life only through the power of the A-bomb.

By then the atom smashers were revealing all kinds of new and peculiar particles, whose mass was created out of the energy of motion. Most of them died out in incredibly brief periods—on the order of a billionth of a second—but their trails could be photographed, and their presence raised new questions. How did they disintegrate? Were they complex structures in themselves?

Feynman was one of the Young Turks of physics who in the nineteen-fifties addressed themselves to these thorny questions. (He had already earned a formidable reputation in theoretical physics because of his efforts in another area—applying quantum mechanics to electromagnetic radiations. For this work, 16 years later, he was to share the Nobel Prize with Dr. Julian Schwinger of Harvard and Dr. S. Tomonaga of Japan.)

Feynman's interest centered around a phenomenon that had intrigued scientists for years—the emission of fast-moving electrons from radioactive substances. This process, which goes under the name of "beta decay," had introduced physicists to a new force in the nucleus, a force quite different from the "strong interaction" that holds it together. Feynman was fired by the challenge of this insight and the subsequent revolutionary developments.

For one thing, physicists in the nineteen-fifties were discovering that the new force—or "weak interaction," as it came to be called—was far more widespread and manifested itself in many more reactions than beta decay. Indeed, it was on a par with the strong interaction, and with the two other universal forces known to science: electromagnetism, which keeps electrons perpetually spinning around a nucleus, and gravity, the weakest force of all. The weak interaction, which is now known to be involved in the decay of many strange particles, is 100,000 times weaker than the electromagnetic force. However, it is exceedingly more powerful than gravity, which is so incredibly feeble compared with the strong interaction that it takes a fraction with 42 zeros to describe its relative strength. This kind of comparison delights Feynman. "Isn't nature wonderful," he says, raising his hands ecstatically, "to make something with 42 zeros!"

Another important development in physics in the nineteen-fifties was the overthrow of one of the fundamental laws in nature. It had long been thought that nature operates with a number of conservation laws, ranging from the familiar indestructibility of energy and matter to the conservation of lesser-known properties of the atom, such as those that explain the stability of the proton and the reason why some particles are created in atom smashers only in multiplets. These laws were regarded as unchanging and universal. One of the most important of them was the one known as "the law of the conservation of parity." It said that if an object had a mirror image, that image would obey the laws of physics just like the real object. To satisfy this law, particles in the sub-atomic world could exist in one of two ways. The particle and its mirror image could be completely identical—like the word MOM, which reads the same in the real world and in the looking-glass world. Or there could be two particles, a "left-handed" one and a "right-handed" one—one the mirror image of the other, like the words MAY and YAM.

Since the strong interactions obey this rule of parity, it was assumed that the weak interactions should also. But a striking thing was discovered in atom-smashing experiments involving a weak interaction. A particle was found that did not have an image fitting the pattern of MOM.

Were there actually two particles, with reversed symmetry, like MAY and YAM? But that suggestion did not jibe with further experiments, which continued to point to the existence of just one particle. In an inspired moment, Feynman and another physicist, Martin Block, offered the view that the law of parity might have failed for this particular weak interaction.

It was a prophetic suggestion. In an epic-making paper, two Chinese-born scientists, C. N. Yang and T. D. Lee, then of the

Institute for Advanced Study at Princeton and Columbia University, suggested that perhaps *all* weak interactions violate the law of parity. They proposed experiments, which were carried out and proved them right. Their intuition won them the Nobel Prize in 1957. More important they turned nuclear physics topsy-turvy.

Freed from the confines of parity, Feynman and Gell-Mann (along with E. C. G. Sudarshan and R. E. Marshak) tackled the problem of finding a way to describe the law of the weak interactions. In 1957, they developed a theory that shows how this force depends on various properties of the particles, such as their directions of spin, thus providing what is now generally regarded as a major contribution to our understanding of the nucleus.

Feynman says that the discovery of this new law was the most exciting thing in his life, far more exciting than his earlier work that led to his Nobel Prize. "I won the prize for shoving a great problem under the carpet," he says, "but in this case there was a moment when I knew how nature worked. It had elegance and beauty. The goddam thing was gleaming." So shiny was the new law that when several eminent physicists conducted experiments that seemed to vitiate it, Feynman insisted the experiments must be wrong. And so indeed they proved to be.

Gell-Mann experienced the thrill of another major and beautiful discovery a few years later. By then the number of particles emerging from the nucleus was increasing fantastically. Almost 100 had been counted by 1962. They had been classified into two main groups known as leptons (weakly interacting particles), or weaklies, as Feynman calls them, and hadrons, or stronglies. Examples of the first group are positive and negative electrons, muons and neutrinos; the second group includes neutrons, protons and pions. (Just to confuse matters, each of these particles has an antiparticle carrying an opposite charge which annihilates the particle on contact.)

A subdivision of the hadrons is a group of particles which are known as "strange particles" because, instead of dying out as they should, they live to a relatively ripe old age. To round out this picture, there is also the photon, a particle that carries the electromagnetic force—and, supposedly, there is a graviton for gravity, though this particle is yet to be found.

To bring some order into this nuclear grab bag, Gell-Mann introduced two new concepts. The first, which had developed as early as 1952, was a quality which he called "strangeness." As with the quark, it had a literary counterpart, this time in Sir Francis Bacon's line: "There is no excellent beauty that hath not some strangeness in the proportion."

Each particle could be assigned a degree of strangeness, depending on the number of steps in its disintegration, and thus it could be distinguished from its neighbors—just as a neutron can be distinguished from a proton by its different electric charge. (Gell-Mann did not know until later that a Japanese scientist named Nishijima working independently in Tokyo came to the same conclusion at about the same time.) With the differences known, Gell-Mann set about seeing in what ways the particles were similar and whether they could all be slipped into a neat, organizational chart, more or less as Mendeleev had done with his periodic table of the chemical elements in the 19th century.

Gell-Mann recalls that he and Feynman tried one pattern after another without luck. Finally, one scheme seemed to work. The particles seemed to fit into families of eight or ten members, with similar characteristics of strangeness, electric charge and other properties, such as mass and spin. Even while Gell-Mann was doing this, Yuval Ne'eman, an Israeli military attaché in London, studying for his doctorate in physics while trying to buy guns for his country, came upon the same scheme.

However, one family of particles in the table had only nine members instead of ten. It seemed incomplete. Gell-Mann thereupon predicted that, if a new member were found, it would have certain properties as indicated by its relatives in the same family of particles. Experimental physicists took up the hunt.

A couple of years later, a team of 33 scientists at Brookhaven National Laboratory hit pay dirt. They had bombarded nuclei and peered at more than 100,000 photographs of the interactions. In one of those pictures they saw the track of the missing particle, which was called omega-minus. It had a life expectancy of a 10-billionth of a second, and it had the basic properties predicted by Gell-Mann. The existence of the omega-minus was shortly verified by scientists at the University of Maryland and thereafter independently at CERN, the great nuclear establishment in Switzerland.

Gell-Mann, with his flair for literary analogy, called his chart the Eightfold Way, as in the Buddhist dictum: "This is the noble truth that leads to cessation of pain. This is the noble eightfold way—right views, right intentions, right speech, right action. . . ." More prosaic physicists call it the SU-3 theory because it is a symmetrical structure based on a triplet of fundamental particles.

The Eightfold Way hit physics like a bombshell. Gell-Mann occasionally marvels at the apparent simplicity of nature that is revealed in the scheme. "Why should an esthetic criterion be so successful so often?" he asks. "Is it just that it satisfies physicists?" Then, echoing Feynman, he declares: "I think there is only one answer—nature is inherently beautiful."

In recent months, a number of physicists have tried to go beyond the Eightfold Way and explain why nature operates with so many particles in this rather neat and poetic style. At Harvard, Dr. Julian Schwinger claims to have developed a simple mathematical theory to explain it all. Others, following Gell-Mann, have constructed a "quark model" in which neutrons and protons behave as if they were made of quarks—and, more than that, as if they were made of three quarks, each of which may come in three forms. The reason why a number of scientists are seriously hunting real quarks (though Gell-Mann himself is not sure that they exist) is that theoretically they cannot decay into something else and thus a stable quark must be somewhere around, and may indeed have lasted since the birth of the universe.

Not all physicists agree, of course. At the University of California in Berkeley, Dr. Geoffrey Chew has taken a radical approach to the entire problem. He has developed a theory, known whimsically as the "bootstrap theory," which says that there really is no rock-bottom fundamental particle like the quark or anything else; indeed, that the strong particles are made of one another, pulling themselves into existence, so to speak, by their own bootstraps. "At first glance, this theory and our quark model may seem contradictory," Gell-Mann says, "but they may actually be quite compatible—and both may even be right—especially if the quark should turn out to be, as is likely, a useful mathematical figment rather than a concrete building block of matter."

Although Gell-Mann and Feynman were both born in New York City of middle-class families, they came to theoretical physics by different routes. Feynman traces almost everything in his make-up to the influence of his father.

"When I was a boy," he says, "Dad and I took long walks in the woods and he showed me things I would never have noticed by myself. He told me about the world and how it looked many years ago. He would say, 'See this leaf? It has a brown line; part of it is thin and part thick. Why?' And when I tried to answer, my father would make me look at the leaf and see whether I was right and then he would point out that the line was made by an insect that devotes its entire life to that project. 'And for what purpose? So that it can leave eggs which turn into new insects.'

"My father taught me continuity and harmony in the world. He didn't know anything exactly, whether the insect had eight legs or a hundred legs, but he understood everything. And I was interested because there was always this kick at the end—a revelation of how wonderful nature really is."

Dick's love of science flowered rapidly, and occasionally it got an unexpected boost. In Far Rockaway High School, which he found pretty dull, a teacher disciplined him for talking too much in class and not paying attention. He was sent to the back of the room and given a book. "After you read this," the teacher said, "you can open your mouth again."

"So I learned calculus," says Feynman. He went on to M.I.T., where he graduated with honors in 1939, and did his graduate work at Princeton. In World War II, he ended up as a group leader at Los Alamos working on theoretical aspects of the material in the A-bomb. He was present at the first test explosion at Alamogordo in July, 1945.

As befits one who challenges the fundamental laws of nature,

Feynman is an inherent iconoclast. He loves to play the bongo drums, and he is probably the first physics professor in history— certainly the first Nobel Prizewinner—to have a picture of himself on the drums included in the introduction to a three-volume college textbook of physics.

Gell-Mann's extracurricular tastes run in more erudite directions. With his wife, who studied archeology at Cambridge, he often enjoys digging for artifacts in such places as Greece and Palestine. He is also a devotee of linguistics; he has studied many languages, including some old dialects of Africa and the Middle East. "I like diversity," he says, "and I like the natural history behind diversity. Why are there so many different tongues, so many different birds, even so many different human neuroses? It's interesting to find the pattern behind them."

Gell-Mann, the son of a language teacher and a prodigy who entered Yale at 15, says he came into physics almost inadvertently. "I had to fill out an application form," he recalls, "where I had to list my future occupation. I started to put down archeologist but my father said I'd never make a living in archeology, and suggested engineering instead. I couldn't stand engineering, so I put down the closest thing, physics."

He went on to get his doctorate at M.I.T., and then to Princeton, where he worked with Oppenheimer. The Gell-Mann and Feynman merger occurred in 1954, during a visit by Gell-Mann to Pasadena. Some words were passed between them, along with howls of laughter over jokes they both found funny, and the next day, Gell-Mann recalls, he was being interviewed by the dean of Cal Tech. He joined the staff as an associate professor in 1955, and became a full professor the following year.

In the last few years, Gell-Mann has been a missionary for the development of the world's largest atom smasher, the proposed 200-billion-electron-volt machine scheduled to be built at Weston, Ill. Along with other top physicists, he believes the $200 million machine is vital to maintain United States supremacy in particle physics.

"I think particle physics is where atomic physics was in the early years of the century," Gell-Mann says. "We're getting an outline of an underlying structure, but there is still no complete theory of either strong or weak interactions which enables us to understand what is really happening at the bottom of everything.

"Recently an experiment performed by Princeton physicists has shown the violation of another law of symmetry that was thought to be valid (like parity 10 years ago). Some theorists went so far as to speculate that a fifth natural force was involved, but that doesn't seem to be true. How is the violation occurring? Nobody seems to know at the moment, but I think we are on the verge of an important discovery."

Feynman says much the same, but in terms of a metaphor—playing chess with a Martian. "If you don't know the rules," he says, "and you see only parts of the board, how do you know how to play? If you know all the rules, can you tell what's in the Martian's mind when he moves the pieces in a certain way?

"The biggest mystery of physics is where the laws are known, but we don't know exactly what's going on. We don't know the strategy in the middle game. We know castling, or how the different pieces move, and we know a little bit about the end game, but nothing in the middle.

"We get reports from the experimentalists, the watchers of the chess game, and we try to analyze the information. We may even suggest a new experiment. But we're still waiting and hoping for the big strategy. Then maybe we'll really understand how wonderful is nature."

Jonas Salk

What is the role of a scientist? He isn't a politician, and he isn't a propagandist. He observes and classifies facts, tests hypotheses, reaches conclusions on the basis of the data at his disposal. The scientist must be objective, impartial, clear. He must avoid being influenced by the pressures on him or even by the bias of his hypotheses.

Until 1953, poliomyelitis was one of the most dreaded diseases in the world. Although it had been designated as a virus early in the twentieth century and was studied with the greatest diligence, this form of paralysis seemed increasingly confusing to research scientists. By the later 1940's, it was clear that polio was a general infection rather than a disease of the nervous system; and scientists began to search for a vaccine that would prevent the disease. In 1948, the National Foundation for Infantile Paralysis supported a new virus laboratory at the University of Pittsburgh under the direction of Jonas Salk. Within three years, he and other research scientists had identified three main types of polio virus and by April 1955 Salk's vaccine was licensed for public use.

Jonas Salk was born in New York on October 28, 1914. After graduating from The City College of New York, he studied medicine at New York University College of Medicine (M.D., 1939), interned at New York's Mount Sinai Hospital, and did research on the influenza virus at the University of Michigan and later at the University of Pittsburgh. From 1949 until 1954 he developed his technique of growing polio virus in cultures of nonnervous tissues; in simple terms, he produced "a killed-virus vaccine." Salk went on to teach and do research at the University of Pittsburgh. Currently he is the director of the Salk Institute for Biological Studies in San Diego, California.

What Price Fame—To Dr. Salk

JANE
KRIEGER

NOT LONG AGO Dr. Jonas Edward Salk took an hour off from a scientific conference to go for a swim. On the beach he overheard a group of 10-year-olds arguing. "Sure that's Dr. Salk —I saw him on television," one said. "The hell it is," another said. "What would Dr. Salk be doing in a bathing suit? Anyhow he's much too young to be Dr. Salk."

The incident was noteworthy for several reasons. It was characteristic of the recognition Salk gets everywhere he goes; it was one of the few times he seemed to get a kick out of being a celebrity; and it was one of the few times in the past three months that he has relaxed.

At 40, the once obscure scientist, whose poliomyelitis vaccine was licensed last April 12, was lifted from his laboratory almost to the level of a folk hero. The effect—even upon a man with Salk's internal gyroscope—has been marked.

He has received a Presidential citation, a score of awards, four honorary degrees, half a dozen foreign decorations, offers for his life story from five Hollywood motion-picture studios, grateful letters from thousands of fellow citizens, pointed criticism from a few fellow scientists—and an uncomfortable feeling that he is "treading water till the waves recede." The waves have not receded. Every day new honors, new requests and new demands pour into his office at the University of Pittsburgh's Virus Research Laboratory, which he directs.

Salk's reaction to his sudden success was exemplified one evening last month when City College, from which he was graduated in 1934, gave him an honorary degree as Doctor of Laws. When he walked into the president's office in a dark suit, white shirt and dark tie, the president, assorted deans and faculty members, the members of the Board of Higher Education and their wives, his father and mother and some friends were gathered to greet him.

Salk, looking self-possessed but not entirely happy, shook hands all around, kissed his parents and allowed the publicity people to put him into a cap and gown. As the photographers posed him he looked embarrassed and winked impishly at a friend. His father said, "We have to be content with only a glimpse of Jonas now." A college official said, "Well, Jonas, you're certainly handling this well. I bet ten years ago you wouldn't have believed you could handle fame so well." Salk said, "Ten years ago I wouldn't have believed this could happen." Another man said, "Jonas, how can you stand all the demands on you?" Salk said, "I've learned to say no. I never dared to say no before." A friend said "Jonas, is your appetite good?" He assured her it was. A reporter said, "I hear you're trying to find an anti-cold vaccine now." Salk said, "All I'm trying to do is keep my balance." He turned to the lady who was worried about his appetite and said, "When a reporter approaches I generally find myself wishing for a Martini."

The photographers finished and the party moved out to the corridor on the way to a private dinner in Salk's honor. As they waited for an elevator, a lady asked Salk if he didn't feel like a writer with a successful first novel published—afraid he could never do it again.

Salk said, "I don't want to go from one crest to another. And science isn't like novel-writing. To a scientist, fame is neither an end nor even a means to an end. Do you recall what Emerson said? 'The reward of a thing well done is to have done it.'" The lady looked puzzled and said, "Don't tell me your head hasn't been turned by all this." Salk said she reminded him of the farmer who saw a giraffe for the first time, "Aw, there ain't no such animal."

At the end of the evening, Salk said to a friend, "Say, do you know why those Frenchmen were here? They made me a Chevalier of the Legion of Honor. That was very nice of them."

Despite such very nice tributes, Salk is profoundly disturbed by the torrent of fame that has descended upon him. He is trying hard to keep himself and the scientific method with which he identifies himself from being sucked into a whirlpool of publicity, politics and pressures of various sorts. He talks continually about getting out of the limelight and back to his laboratory. "It's not a question of modesty," he says. "I want to clean up this vaccine job and get on to other things." Although Salk does not doubt his ability, "modest" is the adjective that seems to be most frequently applied to him. This could be because of his genuine distaste for publicity, which he believes is inappropriate for a scientist, and it could also be because he is exceedingly cautious about advancing any claims. "I don't talk about something until I'm sure of it," he says.

Salk has an absolute conviction that scientists are—or at least should be—a breed apart from other men. "What is the role of the scientist?" he was asked. "He isn't a politician," Salk said, "and he isn't a propagandist. He observes and classifies facts, tests hypotheses, reaches conclusions on the basis of the data at his disposal. The scientist must be objective, impartial, clear. He must avoid being influenced by the pressures on him or even by the bias of his hypotheses."

If Salk the scientist sounds austere, Salk the man is a person of great warmth and tremendous enthusiasm. People who meet him generally like him. Washington newspaper correspondents— a skeptical crew—consider him a convincing person. "He could sell me the Brooklyn Bridge, and I never bought anything before," said one reporter.

He enjoys talking to people he likes, and he likes a lot of people. He talks quickly, articulately, and often in complete paragraphs. Besides talking and, of course, working, Salk also enjoys golf, although he hasn't been on a fairway for more than a year; used to like tennis but says with a grin that he's too old now; does a good deal of reading—his tastes are broad and he often quotes

Emerson, Thoreau, Lincoln and Roger Bacon; and likes to look at paintings—his taste is sophisticated (he selected a Paul Klee for his office). He has very little perceptible interest in the things that interest most people—such as making money.

In 1952 Salk was a laboratory research man whose name was known to very few persons outside of his field and the National Foundation for Infantile Paralysis. With a foundation grant he was trying to make a polio vaccine. So were a number of other scientists around the country.

By the fall of 1952 Salk had an experimental vaccine. In January, 1953, he reported on it to a closed conference of his fellow scientists. He expected his findings would be circulated in professional fashion in scientific journals and meetings throughout the scientific world. But a few days after the conference somebody leaked the word that there was a polio vaccine to Earl Wilson, a columnist Salk had never heard of then. Wilson wrote a story headlined "New Polio Vaccine—Big Hopes Seen." At the same time the polio foundation held a dinner to which the press was invited, and announced "tremendous progress" in the development of the vaccine.

The public excitement generated by these reports about Salk's report was deeply disturbing to Salk. He felt responsible for seeing to it that there were no disappointed hopes, so he went to Harry Weaver, the polio foundation's director of research, and Basil O'Connor, its president, and said he thought the claims should be toned down. "I'd better go to the public myself and try to set the pitch in middle C instead of high C," he said.

O'Connor, a man who knows a great deal about how to get things over to the public, arranged a radio appearance, a press conference and a television clip. Salk picked the date—March 26, 1953—because that was the day the Journal of the American Medical Association was publishing his first piece on the vaccine and he didn't want any sensational press releases on it.

It was a rough day for Salk, still unused to the limelight, but when it was over he felt he had done what he set out to do—to warn the public against overoptimism with regard to something that was still in the experimental stage. Thereafter he appeared on a few other programs and repeated his warnings. He was surprised and hurt when some of his colleagues criticized him for not confining his reports to scientific journals. "Well, Jonas," one scientist said to him, "the only time I see you these days is on television."

That series of events foreshadowed Salk's future, although he was unaware of it. He still believed that, once the field trial of the vaccine was completed and the evaluation in, his role as a public figure—a relatively minor one at that time—would be ended.

On Tuesday, April 12 of this year, Salk sat in an Ann Arbor, Mich., auditorium with a group of other scientists as Dr. Thomas Francis Jr. announced that the Salk vaccine had been found to be safe and up to 90 per cent effective against paralytic polio. "There was a minor earthquake," he said later. "What was so minor about it?" the public relations people asked.

Within the next few weeks Salk received—and rejected—enough invitations to speak, sponsor, dine and promote to keep him busy seven nights a week for three or four years, at an income that he never bothered to estimate but that would have been very large indeed. "Most of this belongs in the category of mink coats and Cadillacs—unnecessary," he said.

Basil O'Connor, who by that time had become a close friend of Salk, said, "It's a problem, educating a fellow like that who has lived in the dark of his laboratory for twenty years."

Salk does not scorn what he considers to be genuine approaches, provided they do not take up much time. For instance, when strangers come up to him, as they are forever doing, and thank him for developing the vaccine, he reacts with pleasure and warmth.

But for the most part, he is appalled at the demands on the public figure he has become and resentful of what he considers to be the invasion of his privacy. "Why do they want to know what I have for breakfast?" he asks irritably.

The vaccine that made Salk such a public figure has now been given to about 7,500,000 children in the United States and abroad.

Although Salk is always quick to point out that many scientists besides himself were involved in its development, and equally quick to point out that the Public Health Service is now in charge of it, he still seems to regard the vaccine with something of the emotional feeling of a mother toward her child.

This was evident during the recent controversy over whether the nation should continue with the vaccination program. The controversy began when some persons injected with vaccine produced by the Cutter Laboratories developed paralytic polio. Salk was horrified. "I know it's purely emotional," he told a friend, "but I cannot escape a terrible feeling of identification with these people who got polio."

It is related that after the Cutter incident, Salk went down to Washington and sharply chastised the Public Health Service for failing to enforce certain of the safety requirements he had recommended. It is also related that Public Health Service officials told him the safety standards were not safe enough for large-scale commercial production.

In any event, the Cutter incident alarmed everybody involved, and that, in turn, resulted in the sequence of stops and starts on the vaccination program, the incredible confusion, the almost daily conferences among Public Health officials, private scientists and vaccine manufacturers, and finally the appointment of a committee of scientists, including Salk, to advise P. H. S. on what to do next.

The period during which all this was taking place—from the end of April until the beginning of this month—was perhaps the most difficult in Salk's life. Wherever he was, his thoughts were likely to be dwelling on the vaccine. His week went something like this: A midnight train from Pittsburgh to Washington; a meeting at the National Institutes of Health from 9:30 A.M. until well after midnight; preparation of memos, reports, suggestions; a conference with the Surgeon General; a conference with the vaccine manufacturers; a plane to Pittsburgh; long-distance telephone calls to Washington and New York; a meeting with polio foundation officials in New York; back to Washington to testify before a Congressional committee or to meet with the Surgeon

General again or to study vaccine manufacturers' reports; back to Pittsburgh to catch up on a few of the most urgent problems of his own laboratory. It added up, conservatively speaking, to a nine-day week.

There were other pressures sharper than time. For Salk, who was absolutely confident that the vaccine, if made correctly, was both safe and effective, the Washington meetings at which some scientists expressed doubts of one kind or another were exceedingly hard to take.

In public, Salk tried to remain in the role of investigator rather than proponent. He made a point of keeping calm at the meetings; he said he didn't lose his temper, he used his temper. Sometimes when he was really angry at his critics, he would go back to his hotel room and write out, in longhand, a speech for delivery next day. Then, having delivered himself of his anger, he would throw the speech in the trash basket and go to bed.

An associate of his said, "That boy really suffers when he sees a paralytic case. You look at him and you see him thinking, 'My God, this can be prevented.' He would like everyone in the country—parents as well as children—to get the vaccine. But he never would make a public plea for it. This was a matter of principle with him. Also, he was certain that, in the end, his vaccine would be used."

A few weeks ago, the Public Health Service and its advisers decided the vaccine should be used. The program is running again —slowly now, but it will pick up steam as more vaccine becomes available. The problems involved in the manufacture of the vaccine seem to have been straightened out; the safety requirements have been tightened; the Public Health Service has set up a new agency to insure the safety, potency and purity of the vaccine.

Salk is pleased. "It's beautiful to see how it has worked out," he says. "This is fine." But for him as well as for the public, the real proof of the vaccine will be in the record, and that will start coming in next month.

Meanwhile, Salk believes that he may have made a more important contribution than the development of the vaccine. "If

anyone asked me what the real contribution was," he said recently,
"I should say that we may ultimately—and I stress the *may*—
be able to show that a killed virus vaccine produces a level of
immunity as high as or even higher than that following an actual
case of paralytic polio."

The Salk vaccine is a preparation of "killed" virus—that is,
polio virus which has been sufficiently inactivated so that it cannot
produce paralytic polio but is still able to stimulate the formation
in the human body of disease-resisting antibodies. Until Salk came
along, tradition and the available evidence favored the use of a
vaccine made from live but "tamed" virus, which, while it had
never been found for polio, had produced a more lasting immunity
against other diseases than a killed virus preparation.

A number of eminent scientists still favor the use of a live
virus vaccine for polio and some predict that it will ultimately be
developed. Salk believes, however, from his own tentative and, he
points out, limited evidence, that the killed virus vaccine may
produce an immunity that will last for years.

It will take time to verify his theories and Salk is eager to get
back to his laboratory. He still wants to find out a number of
things about the polio vaccine: How long will the immunity last?
Are there any children who cannot be immunized? What improve-
ments can be made? Beyond that, he has far bigger goals—"more
in the nature of dreams right now"—involving other diseases.

A few days ago Salk summed up his reactions to his fame.
"You find yourself projected into a set of circumstances for which
neither your training nor your talents have prepared you. It's very
difficult in some respects, but it's a transitory thing and you wait
till it blows over. Eventually people will start thinking, 'That poor
guy,' and leave me alone. Then I'll be able to get back to my
laboratory."

IX
Popular Culture

☐ The democratization of American culture has made most of the representative men of this book popular heroes. Each hero, however, has initially attained his popularity through excellence in some special profession: we know him, first of all, as the politician, the poet, the musician, the scientist. That favorite American question, "What do you do for a living?" is one way of asking, "What kind of person are you? What kind of person have you chosen to be?" And thus, like Othello, we identify the quality of the man through his chosen occupation. The hero of popular culture represents the feelings of Americans in the most direct and commercial sense. His fame depends upon his immediate attractiveness, his ability to evoke response from millions of people. The moment he loses popularity, he renounces his role as hero. He may have a chosen profession—he may be a singer like Frank Sinatra or an editor like Hugh Hefner, or a psychologist like Timothy Leary—but he survives only so long as he can motivate great numbers of people to celebrate him as a cult hero.

☐ The hero of popular culture is the man who most closely represents and illuminates his age. When the age is dominated by religious concerns—as in the Puritan period of America— the hero will be a pious man who represents the finest aspects of the moral life; thus Hawthorne was able to create a tragedy in *The Scarlet Letter* because the ethical hero, Arthur Dimmesdale, had violated the very quality which made him a leader in his Puritan community. When the times are preoccupied with pragmatic problems, a hero like Benjamin Franklin will emerge to represent the interests of people. In an age of political conflict, Thomas Jefferson will speak for the common man. A period of industrial expansion will produce aggressive and ambitious magnates like Rockefeller, Carnegie, and Gould who represent man's desire to be powerful and rich. The contemporary age has produced its own distinctive cult heroes whose common characteristics go far in suggesting the kind of country America has become.

☐ Two basic qualities distinguish the contemporary cult hero: absolute candor and romantic impetuosity. Frank Sinatra, J. D. Salinger, Hugh Hefner, Elizabeth Taylor, Norman Mailer, and Malcolm X have vastly different personal styles, but they share a directness and an honesty that are their most attractive, disarming, and threatening characteristics. They will not tolerate phoniness—that word recurs in their speech as the great modern obscenity—and they speak fearlessly and critically of all those who dissemble. In an age of advertising, these heroes refuse to pretend to be anything but themselves.

☐ Romantic spontaneity has often been a characteristic of the cult hero, but in the modern age it has reached intense proportions. The hero acts on impulse and engages the passions of less confident people. Jacqueline Kennedy will marry a man in defiance of world opinion; Elizabeth Taylor will carry on a romance that runs counter to conventional morality; Timothy Leary will encourage spontaneity and alienation when cautious people tell him to act his age. The magazine that has enjoyed the most extraordinary success in the last fifteen years has been *Playboy*, and it reflects the thinking of many Americans; its "philosophy," as formulated by Hugh Hefner, rests upon the loss of inhibitions, and its popularity is due to "making a success out of people's dreams."

☐ Candor and spontaneity can clearly be dangerous. One might invoke the traditional point of view that considers the Romantic Movement as responsible for modern warfare, for the anarchy that has been loosed upon the world. But one can assert that other interpretation of Romanticism which suggests that the great creativity of the nineteenth and twentieth centuries stems from the unleashing of man's inhibitions, from his new confidence in feeling and the full play of the emotions. The popular cult heroes of America are intensely imaginative, believing, in Emerson's words, "that if the single man plant himself indomitably on his instincts, and there abide, the huge world will come round to him."

Timothy Leary

Light up the candles, let's turn on, tune in, drop out.

One of the most significant and revealing phenomena in American society during the past two decades has been the widespread consumption of drugs. Sleeping tablets, pep pills, marijuana, tranquilizers, LSD, and other assorted drugs act as depressants and stimulants, and serve a multitude of biological needs for millions of Americans. The old take pills to stay alive; the young use drugs to enhance—more often to escape—their lives. Women take pills to prevent birth, obesity, the ravages of age; men consume pills to reduce tension. The drug phenomenon speaks of a deeply troubled people and nowhere more acutely than among the young. Among the young, the man who has arisen as cult hero, called at once "a saint" and the most evil man in America—a professor and a mystic, an actor and a guru, a symbol of sexuality and a revolutionary propagandist, a scientist and a quack, a "frustrated priest" and a "self-inspired chemical Moses"—is Timothy Leary. "Light up the candles," Leary cries, "turn on, tune in, drop out." The young listen; their parents grow fearful.

Timothy Leary was born in 1925 and raised near Boston. He spent two years at the College of the Holy Cross and half a year at West Point, where he discovered Oriental mysticism. Later he was awarded his Ph.D. in clinical psychology at the University of California. Appointed director of psychology research at Oakland Kaiser Foundation Hospital, Leary soon left in 1959 to join Harvard's Center for Research in Personality. After taking a trip to Cuernavaca, Mexico, where he sampled his first hallucinogen, a mushroom derivative called psilocybin,

Leary proclaimed a new religion. He returned to Harvard and experimented with the drug; but when University officials discovered that Leary was involving students in his experiments, they dismissed him from the faculty. Leary went to a 4,000 acre retreat near Millbrook, New York, and soon attracted a wide following. He began to spread his cult throughout the country, conducting "celebrations" and dramatic versions of novels like Herman Hesse's *Steppenwolf*. One of these celebrations is perceptively reported, from the point of view of a sympathetic yet realistic member of Leary's own generation, in Diana Trilling's essay.

Leary claims that there are five levels of consciousness: 1. Sleep or stupor, which can be achieved through alcohol; 2. The waking life, which is a world of words and symbols; 3. A level of sensory consciousness, a state achieved by the use of marijuana; 4. Cellular consciousness, for which LSD is necessary; and 5. "Precellular flash," a state of mind that Leary calls "soul." Leary's famous epigram—turn on, tune in, drop out—suggests that the individual move into a state of active hallucination with LSD ("turn on"), tap new levels of consciousness ("tune in"), and rid himself of cultural conventions ("drop out" of the culture).

The long-range biological effects of LSD are not absolutely clear, but certain conclusions have been accepted by most doctors. The drug affects the central nervous system, causing changes in moods, a certain anxiety, distorted perceptions, hallucinations and at times delusions, and a general depersonalization. "Your ego or central control mechanism falls apart," one expert comments, and controls on the body are generally loosened. LSD may damage brain and bone marrow cells or chromosomes, although evidence is not yet completely conclusive. Sidney Cohen, a psychiatrist who has devoted many years to the subject of drugs, offers a balanced view. "Undoubtedly LSD uncovers hidden conflicts a lot faster than the analyst's couch and so, with certain patients and in careful hands, can be a useful adjunct to psychotherapy. . . . The trouble is LSD attracts unstable therapists as much as it does the neurotic patient. It gives them an intoxicating sense of power to bestow such a fabulous experience on others."

Timothy Leary has said "that nowhere else in the world would he have dared to take the chances he has taken here [in America]: anywhere else, the LSD revolution would have been impossible." In America, where family permissiveness has led to a conflict between young and old, between those in rebellion and those in authority, drugs have given many people a sense of community and permitted them to develop a culture of their own. It is a fact that many of the most imaginative students as well as successful professional people have experimented with different drugs for different reasons: curiosity, kicks, rebellion, amusement, boredom, insight. These people claim that LSD heightens consciousness, that the mind dissociates itself from the self, and that love between people becomes deeper. Leary himself maintains that "sexual ecstasy is the basic reason for the current LSD boom. . . It is almost inevitable, if a man and his mate take LSD together, that their sexual energies will be unimaginably intensified. . . One of the great purposes of an LSD session is sexual union." For every claim, needless to say, there has been a counterclaim.

Whatever may be the truth about the physiological effects of drugs, the cultural impact has been enormous. It is a curious paradox, as Max Lerner has suggested, that though Leary speaks of inner experience, he and those who champion drugs depend on the outer world—in the form of a chemical—to bring that experience about. Still another paradox is the fact that America is a country traditionally proud of its individualism, its aggressiveness, its commitment to self-reliance and the will; yet many young people take a drug that provides a will-less experience, that depends on passivity. These paradoxes—and all the arguments that develop from them—suggest how bewildered Americans are about the world in which they live.

Celebrating with Dr. Leary

DIANA

TRILLING

LTHOUGH we had been told on what was presumably sound authority that the previous Tuesday evening, the opening night of Dr. Leary's scheduled series of Psychedelic Celebrations, the audience had been "tough" and that therefore on our evening too we must expect some element of danger, or at least unpleasantness, actually it would be hard to imagine a milder scene than awaited us at the Village Barn, the small theatre in Greenwich Village to which Dr. Leary's show had suddenly moved from the Village Theatre where it had originally been booked. Here, surely, was nothing for fear on the score of criminality, menace, or even bad manners. My husband and I were meeting friends. There had been confusion about the arrangements because of the change of theatre, so that we arrived almost an hour before the announced curtain time. But the entrance to the Barn was already jammed—no fewer than two hundred people, probably closer to three hundred, were waiting for admission and as time went on the crowd became so dense that it blocked traffic through the street. But the conduct of Dr. Leary's audience was exemplary. There was no sign of impatience about the possibility of not getting seats; no one pushed or showed any of the usual impulse to assert territorial claims. On the other hand I should scarcely describe it as a friendly gathering, and this despite the fact that most of Dr. Leary's audience was of much the same age —under thirty—and of roughly the same situation in life: middle-class dissident, above the average in education.

It was not a crowd that talked or laughed; I saw no exchange of greetings, it was even difficult to particularise couples. The

REPRINTED FROM *Encounter*, JUNE 1967, BY PERMISSION OF THE AUTHOR.

group seemed to be made up of strangely isolated young people
who, if they were acquainted with each other, were not concerned
to further the connection. The general atmosphere was nevertheless one of virtually palpable benevolence. If one can speak of the
face of a gathering, this was the face of an entire, an almost pro-
grammatic, good-will and peaceableness—it reminded me of the
mandatory calm of recent converts to Christian Science. At first
I was surprised by this prevalence of benignity in young people
many of whom might be assumed to be in some degree involved
in the subversive world of drug-taking and who, at any rate, were
all of them dressed in the rather violent contemporary uniforms
of dissent, either harshly black or, at the other extreme, colourful
in refusal of middle-class conformities of dress—until I reminded
myself that, after all, there lies at the heart of the LSD movement
as of most contemporary movements of youthful protest the conviction that it is those who accept, or at least accommodate themselves to, the values of Western society who have lost the knowledge of peace and kindliness. Then, too, LSD would seem to have
a gentling effect on the personality. I have observed this curious
transformation in all the young people I know who have taken
the drug; even after only one or two trips they attain a sort of
supra-humanity, as if they had been purged of mortal error; and
as far as I can make out, this change persists. But one must be
cautious with conclusions drawn only from personal observation.
In our present highly-deficient state of scientific understanding of
LSD, we know with certainty only that its power to work alterations on the brain is enormous: it is 5,000 times more powerful
than mescaline. But the precise nature of the changes it makes
and how far they extend or how long they last we do not know—
which is of course why those who use it or who for whatever
reason do not wish to oppose its use can persuade themselves that
all warning of its danger is without scientific foundation.

We were fortunate in having reserved Press seats for the four
of us by telephone, otherwise we might never have got into Dr.
Leary's show. It was when I was trying to get through the lobby
to pick up our tickets that I had the encounter which stays with
me as summing up the peculiar quality of transcendence that

characterised this audience. A young man blocked my path. I touched his shoulder to ask if I could pass. Although the situation demanded no more than politeness, he turned elaborately, looked down at me from what seemed a divine height and said, "I want you to do anything you want to do." So sublime a response surely had its reference elsewhere than where we stood. Not merely his words but the young man's smile, his bearing, were clearly pointed at some sweeter moral universe than a crowded theatre lobby in Greenwich Village, New York. Yet, even at this early moment in my psychedelic evening, I knew it was a mistake to regard this young man as an extraordinary instance of elevation. It was his personal quality, not mine, that appeared to be the norm of the occasion—in a gathering like Dr. Leary's I had already come to feel cumbersomely earthbound, of a graceless and unloving species. Since my night among Dr. Leary's followers—and followers I must suppose the largest part of his audience to have been, judging not only by appearance and manner but by their conduct in the course of the performance and certainly in the question-and-answer period at the end of the ceremonies—I have seen a special LSD issue of the French magazine, *Crapouillot*, with excellent photographs of people at various stages of LSD intoxication. Some of the subjects appear to be having a grievously bad time but none of them, no matter in what agony, is without his smile of fine imperturbability, which bears about the same relation to our usual notions of self-containment that the smile of classical hysteria (*"la belle indifférence"*) bears to our usual imagination of pleasurable emotion.

Is it perhaps straining for consistency that I found in Dr. Leary's prose, written or spoken, a character not unlike that of his audience—the same imperviousness achieved at an equal cost in substantive actuality? For instance, a placard was posted in the lobby to explain the last-minute switch of Dr. Leary's show from the Village Theatre to the Village Barn. Later I copied it out:

With regard to Dr. Leary's Psychedelic Celebration at the Village Theatre: It is with regret that Dr. Leary has discovered inequities and is experiencing financial problems with the theatre. Therefore he is forced to announce that he will no longer appear at the Village

Theatre. Instead, Dr. Leary will conduct a psychedelic religious celebration tonight at the Village Barn at 9.00. There will be no admission
charge.

Prose like this, at once so plain and "elegant," colloquial and fine,
commonplace and yet formal, almost legalistic, is compounded of
entirely familiar elements of communication. Certainly it has no
shock value. But when we examine it we see that although it is
offered in explanation, it explains nothing; it merely seduces one
into the belief that one has been addressed with a familiar co-
gency. And so with Dr. Leary's spoken language. It creates the
illusion of coherence, it seems to proceed reasonably enough; it is
only when one applies oneself to it that it eludes the grasp. Dr.
Leary's impossible plausibility would not seem, however, to be
consciously contrived, and in this his verbal style differs from that
of more orthodox evangelists. Dr. Leary is nothing if not sincere;
his language could not be less ornate or theatrical. In fact, it is
precisely from its naturalness and sincerity that its hallucinatory
quality derives. Much more than Dr. Leary's speech reminded me
of someone like Father Divine, it put me in mind of the mother
of Lee Oswald, as Jean Stafford describes her in a remarkable little
book, A *Mother in History*, the transcription of a series of interviews between Miss Stafford and Mrs. Oswald. Just as, in the case
of Mrs. Oswald, I began to long for some stage-prop or costume
to assure me that this mistress of the ardently simple and utterly
unconnected statement was only acting, not communicating a
real-life condition, just so as I put myself to Dr. Leary's "honesty"
I came to yearn for the contrivance of theatre.

But, more, what particularly struck me when I came back to
Dr. Leary's notice in the lobby after I had become better acquainted with his mode of discourse was its premise of innocence.
It is of course its innocence that constitutes a chief appeal of
Dr. Leary's doctrine to the privileged young who, perhaps because
they are the offspring of a parent-generation intent on keeping
no knowledge from them, now regard their elders as uniquely
impure in motive and behaviour. If the audience at the Village

Barn was a fair sampling, and I think it was, Dr. Leary's followers are certainly not to be associated with any ordinary image we may have of juvenile delinquency. The class difference, involving as it does not only differences in education but in social assumption, significantly separates the users of LSD from the young world of street gangs and violence. The LSD phenomenon therefore represents a quite separate social problem located, I think, at that special place in society where cultural influences tend to supplant the better-understood social pressures.

Still, nothing I learned in my evening with Dr. Leary proposed the idea that because his young followers make so urgent an option for virtue and purity of motive, they have any special endowment of native goodness, or even any notable sensitivity to ugliness, or inability to sustain it. As to the first, there is no ground for the belief that behind their benevolence there do not lie the usual human angers and aggressions. As to the second, in the course of my evening at the Barn I came to suspect that if we are going to stay with the "frightened generation" explanation of the LSD phenomenon we need to be precise about what we mean. Far from suggesting any extreme vulnerability to the terrors of life, these young people seemed to me to be unduly armoured— and if this is because LSD has reduced their moral alertness, then we must regard the drug as perhaps more dehumanising than we have yet recognised. My point could not be simpler: at the most alarming moments of the evening, when Dr. Leary announced that he knew no child over the age of seven who was not on drugs, or when his coadjutor, Dr. Alpert, in response to a question about 16-, 17-, or 18-year-olds on LSD, said, "Even if they end up in a hospital or prison for a few months, it doesn't bother me," there was no slightest sign of dismay in their audience. Fearful these young people may be, like the rest of us; they have a fearsome world in which to be young. But fear can show itself in a number of ways, and defines character only by the form it takes and the ends it is made to serve. To express concern for the children of Viet Nam and yet remain unmoved by the idea of submitting 7-year-olds to hallucinogenic drugs is surely to obey the dictates of culture rather than of reliable feeling.

Dr. Leary and Dr. Alpert have both been university teachers, teaching psychologists. I daresay my own response to statements as cruelly irresponsible as these—they were casual remarks, really, spoken with an entire ease—is underscored by the importance I assign, the special importance, to their former profession. In a society as mobile as that of America, the school is more than an institution for teaching the intellectual disciplines, it is the matrix of our ongoing culture, the chief source and guardian of our personal and social morality. What the school establishes today, the home will have absorbed by tomorrow—most of the precepts of our post-Freudian family culture were first formulated in our teacher-training programmes. But the problem is that it is exactly because America is so open-ended that youth is valued as it is, beyond its possible emotional and social capacities. And this means that the teacher whose task it is to instruct the young in the complexity of the conditions on which the continuing life of society depends and in the limitations imposed upon the individual by emotional and social reality must himself be able to resist the seductions of rebelliousness for its own youthful sake—which seems to be a difficult demand to make today of anyone of radical spirit and imagination. No one in American public life, certainly no one in government, has the ear of the young like their university instructors, unless it is the advanced social and literary critics, and these are often the same persons, so that if—as now is increasingly happening—the teacher is reluctant to surrender the glamour of youthful rebelliousness and to discover its own grave satisfaction in the exercise of the parental role, he leaves his students in the position of children who have been robbed of the definition they can only achieve when those who train them, and whom they naturally rebel against, have a firm authority of their own; they face emptiness, a world without boundaries. I am not suggesting that the tide of nihilism in which the young appear to be more and more caught up takes its sole or primary force from the school, but only that if anything is to be done to stem it, the salvage will have to be undertaken by the same class of people who did such a successful job of bringing the failure of modern culture to our educated consciousness. Dr. Leary was dismissed, as Dr. Alpert was too, from his Harvard post for engaging his students in his experiments with drugs, but I doubt he would have reached the young as he has were it not for his earlier professional certification.

But, at our evening in the Barn, Dr. Leary was not resting with his pedagogic function. He also made it a religious occasion, and thus drew on the shared fund of recollected church-going his audience, even his young audience, might be supposed to have brought to his celebration. (We keep it in mind, however, that Dr. Leary is under indictment for illegal possession of drugs and if he is to plead freedom of religion under the First Amendment, he does well to put public emphasis on his religious convictions.) His show our night was called "The Incarnation of Christ"; he also does an "Illumination of the Buddha." The ceremonies had been advertised on the theatre rather than the religious pages of the papers, with Dr. Leary "IN PERSON" as the leading attraction. His religious purpose was nevertheless kept dominant. In addition to the film-and-dance portion of the programme, itself ritualistic, there was a sermon, there were prayers by Dr. Leary, and even a moment of silent prayer on the part of the "congregation." Early in the performance Dr. Leary reminded us that while we were gathered here in New York for our religious ceremonies our opposite numbers in India were enjoying the religious ecstasy on the shores of the Ganges, and our opposite numbers in Mexico attaining their exaltation with peyote. Of ecstasy and exultation there might actually be none, either in Dr. Leary's programme or his audience, but unmistakably a spirit of devoutness permeated the auditorium. The religious emotions of Dr. Leary seemed, however, to be considerably interfered with by the strains and temptations of showmanship. And he was very tired, one saw his fatigue from the start as soon as he took his place on the platform in the darkened hall; he might have been managing a hangover. This was a weary impresario and performer, a weary pedagogue, a weary Messiah—the multiplication and confusion of roles that Dr. Leary now assumes are his burden as the leader of a movement which even he could not have guessed would grow so fast.

We had been shown to our seats at a Press table; amusingly, not unexpectedly, a disproportionate space in this small auditorium had been set aside for those Dr. Leary might hope would give his movement still more of the publicity it has already had in such abundance. Although it was legitimate enough that we should present ourselves as members of the Press, at least for me even this means we had used to procure seats added to the self-consciousness I had felt ever since I had arrived at the hall. It is always uncomfortable to sightsee in other people's emotional universe; and after all it had come only as an afterthought, when we were already seated, that I might some time want to write about the occasion and should therefore take notes. Some days later I was to read a review of our evening in the *New York Times*, by a reporter who apparently spotted us for the tourists we were. She got us by name and described us as "initiates of the older cults of politics and psychoanalysis." We were likened—and this is uncommonly vivid reporting for the *Times*—to "atheists attending a religious ritual out of sociological interest . . . our expressions faintly tinged with boredom and distaste." Well, the sociological posture was unquestionably readiest to hand, but I am afraid I was unprotected by scientific distance from the objects of my study. I looked around the theatre at this strangely subdued and isolate audience, and I was painfully aware of the chasm that stretched between the world of these young people and my own at the same age, of the difference between this dedication of theirs and the political dedication of the Marxist '30s in which I had come to maturity. We too, at their age, had pointed to the violence of those in power. My contemporaries, too, had set themselves to make a revolution in consciousness, which would make us "free." But our means had been social and political, and now the very concept of society was inoperative. But if ours had been an ideology of social involvement, not of withdrawal, this could now be no boast—it had led to a blockage of hope which could perhaps never be, certainly had not been, surmounted by a succeeding generation. And for us there had been no atomic bomb. And there had been no such limitlessness in our world, no such vacuum as now passes for the social and personal structure of life. It was not necessary to find any particular emotional vulnerability or even feelingness in Dr. Leary's followers to recognise that they had sufficient ground for confusion and despair, a good bit more even than we had had when we rejected our society as given.

The unease of my situation was much relieved as soon as Allen Ginsberg came to sit at my side, and this is surely not the least interesting aspect of the evening, that by some marvellous transmutation of things as we think them to be, the fact that Ginsberg sat next to me throughout most of the performance was more than a comfort, it provided my chief link with sanity. We had seen him entering the hall and had waved. He had come over to say hello and just then the performance began. To avoid disturbance, Ginsberg sat down at my side. His beard was by far the most lavish in this well-bearded audience; were it still not a blackest black, he should be called the good grey poet of the psychedelic movement, such is his air of venerableness and wisdom, such the authority with which he now seems vested. Time had passed— seven years, eight years?—since I had last seen him. Then, too, it had been a public evening of which I had also tried (not entirely successfully, as it turned out; but, then, one has not the right to ask self-consciousness of one's readers, only of oneself) to report the inevitable reciprocity between the observed and the observer. It was very little later that Dr. Leary mentioned, in all mildness, the presence in the hall of agents from the Narcotics Squad; for a bad instant, as I looked around me and saw no one who met the description, I supposed it might be the four of us Dr. Leary was referring to—except, of course, we had Allen Ginsberg to vouch for us, he was our security in this alien territory. Throughout the ceremonies, speaking in a low steady voice, precise, in firm pedagogic control of knowledge it pleased him to share, this former student of my husband's gave me the assurance I needed of my own identity, unchallenged, in no subtlest degree suborned. The adroitness with which Ginsberg made his aesthetic and critical removal from what was going on onstage while keeping intact his old ties of theoretical and even practical approval of the drug-taking enterprise was something of a triumph. Everything about him indeed, his weight of purpose no less than his canniness, freshly pressed upon me the importance, in the psychedelic universe as elsewhere, of the wish for fame and immortality, that most traditional impulse of the gifted. For what is it, finally, other than the force of this desire, that has sustained Ginsberg, regulated the degree of his involvement in dangerous personal experiment, urged him beyond the anonymousness implicit in the pursuit of selfhood through drugs.

Is Dr. Leary, as well, an exception to the harsh rule of self-eradication in drugs? I doubt it. Certainly drug-promotion is now giving Dr. Leary a rare celebrity. And by the evidence of these religious ceremonies he courts immortality in the largest possible way by identification with immortal principles and personages. But succeed as he may in making converts to his religion, as a self he wears the pale but indelible marks of doom: you see it as soon as he takes the microphone in his hand and invites the spotlight. As a self, he has the invincible anonymousness of a television master of ceremonies, than which surely nothing could be more stricken from the immortal rolls. Dr. Leary looks to be in his mid-forties; he is tall, slim, with a suggestion of willowiness. He is, if you will, handsome, with something of the consciousness of the professional charmer, and I should suppose he is especially comfortable in his stage costume of white trousers and open-necked white shirt. The family background seems to be a little vague: apparently it was Irish Catholic, middle-Western; one reads of an Army father and that he himself went to West Point, but this is not the impression he creates—in appearance and voice he is only "sensitive" deteriorated Harvard, throwing away some considerable advantages of birth. He is fair-haired and tousled, wears a necklace, and performs in bare feet. When he takes the microphone in his hand, one feels it is a natural extension of his infatuate ego and that it will more and more become his staff and his rod, his auxiliary drug, his surrogate selfhood. As the evening wore on, with Dr. Leary up there on the platform and Allen Ginsberg at my side, I had the sense of a certain entertaining ambiguity in the relation of these two psychedelic figures. At least before friends like ourselves from an earlier period in his career Ginsberg seemed to me to make a point of his poetic pride, of his superiority to the leader, even of his superior scholarship, but I may have misread him. At any rate, in the course of the ceremonies, he several times alluded to the need for humour in dealing with the LSD subject. For the poverty of Dr. Leary's show as art he was carefully and courteously apologetic.

There was, first, the darkening of the hall and Dr. Leary's entrance into the spotlight, behind him a white and still-empty screen. From the wings of this makeshift theatre came the soft strumming of a guitar, and immediately the audience was churchy-still—except that the comparison is absurd: church is where people cough and rustle and squirm and there was no coughing or rustling or squirming in the Barn, unless on the part of four unlicensed sociologists. Through the next two hours (I guess the show lasted) Dr. Leary had his audience in entire control; he could be envied by the professionals.

With his opening remarks Dr. Leary effectively formulated, if one can put it so, the incoherence through which I would try to grope for the remainder of the evening. I have a friend who shares his apartment with a painter; one day my friend's mother (this is a Jewish story) came to see him, examined the paintings on his walls and turned to her son with the question, "Who authorised these pictures?" It was the question I would have put to Dr. Leary: Who, or what, had authorised this particular conglomerate of pageant, preachment, classroom, revival meeting, dance, movie, and off-Broadway amateur night? Where had this performance come from, what was the source of its inspiration? How much was it the psychedelic experience itself that was being reproduced for us, how much an "artistic" derivation? How much was Dr. Leary improvising a gospel, and how much was he bearing witness to the accepted doctrine? Where did the play end and pedagogy begin, where did pedagogy end and play begin? Had Dr. Leary and his co-performers recently taken LSD and was the drug thus so-to-speak present in the talk that accompanied the film, or had there been at least the intention of artistic detachment from the actual drugged state? It was reported of the movie, *Flaming Creatures*, whether accurately or not I have no way of knowing, that its actors were all of them under drugs when it was made; this one could credit from the loose automatism of their movements and their dispersed sexuality. Dr. Leary's film and the sporadic miming that took place in front of the screen and the words Dr. Leary himself spoke and those that were intoned antiphonally by the male pantomimist and a woman at the side of the stage were certainly all of them sufficiently lifeless to suggest some similar interference with normal process. Still, I realise that an actor has to be highly skilled to simulate nature unimpeded by human awkwardness. What looked like blocked transmission in Dr. Leary's show may simply have been amateurishness. "You have to go out of your mind to come to your senses." "We don't pray to anyone up there but to what is inside ourselves." Even announcing his best-shaped slogans, Dr. Leary himself, and despite his naturalness and sincerity, failed to take significant shape except in a form already made iconographic by nightclub and television "personalities." The essential quality he conveyed was that of a schoolmaster acting the master of ceremonies in a school show—a good-looking, tired, essentially vulgar, still-boyish teacher, histrionic, equally pleased with his popularity with his students and with the privileges of office which he could exercise as occasion demanded.

He stayed in the spotlight, quite alone, for rather a while. I had no sense it was too long for his audience. His lecture-preachment-patter covered a general territory already well known from repeated accounts of the doctrine. What one had not been sufficiently prepared for was the vagrancy of Dr. Leary's thought, its bold (however tired), bald carelessness of the ordinary rules of reasonableness, of intelligible discourse. For the occasion of ceremony everything was spoken with the cadence of ceremony, something between a croon and a subdued exhortation. *We pray we are not hung up and that you will have a good trip* (did he mean in our next LSD session, or only metaphorically, here in the theatre?). . . . *The voyage is always the same* (did he mean reliable, or was he remarking the singleness of the indicated path?). . . . *We re-new and re-enact the ancient myths* (this could refer to the play, but it could also refer to the sacred journey to which we were being urged). . . . *We pass on what we* (an editorialised Dr. Leary, psychologist?) *have learned in ten years of hard work.* . . . *We* (Dr. Leary and his audience? Dr. Leary and others under the influence of LSD?) *meet in our retinas, we meet on the screen in the vibrating beams of light, also we meet in the liquid canals*

*of the ear; then we move within to resurrect the body, rediscover
the timepiece of the universe: the heartbeat. . . . Then we breathe
together. . . . You should not take a trip without a road map. . . .
Myths are cellular. . . . The myth is a blueprint. . . . Tonight we
invite you to re-live the myth of Jesus Christ. . . . The resurrection
of Jesus Christ has been a rough trip for all of us* (Dr. Leary and
his co-authors? All of us in the 20th century who are the in-
heritors of the Christian tradition?). . . .

*First we ran into Christian backlash, second the backlash from
Jews and atheists. . . . The Christian myth means, once there was
a man who took all the guilts, the shoulds and shouldn'ts, on his
own shoulders and wiped them out. If you experience this myth*
(before you take the drug? afterwards?) *you are free. . . . Go back
and free the world from good and evil. . . . The tolling of the bell
at Millbrook* (here the clanging of a loud bell presumably took
us to Dr. Leary's "institute") *takes us on a voyage of discovery.
You have to have a guide in the person who has been there before
you: an old witch or a frog or a hunchback. Today, your teen-age
child. . . . They have the key to the voyage and it always involves
a chemical tick.* (Trick?) *This is the Chalice, the Holy Communion, and always the Last Supper: goodbye to all back there.
. . . I welcome you in the name of the Father, the Son and the
Holy Ghost. . . . Give thanks as we take the Chalice and let our
thanks ascend. Drink. This is my flesh, bone and blood. . . . As
often as you do this, do this in memory of me.*

Lights had now begun to flash on the screen and Dr. Leary
moved to the side of the stage. His voice rose in intensity. *Open
the naked eye, find the centre!* Great circles of light appear on the
screen, and the show complicates itself:

girl's voice *Can you float through the universe of your body
and not lose your way?*

No one directly answers the question. Mushroom-like patterns
form on the screen. In front of the screen a man in black trousers,
bare above the waist, sways slowly, it would seem painfully, his
arms weaving and reaching in the familiar dance-idiom of tortured quest.

girl's voice *What is happening?*

DR. LEARY   *Float to the centre.*

MAN'S VOICE   *I am drowning in blood. . . . Help. . . . Please make it stop. . . . No, no, don't make it stop.*

GIRL'S VOICE   *Blood to death. . . . Out. . . . Out. . . . Blood to death. . . . Life. . . . Life. . . . Life. . . . Scarlet. . . .*

MAN'S VOICE   *So warm. . . . Drifting down. . . . Melting. . . . Breathing. . . . Breath of life. . . .*

Here my notes indicate a certain amount of groaning on the stage but not who is the sufferer. Unfortunately, I have no shorthand. But if at first I am troubled by my inability to catch every word being spoken on the stage, soon enough as I catch the drift I realise that the drift is all. It is said of LSD that it taps the unconscious in order to add to the store of the conscious; this is indeed its principal and much-vaunted value, that it is supposed to augment consciousness. But surely to call the LSD experience consciousness-enhancing is to merge two meanings of the word "consciousness"—that which we oppose to *un*consciousness and by which we mean those activities of the mind which we can take note of as they proceed, and, second, the honorific meaning, that of active and useful awareness. If one is to judge the LSD state by Dr. Leary's representation or adumbration of it in his ceremonies or by anything one has so far read of it, what happens under LSD may very well be a flooding of the mind with images or emotions from which it is otherwise closed off. But what the mind does with this new material speaks not at all of a significantly enhanced mental activity such as we usually adduce in our appreciation of awareness. The problem is, of course, an old one in aesthetics. It is not without interest that the new Coleridge scholarship demonstrates with some persuasiveness that "Kubla Khan" was not actually an opium dream and that Coleridge offered it as such only in polemic, as a defence of the role of non-reason in the writing of poetry. But it is not solely an aesthetic problem, it is also a scientific problem and a vexing one: how define what we mean by consciousness, especially in the creative process?

The dialogue between male and female voice now peters out and Dr. Leary relinquishes the spotlight so that the full attention of the audience can be focused on the screen. The pictures that appear look to me like magnified blood cells or other organic matter. Then gradually they become more complex, "social," sometimes fleetingly identifiable. Also, the background music now rises in volume, becomes more assertive—Ginsberg whispers to me, "The *Missa Luba*, a Congo version of the Catholic Mass," and obediently I hear what could perhaps be the *Kyrie Eleison*; he whispers "Verdi's *Requiem*" and, more reluctantly, I hear that as well. Without my having quite noted, the guitar has eliminated itself, been replaced by a sound-track to accompany what is apparently intended as a representation, or evocation, of the evolutionary process, a kind of psychedelic March of Time. Ginsberg mentions a word that sounds like *Straboscopia*, which I take to derive from the same root as *Strabismus*: "*Med.* A disorder of the eye in which the optic axes cannot be directed to the same object because of incoordination of the muscles of the eyeballs. . . ." In later dictionary consultation I realise he said *Stroboscopic*, pertaining to "an instrument for observing the successive phases of a periodic motion by means of light periodically interrupted." But the difference is only objective. The camera's wish to catch the speed of psychedelic imagery affects me like a sickness of the eye. From my Press table I no longer see Dr. Leary. I assume he is seated stage right. His voice resumes the incantation:

Let's return to the 20th century and reincarnate Jesus Christ. Let's do it every one of us right now. . . . You have to take on all the guilt, sin and wretchedness of the world. . . . You have to do this for everyone so that there won't be any more. . . . Then we're all through with the good-evil thing and you will be reborn. . . . All-embracing, Dr. Leary invites the police and the narcotics agents to join in the rebirth, and for the first and only time in the evening his audience is vocally responsive. "You're right," come several voices from the audience, soft, devout.

My notes do not say if Dr. Leary is now once more stage centre, in full spotlight, but I recollect him to be. The film has now run its spotty course, from our unicellular origins to our modern metropolitan mediocrity, and we can have the sermon. Certainly it is in fullest stage centre that Dr. Leary makes his biggest pitch of the evening, inviting someone to come up from the audience on to the platform, take off his clothes and be nailed to the cross. *Let's look in the bag. There are some nails here and a crown of thorns.* The audience remains unmoving. Dr. Leary is apparently not surprised, he had expected no volunteers; one wonders, in fact, what he would do if a too-eager listener proffered his services. He repeats: *Will anyone volunteer to be nailed to the cross if we guarantee you there will be no more evil in the world?* He dissipates the reverential hush, or at least lifts it a fraction, with a prepared comment: Dr. Leary confides to us that he had been warned that if he made such a proposal in this setting, "four hundred and ninety-seven exhibitionists, sado-masochists and faggots would storm the platform." There is no laughter. *No, we must not do it that way, we must do it with our clothes on, or even our uniforms. . . . But let's do it.*

There follows the more formal sermon, wholly Dr. Leary's own show and, like all sermons, lengthy. Its text, Dr. Leary announces, is from William Blake *who had been in our profession a couple of hundred years ago* (sic). *. . . He who is a fool persists in his folly* (sic). *. . .* We must start a new religion, says Dr. Leary, and start a new country. *We have been working six years*—it had been ten, I recall, a few minutes back—*to work out a plan to turn on this country and this planet. . . . Starting a new religion is like starting a new business. Or a garden. There are inevitable sequences. . . . A series of ordeals or tests. . . . We have no paranoia or hostility about our opposition, it's a rough business starting a new religion. It's a rough business but highly-stylised, more classic than baseball or football. . . . We must turn on, tune in, and drop out. . . . Turn off your mind and go within. . . . You need a sacrament and today it is a chemical. The chemicals we use are ancient. . . . Treat these sacraments with the respect they deserve. Before you turn on you must be in a state of grace. You must look into yourself and see where you have sinned. On your own chessboard. You are the only one who can forgive yourself. You look in your mirror, in your retina is the history. You confess to yourself. If you don't go to confession before you take a sacrament you may writhe, suffer, call for a doctor. . . . Once you turn on, then you tune in, show others what has been shown to you.* Dr. Leary calls on Rudi and Jackie, assistants, to come forward and testify. They have apparently helped to put the show together, now they will help us tune in.

DR. LEARY *Rudi, where are we now and where are we going?*

RUDI (thinking) *We are working from a core which is a circle of love. A very beautiful and pure thing.*

DR. LEARY *Jackie, where are we?*

JACKIE (who is a girl) *We are here and happy to be here. And we are going from here out, to turn on the world.*

DR. LEARY *We have to work with the young, the artists, the underground groups for a new breakthrough. Artists change consciousness and the change lasts. . . . We work to change family life. . . . Encourage husbands and wives to take LSD together. . . . I can't imagine a husband being turned on without wanting to turn on his wife. I can't imagine parents being turned on without wanting to turn on their children. I know no child over the age of seven who hasn't been given drugs and I know many of them. The parents turn on the children.*

Dr. Leary has a practised device of irony. He echoes his outrages of decency in the voice of outraged respectability:

Imagine turning on children!

There is a pregnant pause, and Dr. Leary recapitulates:

The psychedelic experience is one you want to share with those you care most about. . . . Inconceivable that parents would take LSD and not want their children to share the experience.

The audience continues to be dead still: no one stamps, hisses, rises to object. No one leaves the theatre. (And no reporter, to my knowledge, undertakes to report what we all of us at Dr. Leary's Press tables so clearly heard.) From this point forward, the rest of Dr. Leary's sermon is bound to be anti-climax:

We are now in a legal and political phase. . . . Several million Americans are taking LSD, more taking marijuana, for serious purposes. . . . They need an institution. . . . We are working with the courts to license small groups to take LSD. . . . After you tune in you drop out. It happens so gracefully. . . . A detachment from old ambitions and drives. . . . What we meet and work for is what you want and know is possible. . . . We need and invite your comments and questions.

The comments and questions that comprise the remainder of the programme may be what Dr. Leary invites, they cannot be what he needs. But then, what speaker ever gets the questions he needs, and these were at least intended neither to provoke nor challenge. Dr. Leary fares better than most public speakers when they finish a talk and discover to whom they have been speaking and what they are thought to have said. A man rises from the audience to say that he has confronted the beast: Is this what Dr. Leary meant by confrontation with the wolf? Myself, I had heard no mention of wolves, singular or plural. I wonder if the questioner has in mind the beast one confronts in the mirror when one confesses to oneself, or merely an encounter on the psychedelic journey. Dr. Leary is perhaps himself confused. At any rate, he chooses this moment to call to the stage "his well-known colleague" Dr. Richard Alpert, recently returned from California. Together, Dr. Leary and Dr. Alpert respond to the question that has been asked by examining the uterine recapitulation of man's long slow evolution. *Memory cards flash through your brain when you take LSD, so it doesn't fit your tidy 20th-century mind.* I conclude from this that when you take LSD you return to the womb and re-live the pre-natal development.

The second questioner is a priest; he is recognised by Dr. Leary and Dr. Alpert as a friend. The priest wants to know whether after many trips you could not have the same experience without taking the drug. It is Dr. Alpert who undertakes to reply: *After a trip you get depressed by your new sense of your daily life. After enough of this, you stay high all the time because you have revised your life. . . . LSD is not a substitute for the conscious effort of digging here and now. . . . LSD is a constant reminder of our divinity. We mustn't stop because we are too busy. . . . Find someone not on LSD and find out how he and I are us.* This is the point at which I recall, with a certain syntactical confusion, the priest in Ilf and Petrov's wonderful *The Little Golden Calf* of whom the verb "befuddle" is used as an active verb of expression: "Yes," befuddled the priest—"No," befuddled the priest. But of course this was in another country. . . . The priest sits down; he is apparently satisfied with the answer that has been given him.

And now the master of ceremonies introduces Allen Ginsberg from the audience, calls him to the stage. Ginsberg rises modestly but readily—had he been forewarned?—to join the circle on the platform. While he is threading his way through the audience, Dr. Leary intersperses some remarks on electrons, heightens the scientific authority of the occasion. He also addresses himself to the subject of people killing themselves under the effects of LSD; the percentage is negligible, he assures us, and anyway those are the people who failed to go to confession and expunge their guilts. Dr. Leary gives the nod to the next questioner.

This time the question, although manifestly not intended to give offence, does suggest criticism; it is carefully larded with apology. It seems that although the questioner himself understands the moral nature of the LSD enterprise, there are people of his acquaintance who take the drug just for kicks. Would Dr. Leary comment on this? From the other side of the theatre, I have no trouble hearing the question. But Dr. Leary seems to have difficulty; he turns to his coadjutors in appeal but meeting no help he invites his interrogator to the stage. But on his way, this young men is checked by another member of the audience who rises to protest that such a question can only come from someone caught "in the game"—which is to say, someone under the influence of this-worldly, non-psychedelic, values. A moment of tension develops between the two men at the foot of the platform—it represents something of a relief amidst all this benignity—and then Allen Ginsberg intervenes: *You're taking it too seriously, keep some humour.* The questioner addresses the stage in self-defence: *But I want a successful revolution.* To which Leary responds soothingly: *Tell us why, how are we sliding back from the centre?* The questioner identifies himself as an instructor in a college in South Jersey. Grievingly he explains that some of his students fail to understand the moral purpose of LSD, they take it for the sensation, they are not *serious.* (He hits the word as I have not heard a word hit since the days when the comrades would accuse each other of being *subjective.*) *And I want you to win, I want a revolution like you do.* The troubled comrade from South Jersey is at last disposed of by Dr. Alpert, judiciously: *It doesn't matter from what motive these kids of 16, 17, or 18 take LSD, if*

*they turn on for 30 seconds the experience is so profound. Even
if they end up in a hospital or prison for a few months, it doesn't
bother me. . . . The confusion is the greatest kind of confusion
for these kids, at any age. It opens the door and makes a mensch
of them.* The audience is relieved and ready for the catharsis of
humour after such unblessed controversy.

The necessary humorous relief is supplied by a Negro, a solid
and comely man who rises at the rear of the hall and announces
in a big resonant voice that he has only a single question to ask:
What is LSD? Although he has produced through the hall the
only titter of the evening, he meets a wall of impenetrable silence
on the stage. The questioner repeats his question, once, twice, a
third time. He becomes insistent: *I'm just asking a single question.
I hear you all talking about LSD. What I want to know is, what
is LSD?* After what seems forever—the audience is becoming res-
tive—someone onstage has the presence of mind to answer firmly:
It is a chemical. And the subject is closed; the questioner sits
down. Dr. Leary makes a few remarks about his LEAGUE FOR
SPIRITUAL DISCOVERY, much in the spirit of a preacher before the
plate is passed; no plate is passed, the evening has been an expense to no one. *We in the League are working, at risk, to legalise
marijuana and LSD. . . . It is an intimate family thing we're doing.*
Allen Ginsberg steps forward and announces an anti-war rally on
the following Saturday—no, not an anti-war rally, a "peaceable
march, a transcendence over anger." The meeting is at an end.

There is again no elbowing or pressing as the crowd begins to
leave the hall. Now, as not before the performance started, I begin
to see couples, pairs of boys and girls holding hands, much as
married couples leave funerals or weddings with clasped hands,
bound in the intimacy of shared deep emotion. (Dr. Leary, incidentally, could not be more pious than he is about coupling: approaching the sexual subject, he speaks only of "making love to
your wife.") It also becomes possible, here and there, to particularise other sightseers among the dedicated: the slowed-down
man in his late thirties who wears the mark of yearning, of loneliness, of the failed artist; the dykish, tight-lipped girl who belongs at the side of the swimming-pool of a women's "Y"; the

bookkeeper, as I am certain, who stands out in the crowd for her
excruciating neatness and spinsterishness no less than for her advanced years—it is she whom I overhear greeting an acquaintance:
"What did you think of it? Weren't you *impressed?*" These are
the wanderers between worlds.

But for the most part the audience is as one had first perceived
it: young, Village but middle-class, good contemporary faces of the
kind one wants to trust, the faces of people to whom intellectual
leadership might be thought appropriate, except that they had
made another choice and the signal of it is in their eyes. The four
of us appeal to each other: Is it only the gifted who go in for this
sort of thing? Are these the best, the brightest, of their generation? We of course haven't the answer, any more than we have
the answer to a corollary question, How can any enlightened person of whatever age take this psychedelic leader with intellectual
seriousness, assent in an ideology so barren of ideas? As we move
out on to the street, away from the theatre—unregenerate, we are
looking for a beer—this becomes, in fact, the nub of our anxiety.
For us, Dr. Leary's religious ceremony had been ridiculous when it
had not been despicable, but we had been surrounded by young
people of good education who not only could take Dr. Leary's drug
and this celebration of it but had also somehow managed to issue
to the whole subject of LSD a safe-conduct which exempted it
from rational inspection, creating—or perhaps only responding
to?—an atmosphere in which whoever would put it to adverse
question is automatically taken to be repressive, retrograde, lacking
in imagination, deficient indeed in scientific open-mindedness.

But Dr. Leary's epiphany gave rise to perhaps even bleaker
thoughts than these. In the past month I had heard of four
more young people, four adolescent children of friends, who
had broken down as a result of LSD—two college boys and a college girl who had had to be hospitalised, a high school boy who,
on the edge of psychosis, had had to be withdrawn from school.
This made, so far, seven LSD casualties within my own small
circle of acquaintance. Of course, some or all of them may have
been predisposed to mental breakdown. And we had no figures
to tell us whether they were in any way representative of what
could happen to Dr. Leary's followers. This being so, how long

were we to wait for the statistics to accumulate and be got in order?

For Dr. Alpert there were surely no such anxieties. "These kids" were simply casualties of the new dispensation, eggs that had to be broken to make Dr. Leary's omelette. But I could no more shrug off this concern, retreat into "scientific" or ironic detachment, than I could muster "objectivity" to meet the destruction of the young for the sake of some new Jerusalem of the political imagination. The destruction of a person's mental powers is *actual*, like hunger, poverty, death. It happens in actual life; it entails actual anguish. No, the nub of my anxiety as I left Dr. Leary's show was not that his audience could give credence to the nonsense he spoke—clever as so many of his young followers are, they have no doubt already learned to trust the LSD tale rather than its teller—but the recognition that the direction we take from our present-day assumption that the new and dissident are good in themselves, no matter what their form, may very well lose for us the basic and ordinary knowledge of human decency, including the knowledge that the human mind, even in all its weakness and error, is valuable.

Frank Sinatra

But now the days are short

I'm in the autumn of the year

And now I think of my life

As vintage wine

From fine old kegs. . .

There have been many entertainers who have performed before the American people since 1940—actors, singers, and comedians—but most of them have been as ephemeral as the passions that provoked their popularity. Frank Sinatra achieved fame early, faded temporarily, and then rose again to create so great a legend that he is now considered the show business version of a Renaissance Man: an actor and a director, a television star, business tycoon, and—primarily—a singer. A Sinatra version of a song is inimitable. One knows the voice, for it is part of the sound of our time, reflecting the life style of many Americans.

Born on December 12, 1917, in Hoboken, New Jersey, Frank Sinatra began singing as a young waiter of twenty at the Rustic Cabin in New Jersey. In the late 1930's he joined the bands of Harry James and Tommy Dorsey, whose smooth phrasing on the trombone he admired and began to imitate. His popularity grew quickly during the war years when he sang "slow, dreamy love songs" for crooning young people and appeared on a weekly radio program as well as in the movies, on theater stages and public platforms, throughout the country. Although his popularity declined in the late forties and early fifties, Sinatra entered an even broader phase of his career after his appearance in *From Here to Eternity*—his performance as Maggio resulted in the Academy Award for best supporting actor. From 1953 until the present day he has acted in many movies: *Guys and Dolls, Not as a Stranger, The Tender Trap, The Man with the Golden Arm, Pal Joey, The Manchurian Candidate, Come Blow Your Horn, None But the Brave,* and *The Detective.* He has also invested his money wisely and become extremely wealthy and powerful in the world of Hollywood. His professional interests have been diverse, but the most important phase of his career has always been his singing. It is no accident that Americans have dubbed him with the conclusive title of "The Voice."

Apart from his obvious talents as a singer—his well-modulated tone, his superb phrasing, his intimate and sensual interpretation of a song—Sinatra has always possessed the character of a nonconformist in an age of conformity. He uses the license of his wealth, fame, and power to do what he wants when he wants to, irrespective of public reaction. "A man possessed of as much charisma as anyone on public view," as one commentator puts it, "he is the senior swinger of the land." He seems the essence of youth and "in an age when the young seem to be taking over . . . Frank Sinatra survives as a national phenomenon." He can be the swinger, as in his madcap adventures with other stars like Dean Martin and Sammy Davis, Jr.; he can be the boss, reigning over many financial adventures; he can be the political activist or the defender of minority groups; he can be the temperamental star, by turns angry and happy, brooding and gentle. Behind all of these aspects of his personality, however, is a man who seems absolutely genuine. That quality enters into his singing. As a critic has remarked, he gives "the impression that he believes all the sentiments he is obliged to express, an accomplishment that is at times heroic."

A Measure of Sinatra

BURT

KORALL

DESPITE RUMORS to the contrary, no thunderclaps were heard when Frank Sinatra arrived on the national music scene in 1939. A matchstick of a man with a shock of curly hair, blue eyes, and Indian-high cheekbones dominating a memorably thin face, he joined Harry James's band after extensive freelancing in the New York area. Seemingly, still another pleasant, one-chorus, romantic singer of quiet interludes between instrumentals had been added to a faceless lot.

"But he had a quality; he touched people," recalls Johnny Richards, composer of the melody of "Young at Heart," one of Sinatra's biggest record sellers. "It wasn't something you could put your finger on. Yet each time he got up in front of Harry's band and sang, it happened; you could feel it."

From the outset Sinatra believed in the popular song as a vehicle for projection of feelings, and he thoroughly devoted himself to using it well. Like the many jazzmen with whom he had close contact during his six-month tenure with James and the subsequent two years within the Tommy Dorsey orbit, he sought to bring something extra to music. He dug for the meaning of each song, paying particular heed to enunciation and word shading, and he became concerned about breath control.

Night after night he heard trombonist Dorsey play long, mellifluous melody lines, sometimes extending to sixteen bars without obvious intake of breath. By applying the Dorsey concept to singing, Sinatra felt he could give more graphic and affecting readings of the lyric stories of songs. Much like a boxer in training,

REPRINTED FROM BURT KORALL, "A MEASURE OF SINATRA," *Saturday Review*, OCTOBER 15, 1966. COPYRIGHT 1966 SATURDAY REVIEW, INC.

he expanded the capacity of his lungs by swimming and running, developing to the point where with one breath he could take in almost 40 per cent more air than the average person. This, and his having learned to breathe through his nose while singing, brought a floating, easy feeling to his work. The vocal line, even on some of his Dorsey-RCA Victor recordings, seemed to flow unimpeded from one natural pause in the song to another. He worked carefully, thoughtfully, utilizing silences and glissandi for dramatic effect. Songs assumed graceful shapes.

All of this became more apparent after Sinatra left the Dorsey orchestra to go out on his own. He recorded a series of songs for Columbia, including "That Old Black Magic," "Sunday, Monday, or Always," "Nancy," and his theme, "Put Your Dreams Away," against a cushion of vocal or instrumental sound romantically arranged by Axel Stordahl. Touching, in a wistful manner, upon things of which dreams are made, he caught the country's fancy. The timing was right. Young girls were lonely. Men in the service sought a voice that spoke the language of fantasy, hope, and home. The young Sinatra, personifying the boy next door, filled a need. More importantly, he caught the temper of the times and its youth.

The type of material he recorded through the 1940s and the manner in which he sang supported his fantasy-youth image. He sounded shy rather than sure as he asked, yearned, for love. (Remember "Five Minutes More"?) The youthful sound of his voice in combination with his curiously believable lyric readings and unflagging dedication to musical detail, even his manner of dress —the casual sports coats and floppy bow ties—further defined this image.

As we turned the corner into the 1950s, there was a downward glide in Sinatra's fortunes. His voice began to slip away. Other singers, particularly the emerging Billy Eckstine, took his place in the affections of the public. The bottom seemed to have fallen out. Love ballads weren't selling as well as before. The music business had moved into a period of transition. Novelty recordings occupied top slots on the popularity charts. Sinatra, the romantic balladeer, was out of step and fast losing ground.

There is nothing as outdated as a fallen champion. Sinatra

tried television with varying results. He couldn't "buy" a hit record. An engagement in this period at New York's Paramount, the site of past triumphs, was indicative of the situation: The people just didn't come.

Then, after the release of his first Capitol records in 1953, the darkness that had hovered over Sinatra's career began to lift. The tempo of his life changed, and so did the tempo of his songs. He who had never sung rhythm songs with any great distinction made them the staff of his presentations. Nelson Riddle, Billy May, and others helped establish a more liberated Sinatra. Their arrangements pulsed and kicked, and Sinatra moved around within them with an abandon unknown during his association with Columbia Records. He took chances, improvised, sometimes changed lyrics to suit himself, experimented with rhythms. And always, as in *A Swingin' Affair* (Capitol W 803), the prototype album of the new Sinatra, there was swaggering strength, grabbing you by the lapels. Sinatra had become a fingersnapping, jazz-oriented swinger who sang about things the way they really are, using standards as his medium—his voice deeper, more flexible, tougher, less perfect. Little Boy Blue had faded in favor of a more realistic figure—the guy on the block who hung out on the corner, then left town and made it.

What had remained latent during the early years—the man himself—came through. Sinatra's work in other creative areas, particularly following his Academy Award-winning performance in *From Here to Eternity* (1953), reiterated the feeing established on records. In films he was our Pal Joey, the man on the town in *The Tender Trap* and *Come Blow Your Horn*, an Army major in *The Manchurian Candidate* . . . but unmistakably Sinatra.

Time and trouble, it would seem, had informed him and lent depth to his work. But, because the taste of comeback remains pungent years after the fact, there have been excesses—carelessly recorded performances and some films made with his friends (Dean Martin, Sammy Davis, Joey Bishop, etc.) which seem little more than home movies for public consumption. For all this, the size of Sinatra the artist is inescapable. When he cares, the results can be particularly moving.

Sinatra's fiftieth birthday late last year was the occasion for the release of a two-record set and a ballad collection worth savoring. Not intimidated by the passage of time, he pauses to talk and take stock of his career on *Sinatra: A Man and His Music* (Reprise R-1016), which contains recent remakes of his most popular recordings. He moves from his James hit, "All or Nothing at All," through Dorsey highlights such as "There Are Such Things" and "I'll Never Smile Again," through "Young at Heart" and "Witchcraft," to "Softly as I Leave You," "My Kind of Town," and "September of My Years."

For those of us over thirty, this retrospective package stirs memories and makes for contemplation of our youth. But the music and its interpretation do not trap the listener in a net of nostalgia, as is typical of projects of this genre. On the contrary, the set gives a true picture of the contemporary Sinatra. The lines show in the voice; the softer contours are gone. In lieu of youth, he offers experience, illuminating the inner nature of his songs as only a veteran can.

On *The September of My Years*, the second album in question, Sinatra muses on the private side of his past, thinking aloud via songs by Cahn and Van Heusen, Gordon Jenkins, Ervin Drake, Strouse and Adams, Wilder and Engvick, Bart Howard, Don Hunt, and Weill and Anderson. From all indications, this was a "special" album for him. There are few, if any, mistakes. Notes are beautifully sustained; melody and lyrics meld in the creation of telling vignettes. Given a free field within Gordon Jenkins's spare arrangements, he sings with facility and with the depth of feeling of one who cares, respects his art, himself and his audience. Listen to Drake's reflective "It Was a Very Good Year"; it is indicative of the flavor of this album—in sum, a measure of Sinatra.

Bob Dylan

How many years can some people exist
Before they're allowed to be free? . . .
The answer, my friend, is blowin' in the wind,
The answer is blowin' in the wind.

No singer of the 1960's has appealed to young people more than Bob Dylan. The reasons for his popularity reflect those of many other contemporary cult heroes: he has created his own distinct image of nonconformity; he defies authority of all kinds; he mocks the establishment; he is anti-intellectual; he protests social abuses and militarism; he is an advocate of the little man; and he gives the air of being absolutely authentic. He has been compared to Tom Paine, Huck Finn, and James Dean. He has suggested suffering to some people, lack of discipline to others. He has talked, in one man's view, "for every hung-up person in the whole wide universe" but to another he "is soon to be forgotten." Whatever the conflicting opinions may be, it is clear that Dylan has spoken for a whole new generation and in his personality one discovers some of the special characteristics of the young today.

Bob Dylan was born Robert Zimmerman on May 24, 1941, in Duluth, Minnesota, the older of two sons of Abraham Zimmerman, an appliance dealer. The family moved to Hibbing, Minnesota, where the boy taught himself to play the guitar at the age of ten. By fifteen he had mastered the piano, the autoharp, and the harmonica. Dylan has mentioned the various musicians who influenced his style during this formative period of his life: Woody Guthrie, the famous folksinger

of the thirties; Leadbelly, the Negro blues singer; Big Bill
Brownzy and Big Joe Williams, white country music figures;
Jimmy Rodgers, Hank Williams, and Hank Snow, western
country singers; Sonny Terry, the harmonica player; and the
actor, Charlie Chaplin. By the time young Robert Zimmerman had reached the age of eighteen he had run away from
home five times, and though he entered the University of
Minnesota on a scholarship in the spring of 1960, by the fall
he had already decided that he could not tolerate academic
discipline. He left his home and traveled to Texas, New
Mexico, California, Washington, Kansas, and elsewhere; in
1962, Zimmerman changed his name to Dylan, in honor of
Dylan Thomas whom he deeply admired, and the transformation from hillbilly to city billy was complete. Even Dylan's
name, one critic has said, "is an attempt to shift the blame
elsewhere."

In New York City, where he finally settled, Dylan liven in
the East Village and sang in coffee houses and small clubs.
In a short time he had achieved wide popularity. His records
in the country-style vernacular influenced, at the same time as
they represented, the sensibility of young people. "Blowin' in
the Wind" was an appeal for human compassion; "Bob
Dylan's Dream" suggested his own personal troubles; "With
God on Our Side" was an attack on people who justify war
in the name of religion; "The Times They Are a-Changin' "
considered the gap between the generations, Dylan naturally
sympathizing with younger people. "Until Bob Dylan came
along," a recording executive has remarked, "all of the hit
songs were lachrymose teen-age laments about unhappy high-
school love affairs. But now to an amazing degree, the hits
are about things like war, foreign policy, and poverty. . . .
All in all, Dylan has had a great deal of responsibility for the
surprising interest the younger generation has today in serious
questions like civil rights and Vietnam."

This mood of protest might be called Dylan's first period,

when his lyrics reminded many of the protest songs of the 1930's, the songs, for example, of Maxwell Anderson. Bob Dylan has been a restless performer and has not been content to repeat his early success. He has moved from country-blues singing, in which he accompanies himself with an unembellished guitar, to the use of an accoustical guitar; still later he invented folk-rock, in which he combines the folk song with the electronic beat of rock 'n' roll. Soon after his initial success, to use his own words, he gave up "finger-pointing songs . . . I don't want to write *for* people any more. You known—be a spokesman. . . . From now on, I want to write from inside me, and to do that I'm going to have to get back to writing like I used to when I was ten—having everything come out naturally. The way I like to write is for it to come out the way I walk or talk." This statement leads in turn to his current view that "I define nothing. Not beauty, not patriotism. I take each thing as it is, without prior rules about what it should be."

In his most recent record, *John Wesley Hardy*, Dylan returned to the accoustical guitar and to a fervent morality, claiming that "A song is moral just by being a song." Dylan had not been seen since May 1966 because of a near-fatal motorcycle accident. But his return was welcomed with enormous popularity. He is, as one writer puts it, "Youth's Absolute Hipster," a singer who attacks society but who is affirmative in that he expects his audience to understand exactly what he is saying. He has awkward syntax, imprecise diction; he is formally a mediocre singer. But his special combination of idealism and skepticism; his ability to capture the idiomatic speech rhythms; his vitality and wit and authenticity—these characteristics have made him a cult hero of the younger generation.

"The only thing where it's happening," Dylan has remarked, "is on the radio and records. That's where people hang out. It's not in book form; it's on the stage. All the art they been talking about, it just remains on the shelf." And yet, paradoxically, it is precisely his lyrics that have given Dylan the added dimension so many singers lack. "I write the song," he claims, "because I need something to sing. It's the difference between the words on paper and the song. The song disappears into the air, the paper stays. They have little in common. A great poet, like Wallace Stevens, doesn't necessarily make a great singer. But a great singer always—like Billie Holiday—makes a great poet."

The Sound of Dylan

ELLEN

WILLIS

NEARLY TWO YEARS AGO, Bob Dylan had a motorcycle accident. Reports of his condition were vague and he dropped out of sight. Publication of his book, *Tarantula*, was postponed indefinitely. New records appeared, but they were from his last album, *Blonde on Blonde*. Gruesome rumors circulated: Dylan was dead; he was badly disfigured; he was paralyzed; he was insane. The cataclysm his audience was always expecting seemed to have arrived. Phil Ochs had predicted that Dylan might someday be assassinated by a fan. Pete Seeger believed Dylan could become the country's greatest troubadour, if he didn't explode. Alan Lomax had once remarked that Dylan might develop into a great poet of the times, unless he killed himself first. Now, images of James Dean filled the news vacuum. As months passed, reflex apprehenson turned to suspense, then irritation: had we been put on again? We had. Friends began to admit, with smiles, that they'd seen Bobby; he was rewriting his book, he was about to sign a contract with MGM Records. The new rumor was that the accident had been a cover for retreat. After *Blonde on Blonde*, his intensive foray into the pop demi-monde, Dylan needed time to replenish his imagination. According to a less romantic version, he was keeping quiet till his contracts expired.

The confusion was typical. Not since Rimbaud said "*I* is another" has an artist been so obsessed with escaping identity. His masks hidden by other masks, Dylan is the celebrity-stalker's ultimate antagonist. The original disparity between his public pose as rootless wanderer with Southwestern drawl and the private facts of home and middle-class family and high school diploma in Hibbing, Minn., was a commonplace subterfuge, the kind that pays reporters' salaries. It hardly showed his talent for elusiveness; what it probably showed was naïveté. But his attitude toward himself as a public personality was always clear. On an early recording, he used the eloquent pseudonym, "Blind Boy Grunt," "Dylan" is itself a pseudoynm; possibly inspired by Dylan Thomas (a story Dylan now denies), possibly by a real or imaginary uncle named Dillon, who might or might not be the "Las Vegas dealer" Dylan once claimed was his only living relative.

In six years. Dylan's stance has evolved from proletarian assertiveness to anarchist angst to pop detachment. At each stage he has made himself harder to follow, provoked howls of execration from those left behind, and attracted an ever-larger, more demanding audience. He has reacted with growing hostility to the possessiveness of his audience and its shock troops, the journalists, the professional categorizers. His baroque press conference inventions are extensions of his work, full of imaginative truth and virtually devoid of information. The classic Dylan interview appeared in *Playboy*, where Nat Hentoff, like a housewife dusting her furniture while a tornado wrecks the house, pursued the homely fact through exchanges like: "Do you have any unfulfilled ambitions?" "Well, I guess I've always wanted to be Anthony Quinn in *La Strada*. . . . I guess I've always wanted to be Brigitte Bardot, too; but I don't really want to think about *that* too much."

Dylan's refusal to be known is not simply a celebrity's ploy, but a passion that has shaped his work. As his songs have become more introspective, the introspections have become more impersonal, the confidences of a no-man without past or future. Bob Dylan as identifiable *persona* has been disappearing into his songs, which is what he wants. This terrifies his audiences. They could accept a consistent image—roving minstrel, poet of alienation, spokesman for youth—in lieu of the "real" Bob Dylan. But his progressive self-annihilation cannot be contained in a game of let's pretend, and it conjures up nightmares of madness, mutilation, death.

The nightmares are chimerical; there is a continuing self, the

Bobby Dylan friends describe as shy and defensive, hyped up, careless of his health, a bit scared by fame, unmaterialistic but shrewd about money, a professional absorbed in his craft. Dylan's songs bear the stigmata of an authentic middle-class adolescence; his eye for detail, sense of humor, and skill at evoking the archetypal sexual skirmishes show that some part of him is of as well as in the world. As further evidence, he has a wife, son and house in Woodstock, N.Y. Instead of an image, Dylan has created a magic theater in which the public gets lost willy-nilly. Yet he is more—or less—than the sum of his illusions.

Many people hate Bob Dylan because they hate being fooled. Illusion is fine, if quarantined and diagnosed as mild; otherwise it is potentially humiliating (is he laughing at me? conning me out of my money?). Some still discount Dylan as merely a popular culture hero (how can a teen-age idol be a serious artist—at most, perhaps, a serious demagogue). But the most tempting answer—forget his public presence, listen to his songs—won't do. For Dylan has exploited his image as a vehicle for artistic statement. The same is true of Andy Warhol and, to a lesser degree, of the Beatles and Allen Ginsberg. (In contrast, James Dean and Marilyn Monroe were creatures, not masters of their images.) The tenacity of the modern publicity apparatus often makes artists' personalities more familiar than their work, while its pervasiveness obscures the work of those who can't or won't be personalities. If there is an audience for images, artists will inevitably use the image as a medium—and some images are more original, more compelling, more relevant than others. Dylan has self-consciously explored the possibilities of mass communication just as the pop artists explored the possibilities of mass production. In the same sense that pop art is about commodities, Dylan's art is about celebrity.

This is not to deny the intrinsic value of Dylan's songs. Everyone interested in folk and popular music agrees on their importance, if not their merit. As composer, interpreter, most of all as lyricist, Dylan has made a revolution. He expanded folk idiom into a rich, figurative language, grafted literary and philosophical subtleties onto the protest song, revitalized folk vision by rejecting proletarian and ethnic sentimentality, then all but destroyed pure folk as a contemporary form by merging it with pop. Since then rock-and-roll, which was already in the midst of a creative flowering dominated by British rock and Motown, has been transformed. Songwriters have raided folk music as never before for new sounds, new images, new subject matter. Dylan's innovative lyrics have been enthusiastically imitated. The folk music lovers who managed to evolve with him, the connoisseurs of pop, the bohemian fringe of the literary community, the turned-on searchers after absolute experience and of course teen-agers consider him a genius, a prophet. Folk purists and political radicals, who were inspired by his earlier material, cry betrayal with a vehemence that acknowledges his gifts.

Yet many of Dylan's fans—especially ex-fans—miss the point. Dylan is no apostle of the electronic age. Rather, he is a fifth-columnist from the past, shaped by personal and political non-conformity, by blues and modern poetry. He has imposed his commitment to individual freedom (and its obverse, isolation) on the hip passivity of pop culture, his literacy on an illiterate music. He has used the publicity machine to demonstrate his belief in privacy. His songs and public role are guides to survival in the world of the image, the cool, and the high. And in coming to terms with that world, he has forced it to come to terms with him.

II

By 1960, the folk music revival that began in the fifties had expanded into an all-inclusive smorgasbord, with kitschy imitation-folk groups at one end, resurrected cigarbox guitarists and Ozark balladeers at the other. Of music that pretended to ethnic authenticity, the most popular was folk blues—Leadbelly, Sonny Terry and Brownie McGhee, Lightnin' Hopkins. The response to blues was in part a tribute to the ascendancy of rock-and-roll—Negro rhythms had affected the consciousness of every teen-ager in the fifties. But blues, unlike rock, was free of identification with the dominant society. Its sexuality and rebelliousness were undiluted, and it was about people, not teen-agers. Besides, the

Negro, always a dual symbol of suffering and life-force, was gaining new political importance, and folk blues expressed the restlessness of activists, bohemians, declassé intellectuals. Since younger Negro performers were not interested in preserving a genre they had abandoned for more distinctly urban forms, white city singers tried to fill the gap. Patronized unmercifully by blues purists, the best of them did not simply approximate Negro sounds but evoked personal pain and disenchantment with white culture.

At the same time, there was a surge of folk composing. The Weavers, in the vanguard of the revival, had popularized the iconoclastic ballads and talking blues of Woody Guthrie, chronicler of the dust bowl and depression, the open road, the unions, the common man as intrepid endurer. Pete Seeger, the Weavers' lead singer in the early days and the most prestigious folk musician in the country, had recorded albums of topical songs from the thirties and forties. With the emergence of the civil rights movement, freedom songs, some new, some updated spirituals and union chants, began coming out of the South. Northern musicians began to write and perform their own material, mainly variations on the hard-traveling theme and polemics against racism, the bomb and middle-class conformity. Guthrie was their godfather, Seeger their guru, California songwriter Malvina Reynolds their older sister. Later, they were to acquire an angel— Joan Baez, who would record their songs and sing them at racial demonstrations and peace rallies; an organ—*Broadside*, a mimeographed magazine founded in 1962; and a sachem—Bob Dylan.

Gerde's Folk City, an unassuming, unbohemian cabaret in Greenwich Village, was the folk fan's chief New York hangout. On Monday, hootenanny night, blues interpreters like Dave Van Ronk, bluegrass groups like the Greenbriar Boys, the new topical songwriters—Tom Paxton, Phil Ochs, Len Chandler—would stop in and perform. Established singers came because Gerde's was part of the scene, because they enjoyed playing to the aficionados who gathered after midnight. The young ones came for a showcase and for contact with musicians they admired.

When Bob Dylan first showed up at Gerde's in the spring of 1961, fresh-skinned and baby-faced and wearing a schoolboy's corduroy cap, the manager asked him for proof of age. He was

19, only recently arrived in New York. Skinny, nervous, manic, the bohemian patina of jeans and boots, scruffy hair, hip jargon and hitchhiking mileage barely settled on nice Bobby Zimmerman, he had been trying to catch on at the coffeehouses. His material and style was a cud of half-digested influences: Guthrie cum Elliott; Blind Lemon Jefferson cum Leadbelly cum Van Ronk; the hillbilly sounds of Hank Williams and Jimmie Rodgers; the rock-and-roll of Chuck Berry and Elvis Presley. He was constantly writing new songs. On stage, he varied poignancy with clownishness. His interpretations of traditional songs—especially blues—were pretentious, and his harsh, flat voice kept slipping over the edge of plaintiveness into strident self-pity. But he shone as a comedian, charming audiences with Charlie Chaplin routines, playing with his hair and cap, burlesquing his own mannerisms, and simply enjoying himself. His specialty was composing lightly sardonic talking blues—chants to a bass run guitar accompaniment, a favorite vehicle of Woody Guthrie's: "Them Communists were all around/ in the air and on the ground/ . . . I run down most hurriedly/ and joined the John Birch society."

That fall, *New York Times* folk music critic Robert Shelton visited Gerde's and gave Dylan an enthusiastic review. Columbia Records signed him and released a mediocre first album in February, 1962. It contained only two Dylan compositions, both non-political. Dylan began publishing his topical songs in *Broadside*. Like his contemporaries, he was more propagandist than artist, his syntax often barbarous, his diction crude. Even so, his work stood out—it contained the most graphic descriptions of racial atrocities. But Dylan also had a gentler mood. Road songs like "Song to Woody" strove—not too successfully—for Guthrie's expressive understatement and simple, traditional sound.

In May, 1962, *Broadside* published a new Dylan song:

How many roads must a man walk down before you call him a man?
How many seas must a white dove sail before she sleeps in the sand?
How many times must the cannonballs fly before they're forever banned?
The answer, my friend, is blowin' in the wind, the answer is blowin' in the wind.*

* Copyright © M. Witmark & Sons, 1962.

Set to a melody adopted from a spiritual, "Blowin' in the Wind" combined indignation with Guthriesque simplicity and added a touch of original imagery. It received little circulation until nearly a year later, when Peter, Paul and Mary heard Dylan sing it at a coffeehouse. Their recording of the song sold a million copies, inspired more than 50 other versions, and established topical song as the most important development of the folk revival. The relative subtlety of the lyric made the topical movement aesthetically self-conscious. It did not drive out direct political statements—Dylan himself continued to write them—but it set a standard impossible to ignore, and topical songs began to show more wit, more craftsmanship, more variety.

"Blowin' in the Wind" was included in Dylan's second album, *The Freewheelin' Bob Dylan*, which appeared in May, 1963. This time, nearly all the songs were his own; five had political themes. It was an extraordinary record. The influences had coalesced; the voice, unmusical as ever, had found an evocative range somewhere between abrasion and sentimentality; the lyrics (except for "Masters of War," a simplistic diatribe against munitions-makers) were vibrant and pithy. The album contained what may still be Dylan's best song—"It's A Hard Rain's a-Gonna Fall," a vivid evocation of nuclear apocalypse that owed much to Allen Ginsberg's Biblical rhetoric and declamatory style. Its theme was modern, its spirit ancient. At first hearing, most of the *Freewheelin* songs sounded less revolutionary than they were: so skillfully had Dylan distilled the forms and moods of traditional music that his originality took time to register.

Freewheelin' illuminated Dylan's America—or rather, two Americas. "Hard Rain" confronted the underside, "where the executioner's face is always well-hidden," "where black is the color and none is the number," a world of deserted diamond highways, incipient tidal waves, clowns crying in alleys, children armed with guns and swords, "10,000 whisperin and nobody listenin" and occasional portents of redemption: "I met a young girl, she gave me a rainbow." The satirical "Talking World War III Blues" toured the country's surface: hot dog stands, parking meters, Cadillacs, rock-and-roll singers, telephone operators, cool females, officious doctors. Dylan's moral outrage coexisted with a grudging affection for American society and its foibles. If there was "Masters of

War," there was also "I Shall Be Free"; "My telephone rang, it would not stop, it was President Kennedy callin me up./ He said my friend Bob what do we need to make this country grow I said my friend John, Brigitte Bardot."

For a time, the outrage predominated. Dylan's output of bitter protest increased and his humor receded. He was still learning from Woody Guthrie, but he often substituted despair for Guthrie's resilience: his finest ballads chronicled the disintegration of an unemployed miner's family; the killing of a Negro maid, punished by a six-month sentence; the extremity of a penniless farmer who shot himself, his wife, and five kids. At the same time, his prophetic songs discarded the pessimism of "Hard Rain" for triumph in "The Times They Are a-Changin'" and vindictiveness in "When the Ship Comes In": "Then they'll raise their hands, say we'll meet all your demands and we'll shout from the bow, your days are numbered."

It was Dylan's year. Stimulated by the wide acceptance of his work, inspired by his ideas and images, topical songwriters became more and more prolific. Dylan songs were recorded by dozens of folk singers, notably Joan Baez (at whom he had once sneered, "She's still singing about Mary Hamilton. Where's that at?"). No folk concert was complete without "Hard Rain," or "Don't Think Twice," or a protest song from Dylan's third album, *The Times They Are A-Changin'*. The college folk crowd imitated Dylan; civil rights workers took heart from him; masochistic journalists lionized him. And in the attenuated versions of Peter, Paul and Mary, the Chad Mitchell Trio, even Lawrence Welk, his songs reached the fraternity house and the suburb.

Then Dylan yanked the rug: he renounced political protest. He put out an album of personal songs, and in one of them, "My Back Pages," scoffed at his previous moral absolutism. His refrain —"Ah, but I was so much older then, I'm younger than that now" —seemed a slap at the thirties left. And the song contained scraps of uncomfortably private imagery—hints of aesthetic escapism?

Folk devotees were shocked at Dylan's apostasy. Folk music and social protest have always fed on each other, and the current revival had been political all along. For children of depression activists growing up in the Eisenhower slough, folk music was a way of keeping the faith. When they converged on the Weavers' Town Hall hootenannies, they came as the anti-McCarthy resistance, pilgrims to the thirties shrine. The Weavers were blacklisted for alleged Communist connections; Pete Seeger had been *there*, singing for the unions, for the Spanish Republic. It didn't matter what they sang—in the atmosphere of conspiratorial sympathy that permeated those performances, even "Greensleeves" had radical overtones. Later, as the left revived, folk singing became a badge of involvement, an expression of solidarity, and most important, a history-in-the-raw of struggle. Now, Dylan's defection threatened the last aesthetically respectable haven for believers in proletarian art.

Dylan had written personal songs before, but they were songs that accepted folk conventions. Narrative in impulse, nostalgic but restless in mood, their central image the road and its imperative, they complemented his protest songs: here was an outlaw, unable to settle for one place, one girl, a merely private life, committed to that symbolic onward journey. His new songs were more psychological, limning characters and relationships. They substituted ambition for the artless perfection of his best early songs; "It Ain't Me, Babe," a gloss on the spiritual possessiveness of woman, took three stanzas to say what "Don't Think Twice, It's All Right" had suggested in a few phrases: "I'm thinkin and wonderin, walkin down the road/ I once loved a woman, a child I'm told/ gave her my heart but she wanted my soul." Dylan's language was opening up—doves sleeping in the sand were one thing, "crimson flames tied through my ears" quite another. And his tone was changing: in his love songs, ingenuousness began to yield to self-possession, the spontaneity of the road to the gamesmanship of the city. They were transitional songs, full of half-realized ideas; having rejected the role of people's bard, Dylan had yet to find a new niche.

III

In retrospect, Dylan's break with the topical song movement seemed inevitable. He had modeled himself on Woody Guthrie, whose incessant traveling was an emotional as well as economic necessity, whose commitment to radical politics was rooted in an individualism as compulsive as Dylan's own. But Guthrie had had to organize or submit; Dylan had other choices. For Guthrie, the road was habitat; for Dylan, metaphor. The closing of the iron mines had done to Hibbing what drought had done to Guthrie's Oklahoma, but while Guthrie had been a victim, Dylan was a bystander. A voluntary refugee from middle-class life, more aesthete than activist, he had less in common with the left than with literary rebels—Blake, Whitman, Rimbaud, Crane, Ginsberg.

The beauty of "Hard Rain" was that it exploited poetry while remaining a folk lyric, simple, repetitive, seemingly uncontrived. Now Dylan became self-consciously poetic, adopting a neo-beat style loaded with images. Though he had rejected the traditional political categories, his new posture was if anything more scornful of the social order than before. "It's Alright, Ma (I'm Only Bleeding)" attacked both the "human gods" who "make everything from toy guns that spark to flesh-colored Christs that glow in the dark" and their acquiescent victim, who "gargles in the rat-race choir." "Gates of Eden," like "Hard Rain," descended into a surreal nether-world, the menace this time a psychic bomb, the revolt of repressed instinct: "The motorcycle black madonna two-wheeled gypsy queen/ and her silver-studded phantom cause the gray flannel dwarf to scream." As poetry these songs were overrated —Howl had said it all much better—and they were unmusical, near-chants, declaimed to a monotonous guitar strum. Yet the perfunctory music made the bohemian commonplaces work—made them fresh. Perhaps it was the context: though few people realized it yet, the civil rights movement was losing its moral force; the Vietnam juggernaut was becoming the personal concern of every draft-age man; a new generation of bohemians, more expansive and less cynical than the beats, was about to blossom. The time was right for a reaffirmation of individual revolt.

But Dylan had also been exposed to a very different vision: in May, 1964, he had toured an England transformed by mod fashion and the unprecedented excitement over the Beatles and the Rolling Stones. When his new record came out the following spring, its title was Bringing It All Back Home. On the album jacket, a chiaroscuro Dylan, bright face emerging from ominous shadows, stared accusingly at the viewer. In black suit and striped shirt, he perched on a long divan, hugging a cat, behind him a modish, blank-faced beauty in scarlet lounging pajamas. The room, wreathed in light and dominated by a baroque mantelpiece, abounded with artifacts—*Time,* a movie magazine, a fallout shelter sign, folk and pop records (including earlier Dylan), a portrait, a candlestick, a few mysterious objects obscured by the halo.

Most of side one was devoted to "Gates of Eden" and "It's Alright, Ma." But the most arresting cut on the side was "Mr. Tambourine Man," a hymn to the psychedelic quest: "take me disappearing through the smoke-rings of my mind/ down the foggy ruins of time/ . . . take me on a trip upon your magic swirling ship." Drug-oriented bohemians loved it; it was another step away from the sobersided politicals. It was also more like a folk song than anything Dylan had written since giving up politics, a spiritual road song with lilting, singable melody.

The other side was rock-and-roll, Dylan on electric guitar and piano backed by a five-man band. It was not hard rock. There was no over-dubbing, and Dylan played his amplified guitar folk-style. But the beat was there, and the sound, if not overwhelming, was big enough to muffle some of the lyrics. These dispensed a new kind of folk wisdom. Chaos had become a condition, like the weather, not to analyze or prophesy but to gripe about, cope with, dodge: "Look out, kid, it's somethin you did/ God knows when but you're doin it again." The message was pay attention to what's happening: "Don't follow leaders, watch the parkin meters."

One rock song, "Subterranean Homesick Blues," was released as a single. As Dylan's pop debut it was a modest success, hovering halfway up the *Cash Box* and *Billboard* charts. That summer, Dylan cut "Like a Rolling Stone," the most scurrilous and—with its powerful beat—the most dramatic in a long line of non-love songs:

You used to ride on the chrome horse with your diplomat
who carried on his shoulder a Siamese cat
ain't it hard when you discovered that he wasn't really where it's at
after he took from you everything he could steal.*

It was a number one hit, as "Blowin' in the Wind" had been two years before—only now it was Dylan's own expressive snarl coming over radio and jukebox.

"Rolling Stone" opened Dylan's first all-rock album, *Highway 61 Revisited*. More polished but less daring than *Bringing It All Back Home*, the album reworked familiar motifs. The title song, which depicted the highway as junkyard, temple, and arena for war, was Dylan's best face-of-America commentary since "Talking World War III Blues." The witty and scarifying "Ballad of a Thin Man," which derided the rationalist bewildered by the instinctual revolt, was an updated "Times They Are a-Changin'," with battle lines redrawn according to pop morality. Dylan did not hail the breakdown of sanity he described but merely kept his cool, mocking Mr. Jones (the pop equivalent of Mr. Charlie) for committing squareness: "The sword-swallower he comes up to you and then he kneels/ . . . and he says here is your throat back, thanks for the loan/ and something is happening but you don't know what it is, do you, Mr. Jones?" "Desolation Row" was Dylan's final tribute to the götterdämmerung strain in modern literature—an eleven-minute freak show whose cast of losers, goons and ghosts wandered around in a miasma of sexual repression and latent violence underscored by the electronic beat: "Einstein disguised as Robin Hood . . ./ passed this way an hour ago with his friend, a jealous monk/ now he looked so immaculately frightful as he bummed a cigarette/ then he went off sniffing drainpipes and reciting the alphabet."

The violent hostility of traditionalists to Dylan's rock-and-roll made the uproar over "My Back Pages" seem mild. Not only orthodox leftists but bohemian radicals called him a sellout and a phony. At the July, 1965 Newport Folk Festival, he appeared with his electric guitar and was booed off the stage. . . .

Defiantly, Dylan exacerbated the furor, insisting on his contempt for message songs and his indifference to causes, refusing to agonize over his wealth or his taxes ("Uncle Sam, he's my *uncle*! Can't turn your back on a member of the family!"). In one notorious interview, he claimed he had written topical songs only to get published in *Broadside* and attract attention. Many former fans took the bait. Actually, Dylan's work still bristled with messages; his "opportunism" had absorbed three years of his life and produced the finest extensions of traditional music since Guthrie. But the purists believed in it because they wanted to. Their passion told less about Dylan than about their own peculiar compound of aristocratic and proletarian sensitivities.

Pure folk sound and idiom, in theory the expression of ordinary people, had become the province of middle-class dissidents who identified with the Common Man but whose attitude toward common men resembled that of White Russian expatriates toward the communized peasants. For them popular music—especially rock-and-roll—symbolized the displacement of the true folk by the mass. Rock was not created by the people but purveyed by the communications industry. The performer was incidental to engineer and publicity man. The beat was moronic, the lyrics banal teen-age trivia.

These were half-truths. From the beginning, there was a bottom-up as well as top-down movement in rock-and-roll: neighborhood kids formed groups and wrote songs: country singers adopted a rhythm-and-blues beat. Rock took a mechanized, acquisitive society for granted, yet in its own way it was protest music, uniting teen-agers against adults' lack of sympathy with youthful energy and love and sex. The mediocrity of most performers only made rock more "authentic"—anyone could sing it—and one of the few remaining vindications of the American dream—any kid from the slums might become a millionaire. (The best singers, of course, were fine interpreters; Elvis Presley and Chuck Berry did not have golden voices, but neither did Leadbelly or Woody Guthrie.) Rock-and-roll was further from the grass roots than traditional music, but closer than any other kind of pop. If the *realvolk* did not recognize this, the average adult did, and condemned the music for its adolescent surliness and its sexuality, covert in the lyrics, overt in the beat and in the intense response to idols.

But it remained for the British renaissance to prove that the mainstream of mass culture could produce folk music—that is, anti-establishment music. The Beatles, commercial without apology, delighted in the Americanized decadence of their environment. Yet their enthusiasm was subversive—they endorsed the reality of the culture, not its official myths. The Stones were iconoclastic in a different way: deliberately ugly, blatantly erotic, they exuded contempt for the public while making a fortune. Their cynicism, like Leadbelly's violence or Charlie Parker's heroin, was part of their charisma: unlike traditional folk singers, they could cheerfully censor their lyrics for Ed Sullivan without seeming domesticated—the effect was more as if they had paraded a sign saying "Blank CBS." British rock was far superior to most early rock-and-roll. Times had changed: electronic techniques were more sophisticated, radio stations and record companies less squeamish about sexual candor, and teen culture was merging into a more mature, less superficial youth culture with semi-bohemian tastes. Most important, the British groups successfully assimilated Negro music, neither vitiating rhythm-and-blues nor imitating it, but refining it to reflect their own milieu—white, lower-class, urban, technological, materialistic, tough-minded.

Most folk fans—even those with no intrinsic objections to rock, who had perhaps listened to it when they were teen-agers and not obliged to be serious—assumed that commercial exploitation automatically gutted music. Yet the Rolling Stones were creating as valid blues as any folk singers, black or white. After *Bringing It All Back Home,* the contradiction could no longer be ignored, and those not irrevocably committed to the traditional folk ethos saw the point. Phil Ochs praised *Highway 61*; Joan Baez cut a rock-and-roll record; more and more folk singers began to use electronic instruments. Folk-rock generated an unaccustomed accord between the folk and pop worlds. In *Craw-daddy!,* Richard Fariña lauded "this shift away from open-road-protest-flat-pick-style to more Nashville-Motown-Thameside, with the strong implication that some of us had been listening to the A.M. radio." Malvina Reynolds pronounced the new rock-and-roll "a wonder and delight." By November, 1966, folk-rock had received the final imprimatur—Pete Seeger recorded an album backed by three members of the Blues Project.

Folk-rock was never a form, but a simple-minded inspiration responsible for all sorts of hybrids. At first it was mostly rock versions of Dylan folk songs, social protest rock, and generational trauma rock, a weekend-hippie version of the classic formula, chil-

dren against parents. Then, self-styled musical poets Simon and
Garfunkel began imitating Dylan's apocalyptic songs ("People
bowed and prayed/ to the neon god they made/ . . . the words of
the prophets are written on a subway wall"), starting a trend to
elaborate and, too often, sophomoric lyrics. The Lovin' Spoonful
invented the "good-time sound," a varying mixture of rock, blues,
jug and old pop. Donovan wrote medieval fantasies and pop col-
lages like "Sunshine Superman" and "Mellow Yellow." And there
was acid-rock, the music of new bohemia.

Psychedelic music, like folk-rock, was a catch-all label; it described a variety of products shaped by folk, British rock, Chicago
blues, jazz, Indian music. Psychedelic lyrics, heavily influenced by
Dylanesque imagery, used the conventions of the romantic pop
song to express sexual and mystical rather than sentimental love
and focused on the trip—especially the flight—the way folk music
focused on the road. The Byrds, who had started folk-rock moving
with their hit record of "Mr. Tambourine Man," launched the
California psychedelic sound with "Eight Miles High," which
picked up on the Beatles' experiments with Indian instrumenta-
tion and was ostensibly about flying over London airport (it was
banned anyway by right-thinking disc-jockeys). Though the Byrds
were from Los Angeles, the scene soon shifted north, and a pro-
liferation of underground rock groups—some, like Jefferson Airplane, the Grateful Dead, and Country Joe and the Fish, quickly
surfaced—made San Francisco the new center of avant-garde pop,
superseding Britain.

The California groups came closest to making the term folk-
rock say something. For hippie culture, bastard of the beat
generation out of pop, was much like a folk culture; oral, naive, communal, its aphorisms ("Make love, not war," "turn on, tune in,
drop out") intuited, not rationalized. Pop and beat, thesis and
antithesis of the affluent society, contained elements of synthesis:
both movements rejected intellect for sensation, politics for art,
and Ginsberg and Kerouac glorified a grass-roots America that
included supermarkets and cars as well as mountains and apple
pie. The hippies simplified the beats' utopian anarchism and substituted psychedelic drugs for Zen and yoga; they also shared the
pop enthusiasm for technology and the rainbow surface of afflu-

ence—their music was rock, their style mod. Like Dylan, they
bridged old culture and new—they were still idealists—and they
idolized him. But he did not consider himself their spokesman.
At 25, he was too old ("How can I be the voice of their generation? I'm not their generation") and, though he did not admit it
publicly, too well-read. While "Mr. Tambourine Man" was becoming the hippie anthem, he was saying "LSD is for mad, hateful
people" and making fun of drugs in "Memphis Blues Again."
Dylan was really at cross-purposes with the hippies. They were
trying to embody pop sensibility in a folk culture. He was trying
to comprehend pop culture with—at bottom—a folk sensibility.

IV

It is a truism among Dylan's admirers that he is a poet using
rock-and-roll to spread his art: as Jack Newfield put it in the
Village Voice, "If Whitman were alive today, he too would be
playing an electric guitar." This misrepresentation has only served
to discredit Dylan among intellectuals and draw predictable snip-
ing from conscientious B-student poets like Louis Simpson and
John Ciardi. Dylan has a lavish verbal imagination and a brilliant
sense of irony, and many of his images—especially on the two
Blonde on Blonde records—are memorable. But poetry also requires economy, coherence and discrimination, and Dylan has
perpetrated prolix verses, horrendous grammar, tangled phrases,
silly metaphors, embarrassing clichés, muddled thought; at times
he seems to believe one good image deserves five others, and he
relies too much on rhyme. His chief literary virtue—sensitivity to
psychological nuance—belongs to fiction more than poetry. His
skill at creating character has made good lyrics out of terrible
poetry, as in the pre-rock "Ballad in Plain D," whose portraits of
the singer, his girl and her family redeem lines like: "With unseen
consciousness I possessed in my grip/ a magnificent mantelpiece
though its heart being chipped."

Dylan is not always undisciplined. As early as *Freewheelin'*, it
was clear that he could control his material when he cared to. But
his disciplines are song-writing and acting, not poetry; his words fit
the needs of music and performance, not an intrinsic pattern.

Words or rhymes that seem gratuitous in print often make good musical sense, and Dylan's voice, an extraordinary interpreter of emotion though (or more likely because) it is almost devoid of melody, makes vague lines clear. Dylan's music is not inspired. His melodies and arrangements are derivative, and his one technical accomplishment, a vivacious, evocative harmonica, does not approach the virtuosity of a Sonny Terry. His strength as a musician is his formidable eclecticism combined with a talent for choosing the right music to go with a given lyric. The result is a unity of sound and word that eludes most of his imitators.

Dylan is effective only when exploiting this unity, which is why his free verse album notes are interesting mainly as autobiography (or mythology) and why *Tarantula* is unlikely to be a masterpiece. When critics call Dylan a poet, they really mean visionary. Because the poet is the paradigmatic seer, it is conventional to talk about the film poet, the jazz poet. Dylan is verbal, which makes the label even more tempting. But it evades an important truth—the new visionaries are not poets. Dylan is specifically pessimistic about the future of literature. Far from Desolation Row, "The Titanic sails at dawn/ . . . Ezra Pound and T. S. Eliot fighting in the captain's towers/ while calypso singers laugh at them and fishermen hold flowers." The infamous Mr. Jones, with his pencil in his hand, his eyes in his pocket and his nose on the ground, is a literary man. With the rock songs on *Bringing It All Back Home*, Dylan began trying to create an alternative to poetry. If Whitman were alive today, he might be playing electric guitar; then again, he might be writing advertising copy.

In May, 1966, Dylan recorded *Blonde on Blonde*, a double album cut in Nashville with local musicians. Formally, it was his finest achievement since *Freewheelin'*, but while the appeal of the *Freewheelin'* songs was the illusion of spontaneous folk expression, the songs from *Blonde on Blonde* were clearly artifacts, lovingly and carefully made. The music was rock and Nashville country, with a sprinkling of blues runs and English-ballad arpeggios. Thematically, the album was a unity. It explored the sub-world pop was creating, an exotic milieu of velvet doors and scorpions, cool sex ("I saw you makin love with him,/ you forgot to close the garage door"), zany fashions ("it balances on your head just like a mattress balances on a bottle of wine,/ your brand-new leopard-skin pill-box hat"), strange potions ("it strangled up my mind,/ now people just get uglier and I have no sense of time"), neurotic women ("she's like all the rest/ with her fog, her amphetamine, and her pearls").

The songs did not preach: Dylan was no longer rebel but seismograph, registering his emotions—fascination, confusion, pity, annoyance, exuberance, anguish—with sardonic lucidity. Only once, in "Just Like a Woman," did his culture shock get out of control: "I can't stay in here/ ain't it clear/ that I just can't fit/ . . . please don't let on that you knew me when/ I was hungry, and it was your world." Many of the songs were about child-women, bitchy, unreliable, sometimes vulnerable, usually one step ahead: "I told you as you clawed out my eyes/ I never really meant to do you any harm." But there were also goddesses like Johanna and the mercury-mouthed, silken-fleshed Sad-Eyed Lady of the Lowlands, Beatrices of pop who shed not merely light but kaleidoscopic images: "these visions of Johanna are now all that remain."

The fashionable, sybaritic denizens of *Blonde on Blonde* are the sort of people despised by radicals as apologists for the system. Yet in accepting the surface that system has produced, they subvert its assumptions. Conservative and utopian ideologues agree that man must understand and control his environment; the questions are how, and for whose benefit. But pop culture defines man as a receiver of stimuli, his environment as sensory patterns to be enjoyed, not interpreted (literature and philosophy are irrelevant) or acted upon (politics is irrelevant). "If you want to understand me, look at my surface," says Andy Warhol. And "I like my paintings because anybody can do them." The bureaucrat defends standardization because it makes a complex society manageable. Yet he thinks of himself as an individualist, and finds the idea of mass-produced, mechanized art incomprehensible, threatening— or a put-on. The pop artist looks at mass culture naively and sees beauty in its regular patterns; like an anthropologist exhibiting Indian basket-weaving, Warhol shows us our folk art—soup cans. His message—the Emperor has no clothes, but that's all right, in fact it's beautiful—takes acceptance of image for essence to its logical extreme. *Blonde on Blonde* is about this love of surface.

Dylan's sensitivity to pop comes straight out of his folk background. Both folk and pop mentalities are leery of abstractions, and Dylan's appreciation of surface detail represents Guthriesque common sense—to Dylan, a television commercial was always a television commercial as well as a symbol of alienation. From the first, a basic pragmatism tempered his commitment to the passionate excesses of the revolutionist and the *poète-maudit* and set him apart from hipster heroes like James Dean. Like the beats, who admired the total revolt of the hipster from a safe distance, Dylan is essentially non-violent. Any vengefulness in his songs is either impersonal or funny, like the threats of a little boy to beat up the bad guys; more often, he is the bemused butt of slapstick cruelty. "I've got a woman, she's so mean/ sticks my boots in the washing machine/ sticks me with buckshot when I'm nude/ puts bubble gum in my food."

Dylan's basic rapport with reality has also saved him from the excesses of pop, kept him from merging, Warhol-like, into his public surface. *John Wesley Harding,* released after 20 months of silence, shows that Dylan is still intact in spirit as well as body. The songs are more impersonal—and in a way more inscrutable— than ever, yet the human being behind them has never seemed less mysterious. For they reveal Dylan not as the protean embodiment of some collective nerve, but as an alert artist responding to challenge from his peers. Dylan's first rock-and-roll songs were his reaction to the changes in life-style the new rock represented; *John Wesley Harding* is a reaction to the music itself as it has evolved since his accident. The album is comprehensible only in this context.

As Dylan's recovery advanced, he began making the papers again. He signed a new contract with Columbia—the defection to MGM never came off—and the company announced that he was recording. Dylan was still revered, his near-mythic status only solidified by his long absence from the scene. But whether he could come back as an active performer was another question. It was reported that he had listened to the first few cuts of *Sgt. Pepper* and snapped "Turn that off"; perhaps the new developments in rock had left him behind. On the other hand, perhaps he was leaving rock behind. Many of Dylan's associates—notably Tom

Wilson, his former A&R man—had always insisted that Dylan was much more sophisticated musically than he let on. And in May, a New York *Daily News* reporter quoted Dylan as saying he was at work on "two new sounds."

Ever since the emergence of the Late Beatles and the New Beach Boys, the "serious" rock groups had been producing albums that said, in effect, "Can you top this?" The competition extended to elaborate album covers and titles. By Christmas, the Stones had won the prize—*Their Satanic Majesties Request*, with its 3-D cover, was almost a parody of the whole art-rock phenomenon. How was Dylan going to top *that?* Everyone waited for a revolutionary masterpiece or an extravagant flop. What they got was *John Wesley Harding* in a plain gray jacket with a polaroid snapshot of Dylan and three Indians in the country. The first sound to greet the eager listener was the strumming of an acoustic guitar. The first line of the first song was "John Wesley Harding was a friend to the poor." Dylan had done it again.

The new melodies are absurdly simple, even for Dylan; the only instruments backing his guitar, piano and harmonica are a bass, a drum, and in two songs an extra guitar; the rock beat has faded out and the country and English ballad strains now dominate. The titles are all as straight as "John Wesley Harding": most are taken from the first lines of the songs. The lyrics are not only simple but understated in a way that shows Dylan has learned a trick or two from Lennon-McCartney, and they are folk lyrics. Or more precisely, affectionate comments on folk lyrics—the album is not a reversion to his early work but a kind of hymn to it. Nearly all the songs play with the clichés of folk music. The title song, for instance, seems at first hearing to be a second-rate "Jesse James" or "Pretty Boy Floyd." It starts out with all the catch phrases about the benevolent outlaw, then goes into the story: "It was down in Cheney County the time they talk about/With his lady by his side he took a stand." But the next line goes right out of it again: "And soon the situation was all but straightened out." You never learn what happened in Cheney County or why it wasn't *entirely* straightened out, and the song ends with more stock lines about the bandit's elusiveness and the helplessness of the law. It is not about John Wesley Harding, but about a familiar formula: and this, friends, is how you write the generic outlaw song.

Several of the songs are folk-style fantasies. "Frankie Lee and Judas Priest" is both a folk-ballad (based on another stock situation, the gambler on the road) and one of Dylan's surrealist dream songs; "As I Walked Out One Morning" describes a run-in with an Arthurian enchantress as if she were a revenue agent or the farmer's daughter. This juxtaposition of the conventional and the fantastic produces an unsettling gnomic effect, enhanced in some cases by truncated endings—in "The Drifter's Escape," the drifter's trial for some unknown offense ends abruptly when lightning strikes the courthouse, and he gets away in the confusion; "All Along the Watchtower" ends with a beginning, "Two riders are approaching, the wind began to howl." The aura of the uncanny that these songs create is probably what Dylan meant when he remarked, years ago, that folk songs grew out of mysteries.

But some of the album is sheer fun, especially "Down Along the Cove," a jaunty blues banged out on the piano, and "I'll Be Your Baby Tonight," a thirties-type pop tune that rhymes "moon" with "spoon" for the benefit of those pundits who are always crowing over the demise of "Tin Pan Alley pap." And "Dear Landlord," the best cut musically, is further evidence that Dylan has—well, the only word for it is mellowed:

Dear landlord, please don't dismiss my case
I'm not about to argue, I'm not about to move to no other place
Now each of us has his own special gift and you know this was meant
to be true
And if you don't underestimate me I won't underestimate you.*

In the end, what this album is about is Dylan's reconciliation with his past, with ordinary people, and even—warily, ambivalently—with his arch-enemies, the landlords of the world.

Of course, being Bob Dylan, he has turned this reconciliation into a rebellion. His sudden removal of the mask—see, it's me, a songwriter, I just want to write nice songs—and the apparent step backward could be as traumatic for the public as his previous metamorphoses; Dylan is still in the business of shaking us up.

* Copyright © Dwarf Music, 1967.

John Wesley Harding does not measure up to *Blonde on Blonde*. It is basically a *tour de force*. But it serves its purpose, which is to liberate Dylan—and the rest of us—from the *Sgt. Pepper* straitjacket. Dylan is free now to work on his own terms. It would be foolish to predict what he will do next. But hopefully he will remain a mediator, using the language of pop to transcend it. If the gap between past and present continues to widen, such mediation may be crucial. In a communications crisis, the true prophets are the translators.

Charles Schulz

*No problem is so big or complicated that it
cannot be run away from.*

⌊We live in an age which suspects the heroic gesture. The literary heroes of Bellow, Salinger, and Mailer are comic; the dramatic heroes of Albee are often absurd or pathetic; the fragility of a character like Benjamin in *The Graduate* seems more authentic than the sentimental heroism of movie stars from another period. Comic strips reflect the times in which they are created because their survival depends upon satisfying popular taste. One generation produces a serious version of Superman, Batman, Captain Marvel, and other mythical heroes; another generation uses these heroes for comic effects. "Peanuts," the creation of Charles Schulz, is the comic strip of our age, reaching more than 60,000,000 people in 700 newspapers in the United States, Canada, and 71 other countries. The world is too ferocious for Charlie Brown, Linus, and Snoopy, three of the characters in "Peanuts"; they all agree that "No problem is so big or complicated that it cannot be run away from."⌉

Charles Schulz was born in Minneapolis on November 26, 1922. He had a difficult time in school and did not attend college; but he soon realized his natural gift for drawing and, after teaching at a Minneapolis art school, he turned out a comic strip called "L'il Folks" for the St. Paul *Pioneer Press*. It was soon accepted by Manhattan's United Features Syndicate and in 1950, with the new name of "Peanuts," it appeared in many papers of the country.

The comics had long been featured in American newspapers—ever since "The Yellow Kid" was started in the 1890's. In the 1920's family comics like "The Gumps," "Blondie" (the eternal suburban housewife), and "L'il Orphan Annie" were popular. In the thirties the comic strips turned more dramatic as Dick Tracy shot his way to justice, Terry and the Pirates went to war against the Japanese, Joe Palooka won every fighting match, Buck Rogers and Flash Gordon rode in space, and Prince Valiant represented the medieval hero. There were other forms of solemnity, like "Mary Worth" (the eternal soap opera), "Brenda Starr" (the girl reporter), and "Rex Morgan" (the handsome doctor). Only a few strips were funny in the thirties and forties— "L'il Abner," for example, parodied the whole genre of serious comics by making judges, politicians, and business tycoons seem foolish. "In the fifties the funnies became funny again," to use the words of one comic researcher, as Walt Kelley's "Pogo" featured political satire; Mel Lazarus' "Miss Peach" showed school children satirizing their elders; and Mort Walker's "Beetle Bailey" saw the army through the eyes of an awkward buck private. "The new comics are the real Black Humorists," Al Capp (the creator of "L'il Abner") has observed, and no comic strip fits that description more aptly than "Peanuts."

The leading character of "Peanuts" is Charlie Brown— "everybody's Walter Mitty"—who finds that the world is too much for him. When Charlie calls to apologize for being late to a party, his host replies: "I didn't even know you weren't here." When he carves a girl's initials on a little tree, the tree breaks. Charlie has been called a caricature of the modern American man; his adversary—the modern, aggressive American woman—takes the form of Lucy van Pelt, who plagues Charlie and her younger brother Linus. Linus is the intellectual of the comic strip, who feels that "Security is a thumb and a blanket" and that "Sucking your thumb without a blanket is like eating a cone without ice cream." Snoopy, the dog with a foolish smile and huge ears, is a hedonist. Schroeder is the aesthete who is always playing the music of Beethoven. It is a varied little group, made up of some mean kids who are disturbingly like adults. Charles Schulz, who is a religious man, has didactic intentions. He believes that comic strips should be morally instructive. Whatever his intentions, he has created a highly entertaining and perceptive comic strip which satirizes the age. "Security is having someone to lean on," runs Schulz's famous phrase; and for many readers a little security is provided by knowing that Charlie Brown and his friends are less secure than themselves.

You're a Good Man, Charlie Schulz

BARNABY

CONRAD

ARTOONING is a *fairly* sort of a proposition," said Charlie Brown's creator recently. "You have to be fairly intelligent —if you were really intelligent you'd be doing something else; you have to draw fairly well—if you drew really well you'd be a painter; you have to write fairly well—if you wrote really well you'd be writing books. It's great for a fairly person like me."

For an only *fairly* person, Charles (Sparky) Schulz bids fair to becoming the most successful newspaper cartoonist of all time. "Peanuts," which appears in some 900 newspapers in the U.S. and Canada, plus 100 abroad, has endeared the characters of Charlie, Lucy, Linus, Schroeder and Snoopy to an estimated 90 million readers. Records, films, advertisements, sweatshirts, dolls, books, cocktail napkins and other "Peanuts" paraphernalia have capitalized on the craze to make it a $20-million-a-year industry. The statistics of the triumphs of the strip and its various offshoots are so staggering that its millions of fans—and even its creator—are wondering how the original quality and simplicity of the product can be maintained. As I was interviewing him in his studio—an unexpectedly over-decorated and plush office—near Sebastopol, Calif. (an hour north of San Francisco), the telephone interrupted constantly: A Hollywood producer wanted to talk about a big "Peanuts" musical movie; a caller wanted to know something about the London opening of the hit play "You're a Good Man,

REPRINTED FROM *The New York Times Magazine*, APRIL 16, 1967. COPYRIGHT 1967 BY BARNABY CONRAD. REPRINTED BY PERMISSION OF HAROLD MATSON CO., INC.

Charlie Brown" (now running Off Broadway in New York), another wanted information on his new paperback, "The Unsinkable Charlie Brown." And then there were all the calls from people who wanted him to paint posters for charities, make personal appearances or donate money to this or that cause. Each time Schulz—who, with his crew cut and serious boyishness looks like every freshman's senior adviser—hung up the phone with a sigh. It was not a sigh of exasperation, but rather regret—regret that he was not always able to do the many things that people demand of him.

"I usually get between 400 and 500 letters a week and for years I've managed to answer all of them personally, but I don't know." He leafed through some of the letters. "Most of them are so nice and their requests are so polite and worthwhile—a drawing for a crippled kid, a poster for a special high-school dance. 'Just do a quick sketch of Snoopy,' they ask; 'it'll only take five minutes.' And they're right—it *would* only take five minutes. But they think their letter is the only one on my desk. The five minutes have to be multiplied by hundreds." He looked mournfully at the heap of mail. "Thousands. They forget that I not only have to do some drawing, I occasionally have to do some thinking."

He looked out of his studio window and studied a clump of trees beyond an artificial pond. "It's hard to convince people when you're just staring out of the window that you're doing your hardest work of the day. In fact, many times when I'm just sitting here thinking and therefore working like heck I hear the door open and I quickly grab the pen and a piece of paper and start drawing something so that people won't think I'm just goofing off and anxious to have a little chat. But I like visitors when I'm drawing. It gets lonely up here all day, not like an office or a dentist or somebody who has company around him all the time." Schulz has been termed a recluse but he says: "Oh, we go to San Francisco about once a month, see friends, go to a play. But we aren't night-clubbers or cocktail types. Neither of us drink, never have, just isn't part of our life and our friends just have to accept us like that."

He picked up some more letters. "Lots of people write in ideas.

Some are good, but I don't seem to be able to use other people's suggestions. Here's a pretty good one—'Why not make Snoopy pretend he's a Grand Prix racing driver?' Now that's not a bad idea, and I guess it would work. But first of all, I didn't think of it, and secondly I'd be imitating myself—sort of copying the Snoopy and the Red Baron business. It's always dangerous to copy yourself. Al Capp had a great success with the Schmoos, so then he had to try to repeat with the Kigmies and it wasn't as good. The Red Baron was a good idea but let's not imitate it. My son says he gave me the idea for that—he was working on a World War I model and claims he suggested the Red Baron business, but I don't remember. People think I'm a World War I nut and send me these"—he gestured at shelves of flying books.

I asked him about the hit record "Snoopy and the Red Baron," based on the dog's flights of fancy and aerial encounters with The Red Baron, the king of World War I skies. "I based the Baron on Richthofen because he's sort of the Beethoven of flying. Incidentally, I never heard about this record by the Royal Guardsmen until a friend said, 'Great song you wrote.' I checked with my lawyer the next day and we put a stop to that right away. Or rather we threatened to put a stop until we were included in the success. I understand they've sold two and a half million copies of it already." (Shulz gets a varying percentage of two other hit records as well—Vince Guaraldi's "Jazz Impressions of Charlie Brown" and "Charlie Brown's Christmas," put out by Fantasy Records.)

"Speaking of records, have you heard this?" He picked up the album of "You're a Good Man, Charlie Brown," and played the overture. "I'd like to see the show, but haven't really had time. Maybe next month we'll get to New York, but first I'm taking my wife and four of our five kids and four kids of friends of ours to Sun Valley for our first real vacation in two years. I hear it's a good show—love the music."

The Off Broadway play, made up of prose taken from "Peanuts" strips, opened on March 7 at Theater 80 St. Marks. In his ecstatic review Walter Kerr wrote: "They [the people of 'Peanuts'] have marched clean off that page of pure white light . . . and into forthright, fuming, explosively funny conversation without losing a drop of the ink that made their lifelines so human."

When Schulz talks he is every bit as modest and unassuming as one could want the progenitor of "Peanuts" to be, yet there is a pride of profession in his voice. "Hollywood wants to make a movie of the play and I guess some day we'll do something. There was a nice fellow up here recently who produced 'To Kill a Mockingbird,' and we talked pleasantly. But the moment they start talking about 'their writers' I kind of get chills. I want it to be my words in everything I do. Just as I guess I'm the only cartoonist who doesn't have a helper to do the Sunday strip or fill in backgrounds and stuff. I even do my own lettering. I've thought of it— hiring someone to help. Sometimes I think it would be nice. But then—what would be the point? I don't do this for the money"— he gestured at his big drafting table with several half-inked-in strips on it. "People think I do, but I don't. I do it because I love to draw.

"The things I like to do best are drawing cartoons and hitting golf balls. Now if I hire someone to do my work for me what fun would I get? It'd be like getting someone to hit the golf ball for me. But maybe I'll have to." He glanced balefully at his secretary as she brought in a new stack of mail. "*Life* magazine said I was a multimillionaire—heck, no cartoonist can become a millionaire— but that's what the magazine said and now I'm getting requests for money from all over the world."

Whether or not he is in the millionaire bracket yet, Schulz lives like one. On his 28-acre estate, Coffee Grounds (on Coffee Lane), he has two elegant houses besides his big studio. Then there are stables, a cat, dog and horse per child, a tennis court, a baseball diamond and a four-hole golf course. He is an excellent golfer, 5 handicap, and shoots consistently in the 70's. The highlight of his year is the coveted invitation to the Crosby golf tournament in Monterey. He tries to play golf once a week, but as his success mounts and the work load increases he has to forego more and more games.

Schulz begins his day at 9:30 by walking the quarter mile from his sprawling one-level house across the lawns of his golf holes, past the big swimming pool to his studio. With a secretary in the outer office and a plush living room before you arrive at the place

where he actually draws, it could very well be the office of a successful real-estate broker or a pre-need cemetery-lot salesman.

Clinically neat and organized, Schulz sits at the drawing board
and begins by playing around on a scratch pad with a pencil,
doodling situations and ideas. He tries to conceive of the week's
work as a whole; six separate days' drawings which will somehow
make a unity. When he has the ideas fairly well set in his mind he
takes a 28-inch illustration board, which has the margins of the
four panels printed on it already, and inks in the dialogue. When
he has all six days' strips "dialogued in," he begins to draw the
figures and the action, preferring to draw directly with the pen
with a minimum of penciled guidelines.

One day's strip takes him about an hour to draw. The Sunday
page takes the whole day. He is required by the syndicate to be
five weeks ahead on the daily and eleven weeks ahead on the
Sunday. When I called on him he was just finishing up the strips
for the week of May 8 to May 13, the theme being "Be Kind to
Animals Week." (In one sequence, Snoopy is holding a sign with
that legend on it, and as Lucy goes by he shuts his eyes and
puckers up for a kiss. "Not on your life!" bellows the dear girl,
bowling the dog and his sign over backward. Another day ends
with Snoopy's saying: "This was a good week—I didn't get
kicked.")

Right now Schulz is also busy preparing an hour-and-a-half
film, plus another TV special. (He writes every word, and super-
vised the animation of the other three TV specials.)

The books are a further drain on his time. Since the first one,
called plain "Peanuts," Holt has published some 4,493,000 copies,
and they are all in print. After Holt has had a year or two to sell
a "Peanuts" book at $1, the rights are turned over to Fawcett,
which takes the Holt volume, splits it in two, and sells each copy
for 40 cents. To date Fawcett has sold 12 titles to the tune of 10
million copies. But the publishing doesn't end there. A few years
ago an enterprising San Francisco woman named Connie Boucher
persuaded Schulz to do a book for her Determined Productions
company. It turned out to be "Happiness Is a Warm Puppy," and
it was on *The New York Times*' best-seller list for 45 weeks in
1962 and 1963. This was followed by more "Happiness Is—"

books, plus a Peanuts Date Book, totaling around three million copies in all. In 1965 the John Knox Press published "The Gospel According to Peanuts," being the theological thoughts extracted from the strip, which has been that firm's best seller of all time at more than 635,000 copies.

⌊Which brings one to another consuming interest of Charles Schulz: religion. A member of a Scripture-oriented Protestant nondenominational organization called the Church of God, he keeps 12 Bibles, plus a set of the dozen volumes of the Interpreters' Bible, in his studio. On Sundays he teaches Sunday School in Sebastopol ("to adults only—I could never teach other people's children"). A pushover for charities and organizations designed to help people, he recently consented to accept the chairmanship of the National Aid to the Visually Handicapped and set about organizing a huge golf tourney, to be known as the "Charlie Brown-Lucy Tournament," the proceeds of which will go to the aid of partly blind children. He brooded for weeks over a request to do a poster for Aid for Retarded Children, tried dozens of ideas, and finally had to give up. "There was simply no way to do it without the danger of seeming to mock them."

⌊So this is the hectic world that was created by Charlie Brown/ Schulz (he confesses that they are one and the same person). How did it come about and how did it snowball into these proportions?⌉

Charles Monroe Schulz, as every good "Peanuts" aficionado knows, was born 44 years ago in Minneapolis, Minn. When he was two days old, he was nicknamed "Sparky" by his family for Barney Google's horse Sparkplug, and is still called that by his family and friends. From almost the beginning he wanted to become a cartoonist, thinking it among the noblest of the artistic professions.

"It's a great art," he says now. "I'm convinced it's much harder and more important than illustration. Look at that"—he points to a framed original cartoon page of "Krazy Kat" by George Herriman—"that's art. It was done around 1912 and its humor is every bit as fresh today as then."

Sparky's early life was very Charlie Brownish. "People read a lot into the strip, and I guess what people see in it, that's what's in it. But actually the strip is just about all the dumb things I did when I was little."

In fine Charlie Brown fashion he was the goat on the baseball field, once losing a game 40 to nothing, and even his drawings were turned down by the high-school yearbook. In the Army he was similarly unsuccessful. After being trained as a machine gunner, he discovered he had forgotten to load his weapon the one and only time he was confronted by members of the enemy forces.

"It was the last week of the war and we were going along a road in Southern Germany in a halftrack and somebody said, 'Hey—look over there, there's somebody in that hole over there in the field, shoot him.' So I swung the gun around—50-caliber— pressed the butterfly trigger, and nothing happened. Before I could load he came out with his hands up and I was sure glad I hadn't been able to shoot him."

After the war he got a job lettering a comic magazine, then taught in a Minneapolis art school of the "Draw-me-and-win-a-scholarship" mail-order variety. A fellow instructor was named Charlie Brown, and later unwittingly lent his name to posterity. Another had a pretty blue-eyed sister named Joyce Halverson, and Schulz married her. In 1948 he sold his first cartoon, to *The Saturday Evening Post*. Then he did a weekly cartoon for The St. Paul *Pioneer Press* called "L'il Folks." Within a year it was dropped. After many rejections from other syndicates, it was picked up by United Features in Manhattan. Over Schulz's protests it was renamed "Peanuts." To this day he is still indignant.

"What an ugly word it is," he says disgustedly. "Say it: *Peanuts!* I can't stand to even write it. And it's a terrible title. Now 'Peppermint Patty' is a good title for a strip. I introduced a character named that into the strip to keep someone else from using it. Funny, people don't tell you how to draw or write but EVERYBODY's an expert on titles."

The first month Schulz made $90 with his newly titled strip. A few months later it was up to $1,000 a month. Now, 17 years later, it is close to $1,000 a day.

"Funny," Sparky muses, "I never set out to do a cartoon about kids. I just wanted to be a good cartoonist, like, say, Herriman or my boyhood idol, Roy Crane, who draws 'Buz Sawyer'—a fine cartoonist. I always dreamed of some day coming up with some permanent idea or phrase that would pass into the language, like Snuffy Smith's 'bodacious' or some of Al Capp's gimmicks. I guess maybe 'Good grief' has made it. And perhaps the Great Pumpkin. And the 'Happiness Is . . .' title.

"There are a lot of good cartoonists around. I read all of 'em. Capp, Caniff, 'Miss Peach.' It pleases me that my children seem to like 'Peanuts' as well as any of the others. They know all the books by heart and have favorite strips on their walls and play the records. It's all very gratifying."

When asked about Snoopy, who is my family's favorite character in the strip, he said, "Snoopy's not a real dog, of course—he's an image of what people would like a dog to be. But he has his origins in Spike, my dog that I had when I was a kid. White with black spots. He was the wildest and smartest dog I've ever encountered. Smart? Why, he had a vocabulary of at least 50 words. I mean it. I'd tell him to go down to the basement and bring up a potato and he'd do it. I used to chip tennis balls at him and he'd catch and retrieve 'em." Schulz's sensitive face clouds at the memory. "Had him for years before he died."

[Many psychiatrists who charge a good deal more than Lucy van Pelt's 5-cent consultation fee have tried to analyze the special appeal of "Peanuts." My pedestrian conclusion is that Charles Schulz feels the loss of his dog Spike today as deeply as—or more deeply than—he did a quarter of a century ago, just as he feels the loss of his childhood. Happily for the readers, he is able to translate this long memory and deep feeling into words and pictures. It seems to be universal, either because we had a childhood like that, or wish we had. There's a little Charlie Brown in all of us males and, Lord knows, we've all known, and maybe even married, a Lucy van Pelt, a girl who shouts: "I don't want any downs—I just want ups and ups and ups." Certainly there's been *someone* in each one of our lives ready and eager to pull away the football just as we're about to kick it.

So very often the strip touches chords that remind us of things and homely events we thought we had forgotten. As the catalogue for the recent Whitney exhibition of Andrew Wyeth (Schulz's favorite painter, along with Picasso) stated: "But art arises in the human spirit beyond the reach of words from the levels of deepest memories. We are creatures who need the near and the familiar as well as the exotic."

Emerson wrote in 1838: "A man must have aunts and cousins, must buy carrots and turnips, must have barn and woodshed, must go to market and to the blacksmith's shop, must saunter and sleep and be inferior and silly."]

[Another factor in the strip's popularity with all ages is his sublime handling of how far the fantasy should go. For example, Snoopy's dog house is always shown in profile; we never see it three-quarters view or actually go inside it. We just accept the fact when it is said that Snoopy has a Wyeth and a Van Gogh and a pool table in there, but if we actually saw inside and discovered an unbelievable dog house we would cease to believe in Snoopy as a dog and his relationship with the children. Another all-important factor in Schulz's astonishingly good batting average is his unfailing sense of what is subtly funny.]

"I get letters all the time," he told me, "from optometrists saying, 'How come you're always talking about ophthalmologists' —Linus wore glasses, you know—'why not give us a break?' It's hard to tell them that ophthalmology is somehow funny and the word optometry just isn't. Like Beethoven. My favorite composer is Brahms—I could listen to him all day—but Brahms isn't a funny word. Beethoven is, so I gave him to Schroeder. Like names: Linus is a good name. I borrowed that from a friend, Linus Maurer. Funny, the other night I was trying to think of a good last name for Pigpen—he hasn't got one—and I fell asleep and I dreamed of a new character named José Peterson. That's a good name, isn't it? But I only put him in the strip for a week—he was a baseball player—but he just didn't belong, so out he went, along with some others I've gotten rid of. My strip is not like the kind that depends on variety or new characters. I've got pretty much the same characters and basic idea that I had 17 years ago. I want to keep the strip simple. I like it, for example, when Charlie Brown watches the first leaf of fall float down and then walks over and just says,

'Did you have a good summer?' That's the kind of strip that gives me pleasure to do.

"I liked one I did that I got from one of my children—the only idea I've ever gotten right from something they did or said. We were at the dinner table and Amy was talking away on a real talking streak and finally I said, 'Can't you *please* be quiet?' and she was silent for a moment and then picked up a slice of bread and began to butter it, saying, 'Am I buttering too loud for you?'

"I gave the line to Charlie Brown after Lucy yelled at him. And I like the violent action ones, kids getting bowled over and such things that cartoons were born to do. Too many of these new strips are not cartoons—they're imitations of films, and the movies can do it so much better, beat them at their own game. But I like the quiet ones too. I like it when Linus says, simply: 'Sucking your thumb without a blanket is like eating a cone without ice cream.' I like it when Charlie Brown gets all excited about a big spelling bee and then goes out on the first word because they say, 'Spell "maze," ' and, being the good baseball fan he is, he spells it 'Mays.' I like to keep it all simple. For instance, it seems to me that Snoopy's been getting pretty fantastical lately. I think I'll simplify him, let him just be a dog for a while.

"Incidentally, Snoopy wasn't in the most popular strip I ever did, the one I've had the most mail on. That was the one where the kids are looking at the clouds and Linus says, 'See that one cloud over there? It sort of looks like the profile of Thomas Eakins, the famous portrait painter. And that other group over there—that looks as though it could be a map of British Honduras. And then do you see that large group of clouds up there? I see the stoning of Stephen. Over to the side I can see the figure of the apostle Paul standing.' Then Lucy says, 'That's very good, Linus. It shows you have quite a good imagination. What do you see in the clouds, Charlie Brown?' And Charlie says, 'Well, I was going to say I saw a ducky and a horsey, but I've changed my mind.' "

The phone rang and he talked for a while. When he hung up he said, "That was something about having a helicopter be attacked by the Red Baron. Over Chicago. They've got a real German World War I plane. Publicity stunt of some kind." He shook his head incredulously, and a little sheepishly, at the world he had created. "Where's it all going to end?"

Where, indeed, is it all going to end? Last Thursday I came home from work, hungry for dinner, to find the entire kitchen given over to the making of a two-foot birthday cake for my daughter. It was in the shape and color of Snoopy. Like any other red-blooded male of this generation, I could only look straight out of the panel at the reader and say, "Good grief!"

John Paul Getty

If you can count your money, you
don't have a billion dollars.

"Let me tell you about the very rich," F. Scott Fitzgerald wrote in "The Rich Boy." "They are different from you and me. They possess and enjoy early, and it does something to them, makes them soft where we are hard, and cynical where we are trustful, in a way that, unless you were born rich, it is very difficult to understand. They think, deep in their hearts, that they are better than we are because we had to discover the compensations and refuges of life for ourselves. Even when they enter deep into our world or sink below us, they still think that they are better than we are. They are different."

[Although John Paul Getty—the richest man in America and probably in the world—refutes Fitzgerald in the following essay, his own character seems quite close to the novelist's formulation. "The whole pattern of his life," as one biographer notes, has been "an attempt at reconciliation of the two fundamental ideas in which he was raised, rugged American individualism and privileged *laissez-faire*, combined with a fighting antagonism to the levelling, conformity, and mediocrity of socialism."]

John Paul Getty was born in Minneapolis on December 15, 1892. He attended the University of Southern California at Los Angeles and the University of California at Berkeley, and took graduate work in economics and political science at Oxford University. [By the age of twenty-three, Getty had made a million dollars in Oklahoma oil. After a period as a "playboy," he branched into California oil and by 1923 he was worth $15 million.] Getty became the general manager of George F. Getty, Inc., from 1930–1933; the director of the Petroleum Corporation from 1932–1934; and director of the Tidewater Association Oil Company from 1932–1936. Since 1942 he has been the president and general manager of the Sparta Aircraft Company.

[In the 1960's Getty wrote a series of articles for *Playboy* magazine on "Men, Money and Values in Today's Society." His various maxims read like a twentieth-century version of Poor Richard and express his character so precisely that further analysis becomes unnecessary:

"Luck, knowledge, hard work—especially hard work—a man needs them all to become a millionaire."

"The ability to wait, to resist a quick profit, to save to avoid selling, and to resist the advice of friends who recommend a sale—that adds up to one of the secrets of success."

"Another secret is never to delegate authority other than what's purely administrative. . . . I like Benjamin Franklin's advice: 'If you want it done correctly, do it yourself.' I do it all myself."

"The young men of today are inclined to trade their opportunities for what they call 'security'. . . . These men also tend to overspecialize. They wind up knowing one aspect of business thoroughly, but are often ignorant of the operations of the department a few doors down the hall. You've got to take risks in order to make money."

"I blame at least some of the average man's reluctance to get out on his own and take business risks on the influence women have over him."

"In building a large fortune it pays to be born at the right time."

The World Is Mean to Millionaires

J. PAUL

GETTY

NEVER have the burdens of wealth been greater than they are today, and never have its rewards been slimmer. Rich people once lived in a world apart; today almost the only difference between the multimillionaire and the reasonably well-to-do man earning $15,000 to $25,000 a year is that the millionaire works harder, relaxes less, is burdened with greater responsibilities and is exposed to the constant glare of publicity.

The greatest difference lies in the exposure to publicity. As soon as this is published, I know my mail will increase from an average low of 50 letters a day to 300, 400 or even 1,000. My two secretaries will be working overtime for weeks dealing with long letters from complete strangers, usually written in crabbed, almost indecipherable handwriting, and headed "Dear Paul"—so that they *might* conceivably be from old friends, long lost sight of. Some will be from cranks and religious maniacs, urging me to give away my riches for the good of my soul; but mostly they'll be from people who genuinely need—or at any rate claim to need—financial assistance for themselves or their families, or from perfectly well-to-do people who wish me to contribute to their pet charities. A few, like one I received recently, will demand "one million dollars by return mail since you have so much of the stuff."

I have received up to 2,000 letters a day. Obviously, if I read them all, I'd have time for nothing else. And if I acted on them, I'd be bankrupt very quickly. Calculating the average request at

REPRINTED FROM *The Saturday Evening Post*, JANUARY 2, 1969, BY PERMISSION OF THE AUTHOR.

$500, with an average of 200 letters a day, I would hand out about $100,000 a day for the rest of my life if I obliged every request for funds that is imposed on me.

I want to make it clear that I don't resent this state of affairs. I accept it as part of the penalty of being rich and known. I don't resent such publicity as comes my way. On the contrary, I feel that throughout my life the press has been overwhelmingly fair, even friendly to me. Like the publicity, the letters are part of the price I pay for being a millionaire. I hate rudeness, but I can't reply personally to all the letters I receive. So I have a polite printed reply, a "Mr. Getty regrets," which my secretaries use in most cases.

But this is not to say that I am indifferent to all the unwanted attention. Indeed, it often annoys me. Perhaps it's the lack of consideration of the well-to-do solicitors for charities that irks me most: It doesn't seem to occur to these people that I, too, have charities I'm interested in, and that I'd never dare to do indiscriminate fund-raising among acquaintances of mine, let alone total strangers. As Groucho Marx once said, in an unforgettable hotel-lobby scene: "Boy, what are you shouting my name for? Do I go around shouting your name?"

The charity solicitors, and those who write straightforward begging letters, display an elementary ignorance of the basic financial facts of life which is almost touching. They seem to think that all my wealth is in cash, ready for distribution. It never occurs to them that, as an active businessman, I invest my money, or that I'm in competition, in the oil business, with some of the world's largest corporations. Even successful corporations have to borrow money for expensive, essential development, and no successful corporation, to my knowledge, has ever had a surplus of liquid cash. Why should these people assume that I do?

I first became aware of the penalties of being rich when my father died. I was 37. My father's affairs had never been publicized during his lifetime, and he died a very wealthy man. The size of his estate was commented on in the press. The effect was instantaneous. My mother, Sarah Catharine Getty, his widow, then aged 78, received hundreds of proposals of marriage from total strangers from all over the world. Acquaintances who had never paid particular attention to me would come up and say, "You related to that rich oil man who died the other day?" When I explained, they'd say, "You mean to say he was your *father?*" and I could see in their eyes a sinister glint that hadn't been there before. Constant exposure to this sort of thing has, I suppose, made me wary of the "old friend" who calls up, just because—or so I first suppose —he is glad to see me. I am glad to see him, but I become depressed when I realize that he doesn't really want to see me at all: What he wants is a loan. I have become gun-shy about such people, to the extent of never carrying on my person any sizable amounts of cash.

If I were convinced that by giving away my fortune I could make a real contribution toward solving the problems of world poverty, I'd give away 99.5 percent of all I have immediately. But a hard-eyed appraisal of the situation convinces me this is not the case. The best form of charity I know is the act of meeting a payroll. If I turned over my entire fortune to a charitable foundation, would it do any more good than I do with it? The answer is no. However admirable the work of the best charitable foundation, it would accustom people to the passive acceptance of money—and incidentally deprive of their jobs thousands of hard-working people associated with me.

I disagree, now more than ever, with Scott Fitzgerald's often-quoted remark to Ernest Hemingway: "The rich are different from us." Take the case of the man earning $20,000 a year and compare him with the multimillionaire. Looking at them, more often than not, you simply can't tell the difference. They wear the same clothes, drive the same cars, and live in more or less the same style. In fact, most multimillionaires I've known have been rather frugal in their personal expenditure. I doubt whether many of them spend more on groceries than the man with $10,000 a year. The limousine was once a status symbol. It isn't any longer. Neither are yachts, private planes or world tours. Look at the hundreds of thousands of Americans today who own small yachts (the only kind worth having, in my view) or fly private planes or travel round the world.

One of the few status symbols left to the really rich is art collecting, but even in this field the true value of the picture isn't necessarily in its price. I can prove my point: the best picture I ever acquired was a Raphael, picked up in a sale for $112. Not many modern painters will acquire Raphael's stature, but a small investment in a picture can get you a great picture, if you have taste and a certain amount of luck. The connoisseurs who recognized the genius of Jackson Pollock before he became famous did not only acquire great paintings. They also made a fortune.

When I was a boy, multimillionaires owned huge steam yachts, with large crews. I had one—until 1936. It gave me so much trouble I felt I was in the shipping business. If I ever buy a yacht again, it'll be a small one I can handle—and enjoy handling—myself. As far as I'm concerned, the transatlantic liner of today is more comfortable than the most luxurious private yacht, and the scheduled airliner as comfortable as—and a good deal safer than—the most expensive private plane.

Since multimillionaires have been stripped of so many status symbols and must live very much as other people do, they should, I think, be entitled to the same courtesies. If I go to a doctor, I should be charged the regular fee. If I go to a hotel, I should pay the standard charge for a room. And when I tip, I shouldn't be expected to tip more than the average man. It's rude and inconsiderate to overtip. It only makes things difficult—and embarrassing—for people who are not as rich as I am.

But can really rich people live completely normal lives? It isn't easy. Speaking personally, I find it necessary to insulate myself so I can keep away from professional hangers-on—and I've got awfully good at spotting them. I'm always slightly wary about meeting strangers. Most of my social life revolves round old friends whom I know really well. Not all of them are wealthy—but none of them is obsessed with money. For some years, in Paris, I lived in a hotel room, partly because a hotel provides the same kind of protection from strangers as that afforded by a fleet of servants in a mansion.

I must concede that I'm not overcharged systematically, but some restaurants do inflate my bill, and so do some hotels—and a doctor or two. When that happens, I retaliate very simply by crossing the place, or the specialist, off my list. It isn't quite so easy to cope with the unwarranted attention given to little things

I do, especially if money is involved. There was this business of
the pay phone I had installed in my country house in England
to be used by my guests. When *I'm* staying with friends and have
to make long-distance calls, I make a point of making them from
a pay phone in the nearest town or village. I had the pay phone
installed in my place because I knew that guests preferred it that
way. It saved them the trouble of settling with me afterward, or of
attempting to pay for their phone calls. It saved them trouble.
And yet a spate of letters and cartoons resulted. You might have
thought I was pathologically inclined, instead of taking the simple,
rational step.

Just as a millionaire has to be wary about hangers-on, he has to
be wary about the feminine company he keeps. This is where the
rich man is penalized enormously for being rich. The penalty he
pays for divorce makes many a rich man unwilling to marry in
the first place. Whereas it's generally assumed that the multimillionaire should pay no more than the next man for a meal, a
hotel room or a doctor's bill, it's regarded as normal for a judge
in an American divorce court to impose the maximum settlement
the husband can afford. Old-established family fortunes, usefully
invested for the benefit of society, have been broken by excessive
divorce judgments. The multimillionaire who marries is always
possible prey. His wife may not be the classic gold-digger, but she
may become neurotically intent on obtaining the maximum settlement, either to humiliate her husband or as a kind of revenge.
And lawyers will egg her on and encourage her wildest demands.

We all know of women who make life unbearable for their
husbands, in little ways which can never be proved in court. I
find it incredible that such women can obtain millions of dollars
for having suffered the misfortune of being married to multimillionaires. It is offensive that the more spendthrift and extravagant
such a woman has been during her marriage, the more she can
legitimately claim as being commensurate to her standard of
living. I also find it strange that a woman can claim huge sums
of money earned by her husband's creative talent and without
her help during their marriage.

Most very rich people who end up in the divorce courts have
very unpleasant experiences, and this is perhaps why millionaires

often marry women who have money of their own, and generally mix with people of comparable incomes. There is less risk of an unpleasant situation arising. Most ordinary wives have nothing to gain from divorce. In the case of the millionaire, women have every incentive to behave unscrupulously.

With all these problems, why bother to become a millionaire in the first place? In my case, I inherited a certain amount of wealth and was determined to use this wealth constructively. I take a certain pride in running a corporation, if not more successfully than other people, at any rate just as successfully as most. I could have turned all my assets into liquid cash, instead of working at the drilling business as I do, an average of 12 hours a day— longer hours, incidentally, than your average-income business executive or salary earner. But that, to my mind, would have been running up the white flag and admitting that the responsibilities were too much for me. And I've never felt tempted to give my fortune away to buy my way into a better mood. There are people, of course, who have been destroyed, physically and morally, by their wealth. The same people, born poor, would probably have become alcoholics or thieves.

Though our rewards may be small, we are, if our society is to remain in its present form, essential to the nation's prosperity. We provide others with incentives which would not exist if we were to disappear. As active businessmen, we find it useful to have money simply because a tolerable margin of financial security makes for increased efficiency and competitiveness. If I were not using my fortune usefully, I would have little justification for having it in the first place. And if you then took it away, it wouldn't make all that much difference to me. At least I wouldn't be getting all those letters.

Hugh M. Hefner

I am in the center of the world.

Since World War II there has been a sexual revolution in America. Magazines, movies, books, and plays have enjoyed freer expression than ever before. At the crest of the revolution rides *Playboy: Entertainment for Men,* whose "naked girls," in the words of the editor Hugh Hefner, have become "a symbol of disobedience, a triumph of sexuality, an end of Puritanism." Not everyone agrees with Hefner. Some feel that "Hefner and *Playboy* give the feeling that there is more freedom for everybody around the bend. But it is the kind of freedom children want: doing what they please without concern about whom they hurt." Others believe that "*Playboy* really feeds on the repressed fear of involvement with women, which for various reasons is still present in many other adult Americans." The criticisms are great and varied, but the magazine prospers. At the center of the *Playboy* world, dominating not only over the magazine but also over a vast home of forty-eight rooms and thirty-seven servants ("a Disneyland for adults"), the various *Playboy* clubs spread through the world, the *Playboy* calendars and cufflinks, the *Playboy* anthologies and record clubs, is Mr. Playboy of the Western World, the libidinous Horatio Alger—Hugh Marston Hefner.

Hugh Hefner was born on April 9, 1926, the son of devout Methodists. As a boy Hefner disliked the fundamentalist ethics of his God-fearing parents, although his rebellion against conformity did not manifest itself until later in his life. Hefner concentrated on psychology at the University of Illinois, graduating with a B.S. in 1949. After briefly studying in the Graduate School at Northwestern University he entered the magazine world and was in turn a subscription promotion writer for *Esquire* (1951), a promotion manager for Publisher's Development Corporation in 1952, and circulation manager for *Children's Activities Magazine* in 1953. In 1953 he launched *Playboy* with $1,400, using the famous Marilyn Monroe calendar picture in the first issue. From the outset the magazine was popular, but its sales increased phenomenally when Hefner combined female nudity with female innocence: the "playmate of the month," according to Hefner, is "a young, healthy girl—the girl next door."

"What is a playboy?" the editors of *Playboy* were once asked. "Is he simply a wastrel, a ne'er-do-well, a fashionable bum? Far from it: he can be a sharp-minded business executive, a worker in the arts, a university professor, an architect or engineer. He can be many things, providing he possesses a certain *point of view*. He must see life not as a vale of tears, but as a happy time; he must take joy in his work, without regarding it as the end and all of living; he must be an alert man, an aware man, a man of taste, a man sensitive to pleasure, a man who—without acquiring the stigma of the voluptuary or dilettante—can live life to the hilt. This is the sort of man we mean when we use the word 'playboy.' "

Think Clean

THE BUZZ of cocktail chatter and the clink of ice cubes shrink the vast room with its monumental fireplace, paneled walls, beamed 22-ft. ceiling and two suits of medieval armor. Soft, round girls curl up with boy friends on couches beneath immense paintings by Franz Kline and Larry Rivers. The men are relaxed, confident, plainly well off. A scene straight out of *Playboy* magazine? Precisely. The men are mostly magazine employees, and the girls are some of the 24 bunnies who room upstairs. A couple of centerfold "Playmates," disarmingly pretty and ingenuous-looking in party dresses, sip Pepsi-Cola.

Then stillness and a turning of heads. Down a few steps from a doorway in the corner of the room walk a man and a woman— he, casual in slacks and cardigan sweater; she, sleek in blonde hair and black dress. Simultaneously, a full-sized movie screen begins a silent descent down a side wall. *Playboy* Editor-Publisher Hugh Marston Hefner, 40, sinks into a love seat that has been saved for him beside the 15-ft.-long stereo console. His girl friend, *Playboy* Cover Girl Mary Warren, 23, slips alongside him, puts her head on his shoulder. A butler brings a bowl of hot buttered popcorn and bottles of Pepsi; the lights dim; the movie begins. Last week it was Michelangelo Antonioni's *Blow-Up*, the week before Claude Lelouch's *A Man and a Woman*.

After the movie, buffet supper is served in the bunny dining room. "Hef" (nicknames abound) and Mary chat for awhile, then stroll off to his private quarters. These include a duplex of offices, living room, bedroom (an adjoining room serves as a TV taping studio), all ankle-deep in white carpet. Once Hef has retired, his guests may amuse themselves as they see fit. The top floor of the house, used as a bunny dormitory by the Chicago Playboy club, is

REPRINTED BY PERMISSION FROM THE MARCH 3, 1967, ISSUE OF *Time*, THE WEEKLY NEWSMAGAZINE; COPYRIGHT TIME INC., 1967.

off limits. Very much available, however, is the heated, kidney-shaped first-floor swimming pool (bathing suits, if desired, are supplied by the house). If guests want seclusion, they may swim through a gentle waterfall to a hidden grotto furnished with soft cushions and background music. Privacy is not complete, however, the grotto can be observed through a trap door in the main hall above. The way to a nightcap is a brisk slide down a brass firehouse pole leading to a bar, where a glass wall gives an underwater view of the pool.

Spectator Sex

To some visitors, the trap door and the glass wall are the real symbols of Hugh Hefner's achievement. Bacchanalia with Pepsi. Orgies with popcorn. And 24 girls—count 'em, 24—living right overhead! Not to mention all those mechanical reassurances, like TV and hi-fi. It is all so familiar and domestic. Don Juan? Casanova? That was in another country and, besides, the guys are dead. Hugh Hefner is alive, American, modern, truthworthy, clean, respectful, and the country's leading impresario of spectator sex.

Hefner's pad on Chicago's North State Parkway has become a considerable tourist attraction, with guided tours available to anyone who has a minimum of pull. It is also the monument to a major American business success story. Unlike other Chicago businesses, the enterprise is not founded on steel, grain or transportation, but on a magazine. One of the great publishing successes since World War II, *Playboy* was started in 1953 with a 70,000 press run, now has a 4,000,000 circulation.

The magazine has many things to offer, but the basis of success is the nude or seminude photograph that Hugh Hefner has made respectable in the U.S. prints. America was undoubtedly ready for it anyway, but Hefner seized the moment. He was the first publisher to see that the sky would not fall and mothers would not march if he published bare bosoms; he realized that the old taboos were going, that, so to speak, the empress need wear no clothes. He took the old-fashioned, shame-thumbed girlie magazine, stripped off the plain wrapper, added gloss, class and culture. It proved to be a surefire formula, which more sophisticated and experienced competitors somehow had never dared contemplate.

The Ultimate Life

Apart from the nudes, *Playboy* offers fiction, reportage and interviews, reasonably amusing and bawdy cartoons, some dirty jokes, and discussions by sociologists and theologians. Above all, in vivid color and enthusiastic text, the ultimate life of material and sensual pleasure is abundantly demonstrated for some imaginary man about town. Latest male fashions are on display; so are sleek cars, sumptuous stereo sets and fine wines and foods, with instruction on when, how and to whom to serve them. There is always the suggestion that sex is part of the successful life, that good-looking women are status symbols. Says Paul Gebhard, executive director of Indiana University's Kinsey-founded Institute for Sex Research: "Hefner's genius is that he has linked sex with upward mobility."

Not content just to picture all these pleasures, Hefner has brought many of them to life, sort of. He operates 16 Playboy Clubs. He has opened a Caribbean Playboy resort in Jamaica and has started construction of a $9,000,000 year-round resort near Lake Geneva, Wis. Last year "HMH" enterprises sold $2,400,000 worth of products, ranging from tie clasps bearing the bunny insigne to bunny tail wall plaques.

Hefner has also experienced some commercial failures, including *Show Business Illustrated,* which folded after nine issues with an estimated loss of $2,000,000, and *Trump,* a *Mad*-like humor magazine. On the other hand, the newly formed Playboy Press is thriving; last year, it sold $1,000,000 worth of books, most of them containing reprints from the magazine. At present, *Playboy*'s staff is moving into larger quarters in Chicago's venerable Palmolive Building, leased for 63 years for $2,700,000. Thanks to eager press-agents, the building's famed beacon, whose beam can be seen 500 miles away, has been renamed the Bunny Beacon.

Just Accessories

In both his magazine and its allied enterprises, Hugh Hefner is a prophet of pop hedonism. He instinctively realized what sociologists had been saying for years—that the puritan ethic was dying, that pleasure and leisure were becoming positive and universally adored values in American society. As psychiatrist Rollo May has pointed out, a new puritanism has developed, a feeling that enjoyment is imperative, that to live the full, uninhibited life (in sex as in other areas) is everyone's duty.

Hefner is clearly a new-style puritan, but in many ways he is an old-style one as well. He works to spread the gospel of pleasure with a dogged devotion that would do credit to any God-driven missionary or work-driven millionaire. How much real pleasure his Chicago pleasure dome holds for Hefner is a question his friends and associates sometimes wonder about. There is even something slightly puritanical about the magazine itself. Says Harvard theologian Harvey Cox: "*Playboy* is basically antisexual. Like the sports car, liquor and hi-fi, girls are just another *Playboy* accessory."

Unlike the other accessories, *Playboy*'s girls are out of reach—real in the imagination only. Shapes in the pictures all have an implausible gloss, achieved by lights that flatter and airbrushes that remove blemishes, but most of all by a mind convinced that to be real would not be ideal—and probably obscene. In their creamy perfection, their lack of any natural disorder, their stilted poses and expressionless faces, they recall nothing so much as the ivory-skinned, perfectionist nudes of Victorian and classical paintings, of Ingres, Boucher, and David—the paintings that Grandfather used to steal a glance at on his first trip to Europe.

Beyond Parody

The magazine girls have their living counterparts in the Playboy Club bunnies—700 round little girls in glorified corsets that push their bosoms out, cinch their waists in, run to a sharp V in front and feature a cottontail in the rear. The bunnies also seem unreal (one cynic suggested they are made of plastic), but they are provocative enough for the management to pass a rule against dating the customers. The rule might not be necessary. As the manager of the London Playboy Club, who obviously knows his customers, says: "The basic conventioneer doesn't want to go to bed. He just wants to gawk."

In designing and running the Playboy Clubs, Hugh Hefner has effortlessly soared beyond parody or spoof. No satirist could improve on the thick bunny manual, which commands her, among other things, to remember "your proudest possession is your bunny tail. You must make sure it is always white and fluffy." If it is not, she gets five demerits.

Kinseyan Revelation

"The whole thing," says London *Observer* Columnist Katharine Whitehorn, "is a midwestern Methodist's vision of sin." She is absolutely right. Hefner's parents, Glenn and Grace, had been childhood sweethearts in Nebraska before they married and moved to Chicago. Glenn, an accountant who is now treasurer of *Playboy*, was and is a regular Methodist churchgoer; so is Grace. In his early years, Hefner was the kid across the aisle in school who was always scribbling sketches. He liked to write up the doings of local kids for a neighborhood newspaper, and drew 70 cartoon strips about ornery Western outlaws, an interplanetary space traveler and a diabolical villain named Skull.

After graduating from high school, he enlisted in the Army for an uneventful two years. Discharged, he enrolled in the University of Illinois, largely because of another student there named Millie Gunn. While at Illinois, Hefner read Kinsey's *Sexual Behavior in the Human Male*. It came as a revelation, and he wrote an indignant review in the campus humor magazine. "Our moral pretenses," he said, "our hypocrisy on matters of sex, have led to incalculable frustration, delinquency and unhappiness. One of these days," he promised, "I'm going to do an editorial on the subject."

Aim for the Libido

After 2½ years, Hef graduated from college, married Millie and, with his cartoons tucked underneath his arm, canvassed the Chicago publishing world for a job. Nothing doing, so he took a job with a Chicago firm that produced and printed cardboard cartons. It was, says Hefner, the closest thing to journalism he could get. Eventually he landed a job with the subscription department of *Esquire* magazine. But when, after several months, he asked for a $5-a-week raise, he was turned down. He went to work briefly for a publication called *Children's Activities*, but he decided it was time to start his own magazine—and not for kids. In 1953 he hocked his furniture for $600, scraped together $10,000. He later persuaded a talented designer, Art Paul, to become his art director. Most other magazines for men concentrated on the outdoors, so he shrewdly decided to take up where *Esquire* had left off in catering to indoor tastes. Hefner first wanted to call his magazine *Stag Party*, but a sheet with a similar name protested. Then Eldon Sellers, now an executive vice president with the company, suggested *Playboy*.

Inspired by *Esquire's* popeyed little man about town, "Esky," Hefner picked a bunny to symbolize the new enterprise—because rabbits are the playboys of the animal world. The first issue in December 1953 told readers that "we plan to spend most of our time inside. We like our apartment." Hefner also bought rights to the famed nude calender pictures of Marilyn Monroe, then at the height of her career, and published them for the first time off a calendar. The 48-page issue sold 53,991 copies; even Hef was surprised.

From then on, he aimed *Playboy* straight at the libido. Since sex is part of the whole man, he reasoned, why not devote part of a whole magazine to it? "Would you put together a human being that is just a heart and toenails?" he asks. So he put together a magazine that was largely bosom and thigh and not especially distinguished from other girlie slicks. But he added more substantial content as he went along; today's *Playboy* is a well-stuffed product, bulging with intellectual ambitions and self-confidence.

It even includes some tips from John Paul Getty on how to succeed in business. The humor, however, remains on a fairly primitive level. A typical cartoon shows a playboy in bed with a bunnyesque girl, asking: "Why talk about love at a time like this?"

To begin with, fiction published in *Playboy* was spicy but hardly shocking—long-forgotten efforts by John Steinbeck, Erskine Caldwell, Somerset Maugham, Robert Ruark. *Playboy* also dipped into the ribald classics; despite constant mining, the Boccaccio and De Maupassant vein is still running strong. In the early days, name writers shunned *Playboy*. Today, Vladimir Nabokov, James Baldwin, Kenneth Tynan, Herbert Gold, Ray Bradbury and Ken Purdy regularly provide respectable material. This upgrading of fiction is largely due to Auguste Comte Spectorsky,* 56, who was hired from NBC by Hefner to bring some New York know-how and sophistication (a favorite *Playboy* word) to the magazine. "*Spec*" has done that and more. Last summer he hired as fiction editor Robie Macauley, who had been running the distinguished *Kenyon Review*. "I was familiar with *Playboy*," says Macauley. "The students at Kenyon read it—so did the clergy. Besides, a magazine like this matures as it goes along."

Dream World

Maturing or not, *Playboy* still exists in a rather special world. Partly it can be seen in the ads, some of them for Hefner products. A four-color promotion for the 1967 *Playboy* calendar reads: "Make a date with these twelve Playmates. You won't want to miss a day with this delicious dozen . . . Provocative . . . in captivating new poses. SHARE THE JOY!" Perhaps nostalgic older readers can hear an echo in these lines of the candy butcher during intermission at the burlesque show, peddling the latest "pictures direct from Paris with each and every luscious pose guaranteed the way you gentlemen like it."

In general, though, *Playboy* ads are discreet—no stag movies, no sex manuals. "*Playboy* takes the reader into a kind of dream world," explains Advertising Director Howard Lederer. "We create

* Named for the 19th century French Positivist philosopher who added the word "sociology" to the language.

a euphoria and we want nothing to spoil it. We don't want a reader to come suddenly on an ad that says he has bad breath. We don't want him to be reminded of the fact, though it may be true, that he is going bald."

The dream extends to the magazine's editorial content, but there reality does intrude. Viet Nam has hardly even been mentioned in its columns, but there have been eloquent pleas for abolishing the draft and capital punishment, and a defense of the right to privacy by Senator Edward Long. Long, long question-and-answer interviews, some of them aggressive and stimulating, lately recorded the views of Fidel Castro, Mark Lane and Norman Thomas—just the thing to read aloud to a date in front of the fire, he wearing a Playboy sweater, she wearing Playmate perfume.

The magazine also has its own special crusades. It recently brought enough pressure to win a parole for a West Virginia disk jockey who was serving a one-to-ten-year sentence for a morals offense with a consenting teen-age girl. Another notable success involved a campaign against entrapment tactics practiced by—no, not the CIA but, of all agencies, the Post Office. Seems that postal inspectors were in the habit of placing an ad in a newspaper to the effect that one "swinger" would like to meet another. When letters were exchanged, the unsuspecting hedonist might include a nude photograph or two—whereupon the police arrived and arrested him.* Bowing to a *Playboy*-organized protest movement, as well as complaints from Congress, the Post Office promised to quit the practice.

Playboy has good reason to keep the mails safe for swingers, although the magazine itself has had little trouble with obscenity laws. Hefner was once arrested by the Chicago police after he ran some nude photos of Jayne Mansfield, but the case ended in a hung jury.

Girls *con Brio*

"Every issue of *Playboy*," Hefner has said, "must be paced like a symphony." While there may be a scherzo of cartoons, a

---

* *Playboy* has itself practiced entrapment at times by hiring private investigators who pretend to be eager Johns and ask club bunnies for a date. If the bunnies are dumb enough to accept, they may get fired.

largo of literature, a rondo of reportage, the allegro in each edition is still the girls, and *molto con brio*. Although girl pictures
take up less than 10% of the pages, they remain the main motif.
The style for the centerfold Playmate was set by the maestro himself. He chose a rather average though well-endowed girl named
Charlene Drain who worked in his subscription department. She
said the department needed an Addressograph machine. Sure, said
Hef, provided she would pose in the nude. She agreed, became
"Janet Pilgrim" and appeared in the July 1955 issue. The circulation department got its machine, and "Janet" became, for a while,
head of *Playboy's* readers' service department. She has since married and left for Texas, though she is still listed on the masthead.

Ever since, the magazine has tried hard to make its girls look
ordinary in a wholesome sort of way—just like the Nude Next
Door. The illusion is heightened by the fact that the girls are presented not only nude and in color but also in numerous black and
white pictures in their natural habitat, whipping up a batch of
muffins or playing the guitar. Suggestive poses are out, as are the
accoutrements of fetishism. None of the nudes ever looks as if
she had just indulged in sex, or were about to.

Hefner may have run the Marilyn Monroe shots without her
consent, but now he has no problem finding big-name actresses
eager to appear in the magazine. The album so far includes Carroll
Baker, Arlene Dahl, Ursula Andress, Kim Novak, Susan Strasberg,
Elsa Martinelli and Susannah York. Nor is there any trouble getting unknown girls to pose; hundreds apply. Sometimes, though,
there is a problem in making the copy that goes with them interesting enough. For instance, the latest Miss January, *Playboy* said,
would love to be a nurse. She was "Albert Schweitzer's fairest
disciple. She has read each of the doctor's books at least twice."

The magazine also finds potential Playmates through a network of free-lance photographers. A particularly rewarding field is
wedding parties; a photographer covering the reception will often
spot a comely bridesmaid. If under 21, she must get her parents'
written consent. Photographing her is another matter. Getting a
nonprofessional model, who has never before posed, in the right
mood can take a photographer one whole day, or several. And all
the while the photographer must keep in mind Art Director Paul's

concept of the *Playboy* nude. "The idea," he says, "is to think clean."

Zero Garbo

The selection of the right nude from among hundreds of transparencies is taken at least as seriously by the *Playboy* staff as, say, choosing the proper tribal dance for a lead page in the *National Geographic*. Dialogue between Art Director Paul and Editor Hefner when choosing pictures for the Playmates-of-the-year feature:

PAUL   This is the best shot of her face.

HEF   That shot makes the girl look too Hollywoodish. She doesn't look natural.

PAUL   Don't her breasts look somewhat distorted? . . . It looks as if the shots were made on a foggy day. We don't want to mix the reader up. You can't really be sure that this is the same girl.

HEF (viewing new layout)   There is something wrong with the angle of that shot. Her thighs and hips look awkward. This doesn't do her justice . . . There must be other aspects to her personality.

Hefner knows exactly what he wants. He likes the young, pouty type without complications or excessive intelligence. Riper beauties he summarily dismisses. "Jeanne Moreau is a fine actress," he once said. "But as a woman she tells me zero. And zero to Greta Garbo. I think that when Sophia Loren was 20 she had a fantastic body. But that is all." To Gershon Legman, a Paris-based writer on sexuality, "*Playboy* is for the subvirile man who just wants to look. Basically, he's afraid of the girls." Says the Rev. William Hamilton of Colgate-Rochester Divinity School: "Hefner rightly affirms the goodness of the body, but he misses the beauty and mystery of sexuality."

Bundle of Insecurities

Who reads *Playboy*? Since 85% of its circulation comes from newsstand sales, readership surveys are difficult. But certain clues can be found in a sampling of questions asked of the feature, "Playboy Advisor." Mostly, they deal with insecurities about clothes, food and sex. A Fayetteville, Ark., reader wants to know whether the gas from his CO_2 cork extractor will harm the wine (no). A Bahamas-bound Louisville bachelor wants to know what clothes to take along; a fellow in Elgin, Ill., wonders whether blue or striped shirts are all right after dark (no).

A San Francisco playboy seems to have become involved with a lesbian; the "Advisor" tells him: "Next time she calls, tell her you've lots of authentically male friends for those evenings you wish to spend going out with the guys." An Akron gentleman of 57 pronounces himself "hopelessly in love" with a lovely 49-year-old neighbor. Trouble is, she won't go out with him Saturday nights; she's got a standing date with some other fellow. "Your Saturday nights must indeed be hell," agrees *Playboy*, "but if you insist on your so-called 'rights,' you may force the lady to make a decision that will cause *all* your evenings to be hell."

Despite the occasional appearance in the "Playboy Advisor" of such senior citizens, the magazine is in large measure addressed to the young who worry about the right socks as well as the right line with girls and the right pleasures. In short, it appeals to the undergraduate who wants to act like a sophisticate—or, for that matter, to the high school graduate who wants to act like a college sophomore. And why not? After all, half the magazine's title plainly emphasizes *boy*. Yet this does not do full justice to the range of *Playboy*'s readers. *Playboy* estimates that half have attended college, 70% are between the ages of 19 and 34. Women make up about 25% of its audience, and their reactions are mixed. Says Social Commentator Marya Mannes: There is "the implicit premise that woman is an Object. She has no other function than to be lusted after and lurched at." Other female readers, who apparently don't mind being lurched at, enjoy *Playboy* for its inside view of a man's world and its notion of the latest styles in feminine sex appeal.

The Last Frontier

One of the more surprising facts is that *Playboy*'s readers include quite a number of ministers. Hefner offered the clergy a

25% subscription discount, found that seminarians demanded similar privileges. In some quarters, it is considered the mark of the cool, contemporary minister to mention *Playboy* casually in conversation, quote it in sermons, or even to write for it. In one issue, William Hamilton expounded on God-is-dead theology; shortly after, Bishop James Pike wrote in to argue with him. Harvey Cox of the Harvard Divinity School did an article in praise of the clergy's new grass-roots involvement with social ills and maladjustments; a group of ministers debated the pros and cons of liberalized abortion. "The last frontier is the sexual one," says Allen Moore of the Claremont School of Theology. "Because of Hefner, many in the church have begun to confront this barrier for the first time. Discussion is more open."

To supervise communications between the last frontier and the cloth, Hefner chose onetime Zoologist Anson Mount, the magazine's football editor, appointed·him six months ago to head a new religion department. People who saw this move as a rather amusing put-on overestimate Hefner's sense of humor. It was all very serious, and frivolous staffers were discouraged from making jokes involving "sermon" and "Mount." Recalls the new religion editor: "I found myself over my head with things like personhood, demythologizing, Bonhoeffer. So I went to Hefner and said, 'Man, I've got to go off to school and learn some of this.'" Hef sent him to the University of the South at Sewanee, where he studied hard for one summer and entertained lavishly, as befits an emissary from *Playboy*. The theologians grew so used to stopping by his house at cocktail hour that eventually they even ventured as far as Hef's Chicago mansion for discussions. "At first, they entered the house as if it were Dante's inferno," says Mount. "But now those cats are used to it."

Enlightenment Simplified

Ministerial interest was greatly stimulated by Hefner's earnest, marathon attempt to spell out the "*Playboy* philosophy." It took 25 installments and a quarter of a million words. Hefner's thesis was that U.S. society had too long and too rigorously suppressed good, healthy heterosexuality. Since its growth had been stunted,

Hefner argued, all sorts of perversions flourished in its place. "You get healthy sex not by ignoring it but by emphasizing it," he maintains. And the villain at the bottom of all this? Organized religion, announced Hefner with an unabashed air of discovery. Hefner revived puritanism long enough to condemn it for being as "stultifying to the mind of man as Communism or any other totalitarian concept."

As it poured through the magazine's columns, the *Playboy* philosophy was often pretentious and relatively conventional. Hefner is a kind of oversimplified Enlightenment thinker with what comes out as an almost touching faith in the individual's capacity for goodness. Release a man from repression, thinks Hef, and he will instinctively pursue a "healthy" life in business and sex alike. Hefner also exhibits a tendency to "situation ethics," which calls for judging acts within their special context rather than by a more fixed morality. Some use this formula to justify homosexuality, but Hefner firmly draws a heterosexual line. He does not endorse extramarital sex, though he approves of the premarital variety.

No one has ever accused Hugh Hefner of being lyrical, but he can grow almost eloquent about sex, sounding approximately like D. H. Lawrence as rewritten by Alfred Kinsey. Sex, he is on record as saying, "can become, at its best, a means of expressing the innermost, deepest-felt longings, desires and emotions. And it is when sex serves those ends—in addition to, and apart from, reproduction—that it is lifted above the animal level and becomes most human."

Bedwork

With many more endorsements like that, Hefner might just possibly make sex go out of style. Whatever his philosophy may amount to, he does not belong to the peripatetic school. Is he out bunny-hugging every night in his sports car or carousing through his clubs with Playmates on either arm? Not at all. His Mercedes-Benz sits forlornly in the garage; his clubs never see him. Lean, rather gaunt, with piercing dark eyes, he has succumbed to the work ethic. He explains that he does not want to face all the outside world's trivia—small talk, party joining—that might distract him from his work. Nor does he have the distractions of a family. Hefner was divorced from Millie eight years ago. Their two children live with his ex-wife, who has remarried.

He does a lot of that work in bed—a round bed, 8½ ft. in diameter, which revolves or vibrates at the touch of a button. By rotating the bed toward the fireplace or the bar or the television, Hefner has the feeling that he is moving from one room to another. A life-sized epoxy sculpture of a seated nude girl by Frank Gallo crouches beside the fireplace, and a TV camera can be trained on the bed.

He does visit the office, but mostly he uses dictating machines to communicate with his staff, sometimes producing recorded memos 30 pages long. Two secretaries, one on day shift, the other on night shift, transcribe the flow. The complete man of electronics, he avoids face-to-face contact and gets his information on the outside world from newspapers, magazines and eight television monitors. He rarely watches a TV show when it is on the air, has it taped for later viewing, and also keeps a stock of several hundred taped movies.

No Daylight

Within his sealed capsule, Hefner loses all sense of time and season. He loves the night. By keeping his shades always drawn, he has effectively banished daylight from his life. He eats when he pleases—a kitchen staff is on duty 24 hours a day. But then he subsists largely on Pepsi-Colas, which are stocked in small refrigerators scattered through his quarters, including one in the headboard of his bed. Often he doesn't even know what day it is. A friend suggested giving him a set of seven pajamas with the day embroidered on each—in reverse writing so that he would just have to look in the mirror while shaving to see where he was in the week.

There is evidence that he might be looking in new directions. He sometimes sounds as if he thought the sexual revolution were over, thanks to *Playboy*, and that it is now time to move on to other social and economic challenges. Even the country's gross national product seems to interest him. "A publication," he wrote, "that helps motivate a part of society to work harder, to accomplish more, to earn more in order to enjoy more of the material benefits described—to that extent, the publication is contributing to the economic growth of the nation."

Like sex, G.N.P. has three letters. But for a real hedonist, it's hardly the same thing.

Jacqueline Onassis

*Happiness is not where you find it. I'm determined not to worry. So
many people poison every day worrying about the next.
I've learned a lot from Jack.*

The popular magazines of America have always filled their
pages with fascinating women, from movie stars to the wives
of important public officials. Few women have been the
subject of more analysis, gossip, and adulation than the former
first lady of America, Jacqueline Onassis.

She has been—publicly, at least—a lady rather than a
woman. Born in 1929 the daughter of John Vernou Bouvier
III, a wealthy lawyer, she grew up in New York and East
Hampton in elegant surroundings. Her mother remarried in
June 1942, and as the stepdaughter of the wealthy financier
Hugh Auchincloss, Jacqueline Bouvier spent her winters in
Virginia and her summers in Newport, Rhode Island. She
attended a series of exclusive schools—Miss Chapin's in New
York and Miss Porter's in Farmington, Connecticut—and
went to Vassar College for two years. In her junior year she
studied at the University of Grenoble and the Sorbonne, and
then returned to take her baccalaureate at George Washington University.

At the age of twenty-two Jacqueline Bouvier became an
Inquiring Camera Girl for the Washington *Times-Herald*
and met the rising senator from Massachusetts, John F.
Kennedy. They married on September 12, 1953, and had two
children: Caroline in 1957 and John, Jr., in 1961. On November 22, 1963, her husband, then President, was assassinated in

Dallas, Texas. At the funeral that followed, televised continuously throughout America, Jacqueline Kennedy received
wider and more intense publicity than probably any other
woman in human history. She brought to the death of her
husband a kind of tragic dignity. If he had been fixed in the
minds of Americans as a hero, more a myth than a man, she
encouraged adulation too, for she emerged from the funeral
as the nation's heroine. The myth ended in October 1968,
when Jacqueline Kennedy married Aristotle Onassis, a wealthy
Greek shipowner.

When we speak of the qualities that inform the public
image of Jacqueline Onassis, certain obvious traits come to
mind: her exclusive education; her beauty; her wealth and
high family status; her intelligence and impeccable taste; her
grace, her poise, her seemingly effortless charm; and finally
her stoic courage and dignity when confronted with tragedy.
Many of these characteristics differ from those associated
with people in an egalitarian, democratic society; indeed few
women enjoy the luxuries accorded Jacqueline Onassis. And
yet, despite the fact—some people would say because of the
fact—that her private life was so different from the private
lives of most women, she became the symbol of the lady in
America. Analyzed so exhaustively by the public media, she
has kept her private life remarkably secret. One thinks in
terms of the playwright Pirandello. She has become the role
she was trained to perform—a lady, but never a woman.

Most of the treatment of Jacqueline Onassis has been pure
hagiography. She has seemed—at least before her marriage
to Aristotle Onassis—invulnerable to public criticism. Paul
O'Neil's essay, as the reader will see, is not in that tradition.

For the Beautiful Queen Jacqueline, Goodby Camelot, Hello Skorpiós

PAUL

O'NEIL

Bᴜᴛ look carefully at this island in its indigo sea; observe the yacht with the golden bathtub spigots and 42 telephones; see the swimming pool; see the scarred hill where the castle will be built and while doing so think of the money piled up by the little fellow in dark glasses who owns it—one thousand million dollars. Ladies . . . ladies . . . you've had a week to be scandalized, but now we must insist that you cease sputtering and be serious—those of you over 30, at any rate, who know husbands are to be endured. And gentlemen . . . we're all carnivores here although you need not say so aloud. Are there any of us who really suspect that Jackie is not capable of enormous satisfaction at a union so rich in drama, creature comfort, power, sudden independence of social constraint—and the sweet knowledge of breast-heaving by a million indignant and defeated females—or that Onassis is not bursting with pride at his bauble of baubles?

A great deal has been said during the last few days about the martyred heroine of Camelot whose image was shattered when Jackie's social secretary broke the news in that absurdly formal statement: "Mrs. Hugh Auchincloss has asked me to tell you that her daughter, Mrs. John F. Kennedy, is planning to marry. . . ." Cab drivers have volunteered their opinion by the thousands: "She don't need the money . . . she must be nuts!" So

REPRINTED BY PERMISSION FROM *Life*; © 1968 TIME INC.

has the great American housewife. "I feel almost as badly," said a helpmeet in Atlanta, "as when Jack was assassinated." "German women saw a halo around her head," said an editor of Hamburg's illustrated weekly, *Stern*, "but now it is gone with the wind." Paris' *France-Soir* told its readers: "A serious blow to the Democratic party and its candidate . . ." In Hong Kong and Taipei women were splendidly incensed though none of them had ever heard of the bridegroom before.

⌈One does not need to deny the existence of the heroine, the loving and thoughtful mother, or even the romantic and sensitive girl who married Jack Kennedy to conclude that all this is utter nonsense—and that the participants in last week's wildly heralded marriage of convenience on the island of Skorpiós were better matched than most of the other husbands and wives on our curious planet. The public's view of Jackie, for one thing, has been less than completely accurate. The romantic girl was more worldly, the mother more practical and the heroine of Camelot a great deal tougher, more competitive and more willful than her manners, her innocent beauty and her soft, whispering voice ever suggested. And the public demands on Jackie, the prying, the sympathy heaped upon her after the appalling disasters she went through, all surely had their effect on her. And still the public insisted she remain the Queen.

But queens deprived of court and clout need kings or must make do with half-measures. There have been very few rich, ruthless, unrestricted, old-fashioned to-hell-with-you-Jack kings around of late—particularly unmarried ones. Aristotle Onassis— a fellow who doesn't think much of today's actual monarchs ("All that counts now is money. It's people with money who are the real royalty these days")—has been one of very few.⌉He is a small man—5 feet 5 to Jackie's 5 feet 7— who tends toward blue suits, blue shirts and blue ties when ashore, strips to the waist when he is aboard his glittering yacht and likes those gangster-movie dark glasses.⌈He is not a philanthropic, socially conscious rich man; he is a self-centered, Onassis-conscious rich man.⌉

He holds both Greek and Argentinian citizenship but takes a cool, catholic and apolitical view of governments. He is not a chap

who is given to indignation about sin or who is above dealing
with less than democratic politicos, like the present Greek junta,
on the best terms he can get. He likes dirty jokes and is delighted
to announce that the barstools on his yacht are covered with
leather from the testicles of whales—he once owned a whaling
fleet but sold it to the Japanese at big profit when business began
trailing off.

Onassis has other sides. He is surly when crossed but is also
modest, unassuming, a natural story-teller and, more interestingly,
a rapt listener. These qualities have been at the heart of his
success as a collector of celebrities (Winston Churchill), beautiful
female yachting guests (Greta Garbo) and, of course, his companion of 10 years—dumped only a few months ago—opera star
Maria Callas. Not surprising in a man who built a stupefying
fortune from $250, he is shrewd, courageous, hard-headed—a
gambler who always, apparently, wins, and seems indifferent to
the size of the stakes.

Now why in the name of undulating Aphrodite did bride and
groom, who first met about 15 years ago, find it necessary to
marry with such breakneck precipitousness? Why the sudden
rush to Greece? Why the necessity—so delightful to headline
writers but so disconcerting to the victims—of heaving 90 passengers off Onassis-owned Olympic Airway Flight 412 to Athens?
Even the bride's mother didn't seem to know: "I didn't suspect
they were planning to get married. I was at Stratford Hall in
Virginia and Jackie called and asked, 'Could you get on a plane
tomorrow afternoon, Mummy?'—and I very nobly did!" Precipitousness, plus the fact of marriage to a divorced man by a woman
who could only be described as a member of Catholic aristocracy,
lit off whole fireworks of rumor and speculation. Why? Why?
Why?

But one could also ask: why not? Perhaps Rome could find
some legalism sanctioning the marriage as it had for her sister
Lee. Said one who professed to have "known," Jackie had decided
to marry only after Bob Kennedy's death—since she had felt
marriage would have damaged his cause as a candidate—but having made up her mind, later grew mortally afraid of a leak in the

press and assaults by waves of reporters and cameramen. Thus the hurry. Fascinating! But immaterial to our essential thesis which is, namely: it was inevitable. Society Columnist Suzy Knickerbocker, a Jackie-watcher of the first rank, puts it this way:

"They were made for each other. She can give him what he needs; he can give her what she needs. What greater celebrity in the world to collect than Jackie Kennedy? She's a living legend." Onassis, on his part, says Suzy, will supply trappings of wealth in the royal sense, put a navy and an airline at her disposal. And he will keep her in the newspapers—her way. "Jackie has this love-hate thing about publicity," Suzy continues. "If she had really wanted privacy, the way she says, she could have gotten it. But publicity is like dope and she's got to have that front-page fix."

Consider further the inevitability of her metamorphosis from First Lady to Queen of Skorpiós. It was a metamorphosis based not only in loss but in restlessness and a curious kind of thirst for power. Perhaps it might be more accurate to say she sought absolute control of her own environment, the power to impose her own tastes and wishes on those around her. She seemed to feel little regret at leaving Washington—it is a one-industry town, and the industry, politics, was a phenomenon she had only tolerated. But when she reverted, in New York, to the jet set, the beautiful people, the name artists, name singers, name dancers who had been her companions before the White House, she did so as a world figure and with a certain new imperiousness.

She did not hesitate to order planes to circle before landing while she prepared herself to meet the press at airports. She developed an aversion to dinner parties given by *others*, backed out of them with little compunction, made it plain she wished to see certain people only under certain conditions set by herself. But she also developed an impatience with the "stained-glass image" which made such behavior possible, and apparently a kind of restiveness at being accountable to the Kennedy clan, without actually being of it.

And then there was the man problem. She had no more than three close women friends but, in the words of one sharp-tongued lesser observer, she "borrowed husbands the way other women borrow a cup of sugar."

Wives were sometimes invited along on the trips and social occasions this practice involved, but two who have since gotten divorces make plain to their intimates that they did not contribute manpower to this escort service with enthusiasm. The list is long: it includes Historian Arthur Schlesinger Jr., Composer-Conductor Leonard Bernstein and former Defense Secretary Robert McNamara. Bachelors were not excluded. New York *Paris-Match* Bureau Chief Paul Mathias did his bit. So did Spain's Vatican Ambassador Antonio Garrigues. Lawyer Michael Forrestal tore off to Cambodia with her as, of course, did Britain's Lord Harlech. Harlech was the most popular choice for husband, but that proved to be short-sighted. He just wanted to putter about his digs and, presumably, watch the rain.

So how could Onassis not have been the inevitable choice—the very fellow, as we are now agreed, that she simply had to marry and who simply had to marry her? She saw him frequently. The gossips dismissed "Telis" as "simply impossible, of course," but Jackie herself, we are assured, did not behave as though he was. Our source is Nikos Mastorakis, a Greek reporter who sneaked aboard the yacht posing as the manager of an Athens bouzouki band which played aboard the yacht for Jackie and Onassis last August and also for Ted Kennedy, a "laughing cowboy from Texas," and two pretty girls, one blond "with cerulean eyes" and the other dark and with one leg in a cast. "All, including Jackie and Telis, seemed pleased with their lives," said Mastorakis. "They eat black caviar and red tomatoes. Ted drinks ouzo. Jackie, who is resplendent in a red blouse and long gypsy skirt, prefers the vodka. She leans close when Telis whispers in her ear. At dinner Onassis eats his lamb like a youth. She eats little and nibbles white grapes. But at 4 A.M. with Mr. Moon above, the sweet Mrs. Kennedy sings with Telis when he starts *Adios Muchachos* and I feel they are close."

No slightest hint of the warmth and companionship suggested by this little tableau was evidenced by the 39-year-old bride and 62- (or was it 68?) year-old groom when they were married last week. Jackie looked drawn and concerned as she went through the half-hour Greek Orthodox ceremony in the tiny, bougainvillea-covered chapel—almost oblivious of Onassis in his blue suit, white shirt and bright red tie. Rain fell steadily outside. The service seemed alien to U.S. guests and doubtless to the bride; she clutched the hand of her 10-year-old daughter, Caroline, rather than her husband's on leaving.

But this was no ordinary wedding. Both parties were launching themselves against the pull of social gravity in full view of the world and, like astronauts at lift-off, should not necessarily have been expected to smile and wave. Neither should they have been expected to anticipate a teen-age rapture. Theirs was a merger from which both parties could expect to enjoy something far more invigorating—a heady stimulation of the ego.

Jackie was going to have her cake and eat it, too, and all without being beholden, except, of course, to the Golden Greek. And he was a man who is kind to women and who would gain the splendid gift of "instant class" by indulging her. Her power remained undiminished; not one of the beautiful people had nerve enough to say one word for attribution after the wedding. More touching yet, Boston's crusty, old, Kennedy-oriented Richard Cardinal Cushing rose to say that talk of her having excommunicated herself was "a lot of nonsense." He reported that for months he had been fighting off criticism of the match from sources close to the Kennedy family and to the late President's administration. With some heat, he demanded charity for the lady.

And there was something else about the union which deserved to be weighed. All marriages involve some kind of balance of emotional power—or the lack of it. What other man could marry Jackie Kennedy without simultaneously being dominated by her and the memory of her departed husband? What other man, in fact, could dump her, if he chose to later, without being destroyed by public opinion? But what other woman—so splendid a mirror of accomplishment and self-esteem—could be so utterly indispensable even to a bauble-collecting billionaire? How could they fail, in short—though they fought like wildcats for the next decade—to live happily ever after?